JAZZ
IN THE MOVIES

A Guide to Jazz Musicians 1917-1977

JAZZ
IN THE MOVIES

A Guide to Jazz Musicians 1917-1977

by
David Meeker

ARLINGTON HOUSE·PUBLISHERS
NEW ROCHELLE, N. Y.

Published by Talisman Books
27 Sumatra Road
London NW6 1PS

Library of Congress Catalog Card No. 77-30238

Designed by Richard Dewing 'Millions'
Printed in England by A Wheaton &
Company, Exeter

Introduction

I am always astonished by the work of that small, dedicated, diligent, extremely hard-working and, above all, enthusiastic group of people that the world luckily possesses who spend an incredible amount of time compiling and preserving the facets of civilization that make society's life better and more meaningful. The world should treasure them; instead, I'm afraid, they're either taken for granted or, worse, almost totally ignored. David Meeker is one of that group, but I hope that enough people acquire this book so that he realises the public acclaim he so justly deserves, apart from his own self gratification.

I am equally astonished by the use to which jazz has been put – though certainly not nearly enough – in as many films as this book contains and Meeker, moreover, not only gives us the pertinent statistics, but also a concise and sufficient description (and capsule judgment) of what the films are all about.

I think the work is not only indispensable for any researcher into the history of jazz in film, but also makes wonderful and evocative reading for the true film and jazz fan. I submit it will surely rank as one of the most important contributions in that small, unfortunately, list of essential jazz literature.

Norman Granz

Acknowledgements

Grateful thanks are due to Karl Emil Knudsen (Copenhagen) for allowing me access to his files and to John Jeremy (London) for letting me see his film collection. From Hollywood David Shire, David Raksin, Bud Shank, Hugo Montenegro and Danny Gould have patiently answered my seemingly inconsequential questions, while useful contributions have been received from many enthusiasts, particularly Brian Priestley (London), Joe Showler (Toronto), Bob Rhodes (Bradford), J. J. Mulder (Bunde), Ken Crawford (Pittsburgh), Derek Coller (Sawbridgeworth), Victor Schonfield (London), Roger Richard (Brioude), Ean Wood (London), Tony Middleton (London), Robert Daudelin (Montreal)

For many facts and figures I have mercilessly plundered the pages of The *Monthly film bulletin, Variety, Motion picture herald, Jazz journal, Crescendo international, The standard Kenton directory,* Jorgen Jepsen's *discographies,* Leonard Feather's *Encylopaedia of jazz,* John Chilton's *Who's who of jazz.*

Stills are reproduced with acknowledgement to the original production companies and to Universal, Warner Bros, Columbia, United Artists, 20th Century-Fox, RKO, MGM, Paramount, EMI, Goldwyn, Asa Filmudlejning, TCB Releasing, John Kobal, National Film Archive.

Colleagues at the British Film Institute have helped in many ways often unknowingly. In particular I should like to thank Frank Holland, Elaine Burrows, Tony Sweatman, Peter Flower and the staff of the Information Department.

My inspiration came from Hollywood and its musicians – from Milton M. Rajonsky through Shorty Rogers, The Prince, Roger Short, Boots Brown and Shorty Muggins to Milton Rogers.

My dedication is to Barbara, Paul and Navlika and to Caroline.

Preface

Why should anyone document the work of jazz musicians for the Cinema?

The idea for a book of this nature has been with me for almost twenty years. In the late summer of 1957 a cartoon called *The three little bops* was being shown at a News Theatre in Charing Cross Road and I spent precious pennies on tickets for myself and a reluctant girl friend only to sit, bored to tears, through the 'continuous programme' of newsreel, travelogues and the like. I waited anxiously for the sweet sounds of a Shorty Rogers soundtrack when, for me at least, time would stand still. How I came to learn of that film's existence – or any of the other movies that I chased around town for similar reasons – was a matter of chance. There was obviously a crying need for some sort of reference work to provide details of all the films with jazz content, whether musicians were actually seen on the screen or just heard on the soundtrack. Why had no jazz filmography been produced? Later on, when I found myself professionally engaged in the film world and actively involved in preparing documentation, I began to understand why it had not been attempted. The difficulties in researching such a project would deter any but the lunatic.

Even if it were possible to see and check every movie that had ever been made, film music details are notoriously hard to obtain especially as individual musicians are rarely credited on the screen. Furthermore, many potentially relevant movies are unavailable for viewing or have disappeared for ever. As time passes, the situation worsens – it is estimated that some two thirds of the feature films produced in America alone before 1930 have already been irretrievably lost.

Considering the dedication of jazz enthusiasts to their subject and their almost manic thirst for discographical information, surprisingly little has been published over the years on the jazz musician's involvement with the Cinema. Besides reviews of individual films, a few articles on the subject have appeared from time to time in both jazz and movie periodicals and such devotees as Peter Noble, Ernie Smith, Whitney Balliett and Birger Jørgensen have produced pioneering chapters which have paved the way for a more extensive factual work.

However, it wasn't until 1961 that the first real attempt was made to firmly establish the *genre* with the publication in France of *Jazz au cinema* , an enthusiastic pamphlet in the *Premier plan* series, written by Henri Gautier, whose dedication was particularly commendable as he was still in his 'teens. My own booklet, *Jazz in the movies*, upon which this current book is based, was rushed out through the British Film Institute in 1972, to be followed later that year by Jean-Roland Hippenmeyer's *Jazz sur films* , published in Switzerland. It is to be hoped that my own work, though still far from definitive, will usefully bridge the gap that still exists and might encourage further research in the field, thereby helping to acknowledge the considerable contribution that the jazz musician has made, and will surely continue to make, to the most popular and influential medium of the century.

The compilation of the entries for a work of this nature presented many problems in terms of who to include and who to exclude. There is no agreement on the definition of 'jazz' nor 'jazz musician'. Arguments on the validity of many artists' output have long raged throughout the jazz world. In an attempt to please everyone I have therefore tended to include some of the marginal cases. Where a musician is basically a jazzman, then I have included all his known movie work, whether it is actually jazz or not, but in the case of basically 'straight' musicians – such as André Previn, Michel Legrand, Elmer Bernstein etc., however involved in jazz they may have been from time to time, I have recorded only their jazz work. I have further limited my brief, in terms of the films themselves, by adhering pretty closely to those films that have been available either commercially to cinemas or non-commercially on 16mm, or both. That is to say, material made specifically for TV is excluded unless it has either been available elsewhere or incorporated into theatrical footage. Also excluded are newsreels and other actuality material, advertising commercials, trailers, privately made home movies, 8mm and 9.5mm material.

The basic information against each individual entry gives the original title of the film together with any British/American/ alternative/reissue titles; the country of origin and production/copyright date; the director – or if unknown, the producer – and the original running time. An attempt has then been made to evaluate the movie in a few words, to give an idea of its *genre* and its jazz point of reference. In a few instances this information is incomplete, either because I have been unable to track it down or occasionally because the film is still in production or as yet unreleased. Major jazz names are in bold type and are fully indexed.

A number of films known to have been made are regrettably omitted as research has failed to uncover their titles. For instance, it is known that Albert Nicholas appeared with The Luis Russell Band in a 1932 Paramount feature, Django Reinhardt made a short with the Quintette in 1938, Bud Shank scored a couple of documentaries for Terry Sanders in the 1950s which were never publicly shown, Oscar Pettiford and Benny Bailey participated in a German movie in 1959, Charlie Byrd composed for some US Department of Agriculture films, Julian 'Cannonball' Adderley appeared in non-speaking roles in several Hollywood movies and Speed Webb and His Orchestra made brief appearances in several more films than I have been able to trace.

A word of explanation is required for those readers who are unfamiliar with two specific types of film referred to extensively in the text – Soundies and Snader Telescriptions. RCM Soundies (the initials standing for Roosevelt, Coslow and Mills) were short films produced during the war years for use in a sort of visual juke box. Eight of them were spooled together and projected one at a time via a complicated series of reflectors on to the rear of a glass screen. The Mills Panoram Soundies Machines were rented to thousands of locations across America, mainly bars, hotel lobbies etc. The customer would insert a dime for each three minute selection. The films were produced at a rate of five or six per week and featured most of the popular entertainers of the time, usually performing their current record hits. For technical reasons the films themselves were printed in reverse and when the whole Soundie novelty wore off in 1946 the then-useless prints were sold off to TV and the home movie enthusiasts from where many of them, with a corrected image, eventually found their way to the 16mm and film collectors' markets. Some twenty years later, a similar system appeared in Europe called the Scopitone, made in colour with 16mm magnetic sound (Claude Lelouch was reputed to have made some 400 of them) but they never enjoyed the same success as the Soundies. The same production concept was adopted in the early 1950s by Snader Telescriptions to produce three-minute reels specifically to fill up time on TV; these too eventually wound up on used 16mm lists. Besides having been a fascinating phenomenon, long buried among the details of American popular culture, the RCM Soundie will always retain its importance as a permanent film record of well-known entertainers – many of them distinguished jazzmen – giving their original interpretations of classic musical items. When all is said and done, though within a more specialised area, this is precisely what I have attempted to document.

David Meeker
London
May 1977

Abbreviations used in the text

acc	accordion
alt sax	alto sax
arr	arranger
banjo	banjo
bar horn	baritone horn
bar sax	baritone sax
bas-clar	bass clarinet
bas-flute	bass flute
bas-gtr	bass guitar
bas-sax	bass sax
bas-tpt	bass trumpet
bas-trb	bass trombone
bass	bass
bongos	bongos
clar	clarinet
cond	conductor
conga	congas
cor	cornet
dir	director
drs	drums
elec	electric
fl horn	flugel horn
flute	flute
Fr horn	French horn
gtr	guitar
hca	harmonica
key	keyboards
ldr	leader
mc	master of ceremonies
mello	mellophone
nova	novachord
org	organ
perc	percussion
picc	piccolo
pno	piano
prod	producer
reeds	reeds
sop sax	soprano sax
ten sax	tenor sax
tpt	trumpet
trb	trombone
tuba	tuba
v trb	valve trombone
vibs	vibraphone
vln	violin
voc	vocal

1

A belles dents

France/West Germany 1966 – 105 mins
dir Pierre Gaspard-Huit

Pretentious and glossy romantic-comedy which reveals more of its glamorous heroine than it does imagination. Music score by **Jacques Loussier**.

2

A bout de souffle/Breathless

France 1959 – 90 mins
dir Jean-Luc Godard

Godard's stunning first feature, probably the most influential movie since *Citizen Kane*. Superb. music score by **Martial Solal**.

3

A . . . is for apple

UK 1963 – 11 mins
dir John Burrows, Hugh Hudson

Flashy advertising film sponsored by The Fruit Producers' and The Apple and Pear Publicity Council. Music score by **Jacques Loussier**.

4

A.k.a. Cassius Clay

USA 1970 – 80 mins
dir Jim Jacobs

Straightforward documentary about the boxer Muhammad Ali, with music score by **Teo Macero**.

5

A nous deux, la France!

France/Ivory Coast 1970 – 60 mins
dir Désiré Ecaré

Intelligent, honest comedy which forms the second part of a trilogy about African social problems and French racism. Music by **Memphis Slim**.

6

A poings fermes

France 1949 – 16 mins
dir Marcel Martin

A fantasy on sleep, with music by **Hubert Rostaing** and the **Quintette du Hot-Club de France**.

7

A propos d'un meurtre

France 1966 – 16 mins
dir Christian Ledieu

Fictional short about a woman who murders her lover, with music by **Barney Wilen**.

8

A propos d'une rivière

France 1955 – 25 mins
dir Georges Franju

A poetic evocation of youth and leisure, seen through the eyes of an old man remembering how he used to slip away from school and fish for salmon. Music by **Henri Crolla** and **André Hodeir**.

9

A toute heure en toute saison

France 1961 – 10 mins
dir Roger Fellous, Charley Manchon

Documentary on jam making, from Nicolas Appert to the present day. Music by **Martial Solal**.

10

Abou Ben Boogie

USA 1944 – 7 mins
dir James Culhane

A Universal Walt Lantz *Swing symphony* in Technicolor – a kind of swinging *Thousand and one nights* set in an Arabian nightclub where Sheherazade sings the blues.

11

About face

USA 1952 – 93 mins
dir Roy del Ruth

Unimaginative musical adaptation of the play *Brother Rat* by John Monks Jnr. and Fred F. Finklehoffe, with Gordon MacRae and Eddie Bracken. Paul Smith, *pno*; **Joe Mondragon**, *bass* and **Nick Fatool**, *drs* soundtracked sequences to be used in the film.

12

Accent on girls

USA 1936 – 9 mins
dir Fred Waller

Four numbers from **Ina Ray Hutton** and Her Melodears, supported by the Foster Twins.

13

Accident

UK 1967 – 105 mins
dir Joseph Losey

Harold Pinter adaptation of Nicholas Mosley's novel, beautifully constructed, faultlessly acted and ravishing to look at. Music score by **John Dankworth**.

14

Accord parfait

France 1958 – 10 mins
dir Jean Weinfeld

Accident prevention; with music by **André Hodeir**.

15

Across 110th Street

USA 1972 – 102 mins
dir Barry Shear

Realistic screen adaptation of Wally Ferris's novel *Across 110th* – a virtual blood bath set in Harlem and without a glamorous or romantic character in sight. Suitably percussive music and title song composed and conducted by **J. J. Johnson**.

16

Actualités Gauloises

France 1952 – 10 mins
dir Jac Rémise

Colour cartoon tracing the early history of the Gauls, with music by **Claude Luter**.

17

Actualités préhistoriques

France 1947 – 8 mins
dir J. Rémise, G. Duvoir, C. Guy, M. Young

Animated colour cartoon tracing some of the main events in world prehistory. Music score by **Claude Luter**.

18

Actualités romaines

France 1947 – 7 mins
dir Jac Rémise

An animated cartoon tracing life in Ancient Rome, with music by **Claude Luter**.

19

Adieu Philippine

France/Italy 1960/2 – 106 mins
dir Jacques Rozier

Genuinely fresh and enjoyable comedy, with improvised dialogue and memorable performances from its young players. Music and an appearance by **Maxim Saury**.

20

Adventure in rhythm

USA 1961 – 8 mins
dir Jack Shaindlin

In colour and Cinemascope, a programme of music by The **Tommy Dorsey** Orchestra with vocals by Kaye Ballard.

21

Adventures of an asterisk

USA 1957 – 10 mins
dir John Hubley

Enjoyable colour cartoon with excellent soundtrack music by **Benny Carter** with **Lionel Hampton**.

22

The adventures of Hajji Baba

USA 1954 – 86 mins
dir Don Weis

An unusually spirited Arabian nights romp, suggested by James Morier's work of the title, endowed with a stereophonic, echo chamber theme song sung by **Nat 'King' Cole** which insinuates itself into the soundtrack at every opportunity.

23

An affair of the skin

USA 1963 – 102 mins
dir Ben Maddow

The story of five individuals whose contemporary, big-city America paths cross and intertwine as they pursue their separate and seemingly unrelated goals. On the soundtrack good use is made of **Phineas Newborn**'s recording of 'For Carl'.

24

L'affaire d'une nuit/It happened all night

France 1960 – 95 mins
dir Henri Verneuil

Amusing and entertaining little anecdote of amorous misadventure, with some appealing performances by the leading actors. Music score by **Martial Solal**.

25

Afro-American music: its heritage

USA c1960 – 16 mins
dir Sidney Galanty

Cheaply produced, poorly constructed instructional film for school children which attempts to trace the history of Black American music. Musical illustrations are provided by the **Calvin Jackson** Quartet – Jackson himself on piano; **Buddy Collette**, *ten sax, alt sax, flute;* **Dave Robinson,** *bass* and **Chuck Flores,** *drs.* Jackson also acts as the film's narrator and solos with **Joplin**'s 'Maple leaf rag'.

26

Afro-American worksongs in a Texas prison

USA 1956 – 40 mins
dir Pete Seeger

A simple, leisurely film record of genuine Southern worksongs provided by prisoners working at tree-felling, hoeing and such-like, conveying a deep sense of the pre-history of the Blues.

27

After hours

USA 1961 – 27 mins

Originally produced for TV, a magnificent programme in a night club setting of music by **Coleman Hawkins,** *ten sax;* **Roy Eldridge,** *tpt;* **Johnny Guarnieri,** *pno;* **Barry Galbraith,** *gtr;* **Milt Hinton,** *bass;* **Cozy Cole,** *drs;* Carol Stevens, *voc.* Numbers: 'Lover man' by Jimmy Davis, Roger 'Ram' Ramirez, Jimmy Sherman; 'Sunday' by Chester Conn, Ned Miller, Bennie Krueger, Jule Styne; 'Just you, just me' by Jesse Greer, Raymond Klages; 'Taking a chance on love' by Vernon Duke, John Latouche, Ted Fetter.

28

After seven

USA 1929 – 9 mins

An early fictional Vitaphone short set in a Harlem night club during a dance contest with music by **Chick Webb** and His Band. Identified musicians include **Ward Pinkett**, *tpt;* **Bennie Morton**, *trb;* **Elmer Williams**, *reeds;* **John Truehart**, *gtr* and **Chick Webb**, *drs.* Music includes 'Sweet Sue'.

29

The agony and the ecstasy

USA/Italy 1965 – 139 mins
dir Carol Reed

Over-simplified and vulgar adaptation of Irving Stone's novel about Michelangelo and his Sistine ceiling. Alex North's score includes a solo for lute in 'Contessina' by **Laurindo Almeida**.

30

Ah! Quelle équipe

France 1956 – 96 mins
dir Roland Quignon

Routine comedy in colour with a host of popular French variety stars including **Sidney Bechet** and the orchestra of **André Réwéliotty**.

31

Ain't misbehavin'

USA 1941 – 3 mins
dir Warren Murray

Soundie in which the title number is played, to enthusiastic onlookers, by **Fats Waller**, *pno, voc;* John Hamilton, *tpt;* **Gene Sedric**, *alt sax;* **Al Casey**, *gtr;* Cedric Wallace, *bass;* Wilmore Jones, *drs.*

32

Ain't misbehavin'

USA 1955 – 81 mins
dir Edward Buzzell

Lightweight musical comedy providing little more than mildly diverting escapism. **Fats Waller**'s title number is sung by Piper Laurie; other songs include 'A little love can go a long way', 'The Dixie mambo' and 'I love that rickey tickey tickey'.

▲

Fats Waller in the **Ain't misbehavin'** *Soundie, also used in the 1974* **Ain't misbehavin'**.

33

Ain't misbehavin'

UK 1974 – 85 mins
dir Peter Neal, Anthony Stern

Clumsy compilation exploiting current attitudes to nostalgia and sex, utilising clips from features, shorts and newsreels. Extracts used from Soundies are: 'Honeysuckle Rose' and 'Ain't misbehavin'' by **Fats Waller**; 'Ain't gonna be your dog' by **Meade Lux Lewis**; 'Cabaret echoes' by **Anthony Parenti**'s Famous Melody Boys; 'Shy guy' by the **Nat 'King' Cole** Trio and 'Boogie Woogie at the Civic Opera' by **Albert Ammons** plus soundtrack use of two recordings by **Django Reinhardt** 'Please be kind' and 'The man I love' plus brief clips of 'Londonola' by Roy Fox and a piece by Ivy Benson and Her Orchestra.

34

Air mail special

USA 1941 – 3 mins

Soundie featuring **Count Basie** and His Orchestra presenting the title number, with **Jimmy Rushing**.

35

Al Capone

USA 1959 – 103 mins
dir Richard Wilson

Surface reconstruction of familiar Al Capone background of bootlegging, prohibition and terrorism, with a memorable central performance by Rod Steiger. Musicians playing David Raksin's pastiche jazz score include **Uan Rasey, Lloyd Ullyate, Abe Most, Chuck Gentry, Ray Turner** and **Shelly Manne**.

36

Alabama's ghost

USA 1973
dir Fredric Hobbs

Not yet reviewed – a feature film containing an appearance by The **Turk Murphy** Jazz Band.

37

Alechinsky d'après nature

France/Belgium 1970 – 20 mins
dir Luc de Heusch

Conventional documentary on the life and work of the painter Pierre Alechinsky, with music partly by **Michel Portal**.

38

Alex and the gypsy (Love and other crimes)

USA 1976 – 99 mins
dir John Korty

Nihilistic screen adaptation of Stanley Elkin's novella *The bailbondsman* with a music score by Henry Mancini that makes use of **Django Reinhardt** recordings.

39

Alex Welsh

UK c1963 – 25 mins

Originally produced for BBC TV, a programme of music by The **Alex Welsh** Band with guest star **Henry 'Red' Allen**, *tpt*. Other musicians include **Alex Welsh**, *tpt*; **Roy Crimmons**, *trb*; **Fred Hunt**, *pno*; **Lennie Hastings**, *drs*; **Ron Matthewson**, *bass*; **Al Gay** and **Jim Douglas**. Numbers include 'Beale Street blues', 'New Orleans', 'Way down yonder in New Orleans', 'St James Infirmary', 'Take a closer walk with Thee' and 'When the saints come marching in'.

40

Alfie

UK 1966 – 114 mins
dir Lewis Gilbert

Adaptation of Bill Naughton's successful play, which should have been a good, unpretentious little black and white movie, but isn't. Fine swinging jazz score written by **Sonny Rollins**, though unconfirmed reports suggest that the soundtrack tenor sax work was actually performed by **Tubby Hayes** for contractual reasons. Supporting soundtrack musicians include **Ronnie Scott**, **Keith Christie**, **Stan Tracey** and **Dave Goldberg**.

41

Alfie darling/Oh! Alfie

UK 1975 – 102 mins
dir Ken Hughes

Trivial sequel to *Alfie* inspired by the play of the same name by Bill Naughton. **Annie Ross** has an acting role.

42

Ali Baba goes to town

USA 1937 – 81 mins
dir David Butler

Lavishly produced comedy with music tailored for the debatable talents of Eddie Cantor. Features **Cab Calloway** and The **Raymond Scott Quintet**.

43

L'alibi

France 1936 – 82 mins
dir Pierre Chenal

Melodrama concerning a Parisian dance hostess who is inveigled into providing an alibi for a murderer, with Erich von Stroheim as the mysterious villain of the piece. Features the playing of **Johnny Russell** and an appearance by **Valaida Snow**.

All about loving

see **De l'amour.**

44

The all American bands

USA 1943 – 10 mins
dir Jean Negulesco

Music short featuring four popular big bands. Matty Malneck with 'William Tell overture'; Joe Reichman with 'Night and day'; Freddy Martin with 'Tales from the Vienna Woods' and **Skinnay Ennis** with 'The birth of the Blues'.

45

All colored vaudeville show

USA 1935 – 9 mins
dir Roy Mack

Vitaphone short featuring **Adelaide Hall** and the Nicholas Brothers with 'Lazybones', 'Stars and stripes forever', 'China boy', 'Sweet Sue' and 'Minnie the moocher'.

46

All neat in black stockings

UK 1969 – 99 mins
dir Christopher Morahan

Uncertain in mood, but oddly appealing screen adaptation of Jane Gaskell's novel, beautifully played by its young cast. Robert Cornford's music score features some good tenor work by **Tony Coe**.

47

All night long

UK 1961 – 95 mins
dir Michael Relph, Basil Dearden

A combination of *Othello* and a jazz jamboree that falls flat on both counts. Musicians featured include **Dave Brubeck, Johnny Dankworth, Charles Mingus, Tubby Hayes, Keith Christie, Allan Ganley, Kenny Napper,** Ray Dempsey, **Bert Courtley,** Barry Morgan, **Colin Purbrook,** Johnny Scott and Geoffrey Holder.

48
All star bond rally
USA 1944 – 19 mins
prod Darryl F. Zanuck

A cast of box office names in a featurette produced expressly for the Industry's participation in the Seventh War Loan under the auspices of the Hollywood division of the War Activities Committee. Features **Harry James** and His Orchestra, with Frank Sinatra.

49
All star melody master
USA 1944 – 8 mins
dir Jean Negulesco

Music short featuring four popular bands. Hal Kemp with 'Begin the beguine'; Emil Coleman with 'Just one of those things'; **Skinnay Ennis** with 'Let's do it' and Rubinoff with 'Dark eyes'.

50
All the fine young cannibals
USA 1960 – 122 mins
dir Michael Anderson

Strained and only semi-conscious melodrama based on Rosamond Marshall's novel *The Bixby girls* featuring **Pearl Bailey** as an alcoholic Negro Blues singer acting everyone else off the screen.

51
Almost married
USA 1942 – 64 mins
dir Charles Lamont

Routine second feature comedy with music about an unemployed singer who achieves fame through cabaret engagements. Includes an appearance by **Slim Gaillard**.

52
Amanti
Italy/France 1968 – 88 mins
dir Vittorio De Sica

Glutinous tear-jerker with the more staple clichés of the woman's magazine. The song 'A place for lovers' is sung by **Ella Fitzgerald**.

53
Ambitus
France 1967 – 16 mins
dir G. Patris, L. Ferrari

Pianist **Cecil Taylor** recites one of his poems, backed by music played by His Quartet.

Ambulance
see **Ambulans**.

54
Ambulans/Ambulance
Poland 1962 – 10 mins
dir Janusz Morgenstern

A stark re-enactment of a Nazi wartime practice in which Jewish children were asphyxiated. Music by **Krzystof Komeda**.

55
America, I love you
USA c1943 – 3 mins

Soundie featuring the title number played by **Claude Thornhill** and His Orchestra.

56
An American dream/See you in hell, darling
USA 1966 – 103 mins
dir Robert Gist

Relentlessly sordid and over-heated melodrama based on the novel by Norman Mailer. Music and song 'A time for love' by **Johnny Mandel**.

57
American graffiti
USA 1973 – 110 mins
dir George Lucas

Super-cool fable of the close-down of an era, the Sixties, fairly crackling with the recordings of yesterday including 'Heart and soul' by **Hoagy Carmichael** and Frank Loesser; 'Ain't that a shame' by Domino and Bartholomew, sung by **Fats Domino**.

58
An American in Paris
USA 1951 – 114 mins
dir Vincente Minnelli

One of the best-known of the MGM musicals though not one of the best, partly because of the unimaginative use of the Paris settings and the weak story line. In a café sequence, **Benny Carter**, *alt sax*, with a jazz combo, is prominent playing a Gershwin medley of 'But not for me', 'Someone to watch over me' and 'Love is here to stay'. He also soundtracked alto solo on 'Someone to watch over me' for use in key sequences.

59

American music – from folk to jazz and pop

USA 1969 – 49 mins
dir Stephen Fleishman

An illustrated history of American popular music
with a good section devoted to the story of jazz.
Brief appearances by The **Eureka Brass Band**,
The **Preservation Hall Band**,'**Punch' Miller**,
**George Lewis, Billie and Dee Dee Pierce,
Benny Goodman, Gene Krupa, Duke Ellington,
Big Jim Robinson** and **Billy Taylor**. Also
soundtrack snatches of **Bix Beiderbecke** and
Jack Teagarden.

60

American patrol

USA c1952 – 3 mins

Telescription of **Red Nichols** playing the title
number.

61

The Americanization of Emily

USA 1964 – 115 mins
dir Arthur Hiller

Disappointing anti-war satire scripted by Paddy
Chayefsky from the novel by William Bradford.
Music score by **Johnny Mandel**.

62

L'amour mène les hommes/Desire takes the men

France 1957 – 82 mins
dir Mick Roussel

Formula melodrama of little interest save that it is
outstandingly photographed and it boasts a music
score by **Hubert Rostaing**.

63

An einem Freitag um halb zwolf/On Friday at eleven

West Germany/France/Italy 1960 – 93 mins
dir Alvin Rakoff

Screen adaptation of James Hadley Chase's
novel *The world in my pocket* – a tough thriller
with a robbery theme. Music score by **Claude
Bolling**.

64

Anatomy of a motor oil

UK 1970 – 16 mins
dir Peter de Normanville

An explanation of the chemical contents of a
modern motor oil, produced for Castrol. Music by
Johnny Hawksworth.

▲

Duke Ellington as he appears in **Anatomy of a murder**.

65

Anatomy of a murder

USA 1959 – 160 mins
dir Otto Preminger

Music written by **Duke Ellington** and performed
by His Orchestra provides an exciting backing to
this justly famous – and once notorious – courtroom drama. Ellington also makes an appearance
and delivers a few lines of dialogue. Soundtrack
musicians: **Clark Terry, Cat Anderson, Harold
Baker, Gerald Wilson**, *tpts;* **Ray Nance**, *tpt, vln;*
**Britt Woodman, Quentin Jackson, John
Sanders**, *trbs;* **Russell Procope**, *clar, alt sax;*
Paul Gonsalves, *ten sax;* **Harry Carney**, *bar
sax, clar, bass-clar;* **Jimmy Hamilton**, *clar, ten
sax;* **Ellington**, *pno;* **Jimmy Woode**, *bass;*
James Johnson, *drs.*

66

Anatomy of a performance

USA 1970
dir George Wein, Sidney J. Stiber

One of three documentaries produced around **Louis Armstrong**'s final performances at Newport.

67

And this is free

USA 1963 – 48 mins
dir Norman Dayron

A film impression of Maxwell Street in Chicago where so many bluesmen were given their first chances to perform to the public. Performers appearing include Robert Nighthawk, Johnny Young and 'Louisiana Harmonica' John, with the songs 'Murderin' blues', 'Sweet black angel', 'Goin' down to Eli's to get my pistol out of pawn', among others.

And woman . . . was created

see **Et Dieu créa la femme.**

68

The Anderson tapes

USA 1971 – 99 mins
dir Sidney Lumet

First rate thriller set in New York, based on the novel by Lawrence Sanders. Music by **Quincy Jones** with the soundtrack participation of **Milt Jackson**, *vibs*; **Freddie Hubbard**, *tpt;* '**Toots' Thielemans**, *hca*.

69

The Andromeda strain

USA 1970 – 131 mins
dir Robert Wise

Painstakingly researched but ultimately disappointing screen adaptation of the best-selling novel by Michael Crichton, with music score by **Gil Mellé**.

70

Andy's boogie

USA 1950 – 3 mins

Charlie Barnet and His Orchestra in a performance of the title number with the leader soloing on soprano sax. A Snader Telescription.

Angel baby

see **Engelchen oder die Jungfrau von Bamberg.**

71

Anges gardiens

France 1964 – 21 mins
dir A. Vétusto, F. Reichenbach

The life and obligations of a French policeman. Music score by **Jacques Loussier.**

72

L'Année Sainte

France/Italy 1976 – 90 mins
dir Jean Girault

Listlessly directed, lumbering comedy-thriller in which actor Jean Gabin makes yet another of his comebacks. Bright and witty music score by **Claude Bolling** with harmonica solos by René Gary.

73

The ant and the aardvark

USA 1968 – 6 mins
dir Friz Freleng

Quite funny, though crudely drawn, colour cartoon – the first of a series featuring these two rather unlovable characters. Doug Goodwin's bouncy music score is played by **Pete Candoli**, *tpt;* **Billy Byers**, *trb;* **Jimmy Rowles**, *pno;* **Tommy Tedesco**, *gtr;* **Ray Brown**, *bass;* and **Shelly Manne**, *drs*.

74

The ant from U.N.C.L.E.

USA 1968 – 6 mins
dir George Gordon

Poor colour cartoon in the *Ant and Aardvark* series. As previously, Doug Goodwin's music is played by **Pete Candoli**, *tpt;* **Billy Byers**, *trb;* **Jimmy Rowles**, *pno;* **Tommy Tedesco**, *gtr;* **Ray Brown**, *bass;* and **Shelly Manne**, *drs*.

75

Antipolis/Rendez-vous à Antibes-Juan-les-Pins

France 1952 – 25 mins
dir Robert Mariaud

Aspects and pleasures of Antibes, with music by **Claude Luter**.

76

Antiseptics in hospital

UK 1970 – 18 mins
dir Peter Rawson

The importance of the use of antiseptics in a hospital, produced for I.C.I. Music score by **Johnny Hawksworth.**

77

Antoine et Sébastien

France 1973 – 90 mins
dir Jean-Marie Périer

The story of a father and his adopted son; their friendship, their alliances, their growing understanding of each other. **Claude Luter** and His Orchestra provide sections of the soundtrack music.

78
Anything goes/Tops is the limit

USA 1936 – 91 mins
dir Lewis Milestone

Screen adaptation of the hit Broadway musical set on a ship crossing from New York to Southampton. Whilst justly famous for a host of now-classic Cole Porter songs, included is 'Moonburn' by Edward Heyman and **Hoagy Carmichael**.

79
Apollon – una fabrica occupata

Italy 1969 – 70 mins
dir Ugo Gregoretti

A collective of Italian workers re-enact the labour/management conflict that led to the occupation of their printing plant. Boasts a music score of Free Jazz.

80
Applause

USA 1929 – 82 mins
dir Rouben Mamoulian

Remarkable first feature by one of Hollywood's supreme stylists, based on the novel by Beth Brown. One of the many songs and musical numbers is 'I've got a feelin' I'm fallin' ' by Billy Rose, Harry Link and **Fats Waller**.

81
Appointment with crime

UK 1946 – 98 mins
dir John Harlow

Modest but unusual crime melodrama free from many of the clichés usually found in the second feature thrillers of the period. Dance hall sequences feature The Lew Stone Orchestra and The **Bud Featherstonhaugh** Sextette.

82
Appunti per un orestiade Africana (Notes for an African oresteia)

Italy 1970 – 65 mins
dir Pier Paolo Pasolini

A remarkable film diary of a filmmaker observing himself in the creative process as he makes plans for a film version of the Aeschylus trilogy. Music by **Gato Barbieri**, who is also shown with his group at a recording session.

83
Appunti per un film sul jazz/Notes for a film on jazz

Italy 1965 – 35 mins
dir Gianni Amico

Poorly constructed and clumsily synchronised reportage on the 1965 Bologna Jazz Festival. Musicians appearing include **Mal Waldron, Don Cherry, Johnny Griffin, Ted Curson, Steve Lacy, Annie Ross, Pony Poindexter, Gato Barbieri** and **Karl Berger**. Numbers include 'Now's the time' and 'Tears for Dolphy'.

84
Arabesque

USA 1966 – 105 mins
dir Stanley Donen

Confused, gimmicky adaptation of Gordon Cotler's novel *The Cipher* that fails completely to produce the required dramatic tension. Henry Mancini composed and conducted the score using the talents of **Shelly Manne**, *drs;* **Manny Klein**, *tpt;* **Dick Nash**, *trb;* **Bob Bain**, *mandola;* **Jimmy Rowles**, *pno;* **Jack Sheldon**, *tpt;* **Vince de Rosa**, *Fr horn;* and **Ted Nash**, *alt sax.*

85
Archie Shepp chez les Tourages

France 1971 – 17 mins
dir Théo Robichet

Archie Shepp at the Pan African Festival in Algiers.

86
The arrangement

USA 1969 – 125 mins
dir Elia Kazan

Highly emotional and unnecessarily glossy, romantic melodrama with some bravura performances. Excellent music track by **David Amram**.

87
Art Lund – Tex Beneke – Les Brown

USA 1948 – 10 mins
dir Jack Scholl

One in the series of Martin Block's musical *merry-go-rounds*. 'Ma'm'selle' and 'The sad cowboy' are the two numbers featured by The **Tex Beneke** and **Les Brown** Orchestras.

88
Artie Shaw and His Orchestra

USA 1939 – 10 mins
dir Roy Mack

Vitaphone short featuring **Artie Shaw** and his Orchestra with 'Begin the beguine', 'Let's stop the clock' sung by Helen Forrest, 'Non-stop flight' and 'Press-tschai' sung by Tony Pastor. **Buddy Rich** is on drums.

89

Artie Shaw and His Orchestra in symphony of swing

USA 1939 – 10 mins
dir Joseph Henabery

In a band setting **Artie Shaw** and His Orchestra play 'Jeepers creepers', 'Deep purple' and 'Lady be good' aided by vocals from Helen Forrest and Tony Pastor, with **Buddy Rich**, *drs*.

90

Artie Shaw's class in swing

USA 1939 – 9 mins
dir Leslie Roush

Paramount short subject featuring **Artie Shaw** and His Orchestra with 'I have eyes', 'Shoot the licker to me, John boy', 'Nightmare' and 'Hold your hats'. **Buddy Rich** is on drums.

91

Artistry in rhythm

USA 1944 – 20 mins
dir Lewis D. Collins

A Universal Name Band Musical featuring **Stan Kenton** and His Orchestra playing 'Eager beaver', 'Taboo', 'She's funny that way' and 'Memphis lament' (vocals on latter two by **Gene Howard**), 'Tabby the cat' (**Gene Roland**, *arr;* **Anita O'Day**, *voc*), 'Mother Brady's boarding house' (Dave Matthews, *arr;* **Anita O'Day**, *voc*) and 'Siboney the tailor maid'. Personnel: **John Carroll, Buddy Childers, Karl George, Gene Roland, Mel Green**, *tpts;* **Harry Forbes, Freddie Zito, Milt Kabak**, *trbs;* **Bart Varsalona**, *bass trb;* **Bob Lively,'Boots' Mussulli**, *alt sax;* **Dave Madden, Stan Getz**, *ten sax;* **Bob Gioga**, *bar sax;* **Stan Kenton**, *pno;* **Bob Ahern**, *gtr;* **Bob Kesterson**, *bass;* **Jim Falzone**, *drs*. (**Stan Getz** is heard on the soundtrack but not seen; he was replaced on camera being under age for a movie appearance).

92

Artists and models

USA 1937 – 97 mins
dir Raoul Walsh

Comedy with music set in the advertising world, with Jack Benny taking care of the former. Features a raucous interlude from **Louis Armstrong** and His Band and **Connie Boswell**. Numbers: 'Whispers in the dark', 'Public melody number one', 'Mister esquire', 'Pop goes the bubble', 'Stop, you're breaking my heart' and 'Sasha pasha opening'.

93

Ascenseur pour l'échafaud/Lift to the scaffold/Elevator to the gallows

France 1957 – 89 mins
dir Louis Malle

Louis Malle's first feature film, an intelligent and stylish thriller. The jazz soundtrack was entirely improvised to the image by **Miles Davis**, *tpt*, with an ensemble composed of **Barney Wilen**, *ten sax;* **René Urtreger**, *pno;* **Pierre Michelot**, *bass;* and **Kenny Clarke**, *drs*.

94

Assassins d'eau douce

France 1946 – 23 mins
dir Jean Painlevé

A study of carnivorous fresh-water larvae in which two **Ellington** recordings, 'White heat' and 'Stompy Jones', are used on the soundtrack, both stylistically in accord with the unusual world that is being described.

95

Assault on a queen

USA 1966 – 106 mins
dir Jack Donohue

Preposterous melodrama about a plot to hijack the Queen Mary using an old U-boat. Music score composed by **Duke Ellington** and played by His Orchestra. Soundtrack musicians: **Cat Anderson, Cootie Williams, Conte Candoli, Al Porcino, Ray Triscari**, *tpts;* **Milt Bernhart, Hoyt Bohannon, Murray McEachern, Ken Shroyer**, *trbs;* **Jimmy Hamilton**, *clar, ten sax;* **Bud Shank, Buddy Collette**, *alt sax, flutes;* **Johnny Hodges**, *alt sax;* **Paul Gonsalves**, *ten sax;* **Harry Carney**, *bar sax, clar, bas-clar;* **Ellington**, *pno;* **John Lamb**, *bass;* **Louis Bellson**, *drs*, Catherine Gotthoffer, *harp*.

96

At long last love

USA 1975 – 114 mins
dir Peter Bogdanovich

Embarrassingly limp musical romance featuring 16 Cole Porter songs orchestrated by Gus Levene and **Harry Betts**.

97

At the Club Savoy

USA c 1942 – 3 mins

Soundie featuring comedy-singer Mabel Todd, backed by **Sonny Dunham**.

98

Atlantic City/Atlantic City honeymoon

USA 1944 – 87 mins
dir Ray McCarey

Musical comedy about a young showman who aims to make Atlantic City the centre of the entertainment world. Features **Paul Whiteman** and His Orchestra, **Louis Armstrong** and His Orchestra and Buck and Bubbles. Numbers include 'After you've gone' and 'Nobody's sweetheart'.

Artie Shaw poses for a publicity shot at Paramount Studios.

Atlantic City honeymoon
see **Atlantic City.**

99

Att älska/To love

Sweden 1964 – 95 mins
dir Jörn Donner

Solemn, intellectual sex drama; peculiarly Scandinavian, with all that that implies. Music by Bo Nilsson and **Eje Thelin**'s Quintet.

100

Au Guadalquivir

France 1965 – 15 mins
dir Jean-Loup Puzenat

Documentary about the Guadalquivir valley in the south of Spain. Music by **Jacques Loussier**.

101

Auf wiedersehn

West Germany 1961 – 98 mins
dir Harald Philipp

Heavy comedy about three German-Americans who are caught in the outbreak of war and sent to the USA as spies. Includes an appearance by **Louis Armstrong**.

102

The autobiography of Miss Jane Pittman

USA 1973 – 109 mins
dir John Korty

Adaptation of the novel by Ernest J. Gaines, made originally for US TV. **Odetta** is featured in a small acting role.

103

Autour d'un récif

France 1949 – 15 mins
dir Jacques-Yves Cousteau

Extraordinary underwater documentary exploring the world of tropical fish. Music by **André Hodeir** played by **Don Byas**, *ten sax;* **Kenny Clarke**, *drs;* **Bernard Peiffer**, *pno;* **Hubert Rostaing**, *clar, alt sax;* **Jo Boyer**, *tpt;* **Géo Daly**, *vibs;* **Jean Bouchéty**, *bass,* and Tony Proteau and His Orchestra.

104

Autour d'une trompette

France 1952 – 21 mins
dir Pierre Neurisse

A documentary in two parts. The first deals with the manufacture of trumpets; the second with music on trumpet by **Roy Eldridge** backed by **Benny Vasseur, Claude Bolling, Guy de Fatto, Armand Molinetti, Don Byas** and Belgian singer Yetty Lee.

105

Autumn leaves

USA 1956 – 107 mins
dir Robert Aldrich

A highly coloured piece of emotional fantasy rigidly tailored to the personality and range of its star, Miss Joan Crawford. The title song is sung on soundtrack by **Nat 'King' Cole**.

106

Autumn spectrum

Netherlands 1958 – 6 mins
dir Hy Hirsh

A film collage of images reflected in the water of Amsterdam canals. Soundtrack music by The **Modern Jazz Quartet**.

107

L'Avatar botanique de Melle Flora

France 1965 – 14 mins
dir Jeanne Barbillon

Fictional story of a lonely woman living with a soldier in a small garrison town. Music by **Jacques Loussier**.

108

L'Aventure du jazz

France 1969/70
dir Louis and Claudine Pannasié

Critic Hugues Pannasié's son Louis and daughter-in-law Claudine filmed a number of artistes over a two year period in New York to produce this splendid record of performances by top Swing and Blues musicians. Collective personnel appearing: **Buck Clayton**, *tpt;* **Vic Dickenson**, *trb;* **Budd Johnson**, *ten sax, sop sax;* **Sonny White**, *pno;* **Tiny Grimes**, *gtr;* **Milt Hinton**, *bass;* **Jimmy Crawford**, *drs;* **Memphis Slim**, *pno, voc;* **Milt Sealey**, *pno;* **Bernard Upson**, *bass-gtr;* **Joe Marshall**, *drs;* **Pat Jenkins**, *tpt;* **Eli Robinson**, *trb;* **George Baker**, *gtr;* **Ted Sturgis**, *bass-gtr;* **Cozy Cole**, *drs;* **Sister Rosetta Tharpe**, *gtr, voc;* **Jo Jones**, *drs;* **Milt Buckner**, *org;* **Cliff Jackson**, *pno;* **Zutty Singleton**, *drs;* **John Lee Hooker**, *gtr, voc;* **Willie 'The Lion' Smith**, *pno;* **Dick Vance**, *tpt;* **Buddy Tate**, *clar, ten sax;* **Ben Richardson**, *clar, alt sax, bar sax;* **Eddie Barefield**, *clar, alt sax.* Numbers: 'Chez Pannasié' by **Buck Clayton**; 'Montaubon blues' by **Budd Johnson**; 'Blues is everywhere' by 'Jumpin' at the Woodside' by **Count Basie**; 'One o'clock jump' by **Count Basie**; 'Go ahead' by **Rosetta Tharpe**; 'Caravan' by **Duke Ellington** and **Juan Tizol**; 'Wolverine blues' by **Jelly Roll Morton**; 'When my first wife quit me' by **John Lee Hooker**; 'Relaxin'' by **Willie 'The Lion' Smith**; 'Tin roof blues' by Rappolo-Mares-**Brunies-Ben Pollack**- Stitzel; 'Jokin'' by **Eli Robinson**; 'Boogie Chillun' by **John**

Lee Hooker; 'Beer drinking woman'; 'New Orleans drums' by **Zutty Singleton**; 'Rim shots' by **Zutty Singleton**; 'Basin Street blues'; 'Here comes the band' by **Willie 'The Lion' Smith**; 'Swingin' in Biarritz' by **Milt Buckner, Jo Jones**; 'Tea for two'; 'That's all' by **Rosetta Tharpe**; 'I shall not be moved'; 'The Mooche' by **Duke Ellington**, Irving Mills; 'Drum face no 3' by **Zutty Singleton**; 'Honeysuckle Rose' by **Fats Waller**, Andy Razaf; 'Cozy's drums' by **Cozy Cole**. Also features Lou Parks's remarkable Lindy Hoppers.

109

Les aventures d'un photographe

France 1960 – 13 mins
dir Michel Latouche

The adventures of a photographer during a trip round the tourist sights of Paris. Music by **Martial Solal**.

110
Baby don't you love me anymore
USA 1943 – 3 mins
Soundie featuring vocalist **June Richmond** singing the title number.

111
Baby face
USA 1933 – 68 mins
dir Alfred E. Green
Ruthless but amusing vehicle for Barbara Stanwyck charting her upward progress from the bottom of a New York skyscraper bank to the penthouse. **W. C. Handy**'s 'St Louis blues' is used throughout as a musical linking device.

112
Baby the rain must fall
USA 1964 – 93 mins
dir Robert Mulligan
Likeable, intelligent adaptation of Horton Foote's play *The Travelling Lady* with some charmingly natural performances. Elmer Bernstein's score is arranged by **Shorty Rogers**.

113
Back room blues
USA c1952 – 3 mins
Telescription of **Red Nichols** playing the title number.

Backfire
see **Echappement libre.**

114
Badlands
USA 1973 – 94 mins
dir Terrence Malick
Highly acclaimed venture into recent American mythology based on the true story of a young couple's killing spree across Nebraska in 1958. **Nat 'King' Cole**'s recording of 'A blossom fell' is used on soundtrack.

115
La balade d'Emile
France 1966 – 2 mins
dir Manuel Otéro
Animated cartoon about a man who undergoes a series of transformations. Music by **Martial Solal**.

116
Ball of fire
USA 1941 – 112 mins
dir Howard Hawks
Scintillating comedy, with Gary Cooper and Barbara Stanwyck, based loosely on the theme of *Snow White and the seven dwarfs*, which Hawks was later to remake as *A song is born*. One excellent musical sequence features **Gene Krupa** and His Orchestra playing 'Drum boogie' (vocal by Miss Stanwyck) with Krupa switching from drumsticks to matchsticks for a final coda.

117
Ballad in blue/Blues for lovers
UK 1964 – 88 mins
dir Paul Henried
Flaccid tear-jerker saved only by **Ray Charles**, who plays the leading role with his customary authority and panache. His band, with The Raelets, generates a healthy swing.

Ray Charles with His Orchestra and The Raelets in
Ballad in blue.

118

Ballet in jazz

West Germany 1960 – 15 mins
dir Hans Reinhard

The development of modern ballet from its
classical form, performed by a totally incompetent
group of dancers to turgid Teutonic big band jazz
by Werner Pohl.

119

Ban Nhac Teagarden

Vietnam 1958 – 8 mins

The **Jack Teagarden** Sextet recorded in Saigon
during their 1958/9 tour.

120

Bananas

USA 1971 – 81 mins
dir Woody Allen

Undisciplined but enjoyable series of jokes,
mainly visual; slapstick, broad satire, spoof TV
commercials and one good movie joke.
Orchestrations by **Ralph Burns**.

121

Band of thieves

UK 1972 – 69 mins
dir Peter Bezencenet

Musical comedy about a Traditional jazz band
which makes a name for itself in gaol and, on
release, goes on to better things. Features **Acker
Bilk** and His Band.

122

Band parade

USA 1943 – 10 mins
dir Josef Berne

A couple of numbers performed by **Count Basie**
and His Band with solos from **Buck Clayton** and
Harry Edison, *tpts;* **Don Byas** and **Buddy Tate**,
ten sax; **Jo Jones**, *drs,* and **Basie**, *pno,* plus a
vocal group singing 'Someone's rocking my
dreamboat' plus The **Delta Rhythm Boys**.

The bandit
see **Il bandito**.

123

Il bandito/The bandit

Italy 1946 – 90 mins
dir Alberto Lattuada

Story of a returned ex-soldier, from a camp in
Russia, who finds himself homeless and
abandoned by his family, remorselessly driven to
a life of crime. Soundtrack features **Ella
Fitzgerald**'s recording of 'A tisket-a-tasket'.

124

Bandwagon

UK 1958 – 9 mins
dir Peter Hopkinson

Well above average advertising film made for the
Ford Motor Company which features The **Cy
Laurie** Jazz Band.

125

Bang!

UK 1967 – 8 mins
dir Bob Godfrey

A characteristic Bob Godfrey comedy which
strings together a number of disconnected
Goonish happenings. Music by **Johnny
Hawksworth**.

126

Banning

USA 1967 – 102 mins
dir Ron Winston

Laborious, unconvincing entertainment set in the
artificial world of an exclusive country club. Music
by **Quincy Jones**.

127

Banquet of melody

USA 1946 – 15 mins
dir Will Cowan

Universal short featuring Matty Malneck and His
Orchestra, The **Delta Rhythm Boys**, Peggy Lee
and Rosa Linda. Numbers: 'My blue heaven'; 'Dry
bones', 'Poet and peasant', 'I don't know enough
about you', 'Don't blame me' and 'Stompin' at the
Savoy'.

128

Bar babble

USA c1942 – 3 mins

Soundie featuring **Jimmy Dorsey** and His
Orchestra.

129

Barber shop blues

USA 1933 – 9 mins
dir Joseph Henabery

Vitaphone short with **Claude Hopkins** and His
Orchestra and The Four Step Brothers with
'Trees', 'St Louis blues', 'Nagasaki' and 'Loveless
love'. Personnel: **Albert Snaer, Sylvester Lewis,
Ovie Alston**, *tpts;* **Fernando Arbello, Fred
Norman**, *trbs;* **Gene Johnson, Edmond Hall,
Bobby Sands**, *saxes;* **Claude Hopkins**, *pno;*
Walter 'Joe' Jones, *gtr;* **Henry Turner**, *bass,*
tuba; **Pete Jacobs**, *drs;* and Orlando Roberson,
voc.

130

Barefoot adventure

USA 1961
dir Bruce Brown

Surfing movie little known outside the USA with
soundtrack music composed and played by **Bud
Shank**, *alt sax, bar sax;* with **Carmell Jones**, *tpt;*
Bob Cooper, *ten sax;* **Dennis Budimir**, *gtr;* **Gary
Peacock**, *bass;* and **Shelly Manne**, *drs.*

131

Barefoot in the park

USA 1967 – 105 mins
dir Gene Saks

Excellent adaptation by Neil Simon of his own
highly successful play – a marital comedy. Music
and title song by **Neal Hefti**.

132

Barney Kessel Trio

USA 1962 – 23 mins
dir Steve Binder

Hosted by Oscar Brown Jnr, and originally
produced as *Jazz Scene USA* for US TV, a
bandstand programme by **Barney Kessel**, *gtr;*
Buddy Woodson, *bass;* **Stan Levey**, *drs.*
Numbers: 'Gypsy in my soul', 'In other words',
'April in Paris', 'Danny boy' and 'One mint julip'.

133

Barnyard bounce

USA 1941 – 3 mins

Soundie. One number by The Will Bradley
Orchestra featuring drummer **Ray McKinley**.

134

Bariera/Barrier

Poland 1966 – 83 mins
dir Jerzy Skolimowski

A devastating allegory of the Polish state of mind;
about a national schizophrenia, the barrier
between two generations. Full of dazzling visual
metaphors with suitable music score by **Krzysztof
Komeda**.

Barrier
see **Bariera.**

135

Basie boogie

USA c1950 – 3 mins

Snader Telescription in which **Count Basie** interprets the title number, featuring **Clark Terry**, *tpt;* **Buddy DeFranco**, *clar;* **Wardell Gray**, *ten sax;* **Freddie Green**, *gtr;* **Jimmy Lewis**, *bass;* **Gus Johnson**, *drs.*

136

Basie's conversation

USA c1950 – 3 mins

Telescription of The **Count Basie** Sextet playing the title number and featuring **Buddy DeFranco**, *clar;* **Clark Terry**, *tpt;* and **Freddie Green**, *gtr.*

137

Basin Street blues

USA c1952 – 3 mins

Telescription of **Jack Teagarden** with the title number.

A section of The Louis Armstrong Band in **The beat generation***.*

138

Basin Street revue

USA 1956 – 69 mins

Musical extravaganza with **Lionel Hampton, Sarah Vaughan** and **Nat 'King' Cole** featured. Possibly a compilation of Soundies.

139

The bat people

USA 1974 – 95 mins
dir Jerry Jameson

Low-budget exploitation production on the familiar bestiality theme but using bats instead of birds, worms, fish or what have you. Music score by pianist **Artie Kane**.

140

Bathing beauty/Mr Co-ed

USA 1944 – 101 mins
dir George Sidney

Conventional, brightly coloured nonsense with Esther Williams doing her swimming bit. **Harry James** appears in a speaking role and also with His Music Makers plus Helen Forrest singing 'I cried for you'. Some orchestrations by **Calvin Jackson**.

141

Battle hymn of the Republic

USA c1952 – 3 mins

Telescription of **Red Nichols** playing the title number.

142

Battle stations

USA 1956 – 81 mins
dir Lewis Seiler

Indifferent navy drama, filled with dialogue clichés and hackneyed incidents and characters. **Dick Cathcart**, *tpt*, participated in Mischa Bakaleinikoff's music track.

143

The beat generation

USA 1959 – 93 mins
dir Charles Haas

An enervating mixture of slapstick, religiosity, psychological hokum and grubby sensationalism signifying nothing. Features **Louis Armstrong** and His Band (**Peanuts Hucko**, *clar*) and **Ray Anthony**: the former also supplies a song: 'Someday you'll be sorry'.

144

Beat me daddy, eight to the bar

USA 1940 – 17 mins
dir Larry Ceballos

A Universal featurette in which **Wingy Manone** and His Orchestra, in a salon setting, accompany The Fashionaires, Cathlyn Miller, Alphonse Berg, Maxine Grey and Larry Blake. Numbers include 'Sing, sing, sing' and 'Love is the fashion'.

145

Beat the band

USA 1947 – 67 mins
dir John H. Auer

Unspeakably bad romantic melodrama of a small-town girl who goes to the big city and becomes involved with a bandleader, based on a Broadway play by George Abbott. **Gene Krupa** has a speaking part and appears as soloist with His Orchestra in two rousing numbers, one of which, 'Shadow rhapsody', is so well produced that it could have been made for a different movie. **Gerry Mulligan** is prominent in the band, on alto sax.

146

Beau masque

France/Italy 1972 – 95 mins
dir Bernard Paul

A screen adaptation of a 1950's book by Roger Vailland – a didactic attempt to look at workers' lives and crystallizing it all with a strike. Music by **André Hodeir**.

The Gene Krupa Orchestra in **Beat the band**, *with a young Gerry Mulligan on alto sax.*

▼

Gene Krupa in the memorable production number from **Beat the band**.

147

Le beau militaire

France 1968 – 12 mins
dir Pierre Lambert

Fictional short about a romantic young girl's dreams of a soldier. Music by **Jacques Loussier**.

148

Because I love you

USA c1943 – 3 mins

Soundie in which the title number is sung by **Mamie Smith** backed by The **Lucky Millinder** Band.

Before the revolution

see **Prima della rivoluzione.**

149

Begone dull care

Canada 1948/9 – 8 mins
dir Norman McLaren

A lively interpretation, in fluid lines and colours, of three jazz numbers played by **Oscar Peterson,** *pno;* **Auston Roberts,** *bass;* and **Clarence Jones,** *drs.*

150

The beguiled

USA 1970 – 105 mins
dir Donald Siegel

Outrageous piece of Southern baroque set in the days of the American Civil War, full of atmospherics and sexual symbolism. Percussive music score by **Lalo Schifrin**, and an acting role for singer Mae Mercer.

151

Behind the eight ball/Off the beaten track

USA 1942 – 60 mins
dir Edward F. Cline

Formula vehicle for the three Ritz Brothers
featuring **Sonny Dunham** and His Orchestra and
Ted Lewis's song 'When my baby smiles at me'.

152

Bell, book and candle

USA 1958 – 102 mins
dir Richard Quine

A slender adaptation of John Van Druten's play in
which **Pete** and **Conte Candoli** feature in a short
sequence.

153

Belle of the nineties

USA 1934 – 70 mins
dir Leo McCarey

One of the classic Mae West vehicles in which
she portrays a tough nineteenth-century show-girl
in love with a young boxer. **Duke Ellington** with
all, and sometimes part of His Orchestra provides
the backing, often on screen, for the songs 'When
a St Louis woman goes down to New Orleans',
'Memphis blues', 'My old flame' and 'Troubled
waters'. Part of **Scott Joplin**'s 'Maple leaf rag' is
used for underscore. Musicians involved are:
**Barney Bigard, Johnny Hodges, Otto
Hardwicke, Harry Carney, Sam Nanton, Juan
Tizol, Lawrence Brown, Freddie Jenkins,
Cootie Williams, Arthur Whetsol, Fred Guy,
Wellman Braud, Sonny Greer** and **Ellington**.

154

Belles on their toes

USA 1952 – 89 mins
dir Henry Levin

A sequel to *Cheaper by the dozen* relating further
adventures in the lives of the twelve Gilbreth
children. Features **Hoagy Carmichael**.

*Duke Ellington with His Orchestra at Paramount Studios
in 1934*

Teddy Wilson, Lionel Hampton, Steve Allen and Gene Krupa in **The Benny Goodman story**.

155
Bells are ringing
USA 1960 – 125 mins
dir Vincente Minnelli

Screen version of the hit Broadway play by Betty Comden and Adolph Green. Disappointing except for the impeccable Judy Holliday. Contains a brief appearance by **Gerry Mulligan**.

156
Ben Pollack and His Orchestra
USA 1934 – 9 mins
dir Joseph Henabery

Vitaphone short featuring **Ben Pollack** and His Orchestra, assisted by dancers, playing 'Mimi', 'L'Amour, toujours l'amour', 'I've got the jitters' and 'The beat of my heart'.

157
Ben Pollack and His Park Central Orchestra
USA 1929 – 9 mins

Music short produced by the Vitaphone Corporation featuring The **Ben Pollack** Orchestra.

158
The Benny Goodman story
USA 1955 – 116 mins
dir Valentine Davies

Probably the most watchable of the screen jazz biographies with the musical advantage that **Goodman** himself recorded the soundtrack as well as ghosting clarinet for Steve Allen.
Collective personnel of contributing musicians: **Goodman**, *clar;* **Alan Reuss**, *gtr;* **Teddy Wilson**, *pno;* **Gene Krupa**, *drs;* **George Duvivier**, *bass;* **Blake Reynolds**, *alt sax;* **Hymie Shertzer**, *alt sax;* **Stan Getz**, *ten sax;* **John Best**, *tpt;* **Conrad Gozzo**, *tpt;* **Chris Griffin**, *tpt;* **Irving Goodman**, *tpt;* **Murray McEachern**, *trb;* **Urbie Green**, *trb;*

Jimmy Priddy, *trb;* 'Babe' Russin, *ten sax;* Harry James, *tpt;* Manny Klein, *tpt;* Lionel Hampton, *vibs;* Buck Clayton, *tpt;* Ziggy Elman, *tpt,* (appears but is dubbed by Manny Klein); Kid Ory; Ben Pollack; Alvin Alcorn and vocalist Martha Tilton. Numbers: 'Let's dance'; 'Down south camp meetin'' by Irving Mills, Fletcher Henderson; 'King Porter stomp' by Jelly Roll Morton; 'It's been so long'; 'Roll 'em' by Mary Lou Williams; 'Bugle call rag'; 'Don't be that way' by Goodman, Sampson, Parrish; 'You turned the tables on me'; 'Goody goody'; 'Slipped disc' by Goodman; 'Stompin' at the Savoy' by Goodman, Chick Webb, Sampson; 'One o'clock jump' by Count Basie; 'Memories of you' by Eubie Blake, Razaf; 'China boy', 'Moonglow'; 'Avalon'; 'And the angels sing' by Ziggy Elman, Mercer; 'Jersey bounce'; 'Sometimes I'm happy'; 'Sing, sing, sing' by Louis Prima; Fletcher Henderson is portrayed in the film by Sammy Davis, Snr

159
Berlin og festivalen
Denmark 1963

Impressions of the 1962 Berlin Festival with music by Bjarne Rostvold, Arne Forchhammer and Niels-Henning Ørsted Pedersen.

160
Bernadine
USA 1957 – 95 mins
dir Henry Levin

Uninteresting High School musical comedy from the play by Mary Chase. Jack Costanzo is featured leading his own big band.

161
Bernice bobs her hair/Rites of passage
USA 1976 – 45 mins
dir Joan Micklin Silver

Featurette adaptation of F. Scott Fitzgerald's story about the blossoming of a wallflower in the 1920's. Music by Dick Hyman, performed by Bill Dern Associates.

162
Bessie Smith
USA 1969 – 13 mins
dir Charles I. Levine

Totally artless 'underground' movie exploiting the death of Bessie Smith by intercutting footage from the 1929 *St Louis blues* with footage of a Civil Rights demo in Mississippi backed on sound-track by original Bessie Smith recordings.

163
Best foot forward
USA 1943 – 94 mins
dir Edward Buzzell

MGM Technicolor musical based on the stage play with June Allyson making her feature debut in the role she created on Broadway. Features Harry James and His Music Makers.

164
The best in Cinerama
USA 1963 – 141 mins

A collection of excerpts from previous Cinerama movies which includes the New Orleans jazz sequence in *Cinerama Holiday.*

165
The best man
USA 1964 – 104 mins
dir Franklin Schaffner

Immensely entertaining political comedy scripted by Gore Vidal from his own play; impeccably performed, creatively photographed and intelligently directed. Includes an appearance by Mahalia Jackson.

Best of the blues
see St Louis blues (1939).

166
The best years of our lives
USA 1946 – 182 mins
dir William Wyler

Award-winning, epic-length drama adapted from the book *Glory for me* by MacKinley Kantor about three war veterans, their return home and their re-adjustment problems. Above all, Gregg Toland's cinematography is superlative. Features Hoagy Carmichael and the song 'Lazy river' by Carmichael and Sidney Arodin.

167
Between two worlds
UK 1952 – 19 mins
dir Guy Coté

Ambitious experimental film ballet produced by Oxford University Film Society about a blind artist torn between his love for a girl and a mysterious guide. Soundtrack jazz sequence by Jack Parnell with Ronnie Scott, Jimmy Deuchar, Sammy Stokes and Tony Crombie.

168
Beware
USA 1946 – 45 mins
dir Bud Pollard

An all-Negro musical featuring **Louis Jordan**.

169
Bielles des sables
France 1952 – 20 mins
dir Jean-Claude Huisman

The story of Saharan caravans, with music score by **André Hodeir**.

170
Bienvenue à . . . Duke Ellington
France 1973 – 75 mins
dir Guy Job

Documentary originally produced by ORTF focusing on **Duke Ellington** during one of his last European tours. Includes an excerpt from his ballet *The river*.

171
The big beat
USA 1957 – 82 mins
dir Will Cowan

A series of musical numbers loosely strung together with a skimpy plot, interesting only for appearances by **Charlie Barnet, Buddy Bregman, Harry James, George Shearing** and His Quintet (Percy Brice, *drs*), The **Cal Tjader** Quintet, **Fats Domino** and The **Mills Brothers**.

172
Big Ben
Netherlands 1967 – 31 mins
dir Johann van der Keuken

Documentary on **Ben Webster** in which he is studied and interviewed in Europe, with guest **Don Byas**.

Fats Domino and musicians entertain in **The big beat**.

'Big' Bill Broonzy plays in a Brussels cellar for 'Big' Bill blues.

173
'Big' Bill blues

Belgium 1956 – 18 mins
dir Jean Délire

Pretentious, though valuable, film record of a club performance by **'Big' Bill Broonzy** singing/playing four numbers.

174
'Big' Bill Broonzy

USA – 9 mins

An untitled, unacknowledged film record of **'Big' Bill Broonzy** sitting on a front porch in the sun and playing 'Twelve bar blues', 'John Henry', 'Stump blues' and 'Boogie'. It is thought to date from the early forties.

175
The big broadcast

USA 1932 – 80 mins
dir Frank Tuttle

Pedestrian romantic comedy enlivened by some splendid variety acts by popular broadcasters of the period. The **Mills Brothers** provide 'Tiger Rag'; The three **Boswell Sisters** 'Crazy people'; **Cab Calloway** and His Harlem Maniacs 'Minnie the moocher' and **Benny Carter**'s 'Hot Toddy' and Bing Crosby rehearses 'Please' accompanied by **Eddie Lang**, *gtr.*

176
The big broadcast of 1937

USA 1936 – 99 mins
dir Mitchell Leisen

Little more than a filmed variety show spotlighting a series of popular radio acts. Features **Benny Goodman** and His Orchestra (with **Jess Stacy** and **Gene Krupa**) and the orchestras of Ray Noble and **Ina Ray Hutton**. Numbers: 'You came to my rescue'; 'Here's love in your eye'; 'Your minstrel man'; 'Night in Manhattan'; 'Here comes the bride'; 'Bugle call rag'; 'La bomba' and 'Cross patch'.

Guitarist Eddie Lang accompanies Bing Crosby in **The big broadcast**.

▲

The Benny Goodman Orchestra with Gene Krupa on drums in **The big broadcast of 1937**.

177

The big circus

USA 1959 – 108 mins
dir Joseph Newman

Fast-paced melo running the gamut of every situation familiar to circus stories. **Ted Nash** participated in Paul Sawtell's music track.

178

The big combo

USA 1955 – 81 mins
dir Joseph Lewis

Crisp, professional and unusually violent and ugly gangster thriller with an excellent music score by David Raksin for whom **Shorty Rogers** provided one arrangement.

179

Big fat butterfly

USA c1943 – 3 mins

Soundie featuring **Gene Rodgers** playing the title number.

180

Big fat mamas

USA c1943 – 3 mins

Soundie featuring **'Bull-Moose' Jackson** with the title number.

181

Big noise from Winnetka

USA c1952 – 3 mins

Telescription of The **Bobcats** playing the title number.

182

The big operator

USA 1959 – 91 mins
dir Charles Haas

A characteristic Zugsmith production, purporting to expose American labour rackets while dwelling with relish on scenes of torture and violence. Features **Ray Anthony** with **Vido Musso**.

183

The big shave

USA 1967 – 5 mins
dir Martin Scorsese

An hilarious short film joke in which a man cuts himself while shaving and cuts himself again and again . . . Music: recorded **Bunny Berigan**.

184

The big store

USA 1941 – 83 mins
dir Charles Reisner

One of the weakest of The Marx Brothers comedies with a slight plot used merely as a peg on which to hang the substance of the film – the three let loose in a big city store. Features Virginia O'Brien, Six Hits and a Miss and the song 'If it's you' by Milton Drake, **Artie Shaw** and Ben Oakland.

185

The big TNT show

USA 1966 – 93 mins
dir Larry Peerce

Hollywood's gift to Rock 'n' Roll, an all-star variety show featuring popular recording artistes of the day including **Ray Charles**.

186

Bill Coleman from Boogie to Funk

France 1961 – 9 mins
dir Pierre-A Rocamora

An impression of a Paris jazz club where **Bill Coleman** with **Quentin Jackson, Budd Johnson, Michael Attenoux, André Persiany,** Raymond Fonseque, Max Thomas and Charles Sandrais play 'Bill, Budd and butter' and a snatch of 'Colemanology'. Narration by Sim Copans.

187

Bill Evans

USA 1968 – 17 mins
dir Leland Wyler

A few comments about his work from **Bill Evans** introduce three numbers from the trio at work in a club; 'Jade visions' by **Scott La Faro**, 'Stella by starlight' and 'Emily'. **Bill Evans**, *pno;* **Eddie Gomez**, *bass;* **Arnold Wise**, *drs.* Recorded 27th February 1968.

188

Bill Evans Trio

USA c1968

Originally produced for US TV in their Camera Three series, a programme of music by The **Bill Evans** Trio featuring Jeremy Steig, *flute.* Numbers include 'So what?'

189

Billboard march

USA 1951 – 3 mins

Snader Telescription in which the title number is played by **Les Brown** and His Band.

190

Billy Jack

USA 1971 – 113 mins
dir T. C. Frank (Tom Laughlin)

Curious, bold but ultimately disappointing product of Hollywood radicalism, a plea for the alternative society using the format of the crudest melodrama but made with patent sincerity. Underscore composed and conducted by **Mundell Lowe**.

191

Billy May and His Orchestra

USA 1952 – 15 mins
dir Will Cowan

Universal-International production featuring **Billy May** and His Orchestra backing popular entertainers Marion Colby, The Page Cavanaugh Trio, The Glenns and The Shepard Bell Ringers. Numbers include 'Don't blame me'.

192

The bird

USA 1965 – 4 mins
dir Fred Wolf

Animated colour cartoon depicting the bringing together of two lonely people by a mockingbird. Soundtrack jazz composed and played by **Paul Horn**, *flute.*

193

Birth of a band

USA 1955 – 14 mins
dir Will Cowan

A short story with music about an unsuccessful band that attempts to form a new combo with a girl singer, in the face of their late boss's gangster threats. With the participation of **Joe Maini**, *alt sax*, and singers Connie Haines with 'I can't give you anything but love' and Don Gordon with 'Mr Flamingo'.

194

The birth of Aphrodite

USA – 13 mins
dir Leland Auslender

A highly personal vision of the Aphrodite legend, depicting the birth of the goddess of love and beauty from the Sky God father and the Sea Goddess mother. Music by **Fred Katz**.

195

Birth of the Blues

USA 1941 – 86 mins
dir Victor Schertzinger

A poorly scripted melodrama with Bing Crosby and Mary Martin containing appearances by **Jack Teagarden**. Numbers include 'Memphis blues' and 'St Louis blues', 'Tiger rag', 'Melancholy baby', 'The birth of the Blues' and 'St James infirmary'. Participating on soundtrack are **Danny Polo** (dubbing clarinet for Bing Crosby) and **Poky Carriere** (dubbing trumpet for Brian Donlevy).

196

Black and tan

USA 1929 – 19 mins
dir Dudley Murphy

A rare example of a movie which uses jazz both organically and dramatically, with stunning effect, and with a slight plot that provides a background for the first appearance of **Duke Ellington** on film. On screen is **Duke Ellington** and His Cotton Club Orchestra: **Arthur Whetsol, Freddy Jenkins, Cootie Williams**, *tpts;* **Barney Bigard, Johnny Hodges, Harry Carney**, *reeds;* **Joe Nanton**, *trb;* **Fred Guy**, *banjo;* **Wellman Braud**, *bass;* **Sonny Greer**, *perc;* **Ellington**, *pno*; with The Hall Johnson Choir and Fredi Washington. Musical numbers: 'Black and tan fantasy' by **James 'Bubber' Miley, Duke Ellington**; 'The Duke steps out', 'Black beauty', 'Cotton Club stomp', 'Hot feet', 'Same train' by **Duke Ellington**.

197

The black bunch/Jungle sex

USA 1972 – 67 mins
dir Henning Schellerup

Standard low-budget black vehicle with revolutionary rhetoric, a jungle setting and a quota of sexual push-ups. Music score by **Jack Millman**.

The black glove

see **Face the music.**

198

The black Godfather

USA 1974 – 96 mins
dir John Evans

Black gangster movie – the blacks are the good guys and the baddies are the white Mafia. **Jimmy Witherspoon** plays an elder black leader.

199

Black mama, white mama/Hot, hard and mean

USA 1973 – 85 mins
dir Eddie Romero

The adventures of two women prisoners escaping from a Latin American prison. Music score by **Harry Betts**.

200

Black music in America – from then till now

USA 1971 – 25 mins
dir Hugh A. Robertson

Documentary produced by the Learning Corporation of America on the title subject. Illustrations include **Louis Armstrong, Trummy Young, Ed Hall** during a tour of Ghana; **Nina Simone; Mahalia Jackson; B. B. King** singing 'The thrill is gone'; **Bessie Smith** in 'St Louis blues'; **Count Basie** and His Band; **Billie Holiday** singing 'Fine and mellow' accompanied by **Coleman Hawkins, Gerry Mulligan, Roy Eldridge** etc.; **Duke Ellington** and His Band – including **Johnny Hodges** and **Sonny Greer** – playing 'Take the "A train"', **'Cannonball'** and **Nat Adderley** and soundtrack use of recordings by **'King' Oliver, Jelly Roll Morton** and **Leadbelly**.

201

Black music in transition

USA 1969 – 30 mins

A. B. Spellman discusses the relationship between World War 1, the Harlem renaissance and the migration of Afro-Americans from the South, and traces the evolution of jazz from its origins to its refinement in the back rooms and hot spots of New York.

202

The black network

USA 1936 – 15 mins
dir Roy Mack

Vitaphone short featuring negro entertainers including **Nina Mae McKinney** and The Nicholas Brothers. Songs include 'Something must be wrong with me' and 'Walking with sugar on Sugar Hill'.

203

Black Rodeo

USA 1972 – 87 mins
dir Jeff Kanew

Overlong and repetitive documentary report of the Black Rodeo held in September 1971 at the Triborough Stadium, Randall's Island, New York. Soundtrack music of black performers features **Aretha Franklin, B. B. King, Ray Charles**, Little Richard, Lee Dorsey, Joe Simon, Dee Dee Sharp and Sammy Turner.

204

Black roots

USA 1970 – 61 mins
dir Lionel Rogosin

An attempt to convey some of the suffering, anger and hope of black America through dialogue and music by leading militants including the late Rev **Gary Davis** and singer/guitarist **Larry Johnson**. Incidental recorded music from **Leadbelly, 'Cripple' Clarence Loften, Ray Charles, Memphis Slim** and **John Coltrane.**

205

Black shadows on the silver screen

USA 1975 – 56 mins
dir Thomas Cripps

Cheaply produced, sloppy and misleading documentary on the early black American film industry illustrated by stills and clips from some forty or so productions. Among the personalities revealed are Paul Robeson, Josephine Baker, **Cab Calloway** (in clips from 'Hi de ho' and 'The old man of the mountain') and **Duke Ellington** (in 'Black and tan').

206

The blackboard jungle

USA 1955 – 94 mins
dir Richard Brooks

Contrived, ineffectual melodrama about American educational problems based on the novel by Evan Hunter. In a bar sequence a juke box blares out **Bill Holman**'s 'Invention for guitar and trumpet' played by **Stan Kenton** and His Orchestra. Dramatic use is also made of a recording of 'Jazz me blues' by **Bix Beiderbecke.**

207

The blacksmith blues

USA c1952 – 3 mins

Telescription featuring **Jack Teagarden** playing the title number.

208

Blazing saddles

USA 1974 – 123 mins
dir Mel Brooks

Fast, furious and fond spoof Western raucously mocking everything and everyone that could be crammed into its length. **Count Basie** makes an hilarious appearance calmly swinging 'April in Paris' from a bandstand set in the desert but his band is composed of studio musicians miming to a previously recorded studio playback. Musicians on camera: **Basie**, *pno;* **Marshall Royal, Teddy Edwards**, J. J. Kelson, Fred Jackson, Herman Riley, *saxes;* **Al Aarons, Cat Anderson**, Thomas Cortez, Julius Brooks, *tpts;* **Britt Woodman, Benny Powell, Lawrence Loften**, Maurice Spears, *trbs;* **Red Callender**, *bass;* **Harold Jones**, *drs;* **John Collins**, *gtr.* Recording musicians under John Morris: **Rolly Bundock**, *bass;* **Harry Klee, Wilbur Schwartz**, Jo Soldo, **John Rotella**, Robert Tricarico, *saxes;* **Bud Brisbois,'Snooky'Young, Tony Terran, Pincus Savitt**, *tpts;* **Hoyt Bohannon, Lloyd Ulyate**, Phil Teele, John Bambridge, *trbs;* **Sol Gubin**, *drs;* **Al Hendrickson**, *gtr;* Ralph Grierson, *keyboard;* Tommy Morgan, *hca;* Dale Anderson, *perc.*

209

Bli-blip

USA 1942 – 3 mins

Soundie featuring the song and dance team of Marie Bryant and Paul White, backed by **Duke Ellington** and His Orchestra.

210

'Blind' Gary Davis

USA 1964 – 11 mins
dir Harold Becker

Excellent documentary about the Negro Blues guitarist, including two powerful numbers.

Blind spot

see **The secret fury.**

211

Blindfold

USA 1965 – 102 mins
dir Philip Dunne

Fairly genial example of the spy thriller send-up so popular at this time. Music by **Lalo Schifrin**.

212

Block busters

USA 1944 – 60 mins
dir Wallace Fox

A routine Monogram production glorifying a gang of lazy hooligans, played by The East Side Kids. There is an appearance by **Jimmie Noone**.

Blonde for danger

see **The flamingo affair.**

213

Blood and steel

USA 1959 – 69 mins
dir Bernard L. Kowalski

Perfectly routine low-budget Pacific war movie with little thematic point to it. Has a rather repetitive music score by **Calvin Jackson**.

▲

Count Basie leads a band of studio musicians in **Blazing saddles**.

214

Blood kin/The last of the mobile hotshots

USA 1969 – 108 mins
dir Sidney Lumet

Screen adaptation of Tennessee Williams's play *The Seven descents of Myrtle* – yet another story of Dixie degradation. Music by **Quincy Jones**.

Blood on the streets
see **Borsalino & co.**

Blow-out
see **La grande bouffe.**

215

Blowtop blues

USA 1945 – 3 mins

Soundie featuring **Cab Calloway** and His Band with the title number.

216

Blow-up

UK 1966 – 111 mins
dir Michelangelo Antonioni

Justly renowned masterpiece by one of the Cinema's greatest artists, in which favourite themes are tackled – the disorientation of the contemporary artist and the impossibility of coming to terms with a hostile world. Music composed by **Herbie Hancock**, featuring **Freddie Hubbard** on soundtrack with participating musicians that include **Don Rendell, Ian Carr** and **Gordon Beck**.

217

The blue gardenia

USA 1953 – 90 mins
dir Fritz Lang

Nondescript and far from exciting thriller with such a mediocre script that even Fritz Lang and a good cast can't win. Features an appearance by **Nat 'King' Cole** singing the title song.

218

Blue Harlem

USA 1947

Three numbers by **Billy Eckstine** and His Band with dance creations by Hortense Allen.

219

The blue lamp

UK 1949 – 84 mins
dir Basil Dearden

Coy, theatrical and totally unconvincing melodrama about a pair of young crooks, a robbery, a murder and the ensuing police investigation. A brief club sequence features an English Bop group with **Jack Parnell**, *drs*.

220

Blue tunes

UK 1960 – 9 mins
dir Robert Henryson

Cheaply-made music short presenting three groups in a bandstand setting. First is The Ray Ellington Quartet playing 'I'll close my eyes'. Then **Dill Jones** and His All Stars with 'The gipsy' (Bill Le Sage, *vibs*; Terry Lovelock, *drs*). Finally Eric Delaney and His Band with 'My guy's come back'.

Blues

see **L'Inspecteur connait la musique.**

Blues according to 'Lightnin'' Hopkins *(Fair Enterprises)*.

▼

221

The Blues

USA 1960's – 25 mins
dir Dietrich and Anne Maria Wawzyn

Originally produced for German TV, a study of old ethnic performers and urban bluesmen including **Willie B. Thomas, Mance Lipscombe, Ed Pickens, Black Ace, Alex Moore, 'Lightnin'' Hopkins, Jesse Fuller** and **Lowell Fulson.**

222

The Blues

USA 1973 – 21 mins
dir Samuel Charters

Documents the music and the environment of blues singing in the urban and rural areas of the South, with music sung and played by J. D. Short, 'Baby' Tate, 'Memphis' Willie B., Gus Cannon and **'Sleepy' John Estes**.

223

Blues accordin' to 'Lightnin'' Hopkins

USA 1968 – 31 mins
dir Les Blank, Skip Gerson

An impressionistic study of the man himself using a free-wheeling technique that combines footage of the artiste performing with shots of his environment and friends. Also appearances by **Mance Lipscombe, Ruth 'Blues' Ames** and **Billy Bizor.**

Blues between the teeth

see **Le blues entre les dents.**

224

Il blues della domenica

Italy 1952 – c30 mins
dir Valerio Zurlini

Featurette telling the story of the birth of a revival band and featuring The **Roman New Orleans Jazz Band.**

225

Le blues entre les dents/Blues between the teeth/Blues under the skin

France 1972 – 88 mins
dir Robert Manthoulis

Poorly realised spin-off by writer/director Manthoulis from the superb programme on blues music he made previously *En remontant le Mississippi*. He has utilised some blues interludes around a story of a black ghetto couple and their problems featuring: 'All night long' by and performed by **Mance Lipscombe**; 'John Henry' performed by **Sonny Terry, Brownie McGhee**; 'Nobody loves me but my mother', 'Down and out', 'All I want', 'I need my baby' by and performed by **B. B. King**; 'Someday sweetheart' performed by **Amelia Cortez**; 'When I lay my burden down' performed by **Furry Lewis**; 'Runnin' the Boogie' by and performed by **Roosevelt Sykes**; 'In the shade of the old apple tree' performed by **Louis Armstrong** (soundtrack only); 'My baby done changed the lock on the door' by **Sonny Terry** performed by **Sonny Terry, Brownie McGhee**; 'Jelly roll blues' performed by **Bukka White**; 'Old gal on my door' performed by **Robert Pete Williams**; 'Ships in the ocean' performed by **Junior Wells, Buddy Guy.**

Blues for lovers

see **Ballad in blue.**

226

Blues in the night/Hot nocturne

USA 1941 – 88 mins
dir Anatole Litvak

Drama about a band of musicians and the romantic vicissitudes of their pianist, with a score by Harold Arlen and Johnny Mercer which includes the title number and 'This time the dream's on me'. **Jimmy Lunceford** and His Band appear in one sequence with a solo from **Trummy Young**, *trb*. The soundtrack features **'Snooky' Young**, *tpt*, ghosting actor Jack Carson; **Santo Pecora**, *trb*; and **Stan Wrightsman** dubbing piano for Richard Whorf. The title of the picture was, incidentally, changed after production to reap the success of the title song.

227

Blues in the night

USA 1942 – 3 mins

Soundie featuring **Cab Calloway** and His Orchestra with the title number.

228

Blues like showers of rain

UK 1970 – 30 mins
dir John Jeremy

An introduction to the world of the Blues, from photographs and field recordings made by Paul Oliver on a journey through the Southern States in 1960. With the voices and songs of **Otis Spann, J. B. Lenoir, 'Little Brother' Mongomery, Willie Thomas, Edwin 'Buster' Pickens, Billie Pierce, Wade Walton, Robert Curtis Smith, Lonnie Johnson, Henry Townsend, Sunnyland Slim , Robert Lockwood, Sam 'Lightnin'' Hopkins, James 'Butch' Cage, 'Blind' James Brewer, 'St Louis' Jimmy, Charles Love, Sam Price, James 'Stump' Johnson** and **Speckled Red.**

229

Blues pattern

USA 1956 – 3 mins
dir Ernest Pintoff, John Whitney

An experimental animated cartoon with jazz score by **Shorty Rogers.**

Blues under the skin

see **Le blues entre les dents.**

230

Boarding house blues

USA 1948 – 85 mins
dir Josh Binney

All negro production built around the personalities of leading entertainers in which a slight story introduces a series of vaudeville acts by Dusty Fletcher, Jackie Mabley etc. Features throughout music by **Lucky Millinder** and His Orchestra spotlighting **'Bull Moose' Jackson**, *ten sax, voc;* **Annisteen Allen**, *voc;* **Paul Brickenridge**, *voc.* Also two numbers from **Una Mae Carlisle**, *pno, voc.* Other music includes 'You never know if an apple is ripe before you bite it', 'It ain't like that', 'Let it roll', and 'I love you, yes I do'.

231

Boardwalk boogie

USA 1941 – 3 mins

Soundie featuring drummer **Ray McKinley** with The Will Bradley Orchestra.

232

Bob & Carol & Ted & Alice
USA 1969 – 105 mins
dir Paul Mazursky

More than usually interesting and extremely funny comedy of American morals and mores. Music and song 'I need to be be'd with' by **Quincy Jones**.

233

Bob Crosby
USA 1942 – 3 mins

Soundie number 1802 details unknown.

234

Bob Crosby
USA 1942 – 3 mins

Soundie number 4304 details unknown.

235

Bob Crosby
USA 1942 – 3 mins

Soundie number 4805 details unknown.

236

Bob Crosby and His Orchestra
USA 1938 – 10 mins
dir Leslie Roush

A Paramount music short in which **Bob Crosby** and His Orchestra play 'How'dja like to love me?', 'Pagan love song', 'Moments like this' and 'Romance in the dark'. Personnel on screen include **Eddie Miller**, *ten sax, clar;* **Bob Haggart**, *bass;* **Ray Bauduc**, *drs.*

237

Bob Howard
USA 1942 – 3 mins

Soundie number 16708 details unknown.

238

Bobby Hackett
USA 1961 – 25 mins
dir Bernard Rubin

A studio bandstand programme by **Bobby Hackett**'s Sextet made for the Goodyear Tyre Company. Musicians: **Bobby Hackett**, *cor;* **Urbie Green**, *trb;* **Bob Wilbur**, *clar;* **Dave McKenna**, *pno;* **Nabil Totah**, *bass;* **Morey Feld**, *drs.* Numbers: 'Deed I do', 'The sentimental blues', 'The saints', 'Bill Bailey', 'Struttin' with some barbecue' and **Louis Armstrong**'s 'Swing that music'. Introductory music: 'The good years of jazz' by The **Duke Ellington** Orchestra.

239

Boeing boeing
USA 1965 – 102 mins
dir John Rich

Creaking farce based on the play by Marc Camoletti. Formula music score by **Neal Hefti**.

240

Bonjour cinéma
France 1955 – 17 mins
dir Jacques Guillon

Impressions of a film studio during production. Music by **Sidney Bechet, Claude Bolling** and **Christian Chevallier**.

241

Bonjour tristesse
UK 1957 – 93 mins
dir Otto Preminger

Heavyweight and completely artificial adaptation of Françoise Sagan's grubby little tale of Riviera amorality shot in a blaze of clashing colours. Features **Maxim Saury**.

242

La bonne soupe
France/Italy 1963 – 97 mins
dir Robert Thomas

Pleasantly diverting farce adapted from the play by Félicien Marceau with skittish performances from all concerned. Raymond Le Sénéchal's music-is arranged by **Hubert Rostaing**.

243

Les bons amis
France 1958 – 14 mins
dir René Lucot

The fight against alcoholism, with music by **Christian Chevallier**.

244

Boogie doodle
Canada 1948 – 4 mins
dir Norman McLaren

Experimental animation using various kinds of colouring agents instead of paint. Soundtrack music **Albert Ammons**, *pno;* with **Henry 'Red' Allen**, *tpt;* and **J. C. Higginbotham**, *trb.*

245

Boogie woogie
USA 1944 – 3 mins

Soundie featuring **Meade Lux Lewis** with comedy from Dudley Dickerson.

246

Boogie woogie

Denmark 1946

A short subject featuring **Svend Asmussen** and His Orchestra playing one boogie number.

247

Boogie woogie

Denmark 1966 – 50 mins

A film collage built from odd bits and pieces and set to a music text by **Erik Moseholm**.

248

Boogie woogie bugle boy of Company C

USA 1941 – 7 mins
dir Walter Lantz

A Universal Walt Lantz Swing Symphony in Technicolor charting the effect of hot bugling from a dance band draftee on a squad of roookies.

249

Boogie woogie dream

USA 1941 – 3 mins

Soundie featuring **Albert Ammons, Pete Johnson** and Lena Horne. Originally part of *Boogie woogie dream* (13 mins).

250

Boogie woogie dream

USA 1941 – 13 mins
dir Hans Burger

Short story with music set in the Cafe Society, New York City, featuring Lena Horne, *voc;* **Albert Ammons,** *pno;* **Pete Johnson,** *pno;* **Teddy Wilson,** *pno;* **Emmett Berry,** *tpt;* **Benny Morton,** *trb;* **Jimmy Hamilton,** *clar;* **Johnny Williams,** *bass;* **J. C. Heard,** *drs.* Numbers include 'Boogie woogie dream', 'Unlucky woman (Friday blues)' and 'Evening gown'. Also released as three separate Soundies.

251

Boogie woogie man

USA 1943 – 7 mins
dir James Culhane

A Universal Walt Lantz Swing Symphony in Technicolor about a meeting of swinging ghosts who are influenced by some dark spirits from Harlem and their boogie woogie music.

252

Boogie woogie Sioux

USA 1942 – 6 mins
dir Alex Lovy

Imaginative Walt Lantz Swing Symphony colour cartoon in which Boogie Woogie is brought to the Red Indians by rainmakers Tommy Hawk and His five Scalpers.

253

The book of numbers

USA 1972 – 81 mins
dir Raymond St Jacques

Black orientated period crime drama; a pair of urban dudes set up a numbers racket in a small Southern town. Music performed by **Sonny Terry** and **Brownie McGhee**.

254

Book revue

USA 1945 – 7 mins
dir Robert Clampett

A Blue Ribbon cartoon, produced by Warner Bros. Included are caricatures of many popular entertainers including **Harry James, Tommy Dorsey, Gene Krupa** and **Benny Goodman**.

255

Boom!

UK 1968 – 113 mins
dir Joseph Losey

Highly stylised tale of a confrontation between a penniless poet and the wealthiest woman in the world, which becomes a battle for power. Music for the song 'Hideaway' by **John Dankworth**.

256

Boo's ups and downs

Sweden 1962 – 9 mins
dir Claes Fellbom

Mimed story of a young woman who has a premonition about her lover. Inspired by the music of **John Handy**.

Bop girl

see **Bop girl goes calypso**.

257

Bop girl goes calypso/Bop girl

USA 1957 – 75 mins
dir Howard W. Koch

A thin harmless mixture of Rock 'n' Roll and calypsos made strictly for the under-fifteens. Features **Bobby Troup** in a leading role.

258

Born reckless ʼ

USA 1959 – 79 mins
dir Howard W. Koch

Trite and repetitious yarn bolstered up by innumerable Rock 'n' Roll interludes. Music by **Buddy Bregman**.

259

Born to swing

UK 1973 – 50 mins
dir John Jeremy

A loving tribute to The Swing Era evoked by skilful intercutting of archive material with interview and action footage of ex-**Basie** sidemen shot in New York in 1972. Music by **Buddy Tate**, *ten sax;* **Earle Warren**, *alt sax;* **Joe Newman**, *tpt;* **Dicky Wells**, *trb;* **Eddie Durham**, *trb, gtr;* **'Snub' Mosley**, *trb;* **Gene Ramey**, *bass;* **Tommy Flanagan**, *pno;* **Jo Jones**, *drs;*. and The **Count Basie** Band of 1943. With the participation of **Buck Clayton, Andy Kirk, Gene Krupa**, Albert McCarthy, John Hammond and Richie Goldberg; photographs by Valerie Wilmer; commentary spoken by **Humphrey Lyttelton**.

260

Borsalino

France/Italy 1970 – 126 mins
dir Jacques Deray

A mildly entertaining gangster pastiche based on the book *Bandits à Marseilles* by Eugène Soccomare, with Belmondo and Delon madly exploiting their ready-made tough-guy personae. The soundtrack provides plenty of jingle-jangle jazz by **Claude Bolling**.

261

Borsalino & Co/Blood on the streets

France/Italy/West Germany 1974 – 110 mins
dir Jacques Deray

Alain Delon's undistinguished sequel to his hit gangster picture *Borsalino* set in the early 1930's. Again the music score is provided by **Claude Bolling**.

262

Bosko and the pirates

USA 1937 – 8 mins

MGM cartoon in which a frog colony impersonate coloured entertainers of the day including **Cab Calloway, Louis Armstrong** and The **Mills Brothers**.

The boss
see **El jefe.**

263

Botta e risposta

Italy 1951 – 80 mins
dir Mario Soldati

Musical comedy made up from a series of Music Hall sketches. Features **Louis Armstrong** with **Jack Teagarden, Barney Bigard, Earl Hines, Arvell Shaw, Cozy Cole** and **Velma Middleton**.

264

Les bougnats

France 1966 – 13 mins
dir Manuel Otéro

Fictional story about a couple of coal dealers who use their daughter to recruit assistants. Music by **Martial Solal**.

265

Bound for glory

USA 1976 – 147 mins
dir Hal Ashby

Outstanding screen adaptation of Woody Guthrie's autobiography set in the 30's Depression era. Music supervisor Leonard Rosenman uses songs by both Woody and Arlo Guthrie, Will Geer, **Odetta** and other folk personalities.

266

The boy and girl from North and South Carolina

USA 1946 – 3 mins

Soundie featuring The **Joe Marsala** Band with vocalists Eileen Clarence and Ahmed Rai.

Boy in the tree
see **Pojken i trädet.**

267

Boy! what a girl

USA 1947 – 70 mins
dir Arthur Leonard

All black production with only a slight story and a great deal of clowning. Features The **'Slam' Stewart** Trio, **'Big' Sid Catlett** and His Band, The **Harlem Maniacs** and a guest appearance by **Gene Krupa**, in some eight musical numbers.

268

Boyd Raeburn and His Orchestra

USA 1947 – 10 mins

Columbia featurette with the title band plus vocalists Ginny Powell and Teddy Walters with dancer Nancy Doran. Numbers: 'Temptation'; 'St Louis Blues' and 'Ballerina'.

269

Brands Hatch beat

UK 1964 – 27 mins
dir Brian Gibson

Earle Warren in John Jeremy's **Born to swing** (photo: Valerie Wilmer).

A film record of the 1964 European Grand Prix held for the first time at Brands Hatch. Produced by Castrol. Music by **Chris Barber**.

270
Les bras de la Seine
France 1955 – 16 mins
dir Jean-Claude Bonnardot
Impressions of the Seine floodings in January 1955, with music by **Henri Crolla**.

271
Breakfast in Hollywood/The mad hatter
USA 1946 – 91 mins
dir Harold Schuster
Thin comedy about a popular American radio programme, featuring The **'King' Cole** Trio and including the song 'It is better to be yourself' by **Nat 'King' Cole**.

Breathless
see **A bout de souffle**.

272
La Brigade
France 1974 – 110 mins
dir René Gilson
Based on factual events, a low-key, low-profile look at a resistance group composed mainly of Polish immigrant miners during the last war. Much of the music score consists of wartime numbers by the **Artie Shaw** and **Tommy Dorsey** orchestras.

273
Bright and breezy
USA 1956 – 16 mins
dir Will Cowan
A Universal-International featurette presenting **Charlie Barnet** and His Orchestra, with vocal support, playing 'Redskin rhumba', 'Skyliner', 'You were meant for me', 'Lullaby of Birdland', 'Smooth sailing', 'Shadrack', 'Easy street' and 'Open up your heart'.

274
Bring me the head of Alfredo Garcia
USA/Mexico 1974 – 112 mins
dir Sam Peckinpah
Heavyweight and violent melodrama with a conventional revenge theme, set in Mexico. **Lennie Niehaus** worked as arranger on Jerry Fielding's spare, haunting music score.

Broadway ahead
see **Sweetheart of the campus**.

275
Broadway gondolier
USA 1935 – 100 mins
dir Lloyd Bacon
Routine Warner Bros musical about a singing taxi driver – Dick Powell. Features The **Mills Brothers**.

Broadway jamboree
see **You're a sweetheart**.

276
Broadway rhythm
USA 1944 – 114 mins
dir Roy Del Ruth
Poor adaptation of the Kern-Hammerstein musical, *Very warm for May*; little but a series of routine song and dance numbers. Participating in several sequences is **Tommy Dorsey** with His Orchestra; Lena Horne sings 'Brazilian boogie' and 'Somebody loves me'; **Hazel Scott** plays a boogie number and **Sy Oliver** was responsible for some orchestrations. Other items include: 'Amor, amor, amor', 'I love corny music', 'Pretty baby', 'Oh, you beautiful doll', 'Irresistible you', 'Who's who in your dream life' and Ginny Simms singing 'All the things you are'.

277
Brother, can you spare a dime?
UK 1975 – 109 mins
dir Phlippe Mora
Curious compilation of newsreel, feature and short film extracts centred on The Depression years in the USA. Soundtrack use is made of 'Nobody knows you when you're down and out' sung by **Bessie Smith**; 'Every man a king' sung by **Ina Ray Hutton**; 'Jeepers creepers' performed by **Louis Armstrong**; 'Downtown uproar' by **Cootie Williams** played by The **Duke Ellington** Orchestra; 'Shout and feel it' performed by The **Count Basie** Orchestra. Film clips include: 'Hi de ho' performed by **Cab Calloway**; 'Jealousy blues' sung by **Billie Holiday** from *Symphony in black* and **Benny Goodman** in *Hollywood hotel*.

278
Brother John
USA 1971 – 94 mins
dir James Goldstone
Obtuse mystical melodrama, with spiritual overtones, with Sidney Poitier as a Jesus-like superhero whose sudden return to a small Dixie town irritates the gentry and puzzles his old friends. Music by **Quincy Jones**.

279
The brotherhood
USA 1968 – 96 mins
dir Martin Ritt

Drearily scripted tale of Mafia-ridden brotherly love and conflict. Music by **Lalo Schifrin**.

280
Bubbling over
USA 1934 – 20 mins
dir Leigh Jason

A Radio short featuring **Ethel Waters**. whose songs include 'Harlem express', 'Taking your time' and 'Darkies never cry'.

281
Buck and the preacher
USA 1972 – 102 mins
dir Sidney Poitier

Well-intentioned but dull black Western shot on location in Mexico but somehow lacking the authenticity necessary to hold one's attention. Thundering music score by **Benny Carter** featuring **Sonny Terry** and Brownie McGhee, with the participation of **Emil Richards**.

282
Buck Clayton and His All Stars
Belgium 1961 – 54 mins (in two parts)

A film record of studio performances by **Buck Clayton, Emmett Berry, Dicky Wells, Earle Warren, Buddy Tate, Sir Charles Thompson, Gene Ramey, Oliver Jackson** and **Jimmy Witherspoon**. Produced by Jazz Films SPRL.

283
A bucket of blood
USA 1959 – 65 mins
dir Roger Corman

A macabre satire on beatniks and teenage horror movies, modestly budgeted yet efficiently handled Music by **Fred Katz** with sax solo by **Paul Horn**.

284
Buddy Rich and His Orchestra
USA 1948 – 15 mins

A short in the Thrills of Music series in which a disc jockey introduces the orchestra playing several numbers including 'A man can be a wonderful thing', 'Great head' and 'Kicks with sticks'.

285
Buddy Rich and His Orchestra
USA 1948 – 15 mins
dir Will Cowan

A Universal-International featurette in which **Buddy Rich** and His Orchestra entertain in a nightclub setting supported by dancer Louis Da Pron, singers The Mello-Larks and **Terry Gibbs**, *vibs*. Numbers include: 'Let's get away from it all', 'John had the number', 'One o'clock boogie', 'So long Joe' and 'But no nickel'.

286
A building is many buildings
USA

A short produced by Graphic Films, with music by **Bob Cooper**.

287
Bullitt
USA 1968 – 114 mins
dir Peter Yates

Crisp, technically assured thriller set in San Francisco, with several violent deaths, a good car chase and a self-conscious message. Modernistic music score composed and conducted by **Lalo Schifrin** with contributions from **Howard Roberts**, *gtr;* **Bud Shank**, *flute;* **Mike Melvoin**, *pno;* **Ray Brown**, *bass;* **Larry Bunker**, *drs;* **Bud Brisbois**, *tpt;* **Milt Bernhart**, *trb.*

288
Bundle of blues
USA 1933 – 8 mins

Paramount musical short featuring **Duke Ellington** and His Orchestra with 'Rockin' in rhythm'; a vocal rendering of 'Stormy weather' by **Ivie Anderson** and a tap-dance routine from Florence Mills and Bessie Dudley to 'Bugle call rag'. Personnel: **Marshall Royal, Harry Carney, Barney Bigard, Johnny Hodges**, *saxes;* **'Tricky Sam' Nanton, Juan Tizol, Lawrence Brown**, *trbs;* **Cootie Williams, Arthur Whetsol, Freddie Jenkins**, *tpts;* **Fred Guy**, *gtr;* **Wellman Braud**, *bass;* **Sonny Greer**, *perc;* and **Ellington**, *pno.*

289
Burgundy Street blues
USA 1954 – 3 mins

A film record of Burgundy Street produced by The New Orleans Jazz Club, with accompaniment by The **George Lewis** Trio.

290
The bus is coming
USA 1971 – 113 mins
dir Wendell James Franklin

The story of a confrontation between whites and blacks, told from the Negro side. **Freddie Hubbard**, *tpt,* plays on Tom McIntosh's music track.

291

Busse rhythm

USA 1938 – 10 mins
dir Leslie Roush

Paramount music short featuring **Henry Busse**
and His Orchestra.

Bustin' Out

see **Coonskin.**

292

But not for me

USA 1959 – 105 mins
dir Walter Lang

Strained third screen adaptation of Samson
Raphaelson's stage hit *Accent on youth*. The
Gershwin title song is sung by **Ella Fitzgerald**.

293

Buzz me

USA 1945 – 3 mins

Soundie featuring **Louis Jordan** with His
Tympany Five.

By hook and by crook

see **I dood it.**

294

By request

USA 1935 – 10 mins
dir Roy Mack

Vitaphone short set in a gaudy nightclub featuring
Claude Hopkins and His Orchestra with dancers,
Tip, Tap and Toe and vocalist Orlando Roberson.
Numbers include: 'I would do anything for you',
'Chasing my blues away', 'California, here I
come', 'To call you my own', 'Shine' and
'Chinatown, my Chinatown'. Personnel: **Albert
Snaer, Sylvester Lewis, Ovie Alston**, *tpts;*
Henry Wells, Fred Norman, *trbs;* **Gene
Johnson, Edmond Hall, Hilton Jefferson,
Bobby Sands**, *reeds;* **Claude Hopkins**, *pno;*
Walter 'Joe' Jones, *gtr;* **Henry Turner**, *bass;*
Pete Jacobs, *drs.*

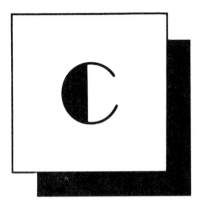

295

Cab Calloway and His Cabaliers

USA 1950 – 19 mins

Snader Telescriptions featuring the title band.

296

Cab Calloway Medley

USA 1943

Soundie featuring **Cab Calloway** with three of his best known songs.

297

Cab Calloway's hi-de-ho

USA 1934 – 10 mins
dir Fred Waller

Paramount music short featuring **Cab Calloway** and His Orchestra playing 'Rail rhythm' and 'The lady with the fan' in a Harlem nightclub setting.

298

Cab Calloway's jitterbug party

USA 1935 – 8 mins
dir Fred Waller

Paramount music short featuring **Cab Calloway** and His Orchestra in a Harlem nightclub setting. The main musical number featured is ' 'long about midnight'.

299

Cabaret

USA 1972 – 123 mins
dir Bob Fosse

Film version of the stage musical by Masterhoff, Kander and Ebb, based on the play *I am a camera* by John Van Druten, adapted from the book *Goodbye to Berlin* by Christopher Isherwood. Music supervision by **Ralph Burns**.

300

Cabin in the sky

USA 1942 – 99 mins
dir Vincente Minnelli

Minnelli's heavily stylised first film: a simple Negro fable, based on a Broadway musical play of the mid-thirties. Features **Louis Armstrong, Duke Ellington** and His Orchestra, Buck Washington, The Hall Johnson Choir, Lena Horne and **Ethel Waters** singing 'Happiness is a thing called Joe'. Also the songs 'Going up' by **Duke Ellington** and 'Things ain't what they used to be' by **Mercer Ellington**. One **Armstrong** session 'Ain't it the truth' was cut from the release prints. Musicians in the **Ellington** band include **Harry Carney, Otto Hardwicke, Johnny Hodges, Lawrence Brown, Ray Nance, Fred Guy, Sonny Greer** and **Ben Webster**.

Cactus

see **Garga M'Bosse.**

301

Cactus flower

USA 1969 – 104 mins
dir Gene Saks

Fresh, unpretentious and beautifully played comedy adapted from the Broadway play by Abe Burrows. Music by **Quincy Jones** whose song 'A time for love is anytime' is sung by **Sarah Vaughan**.

Duke Ellington and His Orchestra play for the dancers in **Cabin in the sky**.

Il cadavere dagli artigli d'acciaio
see **Qui?**

La cagna
see **Liza.**

302
Caio
USA 1967 – 95 mins
dir David Tucker

The impending return of a semi-paralysed fruitstore owner to his wife is the basis of this New York made independent production which enjoyed a brief success at the Venice Festival. Music score by **Ed Summerlin**.

303
Cairo
USA 1942 – 101 mins
dir W. S. Van Dyke II

A smalltown newspaperman, assigned as a war correspondent, becomes involved in spy activities in Cairo and unwittingly becomes the dupe for foreign agents. **Ethel Waters** has a maid's role and contributes one song.

304
Caldonia
USA 1945 – 3 mins
Soundie featuring **Louis Jordan** with his famous arrangement of the title number.

305
Caldonia
USA 1945 – 18 mins
dir William Forest Crouch

Produced by Astor Pictures, an all black musical comedy featuring **Louis Jordan** and His Tympani Five. A slight plot is concerned with film production difficulties. Numbers: 'Caldonia', 'Honey chile', 'Tillie' and 'Buzz me'. Besides **Louis Jordan**, *alt sax, voc*, the group includes **Razz Mitchell**, *drs*.

Calling all cats
see **6.5 special.**

306
Calling all stars
UK 1937 – 75 mins
dir Herbert Smith

Revue spotlighting popular entertainers including Ambrose and His Orchestra, Carroll Gibbons and The Savoy Orpheans, Larry Adler, The Nicholas Brothers and Buck and Bubbles.

307

Campus capers

USA 1941 – 18 mins
dir Reginald Le Borg

Universal music short in which **Jack Teagarden** and His Orchestra play a programme of college favourites supported by Susan Miller singing 'Stormy weather' and 'Walk with me', vocalist Kenny Stevens, dancing comedians Dave & Jack Hacker, The Four Tones and The Crackerjacks.

308

Campus sleuth/Smart politics

USA 1948 – 57 mins
dir Will Jason

A combination of collegiate comedy, danceband entertainment and murder mystery squeezed into 57 minutes. Features **Bobby Sherwood** and His Orchestra.

309

Can I help you?

UK 1966 – 23 mins
dir John Fletcher

The work of Citizens' Advice Bureaux with particular reference to the Stevenage branch where the variety of problems dealt with illustrates the pattern of life in a new town. Music by **Kenneth Graham.**

310

Candide, ou l'optimisme au XXème siècle

France 1960 – 90 mins
dir Norbert Carbonnaux

Weak, updated adaptation of Voltaire's 18th century satirical novel, never more than a disjointed series of revue-type sketches – and ugly ones at that. Music score by **Hubert Rostaing**.

311

Cantagallo

UK 1969 – 23 mins
dir Jeff Inman

Cantagallo is a service station complex on the Autostrada del Sole 250 km from Milan. Its facilities are shown. Music by **Kenneth Graham**.

312

Canyon passage

USA 1946 – 92 mins
dir Jacques Tourneur

An attempt to recreate a broad and fairly detailed picture of true pioneering life in the West of 1856 – the communal loyalty, the rough justice, the isolation of homesteaders etc. **Hoagy Carmichael** is well featured, as the village minstrel, and supplies three of his own songs: 'Rogue river valley', 'I'm gonna get married in the morning' and 'Ol' buttermilk sky'.

313

Caravan

USA 1942 – 3 mins

Soundie featuring the four **Mills Brothers**.

314

Caravan

USA 1952 – 3 mins

Snader Telescription in which **Duke Ellington** and His Orchestra play the title number, with solo by **Juan Tizol**, *v trb*, and featuring **Jimmy Hamilton, Willie Smith, Russell Procope, Paul Gonsalves, Harry Carney**, *reeds;* **Ray Nance, Willie Cook, Cat Anderson**, *tpt;* **Britt Woodman, Quentin Jackson**, *trb;* **Wendell Marshall**, *bass;* **Louis Bellson**, *drs.*

315

Carib gold

USA 1955 – 72 mins
dir Harold Young

Key West, Florida, and its shrimp fishing fleets provide the background for the discovery of a sunken Spanish galleon laden with gold, and the resulting drama. **Ethel Walters** stars and sings the title song.

316

Carmen Jones

USA 1954 – 103 mins
dir Otto Preminger

A CinemaScope screen adaptation of the 1944 Broadway success which provided a modern Negro version of the Merimée story but retained the original Bizet music. There is a performance by **Pearl Bailey** and brief appearances by **Max Roach, Richie Powell, Curtis Counce** plus soundtrack work by **Cozy Cole.**

317

Carnal knowledge

USA 1971 – 97 mins
dir Mike Nichols

Dull, cliché tragi-comedy about sex, as empty as its cardboard characters. Recordings by The **Glenn Miller** Orchestra figure prominently on the soundtrack: 'Moonlight serenade', 'Tuxedo junction;, 'A string of pearls' etc. and also 'Georgia on my mind' by **Hoagy Carmichael** and Stuart Gorrell.

318

Carnegie Hall

USA 1947 – 133 mins
dir Edgar G. Ulmer

Drama of New York's famous music centre. Among the many featured artistes are Vaughn Monroe and His Orchestra and **Harry James** who plays '57th Street rhapsody'.

319

Carousella

UK 1965 – 28 mins
dir John Irvin

Adeptly handled and relatively honest documentary about three girls who perform at a striptease club. Music by **Kenny Graham**.

320

Carry it on/Joan

USA 1970 – 95 mins
dir J. Coyne, R. Jones, C. Knight

Cinéma-vérité portrait of singer Joan Baez which featurs a performance of the song 'Mother earth' by **Memphis Slim**.

321

Case of the blues

USA 1941 – 3 mins

Soundie featuring **Maxine Sullivan** singing the title number, backed by **Benny Carter**.

Castles through the ages

see   Ô saisons, ô châteaux.

322

Cat Ballou

USA 1965 – 96 mins
dir Elliot Silverstein

Consistently attractive Western parody with an original performance by Lee Marvin. Features **Nat 'King' Cole** contributing the song 'The ballad of Cat Ballou'.

323

Cat blues

France 1968 – 9 mins
dir Frédéric Rossif

A cat ballet using slow motion and other devices is intercut with musicians improvising on Blues themes. Features The **Kenny Clarke** Big Band playing the leader's own music.

324

The cat burglar

USA 1961 – 65 mins
dir William N. Witney

Spirited and resolute little suspense tale, constantly on the move. Forceful jazz score by **Buddy Bregman**.

325

Catalina interlude

USA 1945 – 17 mins
dir Alvin Ganzer

Abysmal Technicolor featurette from Paramount concerning the search for a missing girl found singing at the Catalina Salt-Air Club with **Jimmy Dorsey** and His Orchestra. The orchestra soundtracked five numbers: 'Muskrat ramble', 'My ideal', 'Perfidia' and a couple of nondescript pops. Virginia Maxey did the vocals. The band includes **Charlie Teagarden**, *tpt;* **Brad Gowans**, *trb;* **Ray Bauduc**, *drs.*

326

Catch me a spy/Les doigts croisés

UK/France/USA 1971 – 94 mins
dir Dick Clement

Disappointing screen adaptation of the novel by George Marton and Tibor Meray – a lightweight thriller. Music score by **Claude Bolling.**

The cats

see   **Kattorna.**

327

Catuor

Canada 1970 – 4 mins
dir Judith Klein

Pleasant colour cartoon about a talented cat who multiplies himself to become both musician and instrument, as required. A hard-swinging percussive jazz score by Gordon Fleming is played by Fleming, **Herbert Spanier**, Michael Donato and Eric MacDonald.

328

Ce corps tant désiré/Way of the wicked

France 1958 – 98 mins
dir Luis Saslavsky

Laborious romantic melodrama set in a mussel-picking milieu, with Belinda Lee as a reformed prostitute. Music by **Henri Crolla** and **André Hodeir**.

329
Cecil Taylor and Allen Ginsberg
USA 1968 – 10 mins
dir D. A. Pennebaker

Further details unknown.

330
La Cécilia
France/Italy 1975 – 105 mins
dir Jean-Louis Comolli

Perceptive first feature by the editor of the leftist periodical *Cahiers du cinéma* – the story of an anarchist Italian commune formed in Brazil in the late 19th century. Music score by **Michel Portal**.

331
Celebration
Canada 1966 – 16 mins
dir Rex Tasker, William Weintraub

A promotional documentary, composed entirely of colour stills, produced by the National Film Board of Canada on the eve of the Canadian centennial. Swinging music track by The **Oscar Peterson** Trio uses sections of Peterson's own 'Canadiana suite'.

332
Celebrity art
USA 1973 – 11 mins

A short dealing with screen figures whose hobby is painting. Among the personalities on whom it focuses is **Duke Ellington**.

333
Céleste
France/Italy 1971 – 90 mins
dir Michel Gast

Mild comedy charting the romance between a middle aged journalist and his Portuguese maid. Music by **Guy Pedersen**.

334
César et Rosalie
France/Italy/West Germany 1972 – 105 mins
dir Claude Sautet

Routine romantic melodrama with Philippe Sarde's music score orchestrated by **Hubert Rostaing**.

335
C'est la vie Parisienne
France 1953 – 100 mins
dir Alfred Rode

A vintage plot and banal modern trimmings attempt to invoke the Gay 90's with actor Philipe Lemaire as an unlikely jazz trumpeter. Features **Claude Luter**.

336
Cette nuit-là
France 1958 – 100 mins
dir Maurice Cazeneuve

Screen adaptation of the novel by Michel Lebrun about decadent Parisian highlife, with music by **Claude Bolling**.

337
Cette sacrée gamine/Mam'zelle Pigalle
France 1955 – 86 mins
dir Michel Boisrond

A likeably scatterbrained performance by Brigitte Bardot is the only redeeming virtue of this dull comedy – an early screenplay by Roger Vadim. Music by **Henri Crolla** and **André Hodeir**.

338
The challengers
USA 1968 – 120 mins
dir Leslie H. Martinson

Tedious, over-directed motorcar racing melodrama with the usual corny script. Music score by **Pete Rugolo**.

Change of heart
see **Hit parade of 1943.**

339
Change of mind
USA 1969 – 98 mins
dir Robert Stevens

Racial harmony is the message behind this story of a white man's brain transplanted into a black man's body. **Duke Ellington** composed and arranged the score which is played by: **Ellington, Cootie Williams, Willie Cook, Benny Green, Benny Powell, Russell Procope, Paul Gonsalves, Harold Ashby, Harry Carney, Paul Kondziela** and **Rufus Jones**. Numbers include 'What good am I without you?', 'Wanderlust' and 'Creole rhapsody' (with **Ellington** on Fender piano).

340

The changing skyline

UK 1964 – 19 mins
dir Michael Shah Dayan

The siting and construction of a new petroleum chemicals factory in Wales from the reclamation of the sand dunes to the official opening. Music played by **Ted heath** and His Band.

341

Chappaqua

USA 1966 – 82 mins
dir Conrad Rooks

Self-indulgent, semi-autobiographical, hallucinatory movie about Western civilisation poisoned by its own drugs and by a surfeit of images. Features **Ornette Coleman** in a non-speaking role, who also wrote an extended 'Chappaqua suite' for the film which was not used in the final cut – a music track by Ravi Shankar was substituted.

The charge is murder

see   **Twilight of honour.**

342

Charley Varrick

USA 1973 – 111 mins
dir Don Siegel

Thoroughly enjoyable thriller, based on the John Reese novel *The looters*, about a plan to rob a small New Mexico bank, that doesn't work out as intended. Suitably percussive music score by **Lalo Schifrin.**

343

Charlie Barnet and His Band

USA 1949 – 11 mins
dir Charles Skinner

One of the Movietone Melodies series in which **Charlie Barnet** and His Band entertain with special arrangements of popular numbers: 'Redskin rhumba', 'Atlantic jump' and 'My old flame'.

344

Charlie Barnet and His Orchestra

USA 1947 – 14 mins
dir Will Cowan

A Universal-International featurette with **Charlie Barnet** and His Orchestra supported by singers Rita Shore and Della Norell, with Jeanne Blanche and dancers Igor and Tania. **Shorty Rogers**, *tpt,* and **Barney Kessel,** *gtr,* are prominent in the final number. Music includes 'I'll remember April', 'No can do', 'You're a sweetheart', 'Rhumba fantasy', 'I believe in miracles' and 'Murder at Peyton Hall'.

Charlie Barnet and His Orchestra

▼

345

Charlie Barnet and his orchestra

USA 1948 – 11 mins

One of the Thrills of Music series featuring the Orchestra in a programme of music which includes 'Pompton turnpike', 'Stormy weather' and 'Civilisation'.

346

Charlie Barnet and His Orchestra

USA 1951 – 18 mins

Snader Telescription featuring the title orchestra.

347

Chasing the blues

UK 1947 – 10 mins
dir Jack Chambers, Jack Ellitt

Produced for the Cotton Board to encourage mill managers to provide for the welfare of their workers, this film ballet makes its point almost entirely in music and movement. The former is provided by **Jack Parnell**'s Quartet.

348

Le chat dans le sac

Canada 1964 – 74 mins
dir Gilles Groulx

Well-intentioned beginning to the French-Canadian 'new wave', partly an *hommage* to Jean-Luc Godard and partly a love story with political overtones. Besides snippets from Vivaldi, Couperin, Mozart etc. the soundtrack uses four recordings by **John Coltrane**: 'Village blues', 'Naima', 'Blue world' and 'Like Sonny'.

349

Chatterbox

USA 1943 – 76 mins
dir Joseph Santley

Republic vehicle for Joe E. Brown – a burlesque about a cowboy star. Features The **Mills Brothers** and Spade Cooley and His Boys and the musical numbers 'Welcome to Victory Ranch', 'Mad about him, sad without him blues', 'Sweet Lucy Brown', 'With my concertina', 'The guy from Albuquerque' and 'Why can't I sing a love song'.

350

Che!

USA 1969 – 96 mins
dir Richard Fleischer

Very safe movie about an explosive personality, Che Guevara, played by Omar Sharif. Suitable Latin music score composed and conducted by **Lalo Schifrin** using Cuban and Incan instrumen-

tation. On soundtrack, Latin American percussionists include **Mongo Santamaria**, Willie Bobo, Francisco Arvella, Armando Peraza. **Bud Shank** plays Inca flutes, **Larry Bunker** plays electric tom-tom.

351

Check and double check

USA 1930 – 75 mins
dir Melville Brown

Comedy vehicle for Amos 'n' Andy playing a well-meaning pair having trouble over a deed to property. **Duke Ellington** and His Orchestra are featured in a ballroom sequence playing 'Three little words' and 'Old man blues'. Personnel: **Freddie Jenkins, Cootie Williams, Arthur Whetsol**, *tpts;* **Joe Nanton, Juan Tizol**, *trbs;* **Barney Bigard, Johnny Hodges, Harry Carney**, *reeds;* **Fred Guy**, *banjo;* **Wellman Braud**, *bass;* **Sonny Greer**, *perc;* and **Ellington**, *pno.* (**Tizol** and **Bigard** are suitably 'blacked up' for the occasion). The song 'Ring dem bells' is also used.

352

Chemins de lumière

France 1958 – 15 mins
dir René Lucot

Documentary on French railways, with music by **Christian Chevallier**.

353

Cherchez la femme

France 1955 – 95 mins
dir Raoul André

Routine comedy, strictly for the domestic market, involving a journalist and gangsters, kidnappers and diamond smugglers. Features **Maxim Saury**.

354

Cherokee

USA 1951 – 3 mins

Snader Telescription in which the title number is played by **Charlie Barnet** and His Orchestra, including **Claude Williamson**, *pno;* **Bill Holman**, *ten sax;* **Dave Wells**, *trb;* **Bob Dawes**, *bar sax.*

355

Chicago blues

UK 1971 – 50 mins
dir Harley Cokliss

An attempt to show how the tough urban music of Chicago today developed out of the original rural Blues. Features **Johnnie Lewis** with 'Hobo blues', **Floyd Jones** with 'Stockyard blues', **Buddy Guy** with 'First time I met the blues', 'The storefront church chorus' by and sung by **'Muddy' Waters**, 'Hoochie coochie' by Willie Dixon, sung by **'Muddy' Waters** and with **J. B. Hutto** and **Junior Wells**.

356
Chick Corea
West Germany c1961 – 32 mins

Colour study of Circle: **Chick Corea**, *pno;* **Dave Holland**, *bass* and *cello;* **Barry Altshul**, *drs,* working out in a studio and talking about their careers and music.

The chicken
see **Le poulet.**

357
China gate
USA 1957 – 90 mins
dir Samuel Fuller

Appalling melodrama with a preposterous script combining racial prejudice with violent anticommunist propaganda. Features **Nat 'King' Cole** who also sings the title song.

358
Chinatown
USA 1974 – 131 mins
dir Roman Polanski

Masterly, many-layered detective puzzle on lives intersecting in past, present and future, set in 1937 Los Angeles. Among the modest number of contemporary recordings used as source music is **'I can't get started' by Bunny Berigan** and His Orchestra and on Jerry Goldsmith's original music track there is some beautiful solo work by **Uan Rasey**, *tpt.*

A choice of weapons
see **Trial by combat.**

359
Choo choo swing
USA 1943 – 13 mins
dir Josef Berne

Universal short subject devoted to **Count Basie** and His Orchestra playing the title number and 'Swingin' the blues', with The **Delta Rhythm Boys,** Bobby Brooks Quartet, Layson Brothers and **Jimmy Rushing** with 'Sent for you yesterday'. Prominent in the band are **Buck Clayton, Harry Edison, 'Snooky'Young**, *tpt;* **Earle Warren, Buddy Tate, Don Byas, Jack Washington**, *saxes;* **Dicky Wells**, *trb;* **Freddy Green**, *gtr;* **Jo Jones**, *drs.*

360
Chotard et compagnie
France 1933 – 113 mins
dir Jean Renoir

Adaptation of the play by Roger Ferdinand, featuring pianist **Freddy Johnson**.

361
Chris Barber bandstand
UK 1962 – 25 mins
dir Giorgio Gomelsky

A record of The **Chris Barber** Band at the Richmond Jazz Festival. Participating musicians: **Chris Barber**, *trb;* **Eddie Smith**, *banjo;* **Pat Halcox**, *tpt;* **Ian Wheeler**, *clar;* **Dick Smith**, *bass;* **Graham Burbridge**, *drs;* **Ottilie Patterson**, *voc.*

362
Chris Barber's Jazz Band
UK 1956 – 16 mins
dir Giorgio Gomelsky

Jazz Today No 1 produced in association with the National Jazz Federation. A straight programme played by the band with cut-in shots of a Royal Festival Hall audience applauding as if to suggest a live concert performance which it certainly is not. Musicians appearing: **Barber**, *trb;* **Pat Halcox**, *tpt;* **Monty Sunshine**, *clar;* **Dick Bishop**, *banjo;* **Dick Smith**, *bass;* **Ron Bowden**, *drs;* and **Ottilie Patterson**, *voc.* Numbers include 'Lead me on', 'Poor man's blues' and 'Lord you've sure been good to me'.

363
The Christian licorice store
USA 1971 – 90 mins
dir James Frawley

An intriguing movie about a tennis player who succombs to Hollywood, adulation and commercialism and consequently degenerates into an extoller of hair tonic. Visually stunning evocative direction. Music by **Lalo Schifrin**.

364
Le ciel est par dessus le toit
France 1956 – 22 mins
dir Jean-Pierre Decourt

A young couple find the house of their dreams. Music score by **Henri Crolla**.

365
Le ciel sur la tête
France/Italy 1964 – 105 mins
dir Yves Ciampi

Science fiction drama about an aircraft carrier that is threatened by a mysterious satellite from space. Music by **Jacques Loussier**.

366

Cielito lindo

USA 1941 – 3 mins

Soundie featuring The **Mills Brothers** with their interpretation of the Spanish title song.

367

The Cincinnati kid

USA 1965 – 102 mins
dir Norman Jewison

Tight and effectively directed story of a young stud poker player set in the New Orleans of the late thirties. Excellent music score by **Lalo Schifrin** with the title song sung by **Ray Charles**. Also a good New Orleans procession number, **Cab Calloway** in a small acting role and an atmospheric vocal blues by **'Sweet' Emma Barrett**. Other participating musicians seen are: **Emanuel Paul, Jim Robinson, 'Kid' Sheik, George Lewis** and **'Punch' Miller**.

368

Cinderella liberty

USA 1973 – 117 mins
dir Mark Rydell

Appealing adaptation by Darryl Ponicsan of his novel about a sailor's love for a prostitute, set in Seattle. John Williams's music score features harmonica solos by **Jean 'Toots' Thielemans**.

369

Cinderfella

USA 1960 – 88 mins
dir Frank Tashlin

Jerry Lewis as a male Cinderella, with songs and much nauseating sentimentality. Features **Count Basie** and His Orchestra with **Joe Williams**.

370

Cinématographie

France 1966 – 16 mins
dir D. Goldschmidt, J. Meppiel

The Grand Prix of Belgium, an important event in championship motorcycle racing. Music partly by **Michel Portal**.

371

Cinerama holiday

USA 1955 – 119 mins
dir Robert Bendick, Philipe de Lacey

The second of the original Cinerama programmes, shown on a three-panelled screen. Includes a New Orleans sequence with **Oscar Celestin** singing and playing 'Tiger rag' with The **Original Tuxedo Dixieland Jazz Band.**

372

The CirCarC gear

UK 1964 – 10 mins
dir R. Q. McNaughton

The advantages over conventional involute gears of the Wildhaber-Novikov principle of gearing which is used in CirCarC. Music score by **Johnny Hawksworth**.

373

Cisco Pike

USA 1971 – 94 mins
dir Bill L. Norton

Encouraging first feature by a talented screen-writer evoking the rootless, aimless, irresponsible life-style of the pop/drug culture. On the soundtrack fine dramatic use is made of 'Wailin' and whoopin' ' as written and sung by **Sonny Terry**.

374

Cité du midi/The flying trapeze

France 1952 — 25 mins
dir Jacques Baratier

Sharply edited and skilfully shot atmospheric impression of a gymnasium and the backstage world of the circus. Music partly by **Claude Luter**.

375

Clarence the cross-eyed lion

USA 1964 – 92 mins
dir Andrew Marton

Appealing animal movie whose central character is a cross-eyed lion who grows up a gentle beast because faulty vision gives him no chance to develop hunting ability. **Shelly Manne** provides some swinging jazz behind the animated credit titles.

376

Clash by night

USA 1952 – 105 mins
dir Fritz Lang

Expertly played, but slick, pseudo-sophisticated screen adaptation of the play by Clifford Odets. Features The **Benny Carter** Band with **Ben Webster, 'Bumps' Meyers**, *ten saxes*; **Benny Carter**, *alt sax*; **'Keg' Johnson**, *trb*; **Jerry Wiggins**, *pno*; **Charlie Drayton**, *bass*; **George Jenkins**, *drs*. **Ulysses Livingston**, *gtr*, is present only on soundtrack.

377

Class of '44

USA 1973 – 95 mins
dir Paul Bogart

Totally predictable sequel to the earlier *Summer of '42* – a plunge into Forties nostalgia. David Shire's music track incorporates two classic recordings: 'Santa Fe trail' by **Glenn Miller** and His Orchestra and 'Blues in the night' by **Jimmie Lunceford** and His Orchestra.

378

Claude Thornhill

USA c1942 – 3 mins

Soundie number 5808 details unknown.

379

Claude Thornhill and His Orchestra

USA 1947 – 10 mins

Columbia featurette with the title band plus vocalists Fran Warren and Gene Williams. Numbers: 'A Sunday king of love', 'Oh you beautiful doll' and 'Arabian dance'.

380

Claude Thornhill and His Orchestra

USA 1950 – 15 mins
dir Will Cowan

A Universal-International featurette with the title band, vocals from Marion Colby, The Snowflakes and Joaquin Garay plus one number from **'Nappy' Lamare** and His Strawhat Strutters. Numbers include: 'Poor Lil', 'Temptation', 'Sweet and lovely' and 'Everything is Latin in the USA'.

381

Clay pigeon/Trip to kill

USA 1971 – 93 mins
dir Tom Stern, Lane Slate

Exploitation potboiler mixing Vietnam action with drugs and thuggery in a well-worn plot with cliché-bound characters. **Taj Mahal** performed the song 'Whistlin' Dixie' for the soundtrack.

382

Cleopatra Jones

USA 1973 – 89 mins
dir Jack Starrett

Routine addition to the current cycle of black-orientated, inner-city drug melodramas, with the off-beat twist of having a sexy woman detective as the leading character. Music score composed and conducted by **J. J. Johnson**.

383

Close shave

USA 1942 – 3 mins

Soundie featuring the title number interpreted by Aurora Greeley and LeRoy Bloomfield with **John Kirby** among the musicians.

384

Cocksucker blues

USA 1972/6
dir Robert Frank

A rough, mean piece of filmmaking showing the essential violence and resentment that underlies a major pop music event – The Rolling Stones's 1972 American tour. Features among the pop personalities bluesman **Bukka White**.

385

Cocktail magazine no 1

France 1946 – 14 mins
dir Eddie Petrossian

An actuality featurette, part travelogue, with some music from the André Ekyan Quintet with **Henri Crolla**.

386

Les coeurs verts/Naked hearts

France 1966 – 105 mins
dir Edouard Luntz

A story of the juveniles delinquent and near-delinquent who live in the sprawling outer suburbs of Paris. Music credit shared by **Henri Renaud** and Serge Gainsbourg.

387

Coleman Hawkins Quartet

Belgium 1961 – 30 mins

A film produced of the Quartet performing in a Brussels studio, record by Jazz Films SPRL. **Coleman Hawkins** is backed by **George Arvanitas**, *pno;* **Mickey Baker**, *gtr;* Jimmy Woode *bass* and '**Kansas' Fields**, *drs.*

388

College swing/Swing, teacher, swing

USA 1937 – 85 mins
dir Raoul Walsh

A multi-starred spoof of collegiate customs liberally spiced with music and comedy turns. Features **Skinnay Ennis** and the song 'College swing' by Frank Loesser and **Hoagy Carmichael**

389

Colour

UK 1975 – 22 mins
dir Anthony Short

Documentary study of various aspects of colour, including Newton's theories, additive and subtractive colour mixing, the human eye's ability to distinguish and match shades, colour in nature and industry. Music by **Tony Kinsey**.

390

Come back Charleston Blue

USA 1972 – 100 mins
dir Mark Warren

Uneven adaptation of Chester Himes's gangland novel *The heat's on* which continues the adventures of two off-beat, comedic Harlem gumshoes, 'Coffin' Ed Johnson and 'Gravedigger' Jones. Music score composed and conducted by Donny Hathaway, 'supervised' by **Quincy Jones** who also supplied, with Al Cleveland, lyrics for the title song sung by Donny Hathaway and Valerie Simpson.

Come dance with me
see **Voulez-vous danser avec moi?**

391

Come to baby do

USA 1946 – 3 mins
dir William Forest Crouch

Freddie Read, pno, leads The Quartet throughout **The connection**.

Soundie in which the **'King' Cole** Trio present one of their hit recordings.

The comic strip hero
see **Jeu de massacre.**

392

Het compromis

Netherlands 1968 – 83 mins
dir Philo Bregstein

Drama about an American actor living in Holland who is drafted for probable Vietnam service, and his pacifist principles. Soundtrack music by Louis van Dijk, Mozart and **Leadbelly**.

393

Conception

USA 1951 – 3 mins

Snader Telescription in which the title number is played by **George Shearing**, *pno;* **Joe Roland**, *vibs;* **Chuck Wayne**, *gtr;* **Al McKibbon**, *bass;* **Denzil Best**, *drs.*

394

The concert for Bangladesh

USA 1972 – 99 mins
dir Saul Swimmer

▼

Refreshingly straightforward cinematic record of the 1971 Madison Square Garden benefit pop concert for the refugees of Bangladesh. Features **Billy Preston** with his own song 'That's the way'.

395
Confessor
USA 1968/73 – 83 mins
dir Edward Bergman, Alan Soffin

Offbeat work delving into the fading of American myths and the advent of questioning, anguish and frustrations due to the Vietnamese war, political corruption and the problems of minorities. Music by **Chico Hamilton**.

396
The connection
USA 1961 – 110 mins
dir Shirley Clarke

Film adaptation by Jack Gelber of his own highly successful stage play, originally produced by the Living Theatre, about the making of a film of jazz-orientated drug addicts. Plenty of jazz by **Freddie Redd** played by a quartet who are on camera throughout most of the film. **Freddie Redd**, *pno;* **Jackie McLean**, *alt sax;* **Michael Mattos**, *bass;* **Larry Ritchie**, *drs.* **Charlie Parker**'s recording of 'Marmaduke' features prominently in one sequence.

397
Connee Boswell and Ada Leonard
USA 1952 – 14 mins
dir Will Cowan

Universal-International featurette with Ada Leonard and Her All Girl Orchestra furnishing the backing for **Connee Boswell** ('Come on and smile in the sunshine', 'Basin Street blues'); The Freddie Slack Trio ('Pig foot Pete'); violinist Anita Aros ('Brahms's fifth'); comic Bob Hopkins; and their own instrumental ('El cubanchero').

398
Connee Boswell and Les Brown's Orchestra
USA 1950 – 15 mins
dir Will Cowan

Universal-International short subject in which **Les Brown** and His Orchestra provide backing for The Moon Mists; The Dale Sisters; Teddy and Phyllis Rodriguez and finally **Connee Boswell** with two splendid numbers: 'I don't know why' and 'Martha'. **Dave Pell** takes the tenor sax solos, **Ray Sims**, *trb,* and **Jack Sperling** is the drummer.

Connee Boswell and Les Brown's Orchestra.

▼

▲

The Buddy DeFranco Quartet in **Cool and groovy.**

399

Les conquistadores

France 1975 – 100 mins
dir Marco Pauly

A series of asides, readings, talk and sketches making up a tale of a dissatisfied couple seeking adventure under urban pressures and pastoral ennui. Music score by **Joachim Kuhn, Daniel Humair** and **Michel Portal**.

400

Contrast in rhythm

USA 1945 – 3 mins

Soundie featuring **Cecil Scott** and His Orchestra with the title number.

401

Contrechant

France 1963 – 19 mins
dir Claude Boissol

Fictional short about a clarinettist and his wanderings from orchestra to orchestra. Original music by **Maxim Saury**.

402

The conversation

USA 1974 – 113 mins
dir Francis Ford Coppola

Brilliantly manoeuvred account of the tribulations of a professional eavesdropper, and amateur tenor sax, who fears his bugging may lead to a murder. David Shire's superb music track incorporates soundtrack use of several evergreen standards including **Duke Ellington**'s 'Sophisticated lady' together with two original jazz recordings 'Blues for Harry' played by **Pete Jolly**, *pno;* **Ray Brown**, *bass;* **Shelly Manne**, *drs;* **Barney Kessel**, *gtr;* **Al Aarons** or **Bobby Bryant**, *tpt;* **Don Menza**, *ten sax;* and 'Love bug' played by **Shelly Manne**, *drs;* **Ray Brown**, *bass;* **Bud Shank**, *bar sax;* **Al Aarons**, *tpt.* Actor Gene Hackman was ghosted by **Justin Gordon**, *ten sax* and David Shire interpreted his own central piano theme.

403

Conversations with Shakey Jake

USA 1972 – 13 mins
dir Franklin Konigsberg

Telling of a singer's attempt to play the blues.

404

Coogan's bluff

USA 1968 – 94 mins
dir Donald Siegel

Thriller with a first-rate script that doesn't quite

▲

The Chico Hamilton Quintet in **Cool and groovy**.

manage to maintain the brilliance of its opening sequence but nevertheless is sharp, bright and extremely enjoyable. It was extended into a TV series, *McCloud*. Percussive music score by **Lalo Schifrin**.

405
Cool and groovy

USA 1956 – 15 mins
dir Will Cowan

Universal-International featurette with The Conley Graves Trio playing 'Conley's blues' (Conley, *pno*; John Wilshire, *bass*; Billy Schneider, *drs*); The Tune Jesters singing 'Jericho' and 'Dry bones'; The Hi-Los with 'Jeepers creepers'; The **Chico Hamilton** Quintet playing 'A nice day' (**Buddy Collette**, *clar*; **Jim Hall**, *gtr*; **Fred Katz**, *cello*; **Carson Smith**, *bass*; **Chico Hamilton**, *drs*); The **Buddy DeFranco** Quartet playing 'I'll remember April' (**DeFranco**, *clar*; **Pete Jolly**, *pno*; **Bob White**, *drs*; unidentified, *bass*); **Anita O'Day** singing 'Honeysuckle rose' accompanied by The **Buddy DeFranco** Quartet.

406
Cool hand Luke

USA 1967 – 127 mins
dir Stuart Rosenberg

Enjoyable Southern chain-gang drama with allegorical undertones, marred only by the director's fondness for the dreaded zoom lens. Music score by **Lalo Schifrin**.

407
A cool sound from hell/The young and the beat

Canada 1959 – 71 mins
dir Sidney J. Furie

Furie's second feature film, professedly a frank exposition of the Beat Generation as it appears in one particular Canadian city, but only too reminiscent of similar ventures in its incoherence. Music by **Phil Nimmons** featuring guitarist **Ed Bickert**.

408
A cool steady look at the WRAC

UK 1966 – 18 mins
dir John Durst

The reception and early days of a WRAC recruit the opportunities for work and travel etc. Music by **Johnny Hawksworth**.

409

The cool world

USA 1963 – 105 mins
dir Shirley Clarke

Adaptation of Warren Miller's novel and play about a 15-year-old Harlem Negro boy whose primary aim in life is to own a gun and lead his own gang. Jazz score composed by **Mal Waldron** and played by **Dizzy Gillespie**, *tpt;* **James Moody**, *ten sax, flute;* **Kenny Barton**, *pno;* **Chris White**, *bass;* **Rudy Collins**, *drs.* Featured jazz group: **Gillespie, Yusef Lateef, Mal Waldron, Arthur Taylor, Aaron Bell.**

410

Coonskin/Bustin' out

USA 1975 – 82 mins
dir Ralph Bakshi

Part animated, part live-action story of three rural blacks plunging into the urban ghetto maelstrom where non-blacks control the social structure, with music score by **Chico Hamilton**.

411

Cootie Williams and His Orchestra

USA 1944 – 10 mins

Official Films music short featuring the title band with soloists **Cootie Williams, Eddie Vinson, Sam Taylor** and **Bud Powell**. Numbers include: 'Theme' and 'Wild fire'.

412

Cops and robbers

USA 1973 – 89 mins
dir Aram Avakian

Fresh and original robbery movie scripted by the always excellent Donald E. Westlake. Contains a song by Michel Legrand and Jacques Wilson 'It's a world of cops and robbers' sung by **Grady Tate**.

413

Cornbread, Earl and me

USA 1975 – 94 mins
dir Joe Manduke

Adaptation of Ronald Fair's novel *Hog Butcher* about a young black basketball star slain by the police. Music score by **Donald Byrd** performed by The Blackbyrds.

414

Cosmic ray

USA 1962 – 4 mins
dir Bruce Conner

A madly experimental holocaust of images building up a scathing picture of the modern world. The soundtrack uses a recording of **Ray Charles** singing 'What'd I say'.

Cost of loving
see **The prowler.**

415

Count Basie and His Orchestra

USA 1951 – 19 mins

Snader Telescriptions featuring the title orchestra.

416

Count me in

USA 1942 – 3 mins

Soundie in which the title number is played by **Claude Thornhill** with vocals by Martha Wayne and Buddy Stewart.

417

Count me out

USA 1946 – 3 mins
dir William Forest Crouch

Soundie featuring **Red Allen** and **J. C. Higginbotham** heading their combo in the title number.

418

The Count of Monte-Cristo

USA 1974 – 104 mins
dir David Greene

Breathlessly paced screen adaptation of the novel by Alexandre Dumas, but totally lacking in vivacity and atmosphere. Music score by **Allyn Ferguson**.

419

The counterfeit killer

USA 1968 – 95 mins
dir Josef Leytes

A confused and confusing tale of waterfront crime that makes excessive use of sweating close-ups. Music by **Quincy Jones**.

420

Country jazz

Australia 1971 – 11 mins
dir R. Kingsbury

Australian Colour Diary No 37 devoted to impressions of the 25th Australian Jazz Convention held in Dubbo, New South Wales, 26th-30th December 1970. Several local traditional groups are featured plus **Graeme Bell**'s Band.

421

La coupe à dix francs

France 1975 – 100 mins
dir Philippe Condroyer

A firm and acute treatment of familiar situations –
bigotry, the fear of anything different and youthful
problems. Music improvised to film by **Anthony
Braxton** and Antoine Duhamel.

422

Le couteau dans la plaie/Five miles to midnight

France/Italy 1962 – 110 mins
dir Anatole Litvak

Silly, melodramatic thriller landing Anthony
Perkins with another of those stock personalities
based on a wheedling infantilism. **Jacques
Loussier** contributed to Mikis Theodorakis's
music score.

423

Cowboy canteen

USA 1944 – 72 mins
dir Lew Landers

Low-budget musical, Western style, tailored for its
star Charles Starrett, with lots of close harmony
from The **Mills Brothers** and other groups.
Features the song 'Lazy river' by Sidney Arodin
and **Hoagy Carmichael**.

424

Cow-cow boogie

USA 1943 – 6 mins
dir Alex Lovy

A Waltz Lantz Swing Symphony colour cartoon,
being an imaginative parody of the West in which
boogie-woogie replaces 'Home on the range'.
Soundtrack piano is played by **Meade Lux Lewis**.

425

The cradle is rocking

USA 1968 – 12 mins
dir Frank de Cola

An impression of life in New Orleans as it is
today, with memories of the past recalled by
trumpeter **George Cola** who is shown playing
with His **Storyville Jazz Band**. Other music is
provided by The **New Orleans Olympia Brass
Band**.

426

Crashing the gate

USA 1933 – 15 mins
dir Joseph Henabery

Vitaphone short starring Ruth Etting and featuring
among the songs **W. C. Handy**'s 'St Louis blues'.

427

Crawl, Red, crawl

USA 1946 – 3 mins
dir William Forest Crouch

Soundie featuring **Red Allen** and **J. C.
Higginbotham** with the title number, supported
by dancer Johni Weaver.

428

Crazy frolic

USA 1953 – 19 mins
dir Will Cowan

Universal-International musical programmer
featuring **Les Brown** and His Orchestra in a
nightclub setting backing variety acts. Eileen
Wilson sings 'Zing went the strings of my heart';
The Dupree Trio dance two numbers: 'Dance
tropicana' and 'Harlem nocturne'; Lucy Ann
Polk sings 'It's a good day'; Wayne Marlin Trio do
acrobatics; Robert Monet sings 'Venita'. Tenor
sax **Dave Pell** solos during the three band
numbers: 'Ramona', 'It's bigger than both of us'
and 'Montana express'.

429

Crazy house/Funzapoppin'

USA 1943 – 80 mins
dir Edward F. Cline

Disappointing follow-up to *Hellzapoppin'* with
Olsen and Johnson again wreaking havoc
wherever they go. Features The **Count Basie
Band** with **Jimmy Rushing**, The **Glenn Miller**
Singers, The **Delta Rhythm Boys** and the songs
'Rigoletto quartet' and 'Get on board little
children'.

430

The criminal

UK 1960 – 97 mins
dir Joseph Losey

A realistic and unvarnished picture of English
prison life, beautifully directed but marred by an
unconvincing story. Music score by **Johnny
Dankworth** including the song 'Thieving boy'
sung on soundtrack by **Cleo Laine**.

431

The crimson canary

USA 1945 – 64 mins
dir John Hoffman

Routine murder mystery in which two members of
a dance band are suspected of doing away with
their singer during a jam session. Features The
Esquire All American Band Winners, with
**Coleman Hawkins, Howard McGhee, Sir
Charles Thompson, Oscar Pettiford, Denzil
Best** and **Josh White** playing 'Hollywood
stampede'.

432

Croisière pour l'inconnu

France 1947 – 90 mins
dir Pierre Montazel

Formula domestic comedy with a music score by **Hubert Rostaing**.

433

Crossfire

USA 1947 – 86 mins
dir Edward Dmytryk

Classic drama, on a racial theme, concerning three soldier suspects on a murder charge and the task of identifying the real killer. Features **Kid Ory** and His Band.

434

The cruise

USA 1967 – 8 mins
dir John Hubley

Animated cartoon fable of our times, about people and numbers and chance. Music by **Benny Carter**.

435

Cry of jazz

USA 1959 – 33 mins
dir Edward Bland

An informal discussion about jazz and the role of the Negro in America based partly on the director's book *The fruits of the death of jazz*. Music written by **Sun Ra** and **Julien Priester** among others, played by **Sun Ra** and His Arkestra.

436

Cry tough

USA 1959 – 83 mins
dir Paul Stanley

Downbeat account of a young Puerto Rican's struggle to find a place for himself in a slum district of New York, from a novel by Irving Shulman. Music score by **Laurindo Almeida**.

437

Cuckoo patrol

UK 1965 – 76 mins
dir Duncan Wood

An incredibly unfunny farce, with the further embarrassment of a team of grown men – Freddie and The Dreamers – impersonating moronic Boy Scouts. Music by **Kenny Graham**.

438

Cul-de-sac

UK 1966 – 111 mins
dir Roman Polanski

Grotesque drama, set on an island off the Northumbrian coast, that isn't quite sure whether it's a *comédie noire* or an exercise in sick humour. Music score by **Komeda**.

439

Cup glory

UK 1971 – 84 mins
dir Tony Maylam

A brief history of the FA Cup concentrating on the centenary season which culminated in Leeds beating Arsenal at Wembley in May 1972. Music score by **Johnny Hawksworth**.

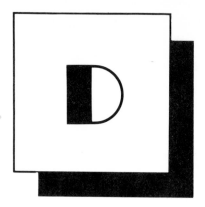

440

D.O.A.

USA 1949 – 83 mins
dir Rudolph Maté

Formula thriller, though with a memorable performance by the always excellent Edmond O'Brian. Features **Lee Young** and **'Illinois' Jacquet.**

Da New York: Mafia uccide
see **Je vous salue Mafia.**

441

Daddy long legs

USA 1955 – 127 mins
dir Jean Negulesco

At least the third screen adaptation of this sentimental old romantic novel but, if nothing else, this version has Fred Astaire and one really good dance sequence, 'Sluefoot', which features **Ray Anthony** and His Orchestra.

442

Dance demons

USA 1957 – 14 mins

Universal music featurette with Lois Ray, Page and Bray, **Stumpy Brown, Butch Stone** and Jo Ann Greer singing with **Les Brown** and His Band of Renown.

443

Dance hall

UK 1950 – 80 mins
dir Charles Crichton

Flat, conventional melodrama about four factory girls who spend their evenings searching for excitement at the local Palais. Features **Ted Heath** and His Music.

444

Dance of renown

USA 1951 – 3 mins

Snader Telescription in which the title number is played by **Les Brown** and His Band.

445

Dance of the vampires/The fearless vampire killers

UK 1967 – 107 mins
dir Roman Polanski

Production difficulties and a good deal of re-editing have rather spoilt Polanski's original conception of this definitive send-up of vampire movies but a few good jokes remain including the now-classic screen credit: 'Fangs by Dr Ludwig von Krankheit'. Music score is by **Krzysztof Komeda**.

446

Dance team

USA 1931 – 83 mins
dir Sidney Lanfield

Fox Film Corp. adaptation of a novel by Sarah Addington, featuring The **Claude Hopkins** Orchestra.

447

Dancers in the dark

USA 1932 – 76 mins
dir David Burton

Light drama adapted from the play *Jazz King* by James Ashmore Creelman about an amorous

▲

Ted Heath and His Music play for the dancers in **Dance Hall**.

taxi-driver and her love for a jazz musician. Features **Duke Ellington** and **Adelaide Hall**.

448

Dancing co-ed/Every other inch a lady

USA 1939 – 4 mins
dir S. Sylvan Simon

College comedy with Lana Turner and a good deal of jitterbugging. Features **Artie Shaw** and His Orchestra playng 'Nightmare', 'Non-stop flight', 'I've got a feeling you're fooling', 'Stars and stripes forever', 'Traffic jam', 'I'm coming Virginia', 'Oh, lady be good' and 'Jungle drums'.

449

A dandy in aspic

UK 1968 – 107 mins
dir Anthony Mann

Disappointingly routine spy thriller adapted by Derek Marlowe from his own excellent book. Music score by **Quincy Jones**.

450

The Daniel jazz

USA 1971 – 14 mins
dir N. H. Cominos

A filmed performance of Louis Gruenberg's *The Daniel jazz*, a work which employs the jazz idiom in classical music. Performed by The Harold Kohon Ensemble at Southampton College in Long Island, N.Y.

451

A dangerous age

Canada 1957 – 69 mins
dir Sidney J. Furie

Probably the first Canadian feature to rate serious criticism: a story of youth, its problems, frustrations and inarticulate rebellions. Music score by **Phil Nimmons**.

452

The dark corner

USA 1946 – 99 mins
dir Henry Hathaway

Good, suspenseful thriller about a private detective framed for murder but ultimately cleared with the help of his secretary. Includes an appearance by **Eddie Heywood**'s Band and the song 'Heywood blues', written by **Heywood**.

453
Dark eyes

USA c1952 – 3 mins

Telescription featuring **Jack Teagarden** with the title number.

454
Dark moves

UK 1974 – 10 mins
dir Peter Austin-Hunt

Cheap exploitation quickie featuring a couple of semi-nude dancers, enlivened only by the splendid jazz soundtrack by **Terri Quaye**, *congas;* **Robin Jones**, *perc;* **Lindsay Cooper**, *bass.*

455
Dark passage

USA 1947 – 106 mins
dir Delmer Daves

A novel by the late David Goodis (*Nightfall, Tirez sur le pianiste*) provided the basis for this tense thriller in the finest Warner Bros tradition. The standard reference books on film music state that **Hoagy Carmichael**'s song 'How little we know' (previously used in the 1944 *To have and have not*) was also used here on soundtrack but this is not so. For the record, the song used throughout is 'Too marvellous for words' with three other numbers used as source music: 'Just one of those things', 'I guess I'll have to change my plan' and 'Someone to watch over me'.

456
Dark waters

USA 1944 – 90 mins
dir André de Toth

Psychological melodrama set in bayou country of Louisiana, featuring **Nina Mae McKinney**.

457
Darling . . .

UK 1965 – 127 mins
dir John Schlesinger

Comedy of English upper-middle-class morals and mores, with music by **John Dankworth**.

A date with a lonely girl
see **T. R. Baskin.**

458
Date with Dizzy

USA 1956 – 10 mins
dir John Hubley

A jazz quintet – **Dizzy Gillespie, Sahib Shihab, Wade Legge, Nelson Boyd, Charlie Persip** – fail hilariously to provide suitable soundtrack music for a cartoon commercial advertising an instant rope ladder.

459
Date with Duke

USA 1947 – 7 mins
dir George Pal

One of the famous series of colour Puppetoons produced by George Pal. **Duke Ellington** provides the music for this one, which is about performing perfume bottles, with extracts from his 'Perfume suite'.

Daughter of horror
see **Dementia.**

460
Dave Brubeck

France 1970 – 32 mins
dir François Leduc

The Quartet – **Dave Brubeck, Paul Desmond, Eugene Wright, Joe Morello** – relaxing and playing together in Vence, before they broke up.

The day and the hour
see **Le jour et l'heure**

461
A day at the races

USA 1937 – 109 mins
dir Sam Wood

One of the best of the wild comedies made by The Marx Brothers during the period of their MGM contract. Controversy still rages as to whether or not a single note of **Duke Ellington**'s music remains in the final release prints; he says he recorded it but he certainly doesn't appear, though **Ivie Anderson** and The Crinoline Choir do.

462
Day of the animals

USA 1976
dir William Girdler

Currently in production, an adventure drama with a music score by **Lalo Schifrin**.

463
The day of the locust

USA 1974 – 143 mins
dir John Schlesinger

Screen adaptation of the novel by Nathanael West – a crystallisation of his Hollywood experiences. Among the many vintage recordings used on soundtrack is 'Jeepers creepers' sung by **Louis Armstrong**.

464

Daybreak express

USA 1953 – 6 mins
dir D. A. Pennebaker

Fast moving impression of an early morning ride into New York along the famed 'Third Avenue El'. **Duke Ellington**'s 1934 recording of 'Daybreak express' is used throughout on soundtrack.

465

Days of wine and roses

USA 1962 – 116 mins
dir Blake Edwards

Ruthless comedy of jargon-ridden PR executives and marital alcoholism; unashamedly sentimental but commandingly played. Henry Mancini's sugary music track owes much to the flawless playing of **Vince DeRosa**, *Fr horn*.

466

De l'amour/All about loving

France/Italy 1964 – 90 mins
dir Jean Aurel

Enjoyable episodic entertainment linked by the general theme of love as seen by Stendhal in his collection of aphorisms on the subject. Music score by **André Hodeir**.

467

De l'autre côté du chemin de fer/The other side of the tracks

France 1967 – 20 mins
dir G. Patris, L. Ferrari

Cecil Taylor talks about his life and work and rehearses with **Jimmy Lyons**, *alt sax;* **Ron Silva**, *bass;* and **Andrew Cyrille**, *drs.*

468

Deacon Jones

USA 1944 – 3 mins

Soundie in which **Wingy Manone** and His Rhythm Band swing through the title number.

469

Dead cert

UK 1974 – 99 mins
dir Tony Richardson

Confused adaptation of the novel by Dick Francis, with a racecourse setting. **Annie Ross** appears in an acting role.

470

Dead to the world

USA 1960 – 87 mins
dir Nicholas Webster

Low-budget suspense melo based on the novel *The state department murders*, with a music score by **Charlie Byrd**. **Eddie Phyfe** was music director and soundtrack drummer.

471

The deadly affair

UK 1966 – 107 mins
dir Sidney Lumet

Sadly underrated screen adaptation of John Le Carré's novel *Call for the dead;* a good old-fashioned thriller with some particularly expert performances. Has a splendid big band jazz score by **Quincy Jones** with a memorable song sung by **Astrud Gilberto**.

472

The deadly companions

USA 1961 – 90 mins
dir Sam Peckinpah

Fascinating, consistently beautiful Western on a revenge theme, adapted by A. S. Fleischman from his own novel. The first feature film by a director who was shortly to become one of the supreme masters of the Western genre. A superb music score by Marlin Skiles contains long passages for two solo guitars, one of which is played by **Laurindo Almeida**.

473

Deadly roulette

USA 1966 – 90 mins
dir William Hale

Vastly entertaining, offbeat thriller on the theme of a man's obsessive conviction that he is the victim of a conspiracy. Percussive score by **Lalo Schifrin.**

Dearest love
see **Le souffle au coeur.**

474

Death of a gunfighter

USA 1969 – 94 mins
dir Allen Smithee (pseud.)

Uneven but highly watchable 20th century Western, started by Robert Totton as director but finished by Don Siegel. Music by **Oliver Nelson** and song 'Sweet apple wine' sung by Lena Horne.

475

A death of princes

USA 1960 – 52 mins
dir John Brahm

Eli Wallach offers a frightening glimpse of degeneracy in this tight little thriller, originally made for US TV. Music score by **Billy May**.

476

Death wish

USA 1974 – 94 mins
dir Michael Winner

Simplistic adaptation of Brian Garfield's novel charting a husband's revenge following his wife's death and daughter's rape by muggers. Suitably atmospheric music composed, orchestrated and performed by **Herbie Hancock** with contributing musicians Fender Rhodes, Bennie Maupin, Paul Jackson, Mike Clark and Bill Summers.

477

Dedans le sud de la Louisiane/Within southern Louisiana

France 1974 – 44 mins
dir Jean-Pierre Bruneau

Documentary about the French-speaking minority in Louisiana, told through their music, culture and language. Music by **Clifton Chenier** and others.

478

Deep jaws

USA 1975 – 89 mins
dir Perry Dell

Flagrantly bad skinflick without even a modicum of intelligence or a trace of genuine humour. Music and vocals by **Jack Millman**.

479

Deep purple

USA 1949 – 15 mins
dir Will Cowan

Universal-International short devoted to **Gene Krupa** and His Orchestra (**Lennie Hambro**. *alt sax;* **Buddy Wise**, *ten sax*), in a nightclub setting, supported by vocalists and acrobats. Numbers include 'Lemon drop', 'Deep purple', 'Bop boogie' and 'Melody in f'.

480

The defiant ones

USA 1958 – 96 mins
dir Stanley Kramer

Two convicts, chained together at the wrists, escape a chain gang; one man is white, the other black. Includes a song 'Love gone' by **W. C. Handy.**

481

The delicate delinquent

USA 1956 – 100 mins
dir Don McGuire

Routine Jerry Lewis comedy on the theme of juvenile delinquency and its treatment. Music score by **Buddy Bregman**.

482

Dementia/Daughter of horror

USA 1953 – 55 mins
dir John Parker

Madly experimental exercise in visual imagery, with wordless soundtrack. An extended nightclub sequence features **Shorty Rogers** and His Giants playing the leader's composition 'Wig alley'.

483

Le départ

Belgium 1966 – 91 mins
dir Jerzy Skolimowski

Polish director Skolimowski brings his own explosive style and considerable visual flair to Brussels, to tell of a young hairdresser with a passion for fast cars. **Krzysztof T. Komeda**'s hard swinging jazz score is an essential contribution. Musicians heard include **Don Cherry, Gato Barbieri, René Urtreger**, Jacques Thollot, **Jean-François Jenny-Clark**, Jacques Pelzer, Edy Louis, Philip Catherine, Luiz Funtez.

484

Département 66

France 1963 – 12 mins
dir Claude Laporte

Documentary on the mountain region of Roussillon, with music by **Jacques Loussier**.

485

Der var engang en krig/Once there was a war

Denmark 1966 – 94 mins
dir Palle Kjaerulff-Schmidt

Warm, humorous and poignant story of a teenager growing up in Denmark during The German Occupation of World War II. Music score by **Leo Mathison** who uses some forties jazz recordings for a party scene that features **Henry Hagemann**, *ten sax*.

La dernière femme
see **L'Ultima donna.**

486

Deryck Guyler

UK 1974 – 13 mins
prod Bill Stevenson

▲

Gene Krupa and His Orchestra, in appropriate bop berets and glasses in **Deep purple***.*

Comedian Deryck Guyler talks about the influence of his Catholic faith on his life and work and plays the washboard with The **Alan Elsdon** Jazz Band.

Designed to cover
UK 1971 – 13 mins
dir Ted Clisby

An exposition of the Triodetic space structure, with music by **Johnny Hawksworth**.

Desire takes the men
see **L'Amour mène les hommes.**

488

Le désordre à vingt ans

France 1967 – 60 mins
dir Jacques Baratier

A documentary looking back at Saint Germain des Prés as it was immediately post war, with film material on most of the personalities of the time: Sartre, de Beauvoir, Artaud, Vian, Cocteau, Greco etc. Music and songs by **Claude Luter** and Alain Vian.

489

Le désordre et la nuit/Night affair

France 1958 – 92 mins
dir Gilles Grangier

Amoral yarn of an ageing detective out to solve the murder of a nightclub owner, with an appearance by **Hazel Scott**.

490

Desperate characters

USA 1971 – 87 mins
dir Frank D. Gilroy

48 hours in the lives of a childless New York couple in the light of the husband's failing business. Soundtrack provided by **Lee Konitz, Jim Hall** and **Ron Carter**.

491

Deux grandes filles dans un pyjama

France 1974 – 95 mins
dir Jean Girault

Screen adaptation of the stage comedy *S.O.S. homme seul* about a married man left alone in Paris over Easter, with music score by **Claude Bolling**.

492

Deux hommes dans Manhattan

France 1958 – 84 mins
dir Jean-Pierre Melville

An essay on friendship, brilliantly created in a New York setting and owing much to Melville's love for the American cinema. Music by **Christian Chevallier** and **Martial Solal**, with an appearance by **Art Simmons**.

493

Les deux plumes

France 1958 – 9 mins
dir Henri Lacam

Animated adventures of two inkwells, with music by **Henri Crolla**.

494

Les deux uraniums

France 1965 – 10 mins
dir Jacques Leroux, Manuel Otéro

Documentary about uranium and its constituent parts, with music by **Martial Solal**.

495

Deviled hams

USA 1937 – 10 mins
dir Milton Schwarzwald

A musical *divertissement*, in a satanic setting, featuring The **Erskine Hawkins** Orchestra with **Wilbur Bascomb**.

496

The devil's daughter

USA c1940 – 70 mins

All Negro production described as 'a burning drama of love and hate in the tropics', featuring **Nina Mae McKinney**.

497

Dexter Gordon

Denmark 1971 – 26 mins
prod Flip Film Productions

A straight record of **Dexter Gordon**, *ten sax*, playing two numbers – one being 'Those were the days' – to an audience in The Montmartre, Copenhagen, accompanied by **Kenny Drew**, *pno;* **Niels Henning Ørsted Pedersen**, *bass;* and **M. Ntshoko**, *drs.* **Ben Webster** is seen briefly among the audience.

498

Dial rat for terror

USA 1972 – 92 mins
dir Larry Cohen

A somewhat clumsy predecessor to the same director's superior *It's alive*, full of wilfully quirky dialogue and heavy-handed parody. Music score by **Gil Mellé**.

499

Dial red o

USA 1955 – 64 mins
dir Daniel B. Ullman

Conventionally tough crime melodrama. Jazz sequences by **Shorty Rogers** and His Giants.

500

Le diamant

France 1970 – 10 mins
dir Paul Grimault

D

Colour cartoon about a traveller who swindles a primitive tribe out of their treasure – the most beautiful diamond in the world. Music by **Jacques Loussier.**

501
Dig
USA 1972 – 25 mins
dir John Hubley

A children's introduction to geology in the form of animated musical fantasy. Music by **Quincy Jones.**

502
Dilemma/A world of strangers
Denmark 1962 – 92 mins
dir Henning Carlsen

Brave, though not entirely successful, attempt at adapting for the screen Nadine Gordimer's novel about apartheid; produced surreptitiously in Johannesburg under the noses of South African authorities believing a musical was in production. Music by Gideon Nxomalo and **Max Roach.**

503
Dill Jones and His All Stars
UK 1960 – 9 mins
dir Robert Henryson

Music short featuring the title group playing 'South of the border', 'Isle of Capri' and 'Cherokee'.

504
Dinah
USA 1944 – 3 mins

Soundie featuring pianist **Bob Howard.**

505
Dirty Dingus Magee
USA 1970 – 91 mins
dir Burt Kennedy

Brash, undisciplined adaptation of David Markson's novel *The ballad of Dingus Magee* with little but Frank Sinatra's professional polish to recommend it. Jeff Alexander's music track includes contributions from **George Roberts,** *bas-trb.*

506
Dirty Harry
USA 1971 – 102 mins
dir Don Siegel

Well-made but shallow glorification of police and criminal brutality with Clint Eastwood as the deadly-accurate super-hero. Modernistic score by **Lalo Schifrin.**

507
Disc jockey
USA 1951 – 76 mins
dir Will Jason

A competent second-feature in the conventional pattern but with interesting appearances by **Tommy Dorsey** and His Orchestra, **George Shearing** and His Quintet, **Red Nichols, Joe Venuti, Red Norvo, Vido Musso, Sarah Vaughan** and **Herb Jeffries.** Musical items include: 'Brain wave' by **George Shearing;** 'Disc jockey' and 'In my heart' by **Herb Jeffries** and Dick Hazard and 'Oh, look at me now' by John De Vris and **Joe Bushkin.**

Disc jockey jamboree
see **Jamboree.**

508
Discovering jazz
USA 1969 – 22 mins

Traces the history of jazz from its roots in 19th century America from Dixieland and Blues through such styles as swing, bop, cool jazz, funky and free improvisation.

509
Dis-moi que tu m'aimes
France 1974 – 90 mins
dir Michel Boisrond

Predictable situation comedy about marital problems encompassing such trendy themes as women's lib and male chauvinism. Music score by **Claude Bolling.**

510
Disneyland after dark
USA 1962 – 46 mins
dir H. S. Luske, W. Beaudine

An impression of Disneyland including a series of musical numbers. Features **Louis Armstrong** and His Band with **Kid Ory** and **Buddy St Cyr.**

511
The distant sounds
USA 1967 – 58 mins

Follows the thoughts and experiences of two black American jazz musicians who travelled from Harlem to Brazil in order to enhance their own understanding of the Afro-American roots of the music which they interpret and communicate to others.

512

Dites-le avec des fleurs

France 1974 – 98 mins
dir Pierre Grimblat

Psychological thriller about Nazi vengeance, adapted from the book by Christine Charrière. Music score by **Claude Bolling**.

513

Dixie jamboree

USA 1944 – 70 mins
dir Christy Cabanne

Routine comedy with music, set on the last surviving Mississippi showboat during a cruise. Features **Cab Calloway** and **Adelaide Hall**.

514

Dixieland droopy

USA 1954 – 7 mins
dir Tex Avery

Highly entertaining MGM colour cartoon about a dog named John Pettybone whose one aim in life is to lead a Dixieland jazz band in the Hollywood Bowl, which he finally does with the aid of a trumpet-blowing flea named Pee-Wee Runt. The music is by Scott Bradley.

515

Dixieland jamboree

USA 1935 – 9 mins

Vitaphone short featuring **Cab Calloway, Adelaide Hall** The Nicholas Brothers and other entertainers performing 'Tiger rag', 'Some of these days', 'I don't know why I feel this way' and 'Nagasaki'.

516

Dizzy Gillespie

USA c1964
dir Les Blank

The trumpeter talks about his work and performs with His Quintet – **James Moody**, *ten sax;* **Kenny Baron**, *pno;* **Chris White**, *bass;* **Rudy Collins**, *drs* – at The Lighthouse, Hermosa Beach. He is also seen in rehearsal and concert with The **Stan Kenton** Neophonic Orchestra.

517

Dizzy Gillespie Quintet

USA 1964 – 29 mins
prods: Ralph J. Gleason, Richard Christian

Produced originally for US TV in KQED's Jazz Casual series, a programme of music and discussion by **Dizzy Gillespie**, *tpt;* **Leo Wright**, *flute, alt sax;* **Lalo Schifrin**, *pno;* **Chuck Lamplin**, *drs;* **Robert Cunningham**, *bass*. Includes an excerpt from 'Gillespiana'.

518

Django Reinhardt

France 1958 – 21 mins
dir Paul Paviot

Documentary on the French guitarist, made five years after his death, with introduction by Jean Cocteau and commentary by Chris Marker, spoken by Yves Montand. Music from **Stephane Grappelly, Henri Crolla, Hubert Rostaing, Hubert Fol, Raymond Fol**, Gerard Leveque, André Ekyan, **Joseph Reinhardt**, Eugène Vees, Emmanuel Soudieux.

519

Do widzenia do jutra/See you tomorrow

Poland 1960 – 85 mins
dir Janusz Morgenstern

Slight but charming and quite memorable story set in the Baltic town of Gdansk about a students' theatre group and their director, played by Zbigniew Cybulski who had himself founded a similar theatre in his student days. Music by **Krzysztof T. Komeda**.

520

Do you love me?/Kitten on the keys

USA 1946 – 91 mins
dir Gregory Ratoff

Conventional Fox musical, expensively and lavishly mounted, with **Harry James** in an acting role and also appearing in musical sequences with His Music Makers. Includes the song 'As if I don't have enough on my mind' by Charles Henderson, Lionel Newman and **Harry James**.

521

Doberman patrol

USA 1973 – 87 mins
dir Frank Defelitta

Enjoyable thriller about a man locked into a department store facing the prospect of being torn to pieces by beautiful but vicious guard dogs. Music track by **Gil Mellé**.

522

Doctor rhythm

USA 1938 – 81 mins
dir Frank Tuttle

Crazy musical comedy with Bing Crosby and Beatrice Lillie. **Louis Armstrong** recorded the number 'The trumpet player's lament' for the film but the sequence was deleted from the eventual release version.

Maureen O'Hara in **Do you love me?** *Behind her are (left) Corky Corcoran,* ten sax *and Willie Smith,* alt sax.

523

Dr Terror's house of horrors

UK 1964 – 98 mins
dir Freddie Francis
Poor horror anthology consisting of five separate short stories. One of these, entitled 'Voodoo' features The **Tubby Hayes** Quintet.

Les doigts croisés

see **Catch me a spy.**

524

Dollars/The heist

USA 1971 – 120 mins
dir Richard Brooks
Suspenseful bank robbery movie with an exhausting chase sequence utilizing some good authentic locales in Germany and finally ending in San Diego. Swinging modernistic music score by **Quincy Jones** played by, collectively, Bobbye Hall Porter, **Milt Holland, Victor Feldman, Larry Bunker, Gene Estes,** *perc*; Paul Humphrey, Ronnie Tutt, *drs*; **Billy Preston,** Paul Beaver, **Artie Kane, Clare Fischer,** Mike Lang, *keyboards*; Eric Gale, Arthur Adams, **Elek Bacsik,** David T. Walker, *gtr*; **Chuck Rainey,** Bill Plummer, *fenders*; Elliott Fisher, *elec vin*; Doug Kershaw, *vln*; Bill Plummer, *sitar*; **Ray Brown,** *bass*; Tommy Johnson, *tuba*; **Jerome Richardson,** *reeds*. Vocals by **Roberta Flack,** Little Richard and The **Don Elliott** Voices. Songs: 'Do it – to it' and 'Money is', words and music by **Quincy Jones.**

525

Don Cornell sings

USA 1952 – 15 mins
Music featurette produced by Universal-International, mainly devoted to a programme of songs by Don Cornell but includes a vocal group, The Skylarks, singing **W. C. Handy**'s 'St Louis blues' and **June Christy** with 'Some folks do and some folks don't'.

526

Don Redman and His Orchestra

USA 1934 – 10 mins
dir Joseph Henabery

Vitaphone short set in another of Hollywood's dream nightclubs featuring The **Don Redman** Orchestra playing 'Yeah man', 'Ill wind', 'Nagasaki' and 'Why should I be tall'. Personnel: **Langston Curl, Sidney De Paris, Shirley Clay**, *tpts;* **Gene Simon, Benny Morton, Quentin Jackson**, *trbs;* **Edward Inge, Rupert Cole, Bob Carrol**, *saxes;* **Don Kirkpatrick**, *pno;* **Talcott Reeves**, *gtr;* **Bob Ysaguirre**, *bass;* **Manzie Johnson**, *drs;* **Don Redman**, *voc* and *mc,* Harlan Lattimore, *voc*; Red and Struggle, *taps.*

527

Don't be a baby, baby

USA 1946 – 3 mins
dir William Forest Crouch

Soundie featuring **Joe Marsala** and His Orchestra with the leader on clarinet and his wife, Adele Girard, on harp.

528

Don't be late

USA 1945 – 3 mins

Soundie featuring **Cecil Scott** and His Orchestra interpreting the title number.

529

Doomsday flight

USA 1966 – 97 mins
dir William Graham

Competent thriller about an aneroid bomb placed on board an aircraft en route for New York. Music score by **Lalo Schifrin**.

530

The Dorsey Brothers encore

USA 1953 – 16 mins
dir Will Cowan

Universal-International short subject bringing **Jimmy** and **Tommy Dorsey** together for a programme with Gordon Polk, Lynn Roberts, dancer Earl Barton and **Tommy Dorsey**'s Orchestra. Numbers include 'Ain't she sweet', 'We'll get it' and 'Jazz me blues' by the brothers' Dixieland Group.

531

Dossier prostitution/Secret French prostitution report

France 1969 – 90 mins
dir Jean-Claude Roy

Semi-documentary report on prostitution, with music by **Jacques Loussier**.

532

Doucement les basses

France/Italy 1971 – 90 mins
dir Jacques Deray

Mild comedy set in Britanny about a young priest – played by Alain Delon – whose past catches up with him. Music score by **Claude Bolling**.

533

Le doulos

France/Italy 1962 – 108 mins
dir Jean-Pierre Melville

A well paced gangster opus with a tale of friendship imbedded in the gunplay, violence and subtle plotting. Piano music by **Jacques Loussier**.

534

Down, down, down

USA 1942 – 3 mins

Soundie with **Louis Jordan** and His Band interpreting the title number.

535

Dragnet

USA 1954 – 88 mins
dir Jack Webb

Crime story in semi-documentary style, based on the immensely popular US TV series. **Dick Cathcart**, *tpt*, participated in Walter Schumann's music track.

Dreamers

see **Fantasterne.**

536

Dreams that money can buy

USA 1944 – 90 mins
dir Hans Richter

Series of episodes depicting the subconscious of its protagonists, based on ideas and scripts of six artists: Léger, Ernst, Ray, Duchamp, Calder and Richter. Songs partly written by **Josh White.**

D

537
Drink hearty

USA 1946 – 3 mins
dir William Forest Crouch

Soundie in which **Red Allen** and **J. C. Higginbotham** combine to present their interpretation of the title number.

538
Drink to me only with thine eyes

USA 1942 – 3 mins

Soundie featuring **Stan Kenton** and His Orchestra backing vocalists Ginger Harmon and Harry Barris.

539
Drive, he said

USA 1970 – 90 mins
dir Jack Nicholson

Confused and disturbing first feature from a talented actor, charting the painful steps towards self-consciousness of an extrovert basketball player. A few bars of 'I cried for you' sung by **Billie Holiday** are used effectively on the soundtrack.

540
Drive-in

USA 1976 – 96 mins
dir Rod Amateau

Quite enjoyable free-style comedy deriving from ideas suggested by the recent spate of disaster movies. Among the many popular songs used on soundtrack is 'Misty' by **Erroll Garner** and Johnny Burke, performed by Ray Stevens.

541
Drum crazy – the Gene Krupa story

USA 1959 – 99 mins
dir Don Weis

Gene Krupa rehearses Sal Mineo for his leading role in **Drum crazy**.

▼

Reasonably straightforward screen biography of the drummer, conventionally scripted but superbly cast and played, particularly by Sal Mineo in the title role, who works wonders matching his movements to **Krupa**'s own soundtrack drumming. Leith Stevens adapted and conducted the score which includes 'Memories of you', beautifully sung by **Anita O'Day**, 'Way down yonder in New Orleans', 'The sunny side of the street', 'Cherokee' and 'Indiana'. **Red Nichols** and **Shelly Manne** as **Dave Tough** have featured roles and there are appearances by **Bobby Troup, Clyde Hurley** and **Al Morgan**. The **Dorsey** Brothers, **Bix Beiderbecke, Bunny Berigan** and **Frankie Trumbauer** are all represented on screen. (**Tommy Dorsey**'s solos were simulated by **Tommy Pederson**).

542
Drummer man

USA 1947 – 15 mins
dir Will Cowan

Universal-International featurette show-casing **Gene Krupa**, vocalist Carolyn Grey, tap dancer Jeanne Blanche, The **Krupa** Jazz Trio and The **Gene Krupa** Orchestra. Numbers: 'Lover', 'Boogie blues', 'Stompin' at the Savoy', 'Blanchette' and 'Leave us leap'.

543
Drums of Africa

USA 1963 – 92 mins
dir James B. Clark

Routine adventure yarn set in equatorial Africa, with music score by **Johnny Mandel**.

544
Dry bones

USA 1945 – 3 mins

Soundie in which the title number is sung by The **Delta Rhythm Boys**.

545
Dry wood and hot pepper

USA 1973 – 98 mins
dir Les Blank

Documentary about the black French-speaking people of southwest Louisiana, made in two parts. The first part centres on the life of the more rural and stable rice farming communities, the second on Zydeco Blues king **Clifton Chenier**.

546
Du sel, du calcaire et du coke

France 1955 – 20 mins
dir Jean Venard

Prize-winning colour documentary on plastics, with a music score by **Henri Crolla**.

547
Du tam-tam au jazz

France 1969 – 70 mins
dir Philippe Brunet

Documentary in three parts showing the influence of the African musical tradition on the American continent. Includes sections on South American music culture, particularly Brazil, Afro-Cuban rhythms, Creole music, Gospel, Spirituals, instrumental blues, blues songs, ragtime and formal jazz.

548
Dubarry was a lady

USA 1943 – 101 mins
dir Roy Del Ruth

Technicolor MGM screen adaptation of Cole Porter's musical comedy about show people, part of which is set in the court of Louis XV. **Tommy Dorsey** and His Orchestra, featuring **Buddy Rich**, *drs*, have two good solo numbers – one in 18th century costume – and also provide backing for vocal/dance routines by the principals, Red Skelton, Gene Kelly, Lucille Ball and Virginia O'Brien plus The Pied Pipers with Jo Stafford and Dick Haymes. Orchestrations in part by **Sy Oliver**.

Duchess of Broadway

see **Talk about a lady.**

549
Duchess of Idaho

USA 1950 – 98 mins
dir Robert Z. Leonard

Handsomely produced MGM musical, set in Sun Valley, featuring Esther Williams's acquatic displays and lively guest appearances from Lena Horne and Mel Torme. **Stumpy Brown**, *trb*, is featured on screen only – the soundtrack was recorded by an MGM staff musician, with 'Skip' Martin as arranger.

550
Duel at Diablo

USA 1965 – 102 mins
dir Ralph Nelson

Tough, action-packed, old-fashioned Western, with a music score by **Neal Hefti**.

551

Duke Ellington and His Orchestra

USA 1943 – 9 mins
dir Jay Bonafield

One of the RKO Jamboree series in which the orchestra plays a straightforward programme of numbers including 'It don't mean a thing if it ain't got that swing', 'Mood indigo', 'Sophisticated lady' and 'Don't get around much any more'. Soloists include **Johnny Hodges, Ben Webster, Ray Nance, Taft Jordan** and **Duke Ellington**.

552

Duke Ellington and His Orchestra

USA 1962 – 25 mins
prod Mike Bryan

A programme by **Duke Ellington** and His Orchestra, produced for the Goodyear Tyre Company. Musicians: **Ray Nance, Shorty Baker, Cat Anderson**, *tpts;* **Lawrence Brown**, *trb;* **Russell Procope, Johnny Hodges**, *alt sax;* **Paul Gonsalves**, *ten sax;* **Jimmy Hamilton**, *clar;* **Harry Carney**, *bar sax;* **Ellington**, *pno;* **Aaron Bell**, *bass;* **Sam Woodyard**, *drs.* Numbers: 'Take the A train', 'Satin doll', 'Blow boy blow', 'Things ain't what they used to be', 'VIP boogie', 'Jam with Sam', 'Kinda Dukish'. Was recorded in New York, 9th January 1962.

553

Duke Ellington at The White House

USA 1969 – 18 mins
prod Sidney J. Stiber

Film record of a reception given at The White House in Washington for President Nixon and his guests at which a presentation is made to **Duke Ellington** on the occasion of his 70th birthday. Musicians appearing include **Shorty Baker, Paul Gonsalves, Billy Eckstine, Cab Calloway, Benny Goodman, Mercer Ellington, Dizzy Gillespie, Dave Brubeck, Paul Desmond, Gerry Mulligan, Clark Terry, Hank Jones, Willie 'The Lion' Smith, Earl Hines, Joe Williams, George Wein, J. J. Johnson, Urbie Green, Jim Hall, Milt Hinton, Louis Bellson**. Commentary spoken by Willis Connover.

554

Duke Ellington – love you madly

USA 1966 – 59 mins
dir Richard Moore

Documentary about **Duke Ellington** and His Orchestra filmed by Ralph J. Gleason over a period of one month and including band performances at North Beach's Basin Street West, Grace Cathedral and at the Monterey Jazz Festival. He is shown relaxing behind the scenes, on the road, and in the company of friends including **Dizzy Gillespie, Earl Hines**, Bunny Griggs and **Jon Hendricks**.

555

Dunderklumpen

Sweden 1973/4 – 138 mins
dir Per Åhlin

A full length colour cartoon for children of all ages; the most ambitious project in the history of Swedish cartoon film making, combining both live and animated figures. Music and songs composed and performed by **'Toots' Thielemans**, who also provides the voice for the character Pellegnillot.

556

Dwaj ludzie z szafa/Two men and a wardrobe

Poland 1957 – 15 mins
dir Roman Polanski

Now classic fantasy-parable about the cost of private lives in the modern world, made by its young director as an exercise while he was still a student at the Polish film school. Light jazz score by **Krzysztof T. Komeda**.

557

Dynamite chicken

USA 1971 – 76 mins
dir Ernie Pintoff

A multi-media mosaic – a kind of screen magazine with a most varied conglomeration of contributors. Briefly features the work of **Eric Dolphy** with 'Iron man', The **'Muddy' Waters** Blues Band and **Luther Johnson**, The Colwell-Winfield Blues Band and **Charles Lloyd** with 'Sombrero Sam' and 'Dream weaver'.

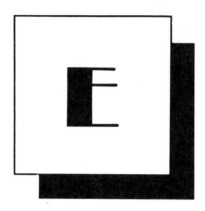

558

Eager beaver

USA 1944 – 3 mins

Soundie in which **Stan Kenton** and His Orchestra play the title number backing tap dancer Jean Ivory.

559

The eagle has landed

UK 1976 – 134 mins
dir John Sturges

Screen adaptation of the novel by Jack Higgins about a kidnap attempt on Winston Churchill in November 1943 by a party of German soldiers. Music score by **Lalo Schifrin**.

560

Earl Carroll sketchbook/Hats off to rhythm/Stand up and sing

USA 1946 – 90 mins
dir Albert S. Rogell

Low-budget Republic musical with a brief appearance by The **Buddy Rich** Band. Numbers: 'I've never forgotten', 'I was silly, I was head-strong and impetuous', 'What makes you beautiful, beautiful?', 'Oh, Henry' and 'Lady with a mop'.

561

Earl Carroll vanities

USA 1945 – 90 mins
dir Joseph Santley

Musical comedy about a European princess who, having been educated in America, prefers Boogie-woogie to Mozart! Features **Woody Herman** and His Orchestra: **Herman**, *clar;* **Ralph Burns**, *pno;* **Marjorie Hyams**, *vibs;* **Billy Bauer**, *gtr;* **'Flip'**

Phillips, John LaPorta, Sam Marowitz, Pete Mondello, 'Skippy' DeSair, *saxes;* Chubby Jackson, *bass;* Dave Tough, *drs;* Ralph Pfiffner, Bill Harris, Ed Kieffer, *trbs;* Neal Hefti, Charlie Frankhauser, Ray Wetzel, Pete Candoli, Carl Warwick, *tpts.* Numbers include 'Apple honey', 'Rock-a-bye boogie' and 'You beautiful thing you'.

562

Earl 'Fatha' Hines

USA 1963/4 – c30 mins
dir Richard Moore

Originally produced by US TV by Ralph J. Gleason in his 'Jazz casual series for KQED, a programme featuring pianist **Earl Hines** in which he talks with R.J.G. about his life and work and provides examples of his music.

563

The early worm gets the bird

USA 1943 – 7 mins
dir Tex Avery

Warner Bros colour cartoon about the friendship between a bird and the worm who saves him from a fox. **Roy Eldridge**, *tpt,* is prominently featured on soundtrack.

564

Earth 11

USA 1971 – 97 mins
dir Tom Gries

A plot-bound space saga made originally for US TV and trimmed by 20 minutes to serve here briefly as a second feature. Music score by **Lalo Schifrin**.

565

Earthquake

USA 1974 – 123 mins
dir Mark Robson

Large-scale hocus-pocus in which Los Angeles is spectacularly razed by a team of special effects men using sets, models, matte work and other undetectable sleights of hand. John Williams provides a suitable music score using among others **Vince De Rosa**, *Fr horn;* **Clare Fischer**, *pno;* and **Shelly Manne**, *drs.*

566

East of Suez

USA 1925 – 75 mins
dir Raoul Walsh

Screen adaptation of Somerset Maugham's 1922 play, with Pola Negri and Edmund Lowe. Somewhere in a crowd scene is **Jesse Fuller**, as an extra, making his first screen appearance.

567

East side of heaven

USA 1939 – 90 mins
dir David Butler

Romantic vehicle for Bing Crosby playing a crooning telegraph messenger. **Mannie Klein** has a small role.

568

Easy to look at

USA 1945 – 65 mins
dir Ford Beebe

Low-budget Universal musical in which The **Delta Rhythm Boys** sing 'Is you is or is you ain't my baby?'.

569

Easy to love

USA 1953 – 96 mins
dir Charles Walters

MGM aqua-musical with Esther Williams's healthy personality and physique set against a background of sun-tan, speedboats and open-air breakfasts. **Pete Rugolo** participated in the Lennie Hayton/George Stoll music track.

570

L'Eau à la bouche

France 1959 – 85 mins
dir Jacques Doniol-Valcroze

A delightful comedy of manners, sadly under-rated at the time of its release. The music track contains two good jazz arrangements by Alain Goraguer, 'Black march' and 'Angoisse'.

571

Ebony parade

USA 1947

Compilation of previously issued Soundies featuring black entertainers including **Cab Calloway, Count Basie, The Mills Brothers, Vanita Smythe**. Mantan Moreland, as a hocus-pocus magician, is used as a linking device.

572

Echappement libre/Backfire

France/Italy/Spain 1964 – 105 mins
dir Jean Becker

Routine situation comedy tailored for Jean-Paul Belmondo's talents. He finds himself travelling for a gang of smugglers and driving a gold-plated car to Bombay. Music by **Martial Solal**.

573

Echo of an era

USA 1957 – 14 mins
dir Henry Freeman

An impression of the history and development of the Third Avenue elevated railway in New York, made shortly before its closure. Jazz score composed and directed by **David Amram**.

574

Eddie Condon

USA 1961 – 26 mins
dir Bernard Rubin

A studio bandstand programme, produced for the Goodyear Tyre Company, featuring **'Wild' Bill Davison**, *cor;* **Cutty Cutshall**, *trb;* **'Peanuts' Hucko**, *clar;* **Johnny Varo**, *pno;* **Joe Williams**, *bass;* **Eddie Condon**, *gtr;* **'Buzzy' Drootin**, *drs.* Numbers: 'Royal garden blues', 'Blue and broken-hearted', 'Big Ben blues', 'Stealin' apples', 'Little Ben blues', 'Muskrat ramble'. Introductory music: 'The good years of jazz' by The **Duke Ellington** Orchestra.

575

Eddie Condon's

USA 1951 – 10 mins

From Columbia's Cavalcade of Broadway series comes this visit to **Eddie Condon**'s jazz club in Greenwich Village. The All Stars, including **'Wild' Bill Davison**, with vocalists Dolores Hawkins and Johnny Ray, play 'For you, my love' and 'Tell the lady I said goodbye'.

576

Eddie Peabody and Sonny Burke's Orchestra

USA 1951 – 14 mins
dir Will Cowan

Universal-International production in which Sonny Burke's Orchestra, in a nightclub setting, provides backing for popular acts: Barbara Perry, dancer; The Cheer Leaders, *vocs;* The **Red Norvo** Trio – **Norvo,** *vibs;* **Tal Farlow,** *gtr;* **Charlie Mingus,** *bass;* – and Eddie Peabody, *banjo,* with a Southern medley and 'St Louis blues'. Other numbers: 'Mambo jambo', 'Live till I die' and 'Anchors aweigh'.

577

Eddie Peabody in banjomania

USA 1927 – 9 mins

Early Vitaphone short featuring music on banjo, mandolin, banjola and harp guitar which includes a performance of **W. C. Handy**'s 'St Louis blues'.

578

Ee baba leba

USA 1947 – 10 mins

An all black production featuring **Dizzy Gillespie** and His Bebop Orchestra presenting, in a stage setting, 'Salt peanuts', 'Ee baba leba' (**Helen Humes,** *voc*) and a number backing tap dancer Ralph Brown.

579

Eggs

USA 1970 – 10 mins
dir John Hubley

Animated colour cartoon representing the dawn of a new day on planet Earth with the Goddess of Fertility sowing the seeds of life bringing her into direct conflict with her partner, Death. Music by **Quincy Jones.**

580

Eins

West Germany 1971 – 115 mins
dir Ulrich Schamoni

Conventional drama about a man with a roulette system and how he cheats his friends. Recordings by **Django Reinhardt** and **Stephane Grappelly** are used extensively on the soundtrack.

Elevator to the gallows

see **L'Ascenseur pour l'échafaud.**

581

Elstree calling

UK 1930 – 86 mins
dir Adrian Brunel

An all star revue, with colour sequences, compèred by Tommy Handley, the performers being drawn from London's musical shows. Remembered mainly for Alfred Hitchcock's credit for direction of 'sketches and other interpolated items'. Includes Teddy Brown and His Orchestra playing 'Ain't misbehavin' by **'Fats' Waller,** Harry Brooks and Andy Razaf.

582

Elvis on tour

USA 1972 – 93 mins
dir Pierre Adidge, Robert Abel

Interesting documentary on the Elvis Presley phenomenon, filmed during a headlong concert tour across the States. Among the many songs featured are 'See see rider' by **Ma Rainey,** 'That's all right' by **Crudup** and 'I've got a woman' by **Ray Charles.**

583

Elvis – that's the way it is

USA 1970 – 108 mins
dir Denis Sanders

Straightforward documentary about Elvis Presley in which he delivers numerous songs from his repertoire, one of which is 'What'd I say?' by **Ray Charles.**

584

Embryo

USA 1975 – 108 mins
dir Ralph Nelson

Serviceable thriller in the style of a science fiction story in which doctor Rock Hudson grows a beautiful young woman in his laboratory. Music score by **Gil Mellé.**

585

The Emperor Jones

USA 1933 – 89 mins
dir Dudley Murphy, William De Mille

Extraordinary adaptation of Eugene O'Neill's play, made in New York for $10,000 and shot in one week, starring Paul Robeson as Brutus Jones. It was **Billie Holiday**'s first film experience – as an extra in a crowd scene.

586

En remontant le Mississippi/Out of the blacks, into the Blues

France/West Germany 1971 – 106 mins
dir Robert Manthoulis

▲

'Furry' Lewis in **En remontant le Mississippi** *(TCB Releasing).*

A rediscovery of the origin of the Blues through a journey along the Mississippi, divided into two sections: 'Along the old man river' and 'A way to escape the ghetto'. Narrator Ted Joans introduces 'Old gal on my door', 'Scrap iron blues' by and performed by **Robert Pete Williams**; 'Poor boy blues' performed by **Bukka White**; 'When I lay my burden down' performed by **Walter 'Furry' Lewis**; 'Jelly roll blues' by and performed by **Bukka White**; 'St Louis blues' by **W. C. Handy** performed by **Walter 'Furry' Lewis**; 'Running the boogie', 'Driving wheel' by and performed by **Roosevelt Sykes**; 'Sweet home Chicago' performed by **Roosevelt Sykes**; 'John Henry' performed by **Sonny Terry** and **Brownie McGhee**; 'In the shade of the old apple tree' as recorded by **Louis Armstrong**; 'Ship in the ocean' by **Junior Wells** and **Buddy Guy**; 'Jelly jam' by and performed by **Willie Dixon**; 'I'm gonna sit right down and write myself a letter' by **'Fats Waller'**; 'Greyhound bus station' by and performed by **Arthur 'Big Boy' Crudup**; 'Four word five letter blues' by **Brownie McGhee**; 'Chain and lock on the door' by **Sonny Terry**; 'You got me down' by **B. B. King**; 'All of your affection' by **B. B. King** and Clark; 'See see rider', 'Rock me baby', 'All night long' by **Mance Lipscombe** performed by him; 'Little bit of love', 'I need my woman' by and performed by **B. B.** King; 'Wrap your troubles in dreams'; 'Low down dirty shame' arranged by James Strotter.

587

End of the road

USA 1969 – 110 mins
dir Aram Avakian

Fascinating, quite beautiful screen adaptation of John Barth's novel often as funny as it is brutal. Superb music supervision by George Avakian whose uses some original music by **Teo Macero** in between bits from Bach and Tchaikovsky and above all superlative use of **Billie Holiday**'s recording of 'Don't worry 'bout me'. (The director was, incidentally, the editor of *Jazz on a summer's day*).

588

The enforcer

USA 1976 – 96 mins
dir James Fargo

Number three in Warner Brothers's *Dirty Harry* series, dutifully built around Clint Eastwood's unyielding macho presence. Jerry Fielding's music track includes one glorious big band number – backing a roof-top chase sequence – featuring gutsy, rip-roaring solos by **Art Pepper**, *alt sax;* **Ronnie Lang**, *ten sax;* and **Bill Perkins**, *bar sax.*

589

The engagement

UK 1970 – 44 mins
dir Paul Joyce

Generally misunderstood comedy scripted by Tom Stoppard, with a music score by **John Dankworth**.

590

Engelchen oder die Jungfrau von Bamberg/ Angel baby

West Germany 1968 – 81 mins
dir Marran Gosov

Ponderous Teutonic sex comedy, with a music score by **Jacques Loussier**.

591

England made me

UK 1972 – 100 mins
dir Peter Duffell

Screen adaptation of Graham Greene's first major novel published in 1935 and set in Nazi Germany. Soundtrack use is made of **Duke Ellington**'s 'It don't mean a thing if you ain't got that swing'.

592

Enrico cuisinier

France 1955 – 20 mins
dir Paul Grimault

A burlesque sketch as played by **Henri Crolla**, who provides his own music.

593

Enter laughing

USA 1967 – 111 mins
dir Carl Reiner

Disastrous attempt to adapt for the screen Joseph Stein's successful Broadway play about show business. Music and title song by **Quincy Jones**.

594

Enter the dragon

USA 1973 – 98 mins
dir Robert Clouse

Hollywood-produced, Orient-filmed spin-off from the crop of violence-drenched Hong Kong melodramas. **Lalo Schifrin** provides the strange music track.

595

Entrance of the gladiators

USA c1952 – 3 mins

Telescription of **Red Nichols** playing the title number.

Epilogue

see **Hvad med os?**

596

The Eric Winstone Band show

UK – 30 mins
dir Michael Carreras

Music featurette in colour and 'Scope with the title band and vocalists plus **Kenny Baker**, *tpt*.

597

Erin éreintée

France 1970 – 30 mins
dir Jean-Paul Aubert

A descriptive essay on Dublin, Irish youth and Irish character, shot at the time that Joseph Strick was making *Ulysses*. Music by **Henri Renaud**.

598

Errand for rhythm

USA 1943 – 3 mins

Soundie featuring **'King' Cole** and His Trio playing the title number.

599

Escape from San Quentin

USA 1957 – 81 mins
dir Fred F. Sears

Aerial escape from San Quentin prison provides the only original touch in this otherwise routine crime story. Music composed and played by **Laurindo Almeida**.

600

Escape to Witch Mountain

USA 1974 – 97 mins
dir John Hough

Disney live-action fantasy concerning the supernatural powers of two psychic children. Music by **Johnny Mandel**.

601

Et Dieu créa la femme/And woman . . . was created

France 1956 – 91 mins
dir Roger Vadim

Basically conventional, though occasionally over-violent, triangle story dedicted almost exclusively to the considerable physical charms of Miss Brigitte Bardot. Music score by Paul Misraki, arranged by the composer and **Bill Byers**.

602

Etoiles en croisette

France 1955 – 10 mins
dir Jacques Guillon

Documentary impression of the stars attending the 1955 Cannes Film Festival, with music by **Sidney Bechet**.

603

Etoiles nucléaires

France 1961 – 23 mins
dir Georges Pessis

Documentary on the European Centre for Nuclear Research in Geneva. Music by **Martial Solal**.

604

Etudes

France 1963 – 8 mins
dir Louis Grospierre

Study of a sculptor and his model, with music score by **Jacques Loussier**.

605

European music revolution

USA 1970

One of two documentaries about the Amougies Festival held in October 1969, featuring the **Art Ensemble of Chicago** with **Don Cherry**.

606

Every day's a holiday

USA 1938 – 78 mins
dir A. Edward Sutherland

Victorian burlesque as a vehicle for its star, Mae West. Contains a brief appeaance by **Louis Armstrong** with the number 'Jubilee' by Stanley Adams and **Hoagy Carmichael**. **Eddie Barefield** is seen playing trombone (*sic*).

Every other inch a lady
see **Dancing co-ed**.

607

Everybody rides the carousel

USA c1970 – 90 mins
dir John Hubley

A view of the stages of life adapted from the works of Erik H. Erikson and told in the form of an animated cartoon, with music by **Bill Russo**.

608

Everything I have is yours

USA 1952 – 91 mins
dir Robert Z. Leonard

Thin MGM Technicolor vehicle for Marge and Gower Champion with musical items that include 'Like Monday follows Sunday', 'My heart skips a beat' and 'Derry down dilly'. **Pete Rugolo** worked with music director David Rose on the music track, as did drummer **Lee Young**.

609

Everything you always wanted to know about sex, but were afraid to ask

USA 1972 – 87 mins
dir Woody Allen

Only the title and some typically inane questions have been borrowed from Dr David Reuben's widely read book on current sexual mores in scripting this zany spoof adaptation by Woody Allen. Music score composed and conducted by **Mundell Lowe**.

610

Eva

France/Italy 1962 – 135 mins
dir Joseph Losey

Losey's stunning study in sado-masochism uses, quite superbly, two **Billie Holiday** recordings 'Willow weep for me' and 'Loveless love'. There's also a fine blues by Michel Legrand called 'Adam and Eve' sung by Tony Middleton.

611

Ex: flame/Mixed doubles

USA 1930 – 73 mins
dir Victor Halperin

A domestic drama based loosely on the 1861 play *East Lynne* and padded out with a few incidental songs. Features **Louis Armstrong** and His Band.

612

The exorcist

USA 1973 – 121 mins
dir William Friedkin

Thin adaptation of William Peter Blatty's supernatural horror novel, for which **Lalo Schifrin** provided a music score which was replaced in the final weeks of post-production by a collage of largely contemporary 'classical' snippets from existing recordings.

613

Eye of the cat

USA 1969 – 102 mins
dir David Lowell Rich

Extravagantly enjoyable thriller which uses cats in much the same way as Hitchcock once used birds. Music score by **Lalo Schifrin**.

614

Eye of the devil

UK 1966 – 90 mins
dir J. Lee Thompson

Ludicrous thriller that is so bad it is constantly hilarious. Music score by **Gary McFarland**.

615
The fabulous Dorseys
USA 1947 – 87 mins
dir Alfred E. Green

Dull, cliché biography of the two brothers, played
by themselves, with a weighty selection of
musical items from their repertoire including
'Marie', 'Green eyes', 'Never say never', 'The
object of my affections' and 'Dorsey concerto' by
Leo Shuken and **Ray Bauduc**. Both The **Jimmy
Dorsey** Orchestra and The **Tommy Dorsey**
Orchestra (with **Alvin Stoller** on drums) appear
with guests Ray Eberly, Stuart Foster, **Mike
Pingatore**, Helen O'Connell, **Henry Busse** and
Paul Whiteman. The only high spot is a jam
session sequence featuring **Art Tatum**, *pno;*
Charlie Barnet, *alt sax;* **Ziggy Elman**, *tpt;*
Tommy Dorsey, *trb;* **Jimmy Dorsey**, *clar;* **Ray
Bauduc**, *drs* plus *bass* and *gtr* with 'Art's blues'.

616
Face the music/The black glove
UK 1954 – 84 mins
dir Terence Fisher

Highly involved and improbable melodrama
scripted by Ernest Borneman from his own novel.
Trumpet theme and special arrangements by
Kenny Baker.

False witness
see **Zigzag.**

617
Fantasie au Vieux-Colombier
France 1953 – 10 mins
dir Yves Allain

A club performance by mime Marcel Marceau,
with music by **Claude Luter**.

618

Fantasterne/Dreamers

Denmark 1967 – 87 mins
dir Kirsten Stenbaek

A zany, madcap comedy with songs and dances, in which a trio of performers thumb their noses at Scandinavian sobriety, sex anxieties and most so-called social taboos. Lively music score by **Erik Moseholm**.

619

Farewell, my lovely

USA 1975 – 97 mins
dir Dick Richards

The third screen adaptation of Raymond Chandler's famous novel, produced as a visually stunning, nostalgic tribute to Hollywood's private eye thrillers of the 1940s. Glorious music score by David Shire who has used some top jazz performers on soundtrack; **Dick Nash**, *trb;* **Ronny Lang**, *alt sax;* **Justin Gordon**, *clar, ten sax;* **Don Menza**, *sop sax;* **Cappy Lewis**, *tpt;* **Artie Kane**, *pno;* **Chuck Domanico**, *bass;* **Al Hendrickson**, *gtr;* **Larry Bunker**, *drs;* **Emil Richards**, *perc.*

The fat and the lean

see **Le gros et le maigre.**

Tommy and Jimmy Dorsey with Janet Blair in **The fabulous Dorseys**.

▼

620

Fathom

UK 1967 – 99 mins
dir Leslie Martinson

A comedy-thriller which manages to impart a charm and freshness to all the best worn clichés of the spy film send-up. Music score by **John Dankworth**.

621

Fats Waller medley

USA 1943 – 9 mins

Soundie featuring three of **Fats Waller**'s best known numbers, compiled from previously issued Soundies?

The fearless vampire killers
see Dance of the vampires.

622

Feather on jazz

USA 1967 – 13 × 10 mins
prod Leonard Feather

Originally produced by MCA TV, a series of jazz programmes introduced on camera by Leonard Feather incorporating short clips from Paramount and Universal productions as well as stills and recordings. Extracts used: 'Tiger rag' from *Birth of the blues;* **Kid Ory** in *Sarah Vaughan and Herb Jeffries;* **Louis Armstrong** in *Every day's a holiday;* **Jack Teagarden** in *Rhythm masters;* **Duke Ellington** in *Murder at the vanities;* **Louis Jordan** in *Follow the boys;* **Billie Holiday** in *'Sugar Chile' Robinson-Billie Holiday-Count Basie Sextet;* **Duke Ellington** in *Symphony in swing;* **Maxine Sullivan** in *Best of the blues;* **Jimmy Rushing** in *Choo choo swing;* **Nat 'King' Cole** in *King Cole and his trio;* **Benny Goodman** in *The big broadcast of 1937;* **Count Basie** in *Choo choo swing;* **Gene Krupa** in *Rhythm and romance;* **Harry James** in *Harry James and The Music Makers;* **Lionel Hampton** in *Lionel Hampton and His Orchestra;* **Red Norvo** in *Jimmy Dorsey's varieties;* **Pearl Bailey** in *Variety girl;* **Sarah Vaughan** in *Sarah Vaughan and Herb Jeffries;* **Louis Armstrong** in *Artists and models;* **Nat 'King' Cole** in *Nat 'King' Cole and Joe Adams Orchestra;* **Anita O'Day** in *Artistry in rhythm;* **June Christy** in *Don Cornell sings;* **Stan Kenton** in *Radio melodies;* **Woody Herman** in *Woody Herman and His Orchestra;* **Charlie Barnet** in *Melody parade;* **Eddie Sauter** and **Bill Finegan** in *The Sauter-Finegan Orchestra;* **Frank Rosolino** in *Gene Krupa and His Orchestra;* **Shorty Rogers** in *Herman's Herd*

623

Featuring Gene Krupa and His Orchestra

USA 1948 – 10 mins

From the Thrills of Music series a straight-forward presentation of numbers from The **Gene Krupa** Orchestra including 'Bop Boogie', 'Sabre dance' and 'The disc jockey jump'.

624

Les félins/The love cage/Joy house

France 1964 – 110 mins
dir René Clément

Undistinguished shocker with a lunatic plot and a few rather nasty sequences. Music by **Lalo Schifrin**.

625

Le femme image

Canada 1960 – 30 mins
dir Guy Borremans

A love story in surrealistic style, with music by **Bobby Jaspar** and **René Thomas**.

626

Des femmes disparaissent/Girls disappear

France 1959 – 85 mins
dir Edouard Molinaro

Tedious, banal and pointless thriller enlivened only by an excellent jazz soundtrack by **Art Blakey** and The Jazz Messengers: **Art Blakey**, *drs;* **Benny Golson**, *ten sax;* **Lee Morgan**, *tpt;* **Bobby Timmons**, *pno;* **Jimmy Merritt**, *bass.*

627

Festival

USA 1967 – 98 mins
dir Murray Lerner

Compilation of material shot at the annual Newport Folk Festival from 1963-1966 with appearances by some 40 artistes including **Sonny Terry** and **Brownie McGhee**.

628

The festival game

UK 1969 – 50 mins
dir Tony Klinger, Mike Lytton

Impressions of the 1969 Cannes Film Festival and interviews with some of the attending celebrities. Jazz score composed and played by **Ronnie Scott** and His Orchestra.

629

Festival of jazz

UK 1961 – 28 mins
dir Giorgio Gomelsky

Kenny Ball's Jazzmen appearing at the N.J.F.'s Richmond Jazz Festival, produced for a TV company and introduced by Steve Race, with title music by **Kenny Graham**. The group includes **Kenny Ball**, *tpt, voc;* **Paddy Lightfoot**, *banjo, voc;* **Ron Bowden**, *drs.* The music: 'Margie', 'Samantha'; 'Down by the riverside'; 'Swing low sweet chariot'; 'Midnight in Moscow'; 'High society'.

630
Feu
France 1970 – 16 mins
dir Claude Jaeger

Impressions of fire-fighting in the mountain regions of France, with music by **Michel Portal**.

631
The fight for life
USA 1940 – 69 mins
dir Pare Lorentz

A story of poverty in American cities, from the book by Paul De Kruif. Music by Louis Gruenberg partly recorded by **Joe Sullivan** and His Sextet.

632
Fighting for our lives
USA 1974 – 58 mins
dir Glen Pearcy

A direct and emotional film record of the 1973 strikes by migrant farm workers in America, produced by the National Farm Workers Service Center, with a music track of Mexican and American folk songs with the participation of **Taj Mahal**, *thumb pno.*

633
Fighting trouble
USA 1957 – 61 mins
dir George Blair

Weaker than average Bowery Boys comedy, with music score composed and conducted by **Buddy Bregman**.

634
Film-vodvil no 2
USA 1943 – 10 mins

A Columbia presentation of vaudeville acts featuring **Cootie Williams** and His Band with **Eddie Vinson**, *vocs,* and Laurel Watson; The Douglas Brothers, dancers, and The Lindy Hoppers.

635
The final programme/The last days of man on earth
USA 1973 – 89 mins
dir Robert Fuest

Elegant but over-derivative science fiction drama, based on the novel by Michael Moorcock. **Gerry Mulligan** takes the sax solos on the soundtrack.

636
Finale
USA 1970
dir George Wein, Sidney J. Stiber

One of three documentaries produced around **Louis Armstrong**'s final performances at Newport.

Fine and dandy
see **The West Point story.**

The Firehouse Blues Five Plus Two
see **Teresa Brewer and The Firehouse Five Plus Two.**

637
The Firehouse Five Plus Two
USA 1951 – 23 mins
Snader Telescriptions featuring the title group.

638
Five guns west
USA 1955 – 73 mins
dir Roger Corman

The prolific Roger Corman's first credited directorial assignment: a slightly above average second-feature Western, with music by **Buddy Bregman**.

639
Five guys named Moe
USA 1942 – 3 mins
Soundie with **Louis Jordan** and His Band.

Five miles to midnight
see **Le couteau dans la plaie.**

640
The Five Pennies
USA 1959 – 117 mins
dir Melville Shavelson

Gaudy VistaVision biopic, suggested by the life of **Loring 'Red' Nichols** and tailored for the talents of Danny Kaye. Music scored and adapted by

F

Leith Stevens; **'Red' Nichols** plays the trumpet solos and there are appearances by **Louis Armstrong, Bob Crosby, Ray Anthony** (as **Jimmy Dorsey**), **Bobby Troup, Shelly Manne** (as **Dave Tough**), **Trummy Young, Billy Kyle, 'Peanuts' Hucko, Danny Barcelona, Joe Venuti, Curtis Counce** and **Clyde Hurley**. **Glenn Miller** and **Artie Shaw** are both represented on screen. Numbers include 'The Five Pennies', 'Indiana', 'Runnin' wild', 'Lullaby in ragtime', 'My blue heaven', 'Follow the leader', 'The saints', 'Bill Bailey', 'Washington and Lee swing', 'The wail of the winds'.

641
Five steps
UK 1968 – 27 mins
dir Joe Mendoza

The training of officer cadets at the Royal Naval College, Dartmouth and at sea. Music score by **Johnny Hawksworth**.

642
Flamingo
USA 1942 – 3 mins
dir Josef Berne

Soundie featuring **Duke Ellington** and His Orchestra playing the title number (**Johnny Hodges**, *alt sax* solo; **Herb Jeffries**, *voc*), supported by the Katherine Dunham Dancers.

643
The flamingo affair/Blonde for danger
UK 1948 – 58 mins
dir Horace Shepherd

Crime story about an ex-commando who robs his employer, featuring **Stephane Grappelly** and His Quintet in a club sequence.

644
Flash
France 1962
dir Allan Zien

Zoot Sims with **Henri Renaud, Bob Whitlock** and **Jean-Louis Viale** at work in the Blue Note in Paris.

645
The fleet's in
USA 1942 – 94 mins
dir Victor Schertzinger

Comedy romance with plenty of music and Dorothy Lamour, featuring **Jimmy Dorsey** and His Orchestra who introduce the now-classic 'Tangerine', plus vocalists Helen O'Connell and Bob Eberly.

Flesh and flame
see **Night of the quarter moon.**

646
Flic story
France 1975 – 110 mins
dir Jacques Deray

Flatfooted tale of cops and robbers, based on the best-selling autobiography of a noted police inspector, Roger Borniche. Music score by **Claude Bolling**.

647
Flight
USA 1960 – 81 mins
dir Louis Bispo

Cool, beautifully photographed independent production shot on the Monterey peninsular in the Big Sur country and based on a story by John Steinbeck. Music by **Laurindo Almeida**.

648
Flying fingers
UK 1961 – 9 mins

Pianist **Dill Jones** and His Orchestra play a programme that includes 'A nightingale sang in Berkeley Square' and 'Penny serenade'.

The flying trapeze
see **Cité du midi.**

649
Follow that music
USA 1946 – 18 mins
dir Arthur Dreifuss

Music featurette spotlighting **Gene Krupa** and His Orchestra in a couple of rousing numbers. Besides the leader, soloists include **Marty Napoleon**, *pno*.

650
Follow the band
USA 1943 – 61 mins
dir Jean Yarbrough

Universal musical about a farm boy addicted to the trombone and his search for success. Musical interludes from **Skinnay Ennis** and The Groove Boys, Alvino Rey, Ray Eberle and The King Sisters among others. Numbers include: 'Melancholy baby', 'What do you want to make those eyes at me for', 'Rosie the riveter' and 'My devotion'.

651

Follow the boys
USA 1944 – 122 mins
dir Eddie Sutherland

Universal's all star tribute to the USO camp
shows with a host of top stars including the
orchestras of **Ted Lewis**, Freddie Slack and
Charlie Spivak plus the **Delta Rhythm Boys** and
Louis Jordan and His Tympany Five singing
'Sweet Georgia Brown' and 'Is you is or is you
ain't my baby'.

652

Too a little ballyhoo
USA 1943 – 3 mins

Soundie in which the title number is sung by **Cab
Calloway**.

653

Fools
USA 1970 – 93 mins
dir Tom Gries

Disappointingly tired romantic comedy that ends
in tragedy for the heroine – as well as for the
film's director. Music score by **Shorty Rogers**.

654

For love of Ivy
USA 1968 – 100 mins
dir Daniel Mann

Coy comedy-romance remarkable chiefly for its
nauseatingly patronising attitude to its coloured
stars. Music and title song by **Quincy Jones**, with
Monty Alexander playing blues piano on
soundtrack.

655

For singles only
USA 1967 – 90 mins
dir Arthur Dreifuss

Quite uninspired romantic comedy with music,
featuring The **Cal Tjader** Band.

For you alone
see **When you're in love.**

656

The form of jazz
USA 1958 – 7 mins

An animated exposition of the approach to
progressive jazz including an analysis of the
instruments used in building the basic rhythms,
produced by the University of California with
narration by **Bobby Troup**. Music by The
Chamber Jazz Sextet – **Allyn Ferguson, Bob**

**Enevoldsen, Roy Roten, Frank Leal, Dent
Hand, Modesto Briseno** – who improvise on
'Three blind mice .

Formula for love
see **Kaerlighedens melodi.**

657

The fortune
USA 1974 – 88 mins
dir Mike Nichols

Lightweight comedy trifle, set in the 1920s, about
a couple of bumbling fortune hunters. Sound-
track music brilliantly scored by David Shire from
Joe Venuti-Eddie Lang recordings: 'I must be
dreaming', 'Pretty Trix', 'My honey's lovin' arms',
'Shaking the blues away', 'Cigarette tango' and
'You've got to see mama every night or you can't
see mama at all'. Soundtrack musicians include
**Mannie Klein, Skeets Herfurt, 'Shorty'
Sherock,'Babe' Russin, Bill Hood, Abe Most, Al
Hendrickson,** Ray Sherman, Bobby Bruce and
Nick Fatool.

658

47th Street jive
USA 1942 – 3 mins

Soundie featuring singer **June Richmond**
accompanied by Roy Milton and His Band.

659

Founded on science
UK 1966 – 25 mins
dir James Allen

Some aspects of sponsor George Wimpey's
research laboratory where experiments are
carried out into problems concerned with building
construction and design. Music score by **Kenneth
Graham**.

660

Four boys and a gun
USA 1956 – 71 mins
dir William Berke

A rather squalid and violent melodrama about a
group of young thugs. Music composed and
conducted by Albert Glasser, with jazz
arrangements by **Shorty Rogers**.

661

Four hits and a mister
UK 1962 – 14 mins
dir Douglas Hickox

Acker Bilk and His Band play four dramatised
numbers.

662

Four jills in a jeep

USA 1944 – 90 mins
dir William A. Seiter

Musical in which four stars appear as themselves on a tour of American army camps in England and North Africa. Features **Jimmy Dorsey** and His Orchestra.

663

The four musketeers – The revenge of milady

Panama/Spain 1974 – 103 mins
dir Richard Lester

Perfunctory sequel to the same company's brilliant *The three musketeers*, with a nondescript music score by **Lalo Schifrin**.

664

Four or five times

USA c1943 – 3 mins

Soundie featuring **Sister Tharpe**, backed by **Lucky Millinder** and His Orchestra.

665

The fox

USA 1967 – 110 mins
dir Mark Rydell

Interesting adaptation of the novel by D. H. Lawrence, beautifully photographed by William Fraker. Music by **Lalo Schifrin**, carefully scored for only ten instruments.

666

Foxtrot

Mexico/Switzerland 1975 – 91 mins
dir Arturo Ripstein

Chic, stylish but ultimately hollow melodrama about a decadent Rumanian aristocrat retreating to a desert island with his wife on the eve of World War 2. Boasts a fine music score by **Pete Rugolo** who superbly evokes period flavour with orchestrations of such tunes as 'Isn't it romantic' and 'Louise' as well as a title tune with lyrics by Jay Livingston and Ray Evans.

667

France Société Anonyme

France 1973 – 100 mins
dir Alain Corneau

Vicious science fiction drama about dope peddling in a chemical culture. Exciting soundtrack use of recordings by **Clifton Chenier**, *acc*, with the participation of **Michel Portal**.

668

Frankenstein: the true story

UK 1973 – 123 mins
dir Jack Smight

A two-hour digest from an original twice the length made for US TV, based on Mary Shelley's novel *Frankenstein*. Music score by **Gil Mellé.**

669

Eine Frau sucht Liebe/A woman needs loving

West Germany 1968 – 96 mins
dir Robert Azderball

Confused romantic melodrama full of sexual and psychological undercurrents, with music by **Jacques Loussier**.

670

Freaky Friday

USA 1976 – 95 mins
dir Gary Nelson

Walt Disney production of Mary Rodgers's 1972 book about a quarrelling mother and teenage daughter who switch personalities for a day. Music score by **Johnny Mandel**, with a theme song, 'I'd like to be you for a day' by Al Kasha, Joel Hirschhorn.

671

Fred McDowell

USA 1969 – 15 mins

A film portrait of one of the last great masters of the Mississippi bottleneck blues style, **'Mississippi' Fred McDowell**, produced by The Seattle Folklore Society. Numbers: 'Shake 'em on down', 'Good mornin' little schoolgirl', 'John Henry', 'Louisiana blues' and 'When I lay my burden down'.

672

Freddie steps out

USA 1946 – 63 mins
dir Arthur Dreifuss

Second-rate musical comedy, without very much of either, featuring **Charlie Barnet**.

673

The French connection

USA 1971 – 104 mins
dir William Friedkin

Carefully detailed, all-location made, documentary-style thriller about the smashing of a major drug-trafficking operation. Superb music score by **Don Ellis**.

674

French connection II

USA 1975 – 119 mins
dir John Frankenheimer

Complementary follow-up to *The French connection* with Gene Hackman repeating his role as Popeye Doyle. Music score again composed and conducted by **Don Ellis**.

Friend of the family

see **Patate.**

675

Frim fram sauce

USA 1945 – 3 mins

Soundie featuring **Nat 'King' Cole**, in a café setting, singing the title number. He is supported by his own Trio, accompanying him on a Panoram screen.

676

Fritz the cat

USA 1971 – 78 mins
dir Ralph Bakshi

Feature length animated colour cartoon about an impenitent cat who indulges joyfully with his two- and four-legged friends in every imaginable social and sexual outrage; based on the comic strip by Robert Crumb. Among the many recordings used on the soundtrack are **Billie Holiday** with 'Yesterdays' and The **Cal Tjader** Band with 'Mamblues'.

677

From here to eternity

USA 1953 – 114 mins
dir Fred Zinnemann

Good, solid, coherent screen adaptation of James Jones's immensely long novel set on an army camp in Honolulu in 1941. Montgomery Clift's bugle playing was ghosted by **Mannie Klein**.

678

The front page

USA 1974 – 105 mins
dir Billy Wilder

The fourth and weakest screen adaptation of the hit play by Ben Hecht and Charles MacArthur. The mock Dixieland soundtrack music was directed by **Billy May**.

679

Frontiers of power

UK 1967 – 22 mins
dir Kenneth Fairbairn

Britain's share in the complex field of developing and producing aero gas turbines and the application of this technology in other fields. Music by **Kenny Graham**.

680

The fugitive kind

USA 1959 – 121 mins
dir Sidney Lumet

Somewhat awesome, mummified screen adaptation of the play by Tennessee Williams, *Orpheus Descending* – a lurid conception of hell on earth. **Jerome Richardson** is prominent in a brief jazz sequence.

681

Funny is funny

USA 1966 – 9 mins

Animated speciality with the voice of Carl Reiner and music by The **George Shearing** Trio.

Funzapoppin'

see **Crazy house.**

682

Fussy-wuzzy

USA 1942 – 3 mins

Soundie featuring music from **Louis Jordan** supported by dancer Ruby Richards.

683

Future one

Denmark 1963 – 8 mins
dir Niels Holt

Impressions of Copenhagen's jazz club, Jazzhus Montmartre, featuring the **New York Contemporary Five: Don Cherry**, *fl horn*; **Archie Shepp**, *ten sax*; **John Tchicai**, *alt sax*; **Don Moore**, *bass*; **John Moses**, *drs*.

684

The fuzzy pink nightgown

USA 1957 – 87 mins
dir Norman Taurog

Mild comedy adapted from the novel by Sylvia Tate, with the music score composed and conducted by **Billy May**.

685
G.I. jive
USA 1943 – 3 mins
Soundie featuring **Louis Jordan**.

686
A game called scruggs
UK 1965 – 46 mins
dir David Hart
Incoherent charade about a young couple in
London. Music by **Johnny Dankworth** with theme
song sung by **Cleo Laine**.

687
The gang's all here/The girls he left behind
USA 1943 – 104 mins
dir Busby Berkeley
Gaudy Technicolor musical with lots of music and
some splendid Busby Berkeley production
numbers. Features **Benny Goodman** and His
Orchestra, with **Lee Castle, Jess Stacy, Louis
Bellson** and **Eugene Porter** plus **Eddie Miller** on
soundtrack. The two **Goodman** numbers are
'Minnie's in the money' and 'Paducah' with 'Soft
winds' used as background music.

688
Garga m'bosse/Cactus
Senegal/Sweden 1974 – 90 mins
dir Mahama Johnson Traoré
Tedious socio-political drama revolving around a
family migrating to Dakar. Soundtrack music:
John Coltrane recordings.

689
Gas-oil
France 1955 – 92 mins
dir Gilles Grangier
Familiar, unadventurous crime drama adapted
from the novel by Georges Bayle with Jean Gabin
in his usual role as the quietly cynical hero. Music
track by **Henri Crolla**.

The gay city
see **Las Vegas nights.**

690
Gene Krupa
USA c1943 – 3 mins
Soundie number 9505 details unknown.

691
**Gene Krupa, America's ace drummer man and
His Orchestra**
USA 1941 – 10 mins
dir Leslie Roush
Paramount music short featuring **Gene Krupa**
and His Orchestra with vocalists Howard Dulaney
and Irene Daye. Numbers include 'Perfidia', 'The
call of the canyon' and 'Jungle madness'.

692
Gene Krupa and His Orchestra
USA 1949 – 15 mins
dir Will Cowan
Universal-International featurette showcasing
Gene Krupa and His Orchestra playing 'Lemon
drop' (soloist **Frank Rosolino**), 'Deep purple' and
'Bop boogie'. There is also an acrobatic quartet.

Gene Krupa poses for a studio publicity shot at Paramount.

693

Genevieve

UK 1953 – 86 mins
dir Henry Cornelius

Light comedy centred around the annual London – Brighton veteran car run. In a nightclub sequence Kay Kendall plays some hot trumpet, suitably ghosted by **Kenny Baker**.

694

Gentlemen marry brunettes

USA 1955 – 95 mins
dir Richard Sale

Brash, strident musical from a novel by Anita Loos with little but the characteristically good-humoured Jane Russell to recommend it. Features a rendering of **Fats Waller**'s 'Ain't misbehavin'' by a gentleman in a gorilla skin.

695

Gentlemen prefer blondes

USA 1953 – 85 mins
dir Howard Hawks

Scrappy, bowdlerised screen adaptation of Anita Loos's musical comedy about two showgirls on the loose in Europe. Features two of **Hoagy Carmichael** and Harold Adamson's songs: 'When love goes wrong' and 'Anyone here for love?'

696

George Shearing Quintet Telescriptions

USA 1951 – 18 mins

Produced for the Snader Telescription Corporation.

697

The George Washington Carver story

USA c1959

Details unknown, thought to be a documentary probably produced on 16mm, but with a music score by **Buddy Collette**.

698

George White's scandals

USA 1945 – 95 mins
dir Felix E. Feist

Routine backstage musical, not to be confused with the superior 1935 version. Features **Gene Krupa** and His Band and the number 'Bolero in the jungle' by Tommy Peterson and **Gene Krupa**.

699

Georgia

USA c1952 – 3 mins

Telescription featuring **Jack Teagarden** with title number.

Get off my back
see **Synanon**.

700

Get outta town

USA 1959 – 62 mins
dir Charles Davis

Routine low-budget production about racketeers and the underworld. Music by **Bill Holman**.

701

Get yourself a college girl/The swinging set

USA 1964 – 85 mins
dir Sidney Miller

Formula teenage caper introducing a string of pop groups but with a bow to modern jazz with appearances by **Stan Getz**, *ten sax;* **Gary Burton** *vibs, bass* and *drs* plus **Astrud Gilberto** with 'The girl from Ipanema' and The **Jimmy Smith** Trio.

702

The getaway

USA 1972 – 122 mins
dir Sam Peckinpah

Screen adaptation of the novel by Jim Thompson about a bank robbery and the ensuing chase to the Mexican border. Packed with material destruction and cinematic razzle-dazzle but its central characters remain ultimately two dimensional. Following early screenings Jerry Fielding's music score was replaced by a suitably percussive track by **Quincy Jones** who uses **'Toots' Thielemans**, *hca,* and The **Don Elliott** Voices.

703

Gettin' back

USA 1974 – 76 mins
dir Gary L. Crabtree

Low-budget documentary of the 1973 Ozark Mountain Folk Fair in Arkansas. Among the many artistes appearing are **Clifton Chenier** and The Red Hot Cajun Band and **John Lee Hooker**.

704

The ghost goes gear

UK 1966 – 41 mins
dir Hugh Gladwish

An embarrassingly artless featurette about a pop group's visit to an ancestral home, with **Acker Bilk** and The Paramount Jazz Band.

705

Gift of gab

USA 1934 – 71 mins
dir Karl Freund

A slight story serves only to introduce a string of screen and radio personalities including **Ethel Waters**, Gus Arnheim and His Orchestra and The Beale Street Boys.

A girl, a guitar and a trumpet
see **Kaerlighedens melodi.**

706

The girl can't help it

USA 1956 – 97 mins
dir Frank Tashlin

Rather dull satire on the exponents and followers of Rock 'n' Roll, padded out with musical items. Features **Ray Anthony** and His Orchestra, **Fats Domino** playing 'Blue Monday', Julie London, Abbey Lincoln and two songs with words and music by **Bobby Troup** 'The girl can't help it' and 'Rock around the rockpile'. (It has been suggested that **Eric Dolphy** is in the instrumental group that backs The Platters on 'You'll never, never, know' but unfortunately the musicians are not seen on screen).

707

Girl crazy

USA 1943 – 99 mins
dir Norman Taurog

Formula vehicle for Judy Garland and Mickey Rooney but with a superb Gershwin score including 'Embraceable you', 'But not for me' and 'Bidin' my time'. **Tommy Dorsey** and His Orchestra are featured in three numbers: 'Treat me rough', 'Fascinating rhythm' and a splendid 'I got rhythm' directed by Busby Berkeley. **Sy Oliver** collaborated as orchestrator.

708

Girl time

USA 1955 – 16 mins

Ina Ray Hutton and Her Orchestra provide the backing for songs by the leader plus acts by Nellie Lutcher, The Costello Twins, Lucita, Tina and Co. Numbers include 'When my sugar walks down the street', 'Granada' and 'Mambola'.

Girls disappear
see **Des femmes disparaissent.**

The girls he left behind
see **The gang's all here.**

709

Girls town

USA 1959 – 90 mins
dir Charles Haas

A concoction of rebellious adolescence, strong-arm sadism, attempted rape, drag racing, fake religious piety and just about everything else – without a mitigating ounce of artistry in it. A leading role is played by **Ray Anthony**.

710

Le Gitan

France 1975 – 102 mins
dir José Giovanni

Agreeable French capter movie with Alain Delon as a gypsy safe-cracker and with a music score by **Claude Bolling** using charts by **Django Reinhardt**.

711

Give me some skin

USA 1943 – 3 mins

Soundie featuring The **Delta Rhythm Boys** with the title number.

712

Le glaive et la balance/Two are guilty

France/Italy 1962 – 140 mins
dir André Cayatte

A tilt at the workings of French justice framed around the story of a double killing on the Riviera. During the opening credits a group appears consisting of **Lou Bennett**, *org*; **Sonny Criss**, *alt sax*; **Sonny Grey**, *tpt*; **Kenny Clarke**, *drs*; Mae Mercer, *voc*.

713

Glamour girl/Night club girl

USA 1948 – 68 mins
dir Arthur Dreifuss

Average second-feature musical about a talent scout's discovery of a singer and their eventual success. Features **Gene Krupa** and His Orchestra with the numbers 'Gene's boogie' and 'Anywhere'.

The glass mountain
see **Szklana góra.**

714

The glass wall

USA 1953 – 80 mins
dir Maxwell Shane

Competent thriller set in New York and ending with a good chase sequence in the United Nations Building. Music by Leith Stevens and a nightclub sequence featuring **Jack Teagarden** with **Shorty Rogers** and His Band – **Jimmy Giuffre** and **Shelly Manne** prominent. Besides his appearance **Rogers**'s trumpet is active on sections of the underscore and he also ghosts trumpet for one of the screen musicians. **Benny Carter** supervised and actor Jerry Paris was ghosted by **Bob Keene**, *clar.*

715

The Glenn Miller story

USA 1953 – 116 mins
dir Anthony Mann

Glossy Hollywood screen biography of the legendary bandleader. The producers have fallen for all the obvious pitfalls in presenting this popular story in unreal, idealised terms but nevertheless there's a great deal of music to enjoy. A good jazz sequence features **Louis Armstrong**

and The All Stars with **Gene Krupa** and 'Basin Street blues' and 'Otchi-tchor-ni-ya'. Trombonist **Joe Yukl** coached and ghosted James Stewart as **Glenn Miller** and other participating musicians include **Ben Pollack, Cozy Cole, Marty Napoleon, Trummy Young, Barney Bigard, Arvell Shaw, 'Babe' Russin, Murray McEachern, 'Chummy' MacGregor, Willie Schwartz, Dick Fisher, Rollie Bundock, Zeke Zarchy** and **Paul Tanner. Miller** numbers include 'Moonlight serenade', 'Tuxedo junction', 'Little brown jug', 'St Louis blues', 'In the mood', 'String of pearls', 'Pennsylvannia 65000' and 'American patrol'.

716

Glory alley

USA 1952 – 77 mins

Dismal melodrama about absolutely nothing, but being set in New Orleans it contains a certain amount of suitable music. Features **Louis Armstrong** and **Jack Teagarden** leading a group

On the set of **The Glenn Miller story**: *Ben Pollack, Gene Krupa, Louis Armstrong, James Stewart, Joe Yukl, Marty Napoleon, Trummy Young, Cozy Cole, Barney Bigard, Arvell Shaw.*

▼

of **Gus Bivona**, *clar;* **Milt Raskin**, *pno;* **Jack Marshall**, *gtr;* **Artie Shapiro**, *bass;* **Frankie Carlson**, *drs.* **Armstrong** sings 'That's what the man said' and other numbers include 'St Louis blues', 'Rampart Street parade', 'Oh, didn't he ramble', 'Free as a bird', 'Glory alley' and 'Jolly Jacqueline'. Orchestrations partly by **Pete Rugolo.**

717

Go, man, go

USA 1954 – 83 mins
dir James Wong Howe

Concise and quite likeable drama built around the Harlem Globetrotters, directed by one of Hollywood's most distinguished and imaginative cameramen. **Sy Oliver** supplies some of the music and there are appearances by **Slim Gaillard.**

718

Goal! world cup 1966

Liechtenstein/UK 1966 – 108 mins
dir Abidine Dino, Ross Devenish

A documentary record of the World Cup football series played in England in July 1966. Music score by **John Hawksworth.**

Going ape

see **Where's poppa?**

719

Going places

USA 1938 – 84 mins
dir Ray Enright

Conventional farce with music and a horse called Jeepers Creepers. Features **Louis Armstrong** and His Band, with **Al Morgan** and **Maxine Sullivan**. **Louis** sings Johnny Mercer's famous number to the horse.

720

Going places

UK 1973 – 28 mins
dir Charles Mapleston

British Road Federation documentary describing the problems of present day transport. Music by **Mike Westbrook.**

721

The golden disc/The inbetween age

UK 1958 – 78 mins
dir Don Sharp

A somewhat vapid plot surrounding a succession of musical numbers by sundry popular entertainers, which include The **Phil Seamen** Jazz Group: **Don Rendell**, *ten sax;* **Ronnie Ross**, *bar sax;* **Bert Courtley**, *tpt;* **Eddie Harvey**, *pno;* **Kenny Napper**, *bass;* **Phil Seamen**, *drs.*

The golden fish

see **Histoire d'un poisson rouge.**

722

Golden ladder

USA 1957 – 15 mins

Universal music featurette with Rod McKuen, Gogi Grant, **Buddy Bregman**, The King Sisters and The Billy Thompson Singers.

723

Golden needles

USA 1974 – 93 mins
dir Robert Clouse

Formula melodrama drawing on the elements of accupuncture and a golden statue with power to exert miraculous virility, set partly in Hong Kong. Equally formula music score by **Lalo Schifrin.**

724

Goodbye, my lady

USA 1956 – 95 mins
dir William A. Wellman

Charming and unaffected story of the relationship between a boy and his uncle and his dog set in the forests and swamps of Georgia. Music composed and played by **Laurindo Almeida** and George Field.

725

The good-for-nothing

USA 1917
dir Carlyle Blackwell

Film adaptation of a successful novel *Jack the good-for-nothing* in which The **Original Dixieland Jazz Band** appear. Believed to be the very first jazz appearance in a fictional movie.

726

Got a penny Benny

USA 1946 – 3 mins

Soundie featuring **Nat 'King' Cole**, *pno, voc;* **Oscar Moore**, *gtr;* and **Johnny Miller**, *bass,* performing the title number.

727

Got to tell it: a tribute to Mahalia Jackson/Mahalia Jackson

USA 1974 – 35 mins
dir Jules Victor Schwerin

Mahalia Jackson talks about her Southern background, then performs eleven numbers in various settings, including 'Down by the riverside', 'Go tell it on the mountain' and 'A closer walk with thee'.

728
La grande bouffe/Blow-out
France/Italy 1973 – 133 mins
dir Marco Ferreri

Vulgar and simplistic allegory of bourgeois behaviour. Music direction by **Hubert Rostaing**.

729
The great gatsby
USA 1974 – 146 mins
dir Jack Clayton

The third screen version of F. Scott Fitzgerald's classic novel, set in 1922. Among the many period pieces of music used on soundtrack is **W. C. Handy**'s 'Beale Street blues' played by **Jess Stacy**.

730
The great Morgan
USA 1946 – 56 mins
dir Nat Perrin.

MGM comedy that includes footage from previous studio productions featuring, among other stars, **Tommy Dorsey** and His Orchestra.

731
The great Waldo Pepper
USA 1975 – 108 mins
dir George Roy Hill

Charming homage to the mystique of daredevilry and deathwish associated with World War One flying aces. Musicians on Henry Mancini's lyrical soundtrack score include **Artie Kane**, *pno* and **Dick Nash**, *bar hom*.

732
The great white hope
USA 1970 – 103 mins
dir Martin Ritt

Pedestrian screen adaptation of Howard Sackler's play about Negro boxer Jack Johnson which should have confined itself to telling its fascinating and true story instead of forcing a message down our throats. Song 'Let me hold you in my arms tonight' composed and sung by **Jesse Fuller**.

733
The Grissom gang
USA 1971 – 128 mins
dir Robert Aldrich

Glossy screen adaptation of James Hadley Chase's gory thriller *No orchids for Miss Blandish*, previously filmed in 1948. 'Ain't misbehavin' ' by **Fats Waller**, Harry Brooks and Andy Razaf is sung in a rehearsal sequence and **Henry Busse** recordings are prominent on soundtrack.

734
Gromaire
France 1967 – 11 mins
dir François Reichenbach

An interview with the painter, engraver and stage designer Marcel Gromaire, now firmly established through numerous exhibitions both in France and in the USA. Music by **Michel Portal**.

735
The groove tube
USA 1974 – 75 mins
dir Ken Shapiro

A satire on TV parodying numerous types of programme intermixed with cod commercials. The music track utilizes 'Mumbles' by The **Oscar Peterson** Trio with **Clark Terry**.

736
Le gros et le maigre/The fat and the lean
France 1961 – 16 mins
dir Roman Polanski, Jean-Pierre Rousseau

A short, wordless fable about the master/slave relationship; the first movie that Polanski made outside Poland. Music by **Krzysztof Komeda-Trzcinski**.

737
Grounds for marriage
USA 1950 – 90 mins
dir Robert Z. Leonard

Formula entertainment from MGM with two of their hottest properties of the time – Van Johnson and Kathryn Grayson. Features The **Firehouse Five plus Two** with 'Tiger rag'. They also recorded 'Five foot two' for use in the Charleston contest sequence and 'Pagan love song' for the exterior shot of the nightclub.

738
Groupies
USA 1970 – 92 mins
dir Robert Dorfman, Peter Nevard

A documentary examination, edited from material shot over a period of nine months, of the lives of some American groupies who reserve their sexual favours for pop musicians. Two songs written by **'Sonny Boy' Williamson**, 'Good morning little schoolgirl' and 'Help me baby' are performed by a pop group.

739

La guerra del cerdo/The pig's war

Argentina 1975 – 90 mins
dir Leopoldo Torre-Nilsson

Screen adaptation of the novel by Adolfo Bioy
Casares – a sinister fable on the generation gap.
Music score by **Leandro 'Gato' Barbieri** who
also recorded the tenor sax solos.

740

The gumball rally

USA 1976 – 106 mins
dir Chuck Bail

Tiresome parody of the car-chase format with
crude intrusions of violence. **Med Flory** makes a
brief appearance.

741

Gunfight in Abilene

USA 1966 – 78 mins
dir William Hale

Well above average Western with some
memorable touches and competent acting by all
concerned. On soundtrack the song 'Amy' is sung
by Bobby Darin, orchestrated by **Shorty Rogers**.

742

Gunn

USA 1967 – 94 mins
dir Blake Edwards

The most successful jazz score written for a TV
series was Henry Mancini's for *Peter Gunn* –
about a jazz orientated private eye. This
monotonous screen treatment of the series uses
some of the original score plus some new
material which at least swings – which is more
than the movie does.

743

Guns, girls and gangsters

USA 1958 – 70 mins
dir Edward L. Cahn

Low-budget thriller about an attempt to rob an
armoured car carrying money from a Las Vegas
gambling house. Music by **Buddy Bregman**.

744

Gyromorphosis

Netherlands 1958 – 7 mins
dir Hy Hirsh

Impressions of construction-sculpture, with the
soundtrack utilizing The **Modern Jazz Quartet**'s
recording of 'Django'.

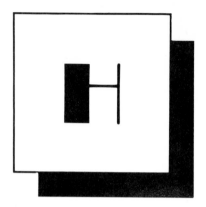

745

Hall alla doerrar oeppna/Keep all doors open

Sweden 1973 – 90 mins
dir Per-Arne Ehlen

Light sex comedy about a locksmith who gets stuck with the title motto of his trade. The soundtrack utilizes several **Fats Waller** recordings.

746

Hallelujah!

USA 1929 – 109 mins
dir King Vidor

Highly successful all negro drama with music – Irving Berlin's 'Waiting at the end of the road' and 'Swanee shuffle' – and several traditional spirituals including 'Goin' home' and 'Swing low sweet chariot'. Features **Nina Mae McKinney, Victoria Spivey** and the Dixie Jubilee Singers.

747

Hamilton in the music festival

UK 1961 – 8 mins
dir John Halas

Unimaginative colour cartoon about a circus elephant who can turn his trunk into various musical instruments. Music by **Johnny Dankworth**.

748

Hamilton the musical elephant

UK 1961 – 8 mins
dir John Halas

Follow-up to *Hamilton in the music festival* in which this most unlovable of elephants takes a job baby-sitting. Music again by **Johnny Dankworth**.

A hand-me-down suit

see **Ubranie prawie nowe.**

The hands of Orlac

see **Les mains d'Orlac.**

749

The hanged man

USA 1964 – 87 mins
dir Donald Siegel

A rather strained and tiresome thriller set in New Orleans during Mardi Gras: a revamping of *Ride the pink horse*. In a nightclub sequence **Stan Getz** impeccably does his Bossa Nova thing.

750

The happiness remedy

USA 1931 – 8 mins
dir Ray Cozine

Paramount music short featuring **Ted Lewis** and His Orchestra with **Jack Teagarden** and **Red Nichols**.

751

The happy hooker

USA 1975 – 98 mins
dir Nicholas Sgarro

Heavily bowdlerised screen adaptation of the autobiographical book by Xaviera Hollander which reduces the author to little more than a typical sexploitation film heroine. Music score by **Don Elliott** who also supplies the music for one song 'Put yourself in my hands'.

752

Harlem after midnight

USA 1947

Three numbers by **Billy Eckstine** and His Orchestra with vocals by the leader and Ann Baker plus a dance by Nicky O'Daniel and Al Guster.

753

Harlem dynamite

USA 1947

Dizzy Gillespie and His orchestra with three numbers featuring vocal by Pancho.

754

Harlem hotshots

USA c1941 – 20 mins

All black production featuring Lena Horne, **Teddy Wilson** and Core Harris and His Orchestra.

755

Harlem is heaven

USA 1932 – 10 mins

Tap routines performed by Bill Robinson and chorus line to the music of **Eubie Blake** and His Orchestra.

756

Harlem jazz festival

USA 1955 – 51 mins
dir Joseph Kohn

Poorly compiled musical revue but contains some good material including **Lionel Hampton** and His Orchestra (**Quincy Jones**, *tpt*; **Milt Buckner**, *pno*, prominent) with two numbers; **Sarah Vaughan**; The **Count Basie** Septet (**Wardell Gray**, *ten sax*; **Buddy DeFranco**, *clar*; **Clark Terry**, *tpt*; **Freddie Green**, *gtr*; **Gus Johnson**, *drs*; **Helen Humes**, *voc*.) with two numbers, one being 'I cried for you'; **Dinah Washington** singing 'My lean baby'; **Nat 'King' Cole** singing and playing 'Route 66' and 'For sentimental reasons'. **Herb Jeffries** is credited but doesn't appear in the version under review.

757

Harlem rhythm

USA 1947

Dizzy Gillespie and His Orchestra playing three numbers with dance creations by Audrey Armstrong and Johny and Henney.

Harlem Rock 'n' Roll

see **Rock 'n' Roll revue**.

758

Harlem serenade

USA c1942 – 3 mins

Soundie with **Lucky Millinder** and His Orchestra plus dancer Edna Mae Harris.

759

Harlem Wednesday

USA 1958 – 11 mins
dir John Hubley

A day in the life of Harlem as reflected in the paintings of Gregorio Prestopino, backed by a jazz score by **Benny Carter**.

760

Harlow

USA 1965 – 126 mins
dir Gordon Douglas

Remarkably restrained adaptation of the biography by Irving Shulman, with Carroll Baker in the platinum blonde role. **Neal Hefti** provides the gently swinging music track.

761

Harmonica rascals

USA c1938 – 9 mins

Vitaphone short in which Borah Minevitch and Band play, among other numbers, **W. C. Handy**'s 'St Louis blues'.

762

Harmony Abroad

UK 1965 – 16 mins
dir Donovan Winter

A visual impression of the activity during the summer holiday season on the Norfolk Broads, with music score by **Johnny Hawksworth**.

763

Harper/The moving target

USA 1966 – 121 mins
dir Jack Smight

Self-conscious attempt to revive for the sixties the cynical corpse-littered thriller of the forties. Music composed and conducted by **Johnny Mandel** with arrangements by Dick Hazard, **Bill Byers** and **Bill Holman**. The song 'Livin' alone' is by Dory and André Previn.

764

Harry in your pocket

USA 1973 – 102 mins
dir Bruce Geller

Well-paced and credible story of a gang of pickpockets, making effective use of locations in Seattle, Victoria BC and Salt Lake City. Music score and song 'Day by day by day' by **Lalo Schifrin**.

765
Harry James and The Music Makers
USA 1943 – 14 mins
dir Will Cowan

Universal-International music featurette in which the band entertain, assisted by vocals from Gale Robbins and a dance routine from Allan and Ashton. Numbers include 'Charmaine', 'I got a crush on you', 'Moanin' low', 'Brave bulls', 'I'm in a jam' and 'Trumpet blue and cantabile'.

766
The hat
USA 1964 – 18 mins
dir John and Faith Hubley

A gently sardonic examination of the origins of international conflict, in cartoon form. Dialogue/music improvisation by **Dizzy Gillespie** and Dudley Moore.

767
Hatari!
USA 1962 – 159 mins
dir Howard Hawks

Long, rambling adventure story set in East Africa about a team of professional hunters attempting to capture wild animals to send to zoos. The music score by Henri Mancini includes the song 'Just for tonight' by Johnny Mercer and **Hoagy Carmichael**.

Hats off to rhythm
see **Earl Carroll sketchbook**.

768
Havre sac
France 1963 – 11 mins
dir Monique Lepeuve

Impressions of France's greatest transatlantic port, with music by **Daniel Humair** and **Guy Pedersen**.

769
Hawaii
USA 1966 – 186 mins
dir George Roy Hill

Respectable screen adaptation of James A. Michener's novel charting the disastrous impact of so-called Christian civilisation on the happy pagans of Polynesia. Music score by Elmer Bernstein with soundtrack participation of **Emil Richards** and **Gene Cipriano**.

770
The hawk talks
USA 1952 – 3 mins

Snader Telescription in which **Duke Ellington** and His Orchestra play the title number, featuring a solo by **Louis Bellson**, *drs,* and **Harry Carney, Willie Smith, Jimmy Hamilton, Russell Procope, Paul Gonsalves**, *reeds;* **Willie Cook, Ray Nance**. **Cat Anderson**, *tpt;* **Britt Woodman, Juan Tizol, Quentin Jackson**, *trb;* **Wendell Marshall**, *bass.*

771
Häxan/Witchcraft through the ages
Sweden 1921 – 76 mins
dir Benjamin Christensen

A history and examination of witchcraft made by one of the cinema's earliest and greatest stylists, re-released in 1968 with added soundtrack, narration by William Burroughs and an interpretative jazz score by **Daniel Humair** played by **Jean-Luc Ponty**, *vln;* **Michel Portal**, *reeds;* **Bernard Lubat**, *vibs;* **Guy Pedersen**, *bass;* **Daniel Humair**, *drs.*

772
Headline bands
USA 1945 – 9 mins

Music short featuring popular entertainers, including Betty Hutton, and the bands of **Woody Herman, Jimmy Dorsey**, Larry Clinton, Rubinoff and Vincent Lopez. Numbers include 'Carolina in the morning', 'Old man Mose' and 'Give me a moment please'.

773
Heads
UK 1969 – 35 mins
dir Peter Gidal

A series of hand-held close-ups on the faces of well known personalities and friends of the director, including **Thelonius Monk**.

774
The heat's on/Tropicana
USA 1943 – 79 mins
dir Gregory Ratoff

Mae West's last big movie before her first retirement – a very unfunny musical comedy. Features **Hazel Scott**.

775

Heaven with a gun

USA 1968 – 101 mins
dir Lee H. Katzin

Agreeably unassuming Western with a nice
performance from Glenn Ford, as usual. Music
score and song 'A lonely place' by **Johnny
Mandel**.

776

Heavenly hideaway

USA c1942 – 3 mins

Soundie featuring a chorus of showgirls with
music provided by **Sonny Dunham**.

777

Heavy traffic

USA 1973 – 75 mins
dir Ralph Bakshi

Crudely animated follow-up to the same director's
Fritz the cat, somehow accomplished without a
touch of artistry. The soundtrack features 'Take
five' by **Paul Desmond**, performed by the **Dave
Brubeck** Quartet.

The heist
see **Dollars.**

778

Hell in the Pacific

USA 1968 – 103 mins
dir John Boorman

The story of two castaways, terrified of each other
merely because their countries happen to be at
war and because they do not understand each
other's language. Music by **Lalo Schifrin.**

779

The hell with heroes

USA 1968 – 102 mins
dir Joseph Sargent

Quasi-melodramatic adventure thriller, lacking in
distinction but competently handled. **Quincy
Jones** provides a conventional music score plus
two jazz sequences in a bar featuring **Ray
Brown**, *bass* and Mae Mercer, *voc.*

Hello! beautiful
see **The Powers girl.**

780

Hello Bill

USA c1943 – 3 mins

Soundie with **Lucky Millinder** and His Orchestra
with the title number.

781

Hello, dolly!

USA 1969 – 148 mins
dir Gene Kelly

Spectacular musical version of Thornton Wilder's
play *The matchmaker* full of visual richness and
sheer size but lacking an essential style. **Louis
Armstrong** appears for one chorus of the title
number.

782

The Hellstrom chronicle

USA 1971 – 90 mins
dir Walon Green

Extraordinary photographic accomplishment
revealing the actualities of everyday insect
existence, flawed only by an unnecessary fictional
commentary. Music by **Lalo Schifrin** who used a
group of percussionists including **Emil Richards**
playing glasses, cymbals, gongs and waterphones
and anything they could lay their hands on.

783

Hellzapoppin'

USA 1941 – 83 mins
dir H. C. Potter

This famous crazy comedy, tailored for Olsen and
Johnson, contains just one excellent jazz
sequence featuring **Rex Stewart**, *cor,* with **Slim
Gaillard, 'Slam' Stewart** and The Lindy Hoppers.

784

Help! my snowman's burning down

USA 1964 – 9 mins
dir Carson Davidson

Mild satire on the contemporary human situation,
with music by **Gerry Mulligan**.

785

Henry Busse and His Orchestra

USA 1940 – 10 mins
dir Jean Negulesco

The title band entertain with a programme of
musical items including 'Hot lips', 'Along the
Santa Fe trail', 'Huckleberry duck' and 'Wang
wang blues'.

786

Henry 9 till 5

UK 1970 – 6 mins
dir Bob Godfrey

Characteristic cartoon about an office worker who
relieves the tedium of his working day by
indulging in sexual fantasies. Music by **Johnny
Hawksworth.**

787

Her highness and the bell-boy

USA 1945 – 111 mins
dir Richard Thorpe

Formula romantic comedy with bell-boy Robert
Walker falling for princess Hedy Lamarr.
Orchestrations partly by **Calvin Jackson**.

788

Herb Jeffries

USA 1950 – 18 mins

Snader Telescriptions featuring the title vocalist.

789

Here comes Elmer/Hitch-hike to happiness

USA 1943 – 74 mins
dir Joseph Santley

Comedy with a certain amount of music and an
early appearance by The **'King' Cole** Trio.
Includes the song 'Straighten up and fly right' by
Nat 'King' Cole and Irving Mills.

790

Here comes the band

USA 1935 – 87 mins
dir Paul Sloane

Romantic musical about a starving musician
fighting for justice and recognition. Features **Ted
Lewis** and His Band, with **'Muggsy' Spanier**.

791

Here comes the groom

USA 1951 – 114 mins
dir Frank Capra

Tedious comedy with lashings of the gratuitous
sentiment that is customary from the director.
Contains a brief appearance by **Louis Armstrong**
and the song 'In the cool, cool, cool of the
evening', the 1951 Oscar winner, by Johnny
Mercer and **Hoagy Carmichael**.

792

Herman's Herd

USA 1949 – 15 mins
dir Will Cowan

Universal-International featurette in which **Woody
Herman** and His Orchestra, in a nightclub setting,
entertain and support The Mello-Larks, Patricia
Lynn, **Terry Gibbs**, *vibs*, Margaret Brown and
Peggy Castle. Numbers include 'Jamaica rhumba'
(solos from **Terry Gibbs** and **Woody Herman**); 'A
great day for the Irish' and 'Lemon drop' (solos
from **Woody Herman, Shorty Rogers, Terry
Gibbs**, *vocs*; **Serge Chaloff**, *bar sax*; **Bill Harris**,
trb.) The band includes **Jimmy Giuffre** and
Shelly Manne.

793

Herning

Denmark 1965
dir Jens Jørgen Thorsen, Novi Maruni

Improvisations by **Erik Moseholm,
Niels-Henning Ørsted Pedersen** and Steffen
Andersen.

The heroin gang
see **Sol Madrid.**

794

He's my guy

USA 1943 – 65 mins
dir Edward F. Cline

Routine, low-budget wartime comedy with music,
set in a factory. Features The **Mills Brothers.**

795

Hey boy! hey girl!

USA 1959 – 81 mins
dir David Lowell Rich

Unpretentious musical vehicle for its two
recording stars, **Louis Prima** and Keely Smith,
who supply most of the musical numbers together
with Nelson Riddle.

796

Hey, lawdy mama!

USA c1942 – 3 mins

Soundie with vocalist **June Richmond** backed by
Roy Milton and His Band.

797

Hey there, it's Yogi Bear

USA 1964 – 90 mins
dir Hanna and Barbera

Hanna and Barbera's first feature length cartoon
recounting the adventures of the TV character
Yogi Bear. Music by **Marty Paich**, (except the
songs).

798

Hey! tojo count yo, men

USA c1943 – 3 mins

Soundie featuring **Louis Jordan**

799

Hi-de-ho

USA 1937 – 9 mins
dir Roy Mack

Vitaphone short featuring **Cab Calloway** and His
Orchestra. Personnel: **'Doc' Cheatham, Irving**

Randolph, **Lammar Wright**, *tpts;* **Claude Jones, De Priest Wheeler**, *trbs;* **'Keg' Johnson**, *trb, gtr;* **Garvin Bushell**, *clar, alt sax, bassoon;* **Andrew Brown**, *alt sax, clar;* **Ben Webster**, *ten sax;* **Walter Thomas**, *ten sax, clar, flute;* **Bennie Payne**, *pno;* **Morris White**, *gtr;* **Milt Hinton**, *bass;* **Leroy Maxey**, *drs,* **Cab Calloway**, *voc, leader.* Numbers: 'I gotta right to sing the Blues', 'Hi-de-ho miracle man', 'Frisco Flo' and 'Some of these days'.

800
Hi-fi à gogo
France 1958 – 20 mins
dir Pierre-A. Rocamora

Music short featuring the orchestras of **Martial Solal**, Benny Bennet and Billy Moore.

801
Hi, good lookin'!
USA 1944 – 62 mins
dir Edward Lilley

Second-feature comedy with music set in a Hollywood radio station, with appearances by **Jack Teagarden** and His Orchestra, Ozzie Nelson and His Orchestra, Tip, Tap and Toe and The **Delta Rhythm Boys**. Includes a performance of **W. C. Handy**'s 'Aunt Hagar's blues'.

802
Hi, Mom!
USA 1969 – 87 mins
dir Brian De Palma

Forgettable satire on sex movies. The soundtrack features a song 'Be black, baby' sung by **Grady Tate**.

803
Hi'ya sailor
USA 1943 – 63 mins
dir Jean Yarbrough

Second-feature musical about four sailors trying to get their buddy's song published. Features **Wingy Manone** and His Orchestra.

Hier, aujourd'hui, demain
see **Mini-midi.**

High and happy
see **Hit parade of 1947.**

804
The high cost of loving
USA 1958 – 87 mins
dir José Ferrer

Painfully sincere domestic melodrama on the theme of insecurity in the modern commercial world, with an acting appearance by **Bobby Troup**.

805
High school confidential!/Young killers
USA 1959 – 85 mins
dir Jack Arnold

Grotesque melodrama involving juvenile delinquency, drug addiction, Rock 'n' Roll and hot-rod racing, featuring **Ray Anthony**.

806
High society
USA 1956 – 107 mins
dir Charles Walters

Flat, uninspired musical remake of Cukor's 1941 comedy of manners *The Philadelphia Story* with a weary Cole Porter score. Features **Louis Armstrong** and His Band with **Trummy Young, Billy Kyle, Edmond Hall, Arvell Shaw** and **Barrett Deems**. Numbers: 'High society calypso', 'Little one', 'Who wants to be a millionaire?', 'True love', 'You're sensational', 'I love you Samantha', 'Now you has jazz', 'Well did you evah?', 'Mind if I make love to you?'

807
Higher and higher
USA 1943 – 91 mins
dir Tim Whelan

Entertaining musical with Michèle Morgan and half a dozen songs from Frank Sinatra. **Charles Mingus** makes his screen bow – as an extra.

Highway girl
see **Return to Macon County.**

808
His captive woman
USA 1929 – 92 mins
dir George Fitzmaurice

Melodrama about a cabaret dancer's adventures in the South Seas with the detective who has been sent to arrest her. Briefly features **'Speed' Webb** and His Orchestra.

809
Histoire de bicyclettes
France 1953 – 14 mins
dir Emile Roussel

Impressions of three different types of bicycle, with music score by **Hubert Rostaing**.

810
Histoire d'un poisson rouge/The golden fish

France 1959 – 20 mins
dir Edmond Séchan

Fastidiously photographed, slightly precious
anecdote about the friendship of a small boy and
his pets, marred mainly by its fraudulent ending.
Lively music score by **Henri Crolla** and **André
Hodeir**.

811
Hit!

USA 1973 – 134 mins
dir Sidney J. Furie

Overlong and very derivative melodrama featuring
a black super-hero: implausible, incoherent and
morally suspect. Music score by **Lalo Schifrin**.

812
Hit parade of 1937/I'll reach for a star

USA 1936 – 78 mins
dir Gus Mains

Musical revue, with a slender thread of a plot,
giving an opportunity to various well-known radio
stars to show their paces. Features **Duke
Ellington** and His Orchestra with **Ivie Anderson**
and the songs 'Sweet heartache', 'Hail, alma
mater!', 'Last night I dreamed of you', 'I'll reach
for a star', 'The lady wants to dance' and 'Was it
rain?'

813
Hit parade of 1943/Change of heart

USA 1943 – 86 mins
dir Albert S. Rogell

*The Count Basie Orchestra, with dancer Dorothy
Dandridge in* **Hit parade of 1943**.

▼

Romantic musical comedy with little story but plenty of music, featuring, among other entertainers, **Count Basie** and His Orchestra (**Buck Clayton**, *tpt;* **Freddie Green**, *gtr;* **Jo Jones**, *drs*) and **Ray Mckinley** and His Band. Numbers: 'A change of heart', 'Do these old eyes deceive me?', 'That's how to write a song', 'Harlem sandman', 'Who took me home last night?' and 'Tahm-boom-bah'.

814
Hit parade of 1947/High and happy

USA 1947 – 90 mins
dir Frank McDonald

Light entertainment with music telling the usual success story of a musical act from its formation through to a Hollywood contract. Features **Woody Herman** and His Orchestra.

815
Hit parade of 1951

USA 1950 – 85 mins
dir John H. Auer

Musical about mistaken identity leading to routine complications. Features The **Firehouse Five plus Two** and numbers include 'Frankie and Johnny'.

816
Hit tune serenade

USA 1943 – 15 mins

Universal Name Band musical featuring **Henry Busse** and His Orchestra.

Hitch-hike to happiness
see **Here comes Elmer.**

817
Hoa-Binh

France 1969 – 90 mins
dir Raoul Coutard

Adaptation of Françoise Lorrain's novel *La colonne de cendres* set in Vietnam: the first movie to be directed by the New Wave's most celebrated cameraman. Music by **Michel Portal**.

818
Hoagy Carmichael

USA 1939 – 10 mins
dir Leslie Roush

A Paramount music short with **Jack Teagarden** and His Orchestra backing **Hoagy Carmichael** compositions, introduced and sung by the composer with assistance from singer Meredith Blake. Numbers: 'Two sleepy people', 'Washboard blues', 'Rockin' chair', 'Stardust', 'Lazybones', 'Small fry' and 'That's right I'm wrong'.

819
The hole

USA 1962 – 15 mins
dir John Hubley

Prizewinning colour cartoon which puts the case for disarmament in a novel and amusing way – two roadworkers discuss the future of mankind. Improvised dialogue by **Dizzy Gillespie**.

820
A hole in the head

USA 1959 – 120 mins
dir Frank Capra

Unashamedly sentimental adaptation by Arnold Schulman of his own play, with music by Nelson

Riddle and two songs: 'All my tomorrows' and 'High hopes'. **Ted Nash** participated on the music track.

821

Holiday

UK 1957 – 18 mins
dir John Taylor

A candid camera view of some aspects of holiday life in Blackpool which does considerable credit to its sponsors – British Transport Films. Music by **Chris Barber** and His Band with **Monty Sunshine**, *clar;* and **Ottilie Patterson**, *voc.*

822

Holiday inn

USA 1942 – 101 mins
dir Mark Sandrich

Light musical comedy tailored for the talents of Bing Crosby and Fred Astaire, later to be remade as *White Christmas* using some of the same Irving Berlin numbers. The **Bob Crosby** Band recorded part of the soundtrack.

823

Holiday rhythm

USA 1950 – 60 mins
dir Jack Scholl

15 songs and 18 vaudeville acts crammed into 60 minutes surround a slight story. Features **Nappy Lamare** with His Dixieland Band.

824

Hollywood canteen

USA 1944 – 125 mins
dir Delmer Daves

A splendid tribute to the real Hollywood Canteen, giving a chance for many top Warner Bros contract artistes to indulge in much singing, dancing and high-powered entertaining. **Jimmy Dorsey** and His Band are on hand to accompany several of the vocal acts and have the floor to themselves for one hard-swinging number – 'King Porter stomp'.

825

Hollywood hotel

USA 1937 – 110 mins
dir Busby Berkeley

In an otherwise disappointing Berkeley musical, **Benny Goodman** and His Orchestra are well featured though a certain amount of their footage was deleted during the editing (it still exists). There is a good number, 'I've got a heartful of music', from The Quartet – **Goodman, Teddy Wilson, Lionel Hampton, Gene Krupa** – and

band numbers include 'Music of love', 'Hooray for Hollywood!', 'Sing, sing, sing' and 'Sing, you son of a gun'. Other music: 'I'm like a fish out of water', 'Let that be a lesson to you', 'Can't teach my heart new tricks', 'Dark eyes' and 'California here I come'. Band personnel: **Benny Goodman**, *clar;* **Harry Goodman**, *bass;* **Jess Stacy**, *pno;* **Allan Reuss**, *gtr;* **Gene Krupa**, *drs;* **Harry James, Ziggy Elman**. Chris Griffin, *tpts;* **Murray McEachern**, Red Ballard, *trbs;* **Vido Musso, Hymie Schertzer, Arthur Rollini**, George Koenig, *saxes.*

826

Hollywood shower of stars

USA 1955 – 9 mins

One of the Columbia Screen Snapshots series featuring the off-screen informality of many Hollywood stars. This one spotlights **Harry James**, among others.

827

Hollywood stars on parade

USA 1954 – 10 mins

Another of the Columbia Screen Snapshots series affording informal glimpses of American entertainers. This edition features, among others, **Harry James** and **Bob Crosby**.

828

The holy mountain

USA/Mexico 1973 – 126 mins
dir Alexandro Jodorowsky

An out-and-out occult trip, shot mainly in Mexico, with the director as guru indulging in excesses of visual high jinks and way-out symbols. The music track is by Jodorowsky, Ronald Frangipane and **Don Cherry**.

829

The homecoming

USA/UK 1973 – 114 mins
dir Peter Hall

Moderately successful attempt to adapt for the screen Peter Hall's original stage production of Harold Pinter's play, set mainly in an outsize living room. Music: a recording of ' 'round midnight' by **Thelonius Monk**, performed by **Monk**, *pno;* **Gerry Mulligan**, *bar sax;* **Wilbur Ware**, *bass;* **Shadow Wilson**, *drs.*

830

L'Homme à femmes

France 1960 – 95 mins
dir Jacques-Gerard Cornu

Loosely constructed murder mystery, based on the novel by Patrick Quentin, with music by **Claude Bolling**.

831

L'Homme de la Nouvelle-Orléans

France 1958
dir Thomas Rowe

A music short featuring **Kid Ory**.

832

Un homme qui me plait

France 1969 – 95 mins
dir Claude Lelouch

Probably one of this trendy director's best pictures, certainly the easiest to watch and the most interesting, set in the USA and telling a love story between a film actress and a movie composer. One sequence is set in **Al Hirt**'s Jazz Club in New Orleans and features singer **'Sweet' Emma Barrett.**

833

Honey chile

USA c1943 – 3 mins
Soundie featuring **Louis Jordan**.

834

Honeysuckle rose

USA 1941 – 3 mins
dir Warren Murray
Soundie in which the title number is played by **Fats Waller**, *pno, voc;* John Hamilton, *tpt;* **Gene Sedric**, *alt sax;* **Al Casey**, *gtr;* Cedric Wallace, *bass;* Wilmore Jones, *drs.*

835

Hong Kong blues

USA c1943 – 3 mins
Soundie in which the title number is presented by its composer, **Hoagy Carmichael.**

836

Honky

USA 1971 – 92 mins
dir William A. Graham
Well-made adaptation of Gunard Solberg's novel *Sheila* about a young black and her relationship with a white youth. Excellent music score, and a quartet of songs, by **Quincy Jones.**

837

The hoodlum saint

USA 1946 – 91 mins
dir Norman Taurog
Unconvincing drama with William Powell pretending he is St Dismas, the patron saint of hoodlums. **Benny Goodman** with His Band (**Mel Powell**, *pno*) recorded 'Sweetheart' for use on the soundtrack.

838

Hooray for Hollywood!

USA 1976 – 100 mins
A cheaply made spin-off from *That's entertainment* consisting of countless extracts from Hollywood movies of the 30s and 40s, mainly from Warner Bros., RKO, Paramount, Fox, Republic and Hal Roach studios. Includes the title song 'Hooray for Hollywood!' from *Hollywood Hotel* featuring **Gene Krupa** and **Harry James** with The **Benny Goodman** Band and some colour footage c1938 of **Henry Busse**.

839

Hooray for love!

USA 1935 – 72 mins
dir Walter Lang
Film adaptation of a popular musical comedy, set against the background of rehearsals and performances of a stage presentation. Features **Fats Waller** and Bill 'Bojangles' Robinson.

Hoppity goes to town

see **Mr Bug goes to town.**

840

L'Horloger de Saint-Paul

France 1974 – 95 mins
dir Bertrand Tavernier
Prize-winning adaptation of a Simenon novel about the effect on a man's life on learning that his son has committed a crime. Orchestrations by **Hubert Rostaing**.

Hot blood

see **The wild one.**

841

Hot car girl

USA 1958 – 71 mins
dir Bernard L. Kowalski
Roger Corman-produced teenager melodrama charting the adventures and fall of a group of defiant delinquents. Music by **Cal Tjader.**

842

Hot chocolate/Cottontail
USA 1941 – 3 mins
dir Josef Berne

Soundie featuring **Duke Ellington** and His
Orchestra playing 'Cottontail', with solos from **Rex
Stewart**, *tpt;* **Ben Webster**, *ten sax;* plus dancing
from Whitey's Lindy Hoppers. Also prominent are
Johnny Hodges, *alt sax;* **Barney Bigard**, *clar.*

843

Hot frogs
USA c1942 – 3 mins

Soundie presented in the form of a musical
cartoon with impressions of **Fats Waller**, Bill
Robinson, **Ethel Waters** and The **Mills Brothers**.

Hot, hard and mean
see **Black mama, white mama.**

844

Hot in the groove
USA c1942 – 3 mins

Soundie featuring **Erskine Hawkins** and His
Orchestra.

Hot nocturne
see **Blues in the night.**

845

**The hot rock/How to steal a diamond in four
uneasy lessons**
USA 1971 – 105 mins
dir Peter Yates

Enjoyable, off-beat crime feature produced on
realistic New York locations with an excellent cast
and a neat, witty script. A fine modernistic score
by **Quincy Jones** is played by **Clark Terry,
Gerry Mulligan, Grady Tate, Ray Brown, Carol
Kaye, Frank Rosolino, Chuck Rainey, Tommy
Tedesco, Victor Feldman, Mike Melvoin, Clare
Fischer, Emil Richards, Jerome Richardson,
Bobbi Porter, Dennis Budimir, Milt Holland**.
Vocals by Tata, The Ian Smith Singers and The
Don Elliott Voices. All music composed,
arranged and conducted by **Quincy Jones**.

846

Hotel
USA 1967 – 124 mins
dir Richard Quine

A truly hoary old melodrama played amid
splendidly garish gilt and plush hotel settings.
Features **Carmen McRae**, appearances by
Andrew Blakeney, *tpt;* **Montudi Garland**, *bass;*
and **Ed Garland** with **Frank Rosolino** contributing to Johnny Keating's soundtrack score.

847

Hotsy footsy
USA 1952 – 6 mins
dir William T. Hurtz

Excrutiatingly unfunny Mister Magoo colour
cartoon in which he mistakes a wrestling ring for
a dance floor. Novelty jazz score by **Milton
'Shorty' Rogers**.

848

House on 52nd Street
USA c1943 – 3 mins

Soundie featuring **Henry 'Red' Allen** and J. C.
Higginbotham with their Band.

849

How does it feel
UK 1976 – 60 mins
dir Mick Csaky

Daft Arts Council investigation into the human
senses and their importance, spotlighting the
creative use made of them by personalities such
as R.D. Laing, Michael Tippett, David Hockney
etc., with **Annie Ross** as narrator.

**How to destroy the reputation of the greatest
secret agent**
see **Le magnifique.**

850

How to murder your wife
USA 1964 – 118 mins
dir Richard Quine

Patchy but generally agreeable comedy, using a
strip cartoon style, written and produced by the
ever-lovable George Axelrod. Music composed
and conducted by **Neal Hefti**.

**How to steal a diamond in four uneasy
lessons**
see **The hot rock.**

851

Howard's house party
USA c1947 – 10 mins

A Century Films production with **Bob Howard**
and **Noble Sissle**.

852

Huckleberry duck
USA c1941 – 3 mins

Soundie featuring **Raymond Scott**'s number sung
by The Martins.

853

Huckleberry Finn

USA 1974 – 117 mins
dir J. Lee Thompson
Embarrassing operetta treatment of Mark Twain's novel, with screenplay, music and lyrics by Robert B. and Richard M. Sherman. The only impression is made by the title song 'Freedom' sung by **Roberta Flack**.

Hunger
see **Sult**.

854

Hurry sundown

USA 1966 – 146 mins
dir Otto Preminger
Slow, meticulous screen adaptation of the giant-sized American novel by K. B. Gilden, set deep down South. Actor Michael Caine mouths an alto sax whenever the script calls for him to wax frustration – finely ghosted by **Ronnie Lang**. The superb music score is by Hugo Montenegro.

855

Hush . . . hush, sweet Charlotte

USA 1964 – 134 mins
dir Robert Aldrich
Shameless follow-up to the same team's fantastic box-office success *Whatever happened to baby Jane?* but not such fun. Features The **Teddy Buckner** All Stars.

856

Hustle

USA 1975 – 118 mins
dir Robert Aldrich
Disappointing thriller with Burt Reynolds as an honest cop trying to preserve a precarious foothold in a corrupt, indifferent city. Some of **Lalo Schifrin**'s music for *Mission impossible* is used on soundtrack and **Med Flory** has a small acting part as a policeman.

857

Hvad med os?/Epilogue

Denmark 1963 – 95 mins
dir Henning Carlsen
The story of an expatriate who returns to his native Copenhagen obsessed with guilt about an incident in the past. Jazz score by **Krzystof Komeda**.

858

Hvor er de tyske studente?

Denmark 1960
A cinematic impression of a demonstration by Provos at Denmark's Thorvaldsen Museum. Music by The **Erik Moseholm** Trio.

859

I can't give you anything but love

USA 1950 – 3 mins

Snader Telescription in which the title number is interpreted by **Cab Calloway** and His Cabaliers, including **Jonah Jones**, *tpt;* **Milt Hinton**, *bass;* **'Panama' Francis**, *drs.*

860

I cried for you

USA c1952

Telescription of **Count Basie** playing the title number.

861

I deal in danger

USA 1966 – 89 mins
dir Walter Grauman

Routine espionage adventure, based on an American TV series, with music partly by **Lalo Schifrin**.

862

I din fars lomme/In your dad's pocket

Denmark 1973 – 73 mins
dir Lise Roos, Anker

Domestic comedy about the everyday life of a small Danish family, with particular emphasis on the antics of their 11 year old daughter. Sound-track jazz improvisations are arranged by Bent Fabricius-Bjerre.

863

I dood it/By hook and by crook

USA 1943 – 102 mins
dir Vincente Minnelli

A crazy comedy of errors produced as a vehicle for Red Skelton and providing plenty of oppor-tunity for song and dance. Features Lena Horne, **Hazel Scott** with **Lee Young**, *drs*, and **Jimmy Dorsey** and His Orchestra plus Helen O'Connell and Bob Eberley. Musical items include 'Star eyes', 'One o'clock jump, 'Swingin' the jinx away' and 'Taking a chance on love'. Among the sound-track musicians are **Barney Bigard** and **Red Callender**.

864

I dreamt I dwelt in Harlem

USA c1943 – 3 mins

Soundie in which the title number is sung by The **Delta Rhythm Boys**.

865

I got it bad and that ain't good

USA 1943 – 3 mins

Soundie featuring **Ivie Anderson**, *voc*, with her classic interpretation of the title song, backed by **Duke Ellington** and His Orchestra with **Johnny Hodges**, *alt sax;* **Barney Bigard**, *clar;* and **Sonny Greer**, *drs*, prominent.

866

I heard

USA 1933 – 6 mins
dir Dave Fleischer

Paramount cartoon featuring Betty Boop, with music by **Don Redman** and His Orchestra. Numbers: 'Chant of the weed' and 'I heard'.

867

I lost my sugar in Salt Lake City

USA 1944 – 3 mins

Soundie in which vocalist Carolyn Gray sings the title number, backed by **Wingy Manone** and His Band.

868

I love my wife

USA 1970 – 95 mins
dir Mel Stuart

Wisecracking marital comedy with some splendid jokes but not much else. Music score by **Lalo Schifrin**.

869

I love you, I hate you

UK 1968
dir David Hart

Details unknown, probably produced on 16mm, but with music score by **John Dankworth**.

870

I met him in Paris

USA 1937 – 75 mins
dir Wesley Ruggles

Conventional romantic farce; the usual story of two men in love with the same girl. The song 'I met him in Paris' by Helen Meinardi and **Hoagy Carmichael**.

871

I tvillingernes tegn/In the sign of gemini

Denmark/Sweden 1975 – 88 mins
dir Werner Hedmann

Soft-core porno spoof about a 1930's record promoter's attempts to contract a girl singer. Original recordings by the late **Leo Mathison** are used extensively on the soundtrack.

872

I want a big fat mama

USA c1943 – 3 mins

Soundie featuring **Lucky Millinder**'s title song.

873

I want a man

USA c1943 – 3 mins

Soundie in which **Annisteen Allen** sings the title number, backed by **Lucky Millinder** and His Orchestra.

874

I want to live

USA 1958 – 120 mins
dir Robert Wise

Highly emotional and uncompromising exposé of police methods and legal execution helped by a good jazz soundtrack composed and arranged by **Johnny Mandel**. **Gerry Mulligan, Art Farmer, Bud Shank, Frank Rosolino, Pete Jolly, 'Red' Mitchell** and **Shelly Manne** appear in the opening sequence. Underscore and source music played by **Jack Sheldon, Al Porcino, Ed Leddy**, *tpts;* **Frank Rosolino, Milt Bernhart, Dave Wells**, *trbs;* **Dave Wells**, *bas-tpt;* **Vince de Rosa**, Sinclair Lott, John Cave, **Dick Parisi**, *Fr horns;* **Harry Klee**, *picc, flutes;* **Abe Most**, *clars;* **Joe Maini**, *saxes, bas-clar;* **Bill Holman**, *saxes, clar;* Marty Berman, *bas-clar, contra bassoon;* **Chuck Gentry**, *bas-sax, contra bas-clar;* **Red Mitchell**, *bass;* **Al Hendrickson**, *gtr;* **Pete Jolly**, *pno;* **Shelly Manne, Larry Bunker, Mel Lewis, Milt Holland, Mike Pacheco**, *perc.* With the participation of **Russ Freeman**, *pno.*

875

I want you

USA 1951 – 101 mins
dir Mark Robson

Recruiting propaganda for the Korean War, technically smooth and expert but the level of writing, with its sentimental evasions, is unworthy of the screenwriter Irwin Shaw. The **Les Brown** Band, minus its leader, was borrowed by MD Leigh Harline to record jukebox and dance-band sequences for the soundtrack.

876

I was here when you left me

USA c1943 – 3 mins

Soundie featuring **Cab Calloway** and His Band with the title number backing vocal by Dotty Saulter.

877

Ich – ein Groupie/Me, a groupie

West Germany 1970 – 103 mins
dir Fred Williams

Slightly better than average sexploitation drama charting the decline and fall of a sweet young thing during her European travels. A disco sequence features **Pony Poindexter** and His Musicians.

878

Idea girl

USA 1946 – 60 mins
dir Will Jason

Light, unpretentious Universal comedy with music about a music publisher's relationship with a dizzy blonde song saleswoman. Features **Charlie Barnet** and His Orchestra with three numbers: 'Xango', 'I don't care' and 'I can't get you off my mind'.

879

The idol

UK 1966 – 111 mins
dir Daniel Petrie

Gloomy psychological melodrama with meaningful undertones. Music score by **John Dankworth**.

880

If I could be with you

USA c1952 – 3 mins

Telescription of **Count Basie** playing the title number, with vocalist **Helen Humes**.

881

If I'm lucky

USA 1946 – 80 mins
dir Lewis Seiler

Musical which for a change has a reasonably plausible and coherent story but not much else for, in black and white, even Carmen Miranda seems to lose her vivacity. Features **Harry James** and His Orchestra.

882

If you can't smile and say yes

USA c1943 – 3 mins

Soundie featuring **Louis Jordan**.

883

If you only knew

USA c1942 – 3 mins

Soundie in which the title number is sung by **Valaida Snow**, backed by The Ali Baba Trio.

884

Il faut vivre dangereusement

France 1975 – 97 mins
dir Claude Makovski

A sort of homage to, and good-natured sendup of, Hollywood private eye movies with Claude Brasseur as part Raymond Chandler and part Mickey Spillane. **Claude Bolling**'s lively music score ranges from modern to Dixieland jazz to electric pop.

885

I'll be glad when you're dead you rascal you

USA 1932 – 8 mins
dir Max Fleischer

Louis Armstrong appears both live and animated in this rather tasteless Betty Boop cartoon to play 'High society', 'Shine' and 'I'll be glad . . .'.

886

I'll be glad when you're dead you rascal you

USA 1942 – 3 mins

Soundie featuring **Louis Armstrong** with the title number.

887

I'll get by

USA 1950 – 83 mins
dir Richard Sale

Undistinguished romantic musical about struggling music publishers. Features **Harry James** and His Orchestra and songs 'There will never be another you', 'I'll get by', 'Taking a chance on love', 'Once in a while', 'I've got the world on a string' and 'You make me feel so young'. Soundtrack musicians on special song numbers: **Red Norvo**, *vibs;* **Red Kelly**, *bass;* **Tal Farlow**, *gtr.*

I'll reach for a star

see **Hit parade of 1937.**

888

I'll tell the world

USA 1945 – 61 mins
dir Leslie Goodwins

Modest comedy, about a radio station, tailored for the talent of fast-talking Lee Tracy. Several specialities are introduced, from tap dancers to cowboy crooners, including a boogie-woogie sequence by **Gene Rodgers**.

889

I'm a shy guy

USA c1943 – 3 mins

Soundie featuring The **'King' Cole** Boys supported by a team of girl dancers.

890

I'm gonna love that guy

USA 1945 – 3 mins

Soundie in which the title·number (**Gene Roland**, *arr.*) is played by **Stan Kenton** and His Orchestra, with **June Christy**, *voc*.

891

I'm home sick, that's all

USA 1944 – 3 mins

Soundie featuring **Stan Kenton** and His Orchestra, with vocal from **Gene Howard**.

892

I'm just a lucky so-and-so

USA c1942 – 3 mins

Soundie in which the title song is sung by Debby Claire, backed by **Ray Bauduc**'s Band.

893

I'm tired of waiting for you
USA c1942 – 3 mins
Soundie featuring Will Bradley and His Orchestra with **Ray McKinley** and a vocal from Lynn Gardner.

894

Imago
USA 1970 – 88 mins
dir Ned Bosnick
Pretentious and confused sexploitation movie analysing a young girl's problems. Music score by **Lalo Schifrin**.

895

Imitation of life
USA 1959 – 124 mins
dir Douglas Sirk
The second screen version of Fannie Hurst's novel, previously filmed in 1934: an inflated essay in twisted values with a veneer of social moralising. Features **Mahalia Jackson** singing 'Trouble of the world'.

896

L'Imprévu
France 1965 – 19 mins
dir Alpha Amadon
Impressions of slowly awakening first love between two young people. Music by **Lou Bennett**.

897

In a lonely place
USA 1950 – 93 mins
dir Nicholas Ray
Excellent adaptation of the novel by Dorothy B. Hughes about an embittered Hollywood screenwriter suspected of murder. A nightclub sequence features singer **Hedda Brooks**.

898

In a mist
Netherlands 1959 – 4 mins
dir Rens Groot
An animated film experiment, on the title music composed by **Bix Beiderbecke**, using on soundtrack the New York City recording of 30th June 1958 by Michel Legrand and His Orchestra.

899

In cold blood
USA 1967 – 134 mins
dir Richard Brooks
Painstaking adaptation of Truman Capote's 'non-fiction novel' – the reconstruction of a real-life crime. First rate music score by **Quincy Jones** using bassists **Ray Brown** and Andy Simkins as musical counterparts of the screen killers, with double stop smears and slides all the way through the picture.

900

In der Werkstatt – Nuremberg Jazz Collegium
West Germany c1970 – 15 mins
dir Hannes Reinhardt
Originally produced for TV, an impression of the work of musician **Werner Heider**, *pno*, in rehearsal with his Quartet (*alt sax, fender bass, drs.*). The music is in 'free' form.

901

In harm's way
USA 1965 – 167 mins
dir Otto Preminger
All star, naval warfare epic adapted from the novel by James Bassett. Jerry Goldsmith's music score provides a song for Diahann Carroll; playing behind her are **Phil Moore**, *pno;* **Milt Hinton**, *bass;* **Earl Williams**, *drs*.

902

In like Flint
USA 1967 – 115 mins
dir Gordon Douglas
A pedestrian sequel to *Our man Flint* which even the engaging James Coburn, as super-Bond, can't manage to salvage. Jerry Goldsmith composed and conducted the score with the theme 'Where the bad guys are gals' and the vocal 'Your zowie face' arranged by **Marty Paich**. Instrumentalists on the soundtrack include **Shelly Manne**, *drs;* **Red Mitchell**, *bass;* **Ronnie Lang**, *alt sax;* **Plas Johnson**, *ten sax;* **Dick Nash**, *trb*.

903

In old Kentucky
USA 1935 – 86 mins
dir George Marshall
The fourth screen version of Charles T. Dazey's famous play charting the feud between the Martingales and the Shattocks, which sadly became Will Rogers's last movie. Features **Nina Mae McKinney** and Bill Robinson.

904
In the cool of the day
USA 1962 – 91 mins
dir Robert Stevens

A mixture of sentimental tragedy and propaganda for the Greek tourist office, based on the novel by Susan Ertz. The title song is sung over the opening credits by **Nat 'King' Cole**.

905
In the heat of the night
USA 1967 – 109 mins
dir Norman Jewison

Fine, intelligent thriller helped by a skilfully written screenplay and excellent performances by a superb cast. Quite memorable music score by **Quincy Jones** includes a title song sung by **Ray Charles** and soundtrack contributions from **Roland Kirk**, *flute;* **Bobby Scott**, *pno;* **Ray Brown**, *bass;* **Billy Preston**, *org;* **Don Elliott**, *voc effects, mello, tpt, bongos.*

In the sign of Gemini
see **I tvillingernes tegn.**

906
In town tonight
UK 1935 – 81 mins
dir Herbert Smith

Revue featuring popular entertainers including Dave Apollon and His Romantic Serenaders, Billy Merrin and His Commanders, Howard Jacobs and His Orchestra and **Coleman Hawkins**.

In your dad's pocket
see **I din fars lomme.**

907
Ina Ray Hutton and Her Orchestra
USA 1943 – 9 mins
dir Leslie Roush

A Paramount *Headliner* music short in which **Ina Ray Hutton** and Her Orchestra entertain, in a bandstand setting, supported by vocalists and the dreaded 'bouncing ball'. Numbers: 'Knock me a kiss', 'Smiles', 'Angry' and 'My silent love'.

The Inbetween age
see **The golden disc.**

Incident at Owl Creek
see **La rivière du hibou.**

The inheritance
see **Karamiai.**

908
The Ink Spots
USA 1955 – 15 mins
dir Will Cowan

Universal-International production featuring **Georgie Auld** and His Auld Stars, in a nightclub setting, backing Joy Lane, *voc;* The Barry Sisters, *vocs;* and The Ink Spots. Numbers include 'If I didn't care'.

Innocent sorcerers
see **Niewinni Czarodzieje.**

909
Inserts
UK 1975 – 117 mins
dir John Byrum

Opportunist reflection on Hollywood's fall from its status as the great dream factory to its current position as little more than a second-hand porn producer. Soundtrack use is made of 'Moonglow' as recorded by **Joe Venuti** and His Orchestra.

910
Inside job
USA 1973 – 85 mins
dir Robert Michael Lewis

Routine cross between a heist movie and a renegade cop saga plus a sprinkling of deprecatory humour. Music by **Oliver Nelson**.

911
L'Inspecteur connait la musique/Blues
France 1955 – 90 mins
dir Jean Josipovici

Dull melodrama, set in a jazz milieu, about an amorous blues singer. **Claude Luter** and **Sidney Bechet** play leading roles as well as providing the music.

912
Instantanes à Juan-les-Pins
France 1953 – 10 mins
dir Robert Mariaud

Humorous aspects of Juan-les-Pins, with music score by **Claude Luter**.

913
International house
USA 1933 – 72 mins
dir Edward Sutherland

Zany comedy about a radio device, invented by a Chinese, and the people who buy it. Features **Cab Calloway** and His Orchestra with 'Reefer man'.

914

International jazz festival

Belgium 1962 – 18 mins
dir Patrick Ledoux

An impression of the 1962 jazz festival at Comblain-la-Tour, in the Ardennes. Features **Julian 'Cannonball' Adderley** and His Group.

915

The international Woolmark

UK 1965 – 16 mins
dir M. L. Broun

The Woolmark as an international symbol and its significance to retailers and consumers. Music by **Dave Goldberg**.

916

The interview

USA 1960 – 5 mins
dir Ernest Pintoff

Brilliantly conceived and extremely funny colour cartoon adaptation of the best-selling disc in which imaginary inarticulate horn-player 'Shorty' Petterstein is interviewed during a gig by a particularly square announcer. Background soundtrack music is part of 'Have you met Miss Jones' recorded by The **Stan Getz** Quintet in New York City on 4th May 1953.

917

Intimate reflections

UK 1975 – 86 mins
dir Don Boyd

Undistinguished melodrama full of slow-motion effects, zoom lens shots, theatrical monologues and long empty scenes of the lead characters discussing *their* boredom. Loud and abrasive music and the songs: 'She's calling to you, Robert', 'Come now, Mrs Hargreaves', 'Jane and Robert' and 'It's only money' by **Mike Gibbs** and Paul Jones, sung by the latter.

918

Introduction to jazz

USA 1952 – 12 mins
dir Denis Sanders

An impressionistic summary of the beginnings of jazz, made for The University of California. Recordings used on soundtrack: 'Take this hammer', by **Huddie Ledbetter**; 'West End blues' by **Louis Armstrong**'s Hot Five; 'Fidgety feet' by The Yerba Buena Band; '1919' by **Kid Ory**'s Orchestra; 'Dr Jazz' and 'Shoe shiner's drag' by **Jelly Roll Morton's** Red Hot Peppers.

919

Intruder in the dust

USA 1949 – 86 mins
dir Clarence Brown

Intelligent, faithful screen adaptation, by Ben Maddow, of the novel by William Faulkner, with strong, clear-cut performances by an excellent cast. A recorded Dixie band is used on soundtrack for a lynching scene; the personnel were **Clyde Hurley**, *tpt;* **Randall Miller**, *trb;* **'Tiny' Berman**, *tuba;* **Don Lodice**, *ten sax;* **Gus Bivona**, *clar;* **Mel Powell**, *pno;* **Red Roundtree**, *banjo;* **Frank Carlson**, *drs.*

920

L'Invention

France 1967 – 14 mins
dir G. Patris, L. Ferrari

Improvisations by **Cecil Taylor**, *pno,* accompanied by **Jimmy Lyons**, *alt sax;* **Ron Silva**, *bass;* and **Andrew Cyrille**, *drs.*

921

Is everybody happy?

USA 1929 – 74 mins
dir Archie L. Mayo

Drama about a family of Hungarian emigrés and their fortunes in the USA. Features **Ted Lewis**, acting and playing, **'Muggsy' Spanier**, in The Lewis Band, and **Don Murray**, who died during the filming. Musical items: 'St Louis blues', 'Tiger rag', 'In the land of jazz', 'Start the band', 'Wouldn't it be wonderful?', 'I'm the medicine man for the Blues', 'New Orleans' and 'Samoa'.

922

Is everybody happy?

USA 1943 – 73 mins
dir Charles Barton

Screen biography of **Ted Lewis** featuring **Lewis** and His Orchestra. Numbers include 'St Louis blues'. Michael Duana impersonates **Lewis**, who dubbed for him on soundtrack.

923

Is you is or is you ain't my baby?

USA c1943 – 3 mins

Soundie featuring The **'King' Cole** Trio with vocalist Ida James interpreting the title number.

Isabel is death

see **Tatu bola.**

924

Isabelle devant le désir

Belgium/France 1975 – 90 mins
dir Jean-Claude Berckmans

Screen adaptation of Maud Frère's novel *La Délice* about the sexual emancipation of a young girl. Music score by **Claude Luter** and Yannick Singery.

925

Isham Jones and His Orchestra

USA 1934 – 10 mins
dir Roy Mack

Vitaphone short with the title band, supported by singers and dancers, playing 'Rachmaninoff prelude', 'Siboney' and 'Why can't this night go on for ever?'

926

Isn't it romantic?

USA 1948 – 87 mins
dir Norman Z. McLeod

Inoffensive family comedy with music, set in Indiana at the turn of the century. **Pearl Bailey**, as a maid, does a couple of comedy songs.

927

Istanbul

USA 1956 – 84 mins
dir Joseph Pevney

Adventure melodrama tinged with nostalgic sentiment and an amnesia sub-plot. Features **Nat 'King' Cole**.

928

Istanbul express

USA 1968 – 93 mins
dir Richard Irving

Uninspired, glossy espionage thriller with a thoroughly cliché script – originally produced for TV. Music by **Oliver Nelson**.

929

It don't mean a thing

Denmark 1967
dir Flemming Quist Møller

Part animated, part live action cartoon about a reluctant princess who eventually dances. Soundtrack music partly by **Dizzy Gillespie**.

It happened all night
see **L'Affaire d'une nuit.**

It won't rub off, baby
see **Sweet love, bitter.**

930

It's all over the town

UK 1963 – 55 mins
dir Douglas Hickox

Pop music revue maintaining a hectic parade of musical numbers. Features Mr **Acker Bilk** and The Paramount Jazz Band whose performance includes an arrangement of 'The Volga boatmen' complete with Russian dancer and tame bear.

931

It's a panic

USA c1935 – 10 mins
dir Roy Mack

Music short in which Benny Meroff and His Band play a programme of numbers including **W. C. Handy**'s 'St Louis blues'.

932

It's a wonderful world

UK 1956 – 89 mins
dir Val Guest

Musical in which composers win popular success by reversing songs, featuring **Ted Heath** and His Music with 'The Hawaiian war chant'.

933

It's been a long, long time

USA 1945 – 3 mins

Soundie in which **June Christy** sings the title number, backed by **Stan Kenton** and His Orchestra.

934

It's great to be young

UK 1956 – 93 mins
dir Cyril Frankel

Simple British comedy revolving around the trials and tribulations of a grammar school orchestra. Part of the music is provided by **Humphrey Lyttelton**'s Band.

935

It's on the record

USA 1937 – 10 mins

Universal music short in which a music store proprietor reminisces on vaudeville days and brings back to life performers that include The **Original Dixieland Jazz Band.**.

Jazz in the movies British style from **It's great to be young**.

936

It's Trad Dad!

UK 1962 – 73 mins
dir Dick Lester

Crazy comedy, full of zest and invention, featuring among others, **Kenny Ball** and His Jazzmen, **Terry Lightfoot** and His New Orleans Band, **Chris Barber** and His Band, **Acker Bilk** and His Paramount Jazz Band, **Bob Wallis** and His Storyville Jazzmen and **Ottilie Patterson**.

937

The Italian job

UK 1969 – 100 mins
dir Peter Collinson

A thinly scripted, routine thriller of perfect crime and inevitable retribution enlivened only by some superb stunt driving. Music score and songs 'On days like these' and 'Getta blooming move on!' by **Quincy Jones**.

938

Ivy

USA 1947 – 99 mins
dir Sam Wood

Dramatic adaptation of the novel by Marie Bellock Lowndes with Joan Fontaine as the predatory murderess. The song 'Ivy' composed by **Hoagy Carmichael**.

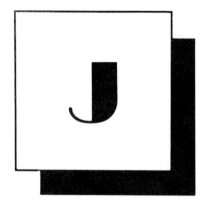

939

Ja da

USA 1942 – 3 mins

Soundie featuring Henry Levine and His Dixieland Jazz Band playing the title number.

940

Jack Armstrong blues

USA c1951 – 3 mins

Telescription of **Jack Teagarden** playing the title number.

941

Jack Johnson

USA 1970 – 88 mins
dir William Cayton

Superb documentary dealing with the life and times of the black boxer who recently received renewed fame as the subject of Howard Sackler's play *The great white hope* and its subsequent screen adaptation. Electric music score by **Miles Davis** co-ordinated by **Teo Macero**. Soundtrack musicians include **Miles Davis**, *tpt;* **Herbie Hancock**, *org;* **John McLaughlin**, *gtr;* **Steve Grossman**, *sop sax;* **Billy Cobham**, *drs;* **Jack de Johnette**, *drs.*

942

Jack Teagarden in Thailand

Thailand 1958 – 15 mins

Documentary on part of **Jack Teagarden**'s 1958/9 tour of Asia including a studio performance of 'St Louis blues' and 'The saints' featuring **Don Ewell**, *pno,* and **Don Goldie**, *tpt.*

943

The Jack Teagarden show

Cambodia 1958 – 10 mins

The **Jack Teagarden** Sextet recorded in Phnom Penh during their 1958/9 tour of Asia.

944

Jack the Ripper

UK 1958 – 84 mins
dir Robert S Baker, Monty Berman

Unambitious version of the 'Ripper' story but successful enough on the level of a routine suspense thriller. A special soundtrack was prepared for the American version which incorporated music by **Pete Rugolo** in collaboration with Jimmy McHugh.

945

Jack, you're playing the game

USA 1941 – 3 mins

Soundie in which The **Delta Rhythm Boys** sing the title number.

J'Ai mon voyage

see **Quand c'est parti, c'est parti.**

946

Jail keys made here

USA c1970 – 10 mins
dir Lee Boltin

Award winning adaptation of the book of photographs by Lee Boltin – a record of advertising signs in urban America. Music by **Dave Brubeck**.

47

ailhouse blues

SA 1929 – 9 mins
r Basil Smith

Columbia short featuring vocalist **Mamie Smith**.

48

am session

SA 1942 – 3 mins
ir Josef Berne

oundie featuring **Duke Ellington** and His
rchestra in a basement club setting playing the
umber 'C jam blues', with solos by **Rex Stewart**,
ot; **Ben Webster**, *ten sax;* **Ray Nance**, *vln;* **Joe**
anton, *trb;* **Barney Bigard**, *clar;* **Sonny Greer**,
rs.

he Charlie Barnet Band against a studio backdrop in
am session.

949

Jam session

USA 1944 – 74 mins
dir Charles Barton

Poorly scripted and altogether uninspired musical,
though rich in performers featuring as it does,
Louis Armstrong and His Orchestra, with
Lawrence Lucie, *gtr,* **Charlie Barnet** and His
Band, Glen Gray and The Casa Loma Orchestra,
the bands of Alvino Rey, Jan Garber, Teddy
Powell plus Jo Stafford and The Pied Pipers.
Numbers include 'St Louis blues', 'No name jive'
and 'Jive bomber'. Recording personnel for
'Cherokee' by **Charlie Barnet** and His Orchestra:
'Peanuts' Holland, Al Killian, Howard McGhee,
Paul Cohen, *tpts;* Bob Swift, **Eddie Bert,**
Trummy Young, Ed Fromm, *trbs;* **Charlie**
Barnet, Steve Cole, George Sivaro, *alt saxes;*
Kurt Bloom, Mike Goldberg, *ten saxes;* **Danny**
Bank, *bar sax;* **Ralph Burns**, *pno;* **Turk van**
Lake, *gtr;* **Chubby Jackson, Oscar Pettiford**,
basses; **Lou Fromm**, *drs.* **Killian, McGhee,**
Holland, Young and **Pettiford** do not appear on
camera, as white actors sat in their places.

J

950

Jam session

France 1951 – 9 mins
dir Pierre Neurisse

A group of French musicians amuse themselves by jamming after work – **Géo Daly, Michel de Villers**, Maurice Meunier, **André Persiany**, Jean Bouchety and Roger Paraboschi.

951

Jamboree/Disc jockey jamboree

USA 1957 – 86 mins
dir Roy Lockwood

A meagre story is used to introduce a series of popular entertainers, mostly as undistinguished as the plot. Appearances, however, by **Count Basie** and His Orchestra with 'One o'clock jump', **Joe Williams** and **Fats Domino** with 'Wait and see' and there is music by **Neal Hefti**.

952

Jamboree no.3

UK – 8 mins

A short produced by Pathé News featuring **Ray McKinley** and His Orchestra.

953

The James Dean story

USA 1957 – 82 mins
dir George W George, Robert Altman

Tactful and tasteful film biography of the actor using purely documentary material – stills, tapes, film tests, interviews etc. Has a good jazz score by Leith Stevens with arrangements by **Johnny Mandel** and **Bill Holman**.

954

Jammin' in the panoram

USA 1942 – 3 mins

Soundie in which **Stan Kenton** and His Orchestra re-enact their rise to fame.

955

Jammin' the Blues

USA 1944 – 10 mins
dir Gjon Mili

Probably the most famous jazz movie of all which was produced by the jazz impresario Norman Granz and remains especially important for the appearance of **Lester Young.** Other participating musicians are **Harry Edison**, *tpt;* **'Illinois' Jacquet**, *ten sax;* **Barney Kessel**, *gtr;* **Marlowe Morris**, *pno;* **John Simmons**, *bass;* **Red Callender**, *bass;* **Sidney Catlett**, *drs;* **Jo Jones**, *drs;* **Mary Bryant**, *voc.* Numbers: 'The midnight symphony', 'On the sunny side of the street' and 'Jammin' the Blues'.

956

Janine

France 1962 – 19 mins
dir Maurice Pialat

Short story about a man in search of his wife, who has become a low-class prostitute. Music by **René Urtreger**.

957

Jasper in a jam

USA 1946 – 7 mins
dir George Pal

A Puppetoon with the action set in a pawnshop where musical instruments come to life at midnight. Music supplied by **Charlie Barnet** and His Orchestra with Peggy Lee. Numbers: 'Pompton Turnpike' and 'Cherokee'.

958

The jay walker

USA 1955 – 7 mins
dir Robert Cannon

One of the best of the many colour cartoons produced by UPA in the 1950's. This one recounts the adventures of an inveterate jay walker and has music provided by **Billy May**.

959

Le jazz à Paris

France 1965 – 5 mins
dir Léonard Keigel

A brief sequence from a *Chroniques de France* programme surveying the current Paris jazz scene. **Lou Bennett**, *org*, and **Kenny Clarke**, *drs*, are shown playing at The Blue Note; there is a short interlude with **Art Simmons**, *pno*, and in a café in The Marché aux Puces a group pays tribute to **Django Reinhardt**.

960

Jazz all the way

UK 1964 – 9 mins

An appalling issue of the *Look at life* series which casts its blind eyes over the subject of jazz in Britain, without any attempt at understanding whatsoever. **Humphrey Lyttelton, Mike Cotton, Dick Charlesworth** and **Acker Bilk** appear briefly with their respective groups and there is one music shot of **Dizzy Gillespie** at The Manchester Festival.

961

Jazz auf Burg Schwaneck

West Germany 1960 – 10 mins
dir Charles Van der Linden

Jimmy Garrison in **Jazz is our religion** *(photo: Valerie Wilmer/TCB Releasing).*

J

Arty-crafty reportage from the magnificent Schwaneck castle near Munich where a group of musicians gather for tuition in jazz. A few recorded bars of **Woody Herman**'s 'Goosey gander' is about all the film is good for.

962
Jazz ball
USA – 60 mins
Compiler Herbert L. Bregstein
A compilation of music extracts and Soundies, with added narration, made for TV. Among those featured are **Cab Calloway** with 'Zaz zuh zaz'; **Duke Ellington** and His Orchestra with 'Rockin' in rhythm', 'Stormy weather' and 'Bugle call rag' – all from *Bundle of blues* – The Mills Brothers with 'I ain't got nobody'; **Ina Ray Hutton** with 'Truckin'; **Louis Armstrong** with 'Shine' from *Rhapsody in black and blue*, **Louis Prima** with 'Chinatown'; **Bob Crosby** with 'How do you like to love me' and 'South Rampart Street parade'; Vincent Lopez and His Orchestra with **Jack Teagarden** and Betty Hutton with 'Dipsy doodle'; **Isham Jones** and His Orchestra; **Henry Busse** with 'Hot lips'; **Jimmy Dorsey** and His Orchestra with **'Wild' Bill Davison; Artie Shaw** with **Buddy Rich** and Sammy Davis, Peggy Lee, Johnny 'Scat' Davis, Lawrence Welk, Hal Kemp, Bob Chester, Russ Morgan and Rudy Vallee.

963
Jazz boat
UK 1959 – 96 mins
dir Ken Hughes
A juvenile crime story of no interest apart from the featured role of **Ted Heath** and His Music.

964
Jazz dance
USA 1954 – 22 mins
dir Roger Tilton
A filmed jazz session at Central Plaza Dance Hall, New York City featuring **Jimmy McPartland**, *tpt, voc;* **Jimmy Archey**, *trb;* **'Pee Wee' Russell**, *clar;* **Willie 'The Lion' Smith**, *pno;* **George 'Pops' Foster**, *bass;* **George Wettling**, *drs.* Music: 'Jazz me blues', 'Ballin' the jack', 'Royal garden blues' and 'The saints'.

965
Jazz festival
USA 1949/1956
dir Well Corsan
Musical extravaganza featuring top jazz talent; a compilation by Universal Pictures of previous music shorts ranging from conventional screen size in monochrome to CinemaScope and colour.

Includes **Count Basie** and His Orchestra, **Lionel Hampton, Duke Ellington, Sarah Vaughan, Stan Kenton** and **Nat 'King' Cole**.

966
Jazz festival
USA 1968 – 26 mins
A Universal Pictures re-issue of two previous shorts; *Pete's place* and *Four hits and a mister.*

967
Jazz from Studio 61
USA 1959 – 30 mins
prod Robert Herridge
Studio performances filmed originally for CBS TV featuring The **Ahmad Jamal** Trio with **Israel Crosby** and a **Ben Webster** group which includes **Buck Clayton**, *tpt;* **Vic Dickenson**, *trb;* **Hank Jones**, *pno;* **Jo Jones**, *drs;* **George Duvivier**, *bass.* Numbers: 'Mop mop', 'Darn that dream', 'Chelsea Bridge' and 'C jam blues'.

968
Jazz Gestern und Heute
West Germany 1953
Details unknown but it features **Hans Koller** and **Albert Mangelsdorff**.

969
Jazz in piazza
Italy 1974 – c80 mins
dir Pino Adriano
Film record, shot on 16mm, of musicians appearing at the 1974 Umbria Jazz Festival: The Perugia Big Band, The **Horace Silver** Quintet, The Gianni Basso – Dino Piana Quintet, The **Gerry Mulligan** Quartet, **Marian McPartland**, The **Charlie Mingus** New Group, The **Thad Jones-Mel Lewis** Big Band, **Keith Jarrett**, The **Sonny Stitt** Quartet, **Anthony Braxton**, and Freedom (**Sam Rivers, Dave Holland, Barry Altshul**). Numbers include 'Stormy weather', **Duke Ellington**'s 'Sophisticated lady' and 'In a sentimental mood', **Horace Silver**'s 'Song of my father' and **Gerry Mulligan**'s 'Line for Lyons'.

970
Jazz is our religion
UK 1972 – 50 mins
dir John Jeremy
A distillation in images, words and music of the jazz life, with photographs by Valerie Wilmer. Music by **Johnny Griffin**, *ten sax,* leading a quintet of **Dizzy Reece**, *tpt;* **Ignatius Quail**, *pno;* **Coleridge Goode**, *bass;* **Terri Quaye**, *conga;* **Rudi Henderson**, *drs,* with **Jon Hendricks**, *voc,*

Art Blakey in John Jeremy's **Jazz is our religion**
(photo: Valerie Wilmer/TCB Releasing).

playing 'That's enuff', 'Now's the time', 'Dean St blues', 'Alone again', 'Livetime' and 'Jaygee blues'. Big band tracks by The **Clarke-Boland** Band with **Alan Shorter,** *tpt,* **Lol Coxhill,** *sop sax,* drum tracks by **Art Blakey, Sunny Murray, Kenny Clare, Guy Warren.** Jazz poems by Langston Hughes and Ted Joans, read by the latter. With the voices of **Raschied Ali, Art Blakey, Marion Brown, Kenny Clare, Andrew Cyrille, Bill Evans, Jimmy Garrison, Dizzy Gillespie, Johnny Griffin, Jo Jones, Jon Hendricks, Blue Mitchell, Sunny Murray, Dewey Redman, Guy Warren** and **Eddie Gomez.**

971

Jazz-jamboree nos. 1, 2, 3.

France 1953 – 10 mins each
dir Edgar Roulleau

Film *reportages* of a concert given in The Arènes de Lutèce in Paris featuring many local musicians including **Sidney Bechet** and **Claude Luter.**

972

Jazz on a summer's day

USA 1960 – 86 mins
dir Bert Stern

Valuable record of the 1958 Newport Festival though made in an irrelevant and obtrusive style. Features **Jimmy Giuffre, Bob Brookmeyer, Jim Hall, Ben Webster, Oscar Pettiford, Rex Stewart, Thelonius Monk, Henry Grimes, Roy Haynes, Sal Salvador, Sonny Stitt, Anita O'Day, Hank Jones, Dinah Washington, Urbie Green, Terry Gibbs, Max Roach, Gerry Mulligan, Art Farmer, Bill Crow, Dave Bailey, Chico Hamilton, Eric Dolphy, Fred Katz, George Shearing,** 'Big' Maybelle, Chuck Berry, **Louis Armstrong, Jack Teagarden, Buck Clayton, Rudy Powell, Jo Jones, Trummy Young, Danny Barcelona, 'Peanuts' Hucko** and **Mahalia Jackson.** Numbers include 'The train and the river', 'Blue Monk', 'Do nothin' 'till you hear from me', 'The wind', 'Sweet Georgia Brown', 'Tea for two', 'Sweet little sixteen', 'Tiger rag', 'Rockin' chair', 'Up a lazy river', 'The saints', 'Blues', 'All of me', 'Rondo', 'Catch as catch can' and 'I ain't mad at you'.

973

The Jazz singer

USA 1927 – 90 mins
dir Alan Crosland

Highly emotional screen adaptation of Samson Raphaelson's play, generally thought of as the first talkie but was in fact principally a silent film with synchronised musical accompaniment, a few songs by Jolson and, more or less as an oversight, a few lines of dialogue. Features pianist **Paul Lingle.**

974

The Jazz singer

USA 1952 – 105 mins
dir Michael Curtiz

Uncomfortable remake of the 1927 movie steering an uneasy course between the Temple and the bright lights, with frequent lapses of taste. Peggy Lee tries hard with some good numbers that include 'The birth of The Blues', 'Lover' and 'Just one of those things'.

975

Jazz the intimate art

USA 1968 – 53 mins
prods Robert Drew, Mike Jackson

Produced by Drew Associates and narrated by Don Morrow, a superficial colour documentary about four jazzmen who are shown interviewed, rehearsing, relaxing and in concert; **Louis Armstrong,** *tpt, voc,* with 'The saints', 'Hello dolly', 'Rose' and 'The kinda love song'; **Dizzy Gillespie,** *voc, tpt,* supported by **James Moody,** *alt sax, ten sax,* with 'Swing low sweet Cadillac'; **Dave Brubeck,** *pno,* supported by **Paul Desmond,** *alt sax,* **Eugene Wright,** *bass,* **Joe Morello,** *drs,* with 'I'm in a dancing mood' and his oratorio 'Light in the wilderness'; **Charles Lloyd,** *flute, ten sax,* supported by **Keith Jarrett,** *pno,* with 'Forest flowers'.

Jazz triptych
see **Tryptyk jazzowy.**

976

Jazzbanditen

West Germany 1959 – 90 mins
dir Bodo Ulrich

A study of The Basin Street Club in Düsseldorf in which young people listen and jive to US jazz records. A very pale shadow of *Momma don't allow.*

977

Jazzoo

USA 1968 – 18 mins
dir John Camie

Colour experimental production about a trip to a zoo in St Louis, Missouri, with an original jazz score by Oliver Lake.

978

Je vous salue Mafia/Da New York: Mafia uccide!

France/Italy 1965 – 88 mins
dir Raoul J. Levy

Thriller about two hired killers sent to France to eliminate a witness to a crime. Music score by **Hubert Rostaing**.

979

Jealous

USA 1942 – 3 mins

Soundie featuring actress Mary Brian and the two-piano team of **Stan Kenton** and Hal Borne.

980

The Jean Goldkette Orchestra on tour

USA 1974 – 5 mins

Recently copyrighted, details unknown.

981

El jefe/The boss

Argentina 1958 – 100 mins
dir Fernando Ayala

Award-winning drama describing the rise and fall of a suburban bully who rules his gang with brutal insight. An early music score by **Lalo Schifrin** is an added asset.

982

Jerry Livingston and His Talk of the Town Music

USA 1939 – 11 mins
dir Lloyd French

Vitaphone short spotlighting popular entertainers including The **Adrian Rollini** Trio.

983

Jesse 'Lone Cat' Fuller

USA 1968 – 25 mins

Rare performances by bluesman **Jesse Fuller** including the songs 'John Henry', 'Red River blues' and 'San Francisco Bay blues', produced by The Seattle Folklore Society.

984

Jeu de massacre/The comic strip hero/The killing game

France 1968 – 95 mins
dir Alain Jessua

The fantastic adventures of a writer of comic strips who investigates a man's claims that he is being hunted by a gang out to kill him. Music score by **Jacques Loussier**.

985

Jeu 1

France 1962 – 15 mins
dir François Reichenbach, Dirk Sanders

Ballet techniques to music by **Jacques Loussier**.

986

Jim Stirling's architecture

UK 1973 – 50 mins
dir Ron Parks

An account of the controversial British architect, made for The Arts Council of GB. Commentator: **George Melly**.

987

Jimmie Lunceford and His Dance Orchestra

USA 1936 – 10 mins
dir Joseph Henabery

Vitaphone music short featuring the title band with The Three Brown Jacks and vocalist Myra Johnson. Numbers: 'Jazznocracy', 'It's rhythm coming to life again', 'Rhythm is our business', 'Nagasaki' and 'You can't pull the wool over my eyes'. Personnel: Eddie Thompkins, **Paul Webster, Sy Oliver**, *tpts;* Elmer Crumbly, Russell Bowles, **Eddie Durham**, *trbs;* **Willie Smith**, Laforet Dent, **Joe Thomas, Earl Carruthers**, *saxes;* **Ed Wilcox**, *pno;* **Al Norris**, *gtr;* Moses Allen, *bass;* **Jimmie Crawford**, *drs,* **Jimmie Lunceford**, *ldr* and *mc.*

988

Jimmy Dorsey

USA c1941 – 3 mins

Soundie details unknown, but features the title leader plus vocalist Bob Eberly.

989

Jimmy Dorsey and His Orchestra

USA 1938 – 10 mins
dir Lloyd French

Vitaphone short in which the title band, with **Ray McKinley**, *drs,* in a nightclub setting, play a programme with vocals from Bob Eberly and Evelyn Oak. Numbers: 'It's the dreamer in me', 'I love you in Technicolor' and 'Dusk in Upper Sandusky'.

990

Jimmy Dorsey and His Orchestra

USA 1940 – 10 mins
dir Leslie Roush

A music programme in Paramount's *Headliner* series featuring the title band with vocalists Helen O'Connell and Bob Eberly. Numbers: 'Bebe', 'My wubba dolly', 'Only a rose' and 'John Silver'.

991

Jimmy Dorsey and His Orchestra
USA 1948 – 15 mins
dir Will Cowan

A Universal-International production featuring the title band backing popular entertainers The Mello-Larks, Dottie O'Brien and Bill Lawrence. Numbers include 'Am I blue?', 'We hate cowboy songs', 'Quien sabe?', 'Jamboree Jones' and 'Lover'.

992

Jimmy Dorsey's varieties
USA 1952 – 15 mins
dir Will Cowan

A Universal Name Band musical in which the title band play seven numbers including 'Sweet Georgia Brown' and 'South Rampart Street parade'. Also features The **Red Norvo** Trio – **Red Norvo**, *vibs;* **Tal Farlow**, *gtr;* **Red Mitchell**, *bass* – playing 'Temptation'.

993

J'Irai cracher sur vos tombes
France 1959 – 105 mins
dir Michel Gast

Melodrama of racial conflict in the deep South involving a white couple and a white-skinned Negro, from the novel by Boris Vian. Jazz compositions and arrangements by Alain Goraguer.

994

Jive busters
USA 1944 – 15 mins
dir Lewis D. Collins

A Universal Name Band musical featuring **Sonny Dunham** and His Orchestra.

995

Jive, little gypsy, jive
USA 1941 – 3 mins

Soundie featuring a gypsy dance by Diana Castillo and a large gypsy band directed by **Bobby Sherwood** with The Three Cheers.

996

Jivin' in be-bop
USA 1947 – 60 mins
dir Leonard Anderson

Crude second feature made for black audiences – a continuous series of musical numbers and dance routines featuring **Dizzy Gillespie** and His Orchestra, including **Milt Jackson**, *vibs;* **John Lewis**, *pno;* **Ray Brown**, *bass;* Kenny Hagood, *voc;* **Helen Humes**, *voc.* Music includes 'Salt peanuts', 'I waited for you', 'Dizzy atmosphere', by **Dizzy Gillespie**, 'Bob a lee-ba' by **Dizzy Gillespie**, John Brown; 'Oop bop sh'bam' by Gil Fuller, **Dizzy Gillespie**, Roberts, 'Shaw 'nuff' by **Charlie Parker, Dizzy Gillespie**, 'A night in Tunisia' by Dizzie Gillespie, Frank Paparelli, 'One bass hit', 'Things to come', by **Dizzy Gillespie**, Gil Fuller, 'Ornithology' by **Charlie Parker**, Benny Harris, 'He beeped when he shoulda bopped' by **Dizzy Gillespie**, Gil Fuller, John Brown, 'Crazy about a man', 'Boogie in C', 'Boogie in D', 'Shoot me a little dynamite eight', 'Grosvenor Square'.

997

Jivin' jam session
USA 1942 – 15 mins
dir Reginald Le Borg

A Universal featurette in which **Sonny Dunham** and His Orchestra entertain supported by Louis Da Pron, Harriet Clark, Jimmie Dodd, The Three Comets and Ray Kellogg. Numbers include 'Don't go west young man', 'Memories of you', 'Nothing' and 'From one love to another'.

Joan
see **Carry it on.**

998

Joe Kidd
USA 1972 – 87 mins
dir John Sturges

Routine Western tailored for the talents of its star, Clint Eastwood, which has its moments but is generally let down by a mediocre story. Melodic, though somewhat twangy, score by **Lalo Schifrin**.

999

Jog along
USA 1946 – 3 mins
dir Dave Gould

Soundie in which the title song is sung by Paula Kelly with **Glenn Miller**'s Modernaires.

1000

John and Mary
USA 1969 – 92 mins
dir Peter Yates

Romantic comedy that succeeds perfectly in doing exactly what it sets out to do – entertain. Music and song 'Maybe tomorrow' by **Quincy Jones**.

1001

The John Coltrane Quartet

USA 1963/4 – c30 mins
dir Richard Moore

Originally produced for US TV by Ralph J. Gleason in his Jazz Casual series on KQED, a rare film record of performances by **John Coltrane**, *ten sax;* supported by **McCoy Tyner**, *pno;* **Jimmy Garrison**, *bass;* **Elvin Jones**, *drs.* Numbers: 'Afro blue', 'Alabama' and 'Impressions'.

1002

John Handy at The Blue Horn

Canada 1965 – 26 mins
dir Brian Guns

Handy talks about his music in a Vancouver jazz club and performs with his group: Michael White, Terry Clarke and Don Thompson.

1003

Johnny Angel

USA 1945 – 79 mins
dir Edwin L. Marin

Routine murder mystery with George Raft, set in New Orleans. Features **Hoagy Carmichael** singing 'Memphis in June' by Paul Francis Webster and **Carmichael**.

1004

Johnny Cool

USA 1963 – 102 mins
dir William Asher

Enjoyable, fast moving gangster movie, based on the book *The kingdom of Johnny Cool* by John McPartland. Music score by **Billy May**.

1005

Johnny Holiday

USA 1949 – 92 mins
dir Willis Goldbeck

Synthetic melodrama about a young delinquent in reform school. Features **Hoagy Carmichael** who also provides the song 'My Christmas song for you'.

1006

The joint is jumpin'

USA 1941 – 3 mins
dir Warren Murray

Soundie in which the title number is played by **Fats Waller**, *pno, voc;* John Hamilton, *tpt;* **Gene Sedric**, *alt sax;* **Al Casey**, *gtr;* Cedric Wallace, *bass;* Wilmore Jones, *drs.*

1007

A jolly bad fellow

UK 1964 – 96 mins
dir Don Chaffey

Awkward and particularly tasteless comedy trying to do what Ealing Studios did much better. Solo jazz organ on soundtrack played by **Alan Haven**.

1008

Jonas

West Germany 1957 – 86 mins
dir Dr Ottomar Domnick

Experimental feature dealing with the problem of guilt-laden loneliness in a big city. The music track features **Duke Ellington**'s composition 'Liberian suite'.

1009

Jordan jive

USA 1944 – 3 mins

Soundie featuring **Louis Jordan**.

1010

Joseph 'n' his brudders

USA 1945 – 3 mins

Soundie with **June Richmond**, backed by dancers performing in an Egyptian setting.

1011

Un jour en Suède

France 1952 – 10 mins
dir Pierre Demarne

A day in the life of a Swedish girl, with music by **Claude Luter**.

1012

Le jour et l'heure/The day and the hour

France/Italy 1963 – 104 mins
dir René Clément

World War II melodrama about an American Air Force pilot shot down over Occupied France in 1944 and his escape to Spain. Music by **Claude Bolling**.

1013

Le journal d'un combat

France 1965 – 18 mins
dir Guy Giles

The story of oil-painting from the bare canvas to the finished work, with music by **Jacques Loussier**.

1014

Journey through Rosebud

USA 1971 – 93 mins
dir Tom Gries

Well-intentioned but insufficiently developed dramatization of the plight of the American Indian in the modern US. Music score by **Johnny Mandel**.

1015

Los jovenes viejos/The sad young men

Argentina 1961 – 101 mins
dir Rodolfo Kuhn

An impressive first feature film by a young Argentine movie buff, about youth's endless search for a *raison d'être*, owing much to Antonioni in general and *L'Avventura* in particular. A superb music score by Sergio Mihanovich, arranged by Oscar López Ruiz, includes several hard-swinging jazz tracks played by Jorge López Ruiz, *bass*; Oscar López Ruiz, *gtr;* Osvaldo Mazzei, *drs*; Rubén López Furst, *pno*; Jorge Barone, *flute*; **Leandro 'Gato' Barbieri**, *ten sax;* Rubén Barbieri, *tpt*; Luis M Casalla, *trb*; Domingo Cura, *conga*; Osvaldo Bissio, *vibs*.

Joy house

see **Les félins**.

The judge and the assassin

see **Le juge et l'assassin**.

1016

Le juge et l'assassin/The judge and the assassin

France 1975 – 125 mins
dir Bertrand Tavernier

Impressive drama charting the relationship between an attorney and a tramp suspected of being responsible for some nasty killings. Music score by Philippe Sarde, directed by **Hubert Rostaing**.

1017

Juke box boogie

USA 1944 – 3 mins

Soundie featuring pianist **Gene Rodgers** with the title number.

1018

Juke box jenny

USA 1942 – 61 mins
dir Harold Young

Formula romance with music about a record salesman who builds a juke box star out of a young singer. Features **Charlie Barnet** and His Orchestra, with **Cliff Leeman**, *drs;* **Wingy Manone** and His Orchestra; The Milt Herb Trio and The King's Men plus the song 'Fifty million nickels' by **Charlie Barnet**.

1019

Juke box Joe's

USA 1944 – 3 mins

Soundie featuring Carol Adams backed by **Wingy Manone**.

1020

Jumpin' at the jubilee

USA 1944 – 3 mins

Soundie with **Louis Jordan** and His Band with dancers The Swing Maniacs.

1021

June Christy with The Ernie Filice Quartet

USA 1950 – 18 mins

Snader Telescriptions featuring the title artistes.

1022

The jungle book

USA 1967 – 78 mins
dir Wolfgang Reithermann

Animated cartoon feature – the last under Disney's personal supervision – based on the 'Mowgli' books by Rudyard Kipling. **Louis Prima** supplies the speaking and singing voice for a character called King Louie of the Apes.

1023

Jungle jive

USA 1944 – 7 mins
dir James Culhane

A Universal *Swing Symphony* cartoon in Technicolor, for which **Bob Zurke** recorded the music only a month before he died.

Jungle sex

see **The black bunch**.

1024

Junior jive bombers

USA 1944 – 10 mins
dir Leroy Prinz

Warner Bros music short featuring interpretations of five popular jazz numbers including 'Blues in the night' and 'Drum boogie'.

J

1025

Junior prom

USA 1946 – 69 mins
dir Arthur Dreifuss

The first production in Monogram's *Teenager* series built around the antics of high school kids. Features **Eddie Heywood** and His Orchestra with 'Loch Lomond' and Abe Lyman and His Orchestra plus vocalist singing 'My heart sings'.

1026

Just a-sittin' and a-rockin'

USA 1945 – 3 mins

Soundie featuring The **Delta Rhythm Boys** with the title number.

1027

Just like a woman

UK 1966 – 89 mins
dir Robert Fuest

A laborious attempt to catch the style and insouciance of the *nouvelle vague* directors, though it is quite pretty to look at. Music score by **Ken Napper**, and an appearance by **Mark Murphy**.

1028

Just routine

UK 1967 – 30 mins
dir Jeff Inman

Ten men and an officer on patrol in the desert around the Persian Gulf attempt to show some attractions of army life. Music by **Kenny Graham**.

1029

Justine

UK 1976 – 90 mins
dir Stewart MacKinnon

Oblique screen adaptation of the novel by the Marquis de Sade in which the dramatic elements have been deliberately pared away to leave a series of tableaux over which the characters recite their lines. A string quartet by **Johnny Hawksworth** is used as soundtrack music.

1030

Jutro premiera/Opening tomorrow

Poland 1962 – c90 mins
dir Janusz Morgenstern

Screen adaptation of the play *The third bell's ringing* by Jerzy Jurandot, set against a background of the theatre. Music by **Krzystof Komeda**.

▲

Louis Armstrong and Velma Middleton having fun in
Kaerlighedens melodi.

1031

Kaerlighedens melodi/Formula for love/A girl, a guitar and a trumpet

Denmark 1959 – 87 mins
dir Bent Christensen

A light-hearted feature with music, mainly a vehicle for its stars Nina and Frederik. **Louis Armstrong, Trummy Young, 'Peanuts' Hucko** and **Velma Middleton** feature in a jazz cellar sequence. The film's musical numbers include 'The formula for love', 'Wonderous, wonderous love', 'Voodoo girl', 'Painting and plugging', 'Blues for Arhoff', 'Hello, pretty one', 'Struttin' with some barbecue', 'So long Emile' and 'For whom the saxes sing'.

1032

Kansas city bomber

USA 1972 – 99 mins
dir Jerrold Freedman

Vulgar, dismally scripted spin-off from the far superior *Roller Derby* with Raquel Welch wasting her undoubted talents as a knockabout roller-skating star. Music score by **Don Ellis**, who also provides music for three songs: 'Rounds and spheres', 'Your way ain't my way, baby' and 'All night market'.

1033

Kansas City Kitty

USA 1944 – 71 mins
dir Del Lord

Low-budget musical comedy tailored for the energetic talents of Miss Joan Davis, featuring **Bob Crosby**.

1034

Karamiai/The inheritance

Japan 1961 – 108 mins
dir Masaki Kobayashi

Quite lunatic but thoroughly enjoyable comedy-drama about the family and friends of a dying industrialist and their pursuit of his fortune. Toru Takemitsu's music score consists entirely of swinging big band jazz tracks heavily influenced by fifties **Gil Evans/Miles Davis** and contains splendid muted trumpet and tenor sax solos.

1035

Kärlek 65/Love 65

Sweden 1965 – 95 mins
dir Bo Widerberg

Bleak, though beautifully observed, autobiographical confession of disenchantment. Juxtaposed on the soundtrack are generous helpings of Vivaldi and **Bill Evans**, the latter playing 'Peace piece'.

1036

Kattorna/The cats

Sweden 1964 – 93 mins
dir Henning Carlsen

Screen adaptation of the play by Valentin Chorelle, set in a laundry and with an all female cast. Music by **Krzystof Komeda**.

Keep all doors open

see **Hall alla doerrar oeppna.**

1037

Keep it cool

USA 1954 – 16 mins

Universal music featurette spotlighting various performers and novelty acts including The **Red Norvo** Trio playing 'How am I to know?'

1038

Kehoe's Marimba Band

USA 1944 – 10 mins

A Columbia vaudeville short presenting the title group, The Winter Sisters, **Glenn Miller** and His Modernaires and Andy Mavo.

1039

Kelly's heroes

USA/Yugoslavia 1970 – 143 mins
dir Brian G. Hutton

Large-scale, old-fashioned war movie with plenty of action and devastating explosions. Music and songs 'Burning bridges' and 'Si tu me dis' by **Lalo Schifrin**.

Kid Ory and His Creole Jazz Band

see **Sarah Vaughan and Herb Jeffries.**

1040

Killer diller

USA 1948 – 80 mins
dir Josh Binney

All Negro production in which a slight plot and a series of vaudeville acts feature popular entertainers Dusty Fletcher, Jackie Mabley etc. Music throughout is supplied by **Andy Kirk** and His Band plus three numbers from The **Nat 'King' Cole** Trio, with **Oscar Moore**, *gtr*, and **Johnny Miller**, *bass*. Numbers include 'Ain't misbehavin'', 'Now he tells me', 'Don't sit on my bed', 'Ooh kick a rooney' and 'Breezy and the bass'.

The killing game

see **Jeu de massacre.**

1041
King Arthur was a gentleman
UK 1942 – 99 mins
dir Marcel Varnel

Dismal comedy vehicle for its star, Arthur Askey, featuring a very young **Victor Feldman**.

1042
'King' Cole and His Trio
USA 1950 – 15 mins
dir Will Cowan

Universal-International featurette with **Nat 'King' Cole, Irving Ashby**, *gtr*, **Joe Comfort**, *bass*, and **Jack Costanzo**, *conga*, supported by **Benny Carter** and His Orchestra plus tap dancer Bunny Briggs, vocalist Dolores Parker and 'Scat Man' Crothers. Numbers include 'Route 66' and 'Ooh kick arooney'.

1043
King Creole
USA 1958 – 116 mins
dir Michael Curtiz

An entangled series of clichés providing a most unattractive vehicle for its star, Elvis Presley; from Harold Robbins's novel. **Al Morgan** appears briefly.

1044
King of burlesque
USA 1935 – 90 mins
dir Sydney Lanfield

Routine 20th Century Fox musical comedy that introduced the songs 'Lonely lady' and 'Shootin' high'. **Fats Waller** is featured playing 'Too good to be true' and 'I've got my fingers crossed'. **Teddy Buckner**, *tpt*, appears with **Waller**.

1045
King of jazz
USA 1930 – 90 mins
dir John Murray Anderson

Spectacular musical extravaganza, in early Technicolor, featuring a variety of popular entertainers of the time. **Paul Whiteman** takes a leading role together with His Band including **Eddie Lang, Joe Venuti, Roy Bargy, Irving Friedman** and the number 'Rhapsody in blue'. Other numbers include 'Happy feet', 'Song of the dawn', 'It happened in Monterey', 'A bench in the park' and 'Ragamuffin Romeo'.

1046
King of kings
USA 1961 – 160 mins
dir Nicholas Ray

Thoroughly tedious, religious spectacular with all the familiar ingredients – battle scenes, orgies, pomp, processions and sentiment, relieved only by Miklós Rózsa's full, rich, music track on which **Shelly Manne** was tympanist.

1047
Kings go forth
USA 1958 – 109 mins
dir Delmer Daves

Conventional US Army melodrama based on the novel by Joe David Brown with a sensitive performance by Tony Curtis. In a dive sequence Tony Curtis borrows a trumpet and solos: the musician he takes it from is **Pete Candoli** who presumably then ghosts the solo. Also in this sequence are **Red Norvo**, *vibs;* **Mel Lewis**, *drs;* **Richie Kamuca**, *ten sax*.

1048
Kiss her goodbye
USA 1958 – 93 mins

Psychological thriller with Elaine Stritch, set in Florida. **Ray Copeland**, *tpt*, and **Frank Socolow**, *ten sax*, are heard on soundtrack with **Johnny Richards**.

1049
Kiss me deadly
USA 1955 – 96 mins
dir Robert Aldrich

Mike Hammer adventure, adapted from a Mickey Spillane story, distinguished by an extraordinary arty style – bold, formalised low-key effects, tilted shots, extreme close-ups, complicated long takes, sometimes *outré* compositions. Frank Devol's score includes a song, 'Rather have The Blues', sung over the opening credits by **Nat 'King' Cole**.

1050
Kiss of death
USA 1947 – 99 mins
dir Henry Hathaway

Influential gangster thriller notable for Richard Widmark's first screen appearance as a sadistic laughing killer. A brief nightclub sequence features a jazz combo with **Jo Jones**, *drs*.

1051
Kiss the boys goodbye
USA 1941 – 85 mins
dir Victor Schertzinger

Routine Paramount musical which includes an appearance by **Connie Boswell**.

Jo Jones in **Kiss of death**.

1052

Kitchen think

UK 1974 – 10 mins
dir Lee Mishkin

An animated cartoon, produced for British Gas, looking at ways that man has developed the art of cooking, with music track by **Johnny Hawksworth**.

Kitten on the keys

see **Do you love me?**

1053

The knack

UK 1965 – 84 mins
dir Richard Lester

Beautifully cast and excitingly photographed adaptation by Charles Wood of Ann Jellicoe's play, marred by a frenzied barrage of unnecessary modish tricks. Jazz organ on soundtrack played by **Alan Haven** and a brief appearance by **George Chisholm** as a porter.

Knife in the water

see **Noz w wodzie.**

1054

København, Kalundborg og –?

Denmark 1934 – 70 mins
dir Ludvig Brandstrup, Holger Madsen

A filmed revue featuring popular radio performers of the period including Erik Tuxen's Orchestra, Roy Fox's Orchestra, Teddy Brown and three terrific numbers from **Louis Armstrong** and His Orchestra: 'I cover the waterfront', 'Dinah' and 'Tiger rag'.

1055

Kongi's harvest

Nigeria/Sweden 1970 – 85 mins
dir Ossie Davis

Satire on contemporary African politics based on the play by Wole Soyinka, with music by **Chris McGregor**.

1056

Lacombe Lucien

France/Italy/West Germany 1974 – 137 mins
dir Louis Malle

Praiseworthy attempt to show how a young person could have been seduced by Fascism purely by force of circumstance; set in southwest France during 1944. Period recordings used on soundtrack include 'Minor swing', 'Manoir de mes rêves', 'Nuages', 'Douce ambiance', 'Fleur d'ennui' and 'Lentement mademoiselle' by The **Quintet of the Hot-Club of France** with **Stephane Grappelly** and **Django Reinhardt**.

1057

The ladies' man

USA 1961 – 106 mins
dir Jerry Lewis

Disappointing second attempt by Jerry Lewis to function as his own producer/director which regresses into infantilism. Features **Harry James**.

1058

Lady and the tramp

USA 1955 – 75 mins
dir H. Luske, C. Geronimi, W. Jackson

Walt Disney's highly successful canine colour cartoon; the first animated feature to be produced in CinemaScope. **Marty Paich** played on and arranged for the music track which includes songs by Peggy Lee and Sonny Burke.

1059

Lady be good

USA 1941 – 111 mins
dir Norman Z. McLeod

Excellent musical, based loosely on the stage production, with a marvellous Gershwin score which includes evergreens such as 'Fascinating rhythm', and 'The last time I saw Paris'. Two additional numbers by Arthur Freed and Roger Edens, 'You'll never know' and 'Your words and my music' add cream to the cake. Features **Jimmy Dorsey** and His Orchestra.

1060

Lady in cement

USA 1968 – 93 mins
dir Gordon Douglas

Uninspired sequel to the same company's *Tony Rome*, based on the novel by Marvin H. Albert and featuring Frank Sinatra as a hang-loose private eye. Bouncy music score composed and conducted by Hugo Montenegro, orchestrated by **Billy May**.

1061

Lady sings The Blues

USA 1972 – 144 mins
dir Sidney J. Furie

Offensively simplified film biography of **Billie Holiday** with Diana Ross as 'Lady Day'. Official credit for the music score goes to Michel Legrand, supervised by Gil Askey, but in fact the latter did about 75% of the scoring, **Oliver Nelson** and **Benny Golson** did two arrangements each and Michel Legrand just wrote the love theme (**Oliver Nelson** was originally hired to do the whole film but cut out after the first week). Soundtrack musicians, conducted by Gil Askey: **Al Aarons, Cat Anderson, Bobby Bryant, Harry Edison**, *tpts;* **Georgie Auld, Buddy Collette, Plas Johnson, Jack Nimitz, Marshall Royal, Ernie Watts**, *saxes;* **George Bohanon, Jimmy Cleveland, Henry Coker, Grover Mitchell,**

Maurice Spears, *trbs;* Max Bennett, Red Callender, *bass;* John Collins, *gtr, bjo;* Earl Palmer, *drs;* Don Abney, Gerald Wiggins, *pno.* Also Teddy Buckner, *tpt;* Chester Lane, *pno;* Arthur Edwards, *bass;* Jesse Sailes, *drs;* John Ewing, *trb;* Caughey Roberts, *clt, sop sax.* Numbers include: 'See see rider blues' by Ma Rainey, ' "Lady" sings the Blues' by Billie Holiday, 'Don't explain', 'Fine and mellow' and 'God bless the child'.

1062
Lambert & Co
USA 1964 – 14 mins
prod R. Leacock, D. Pennebaker

Beautifully observed impression of an audition by Dave Lambert and His Group at the RCA recording studios in Manhattan, brilliantly catching the sheer joyfulness of the music they make. Other singers appearing: Mary Vonnie, David Lucas, Sarah Boatner, Leslie Dorsey.

1063
Lamplight
USA 1941 – 3 mins

Soundie featuring Skinnay Ennis and His Orchestra with Bonnie Kildare.

1064
Lamplighter's serenade
USA 1942 – 3 mins

Soundie featuring a trio of dancers with their partners, backed by Sonny Dunham.

1065
The landlord
USA 1970 – 110 mins
dir Hal Ashby

Based on the novel by Kristin Hunter, Hal Ashby's first feature film as director incisively hits out at all America's sacred cows from motherhood and Sidney Poitier movies to the pervasive myth of the golden liberal heart that beats inside every man of property. Features Pearl Bailey in a leading role.

1066
Les larmes de crocodile
France 1965 – 5 mins
dir Robert Delpire

The story of 'crocodile tears' as told to a small boy by his father. Music by Dave Brubeck.

1067
Larry Johnson
USA 1970 – 20 mins
dir John Hammond Jnr

The young black blues man Larry Johnson sings and plays a programme of traditional blues with confidence and humour.

1068
Las Vegas nights/The gay city
USA 1941 – 87 mins
dir Ralph Murphy

Comedy with music set in Las Vegas, America's last frontier town. Features Tommy Dorsey and His Orchestra with Heine Beau, Johnny Mince, Freddy Stulce, Don Lodice, *saxes;* Joe Bushkin, *pno;* Tommy Dorsey , Lowell Martin, Les Jenkins, George Arus, *trbs;* Jimmy Blake, Ray Linn, Chuck Petersen, Ziggy Elman, *tpts;* Sid Weiss, *bass;* Buddy Rich, *drs,* and The Pied Pipers with Jo Stafford, Connie Haines and Frank Sinatra.

1069
The Las Vegas story
USA 1952 – 88 mins
dir Robert Stevenson

Nicely photographed but otherwise involved story of intrigue, crime and love-hate with possibly the first movie chase sequence to feature a helicopter. Appearance by Hoagy Carmichael as a hack pianist singing 'My resistance is low' and two of his own compositions 'I get along without you very well' and 'The monkey song'.

The last days of man on earth
see The final programme.

1070
The last detail
USA 1973 – 104 mins
dir Hal Ashby

Accomplished screen adaptation of Darryl Ponicsan's novel about two career sailors escorting to a naval prison an underprivileged rating for petty thievery. Johnny Mandel's deliberately spare score uses military airs, notably 'American patrol', with a great deal of drum rolling performed by the ubiquitous Shelly Manne.

1071
The last grenade
UK 1969 – 93 mins
dir Gordon Flemyng

A routine chase thriller with plenty of action and a lot of noise. Music score by John Dankworth.

1072

Last night's gardenias

USA 1941 – 3 mins

Soundie featuring singer Shirley Deane backed by **Bobby Sherwood** and His Orchestra.

The last of the mobile hotshots
see **Blood kin.**

1073

Last of the red hot lovers

USA 1972 – 98 mins
dir Gene Saks

Faithful screen version of Neil Simon's play telling the adventures of one Barney Cashman, happily married for 22 years, trying to make it, 'just once', with another girl. Music score by **Neal Hefti**.

1074

The last of the secret agents

USA 1966 – 92 mins
dir Norman Abbott

Mundane comedy featuring an American duo who make a singularly negative impression. **Neal Hefti**'s song 'You are' is used as backing.

1075

The last safari

UK 1967 – 99 mins
dir Henry Hathaway

Unconvincing jungle adventure, loosely constructed, insecure and unclimactic. Music score by **John Dankworth.**

Last tango in Paris
see **Ultimo tango a Parigi.**

The last woman
see **L'ultima donna.**

1076

Latin lovers

USA 1953 – 104 mins
dir Mervyn LeRoy

A laboured and uninspired melodrama with Lana Turner uncertain as to whether her men friends are more interested in her $37,000,000 than in herself. Orchestrations by **Pete Rugolo.**

1077

Laurence

France 1962 – 9 mins
dir Guy Saguez

Short story about a man's search for his girl, with music by **Lou Bennett**.

1078

The lawbreakers

USA 1960 – 79 mins
dir Joseph M. Newman

Slightly above average 'honest copy in asphalt jungle' thriller: quite watchable. A cool score by **Johnny Mandel**.

1079

Lazy rhythms

USA c1944 – 9 mins

Compilation of three Soundies featuring The **Mills Brothers** with 'Lazy river', 'Rockin' chair' and ' 'til then'.

1080

Lazy river

USA 1944 – 3 mins

Soundie featuring The **Mills Brothers** with **Hoagy Carmichael**'s classic title number.

1081

Lazybones

USA 1941 – 3 mins

Soundie featuring **Hoagy Carmichael** playing and singing his own title composition, plus some comedy dancing by Dorothy Dandridge.

1082

Leadbelly

USA 1976 – 127 mins
dir Gordon Parks

Stiff and lifeless film biography of a black blues singer, played rather well by Roger E. Mosley, inspired by the life of **Huddie Ledbetter**, with songs rendered in an adequate but less than inspired fashion by 'HiTide' Harris. Songs: 'Fannin' Street', 'Governor Pat Neff', 'Cotton fields', 'Bring me li'l' water, Silvy', 'The bourgeois blues', 'Jim Crow', 'Ella Speed', 'The midnight special', 'Ol' rattler/Old Riley' by **Huddie Ledbetter**. **'Blind' Lemon Jefferson** is portrayed by Art Evans. Soundtrack backup musicians include **Brownie McGhee, Sonny Terry**, David Cohen and Dick Rosmini.

1083

The learning tree

USA 1969 – 106 mins
dir Gordon Parks

Sentimental, awkward adaptation by Gordon Parks of his own semi-autobiographical 1963 novel of a youth's struggle toward maturity in a rural Kansas during the 1920's. Parks is also composer of the music score and his title song is sung by **O. C. Smith**. **Jimmy Rushing** has an acting role as a brothel-keeper and sings one blues.

1084
Leave it to Harry
USA 1954 – 15 mins

One day in the life of **Harry James**; recordings, TV sessions etc. Three band spots include 'Don't be that way'.

1085
Legacy
USA 1975 – 79 mins
dir Karen Arthur

Impressive though uneven portrait of a suburban housewife slowly talking herself into madness through a day of domestic routine. Music score by Roger Kellaway, played by Roger Kellaway, *key;* **Gene Cipriano**, *reeds;* Edgar Lustgarten, *cello;* **Chuck Domanica**, *bass;* **Emil Richards**, *perc*.

1086
The legacy of the drum
USA c1970

Documentary featuring **Dizzy Gillespie** in conversation with **Dwike Mitchell** and The **Mitchell-Ruff Duo** plus the voice of **Miles Davis**.

1087
The legend of John Henry
USA 1973 – 14 mins
dir Sam Weiss

Animation emphasising the John Henry character as a folk hero and as an example of the dignity of the 'Black' man. Composer/arranger is Tom McIntosh with new lyrics by Joe Cavella. The narration is sung by **Roberta Flack** backed by **Herbie Hancock, Max Bennett, John Guerin, Victor Feldman** and **Tommy Tedesco**.

1088
Lenny
USA 1974 – 111 mins
dir Bob Fosse

Screen adaptation by Julian Barry of his play about Lenny Bruce and the three people who exerted the greatest influence on his life. Music supervision and scoring by **Ralph Burns** using, among other recordings, 'Well you needn't' by **Thelonius Monk** and 'It never entered my mind'

and 'Tempus fugit' by The **Miles Davis** Quintet. **Jimmy Crawford**, *drs*, appears in one cellar club sequence.

1089
Lenny Bruce without tears
USA 1972 – 85 mins
dir Fred Baker

Uneven documentary about the performer using on soundtrack 'Jazz dance suite' by **Gigi Gryce**.

1090
Leo Reisman and His Hotel Brunswick Orchestra in Rhythms
USA 1929 – 10 mins

Early Vitaphone short with the title band entertaining with a programme that includes **W. C. Handy's** 'St Louis blues'.

1091
Léon la lune
France 1956 – 15 mins
dir Alain Jessua

The life of a tramp in Paris, with music by **Henri Crolla**.

1092
Léon Morin, prêtre
France/Italy 1961 – 117 mins
dir Jean-Pierre Melville

Story of a young widow living in a provincial town in France during the German occupation whose friendship with a young priest develops into love. Music by **Martial Solal**.

1093
Lepke
USA 1974 – 110 mins
dir Menahem Golan

A stiff and po-faced *mélange* of gangster clichés, accurately described by one reviewer as a 'kosher version of *The Godfather*', with Tony Curtis trying hard to build a comprehensible character out of wafer-thin material. One speak-easy sequence features a jazz group which includes **Marshall Royal**.

1094
Les Brown
USA 1948 – 10 mins
dir Jack Scholl

One in the 'Martin Block's Musical Merry-go-round' series in which America's No. 1 disc jockey traces the history of The Band of Renown and its rise to popularity.

1095

Les Brown and His Orchestra

USA c1941 – 3 mins

Soundie No. 704, details unknown.

1096

Les Brown and His Orchestra

USA c1941 – 3 mins

Soundie No. 1207, details unknown.

1097

Les Brown and His Orchestra

USA 1951 – 17 mins

Snader Telescriptions featuring the title orchestra.

1098

Les Brown and The Band of Renown

USA 1949 – 15 mins

dir Will Cowan

Universal-International music short in which the band entertains, supported by The Mello-Larks, Artie Wayne and **Butch Stone**. Numbers: 'Leap frog', 'I've got my love to keep me warm', 'When Francis dances with me', 'I'm the man with the dream', 'I want to be kissed' and 'Bopple sauce'. **Dave Pell**, *ten sax*, is prominent.

1099

Les Brown goes to town

USA 1955 – 15 mins

Universal music featurette with **Les Brown** and His Orchestra plus The Bell Sisters.

1100

Let It Be

UK 1970 – 81 mins

dir Michael Lindsay-Hogg

Straightforward *cinéma-vérité* study of the Beatles at work, with the participation of **Billy Preston**.

1101

Let me off uptown

USA 1942 – 3 mins

Soundie featuring **Gene Krupa** and His Orchestra with the title number. **Anita O'Day** takes the vocal and **Roy Eldridge** is featured on trumpet.

1102

Let no man write my epitaph

USA 1960 – 106 mins

dir Philip Leacock

Sombre melodrama, set in the slums of Chicago in the 1950s, based on the novel by Willard Motley. **Ella Fitzgerald** has an acting role as a dope addict nightclub singer and also briefly sings 'Reach for tomorrow' by Jimmy McHugh and Ned Washington.

1103

Let the good times roll

USA 1973 – 99 mins

dir Sid Levin, Robert Abel

A moving and exciting recreation of 1950's rock 'n' roll frenzy focusing on two revival concerts in 1972 supplemented with other varied footage to present 33 musical numbers. Includes part of a **Fats Domino** performance at Las Vegas's Flamingo Hotel.

1104

Let's do it again

USA 1975 – 113 mins

dir Sidney Poitier

High-spirited yet unassuming entertainment aimed at black audiences, with a particularly funny performance by Bill Cosby. Small acting roles are taken by **Billy Eckstine** and **Med Flory**.

1105

Let's go steady

USA 1945 – 61 mins

dir Del Lord

Teenage musical about two amateur song writers peddling their charts. Features **Skinnay Ennis** and His Orchestra with Mel Tormé and The Meltones.

1106

Let's make music

USA 1940 – 80 mins

dir Leslie Goodwins

Low-budget musical featuring **Bob Crosby** and His Orchestra and the item 'Big noise from Winnetka' by Gil Rodin, **Bob Haggart, Ray Bauduc** and **Bob Crosby**.

1107

Let's make rhythm

USA 1947 – 20 mins

dir Wallace Grissell

RKO-Radio music short; a corny romantic plot strings together a programme of musical items by **Stan Kenton** and His Orchestra: 'Artistry in rhythm', 'Down in Chihuahua' (The Pastels, *voc*, **Pete Rugolo**, *arr*), 'Just a-sittin' and a-rockin'' (**June Christy**, *voc*, **Gene Roland**, *arr*), 'Concerto to end all concertos', 'Tampico' (**June**

L

Christy and The Pastels, *voc*, **Rugolo** and **Roland**, *arr*). Personnel: **Buddy Childers, Ray Wetzel, Chico Alvarez,** John Anderson, **Ken Hanna,** *tpts;* **Kai Winding,** 'Skip' Layton, **Milt Bernhart, Harry Forbes,** *trbs;* **Bart Varsalona,** *bas-trb;* Eddie Meyers, **'Boots' Mussulli,** *alt sax;* **Vido Musso, Bob Cooper,** *ten ax;* **Bob Gioga,** *bar-sax;* **Stan Kenton,** *pno;* **Bob Ahern,** *gtr;* **Eddie Safranski,** *bass;* **Shelly Manne,** *drs*.

1108

Les liaisons dangereuses 1960
France 1959 – 106 mins
dir Roger Vadim

Glossy and superficial adaptation of Choderlos de Laclos's savage novel, updated to 1960. Music score credited to Jack Marray (pseud). Underscore consists of **Thelonius Monk** themes specially recorded in New York by **Monk,** *pno;* **Charlie Rouse,** *ten sax;* **Sam Jones,** *bass;* **Art Taylor,** *drs*: 'Crepescule with Nellie', 'Ba-lue bolivar ba-lues-are', 'Rhythm-a-ning', 'Well you needn't', 'Light blue', 'Pannonica' and one other. Source music for both the nightclub and party sequences composed for the movie by **Duke Jordan** and played by **Art Blakey**'s Jazz Messengers: **Lee Morgan,** *tpt;* **Barney Wilen,** *ten sax, sop sax;* **Bobby Timmons** and **Duke Jordan,** *pno;* **Jymie Merritt,** *bass;* **Art Blakey,** *drs*: 'No problem', 'Prelude in blue', 'Miguel's party' and 'Valmontana'. During the party sequence, the performers on camera (unsynchronised) are **Kenny Dorham,** *tpt;* **Barney Wilen,** *ten sax;* **Duke Jordan,** *pno;* Paul Rovere, *bass;* **Kenny Clarke,** *drs*.

1109

Lies my father told me
Canada 1975 – 102 mins
dir Jan Kadar

A nostalgic, morally black and white fairy-tale which sermonises about the bad effect of immigration on the integrity of a Jewish family. Music director Sol Kaplan uses his own song 'Rags, clothes, bottles' on soundtrack as well as 'I'm just wild about Harry' by **Eubie Blake** and **Noble Sissle,** performed by Tony Carroll.

1110

Life is real
USA c1934

Black-produced movie; details unknown except that it featured **Nina Mae McKinney.**

1111

The life of Riley
USA 1949 – 87 mins
dir Irving Brecher

Domestic melodrama based on a popular US radio feature. With the participation of **Red Callender.**

Life together
see **La vie à deux.**

Life upside down
see **La vie à l'envers.**

Lift to the scaffold
see **Ascenseur pour l'échafaud.**

1112

'Lightnin'' Sam Hopkins
USA 1967 – 8 mins

Produced for the University of Washington Archives of Ethnic Music and Dance, an informal performance by one of the best-known country blues guitar players. Songs: 'Baby, please don't go' ('Another man done gone'); 'Mojo hand' and 'Take me back'.

1113

Limehouse blues
Netherlands 1953 – 3 mins
dir Emile van Moerkerken

Carefully edited compilation of material from the late 1930s illustrating a recording of 'Limehouse blues' by **Duke Ellington** and His Orchestra.

1114

Line/Passionate demons
Norway 1961 – 90 mins
dir Nils Reinhardt Christensen

A rather sensational story about young people in a provincial town, though charmingly played, is backed by a score written by Egil Monn-Iversen played by top Norwegian jazzmen with **Don Byas,** *ten sax.*

1115

The linesman
UK 1965 – 20 mins
dir Peter Griffiths

Men at work on the construction of a transmission line in North Wales carrying power 34 miles from the nuclear power station at Trawsfynydd. Music score by **Johnny Hawksworth.**

1116

Lionel Hampton and Herb Jeffries
USA 1955 – 15 mins
dir Will Cowan

Universal-International music short spotlighting **Lionel Hampton** and His Band with Vicky Lee singing 'Baby, don't love me', Lolay White singing 'Black coffee' and The Four Hamptons gyrating.

1117
Lionel Hampton and His Orchestra

USA 1949 – 14 mins
dir Will Cowan

One of the very best of the Universal-International music shorts, which features the title band (**Ed Mullins,** *tpt;* **Al Grey, Jimmy Cleveland,** *trb;* **Bobby Plater,** *alt sax;* **Wes Montgomery,** *gtr*), plus William 'Carley' Hamner, Lorene (Betty) Carter, *voc,* Sonny Parker, *voc,* Kitty Murray, Joe Adams and Lawrence and Lillian Williams. **Hampton** leads the proceedings and dances as well as soloing on drums, *vibs* and *alt sax.* Numbers include 'Wee Albert', 'Airmail special', 'Robbin's nest', 'Hamp's gumbo' and 'Flying home'.

1118
Lionel Hampton and His Orchestra

USA 1951 – 19 mins

Snader Telescriptions featuring the title band.

1119
Liquid jazz

USA 1962 – 5 mins
dir Joseph Kramer

Abstract images produced from the movement of coloured liquids, accompanied by Dixieland jazz by Trevor Duncan.

1120
The liquidator

UK 1965 – 104 mins
dir Jack Cardiff

Gloomy pastiche of the spy film formula, with music score and title song by **Lalo Schifrin.**

1121
The Lisbon story

UK 1945 – 101 mins
dir Paul L. Stein

Appalling melodrama, with music, full of the usual screen Nazis and Occupied Europe clichés. Features **Stephane Grappelly.**

1122
Listen to Larry

USA 1940 – 9 mins
dir Leslie Roush

Larry Clinton and His Orchestra entertain, supported by vocalists Terry Allen, Helen Southern and Jimmy Curry.

1123
Listen to my music

UK 1961 – 9 mins
dir Robert Henryson

Music short featuring **Ted Heath** and His Band playing 'Sidewalks of Cuba', 'The champ' and 'Ill wind'.

1124
Listen to the bands

USA 1944 – 8 mins
dir Jean Negulesco

Four top bands of the day entertain with popular numbers; Glen Gray, **Skinnay Ennis**, Joe Reichman and Milt Britton.

1125
Little cigars

USA 1973 – 92 mins
dir Chris Christenberry

A gang of midget bank robbers embark on a cross-country crime spree. Music score by **Harry Betts.**

1126
Little girl

USA c1952 – 3 mins

Snader Telescription in which **Nat 'King' Cole,** *pno, voc,* interprets the title number, supported by **Irving Ashby,** *gtr;* **Joe Comfort,** *bass;* **Jack Costanzo,** *conga.*

1127
Little murders

USA 1971 – 108 mins
dir Alan Arkin

Jules Feiffer's screen adaptation of his own play: a fantasy about a family under siege from the massed horrors of American urban life. The soundtrack utilises 'Skating in Central Park' by **John Lewis,** performed by The **Modern Jazz Quartet.**

1128
The little shop of horrors

USA 1960 – 70 mins
dir Roger Corman

Good-humoured, low-budget horror comedy which is rumoured to have been shot in the incredible time of two days. Music score by **Fred Katz.**

L

1129

Live and let die

UK 1973 – 121 mins
dir Guy Hamilton

The eighth James Bond movie, packed with
memories of the old Saturday morning serials . . .
Contains two brief appearances by The **Olympia
Brass Band** and a small speaking role goes to
trumpeter **Alvin Acorn** as an assassin.

1130

Live it up

UK 1963 – 74 mins
dir Lance Comfort

A slight story is used as a peg on which to hang
a string of musical numbers mainly in the popular
idiom. Features **Kenny Ball** and His Jazzmen,
one of whose numbers is a perversion of the
'Turkish' March from Mozart's *A Major Piano
Sonata*, K331.

1131

Living jazz

UK 1961 – 43 mins
dir Jack Gold

An attempt to convey something of the life of a
professional jazz musician in Britain, featuring
The **Bruce Turner** Jump Band with **Turner**, *alt
sax;* **John Chilton**, *tpt;* **John Mumford**, *trb;*
Collin Bates, *pno,* **Jim Bray**, *bass;* **Johnny
Armitage**, *drs.* All the music written and arranged
by **Bruce Turner**.

1132

Liza/La cagna

France/Italy 1972 – 100 mins
dir Marco Ferreri

Harsh, oblique look at society today and those
who negate it, adapted from a book by Ennia
Flaiano. Philippe Sarde's music score includes a
theme played on clarinet by **Hubert Rostaing**,
with violin solos by **Stephane Grappelly**.

1133

Le locataire/The tenant

France 1976 – 126 mins
dir Roman Polanski

Unconvincing screen adaptation of Roland
Topor's bizarre novel *Le locataire chimérique* – a
story of a bureaucratic clerk's paranoid
breakdown. Suitably gloomy music score by
Philippe Sarde, directed by **Hubert Rostaing**.

1134

Lol Coxhill

UK 1973 – 25 mins
dir Mick Audsley

A portrait of the musician, produced by the Royal
College of Art's Department of Film and
Television.

▲

Lol Coxhill (TCB Releasing).

L

1135

London Town/My heart goes crazy

UK 1946 – 119 mins
dir Wesley Ruggles

Disastrous attempt at making a Technicolor British musical featuring comedian Sid Field, with an appearance by **Jack Parnell**.

1136

The loneliness of the long distance runner/ Rebel with a cause

UK 1962 – 104 mins
dir Tony Richardson

Fashionable drama of a young, disingenuous, social outlaw, adapted by Alan Sillitoe from his own short story: all fussy stylistic devices and restless tricksiness. John Addison's music score contains a jazz sequence played by **Pat Halcox**, *tpt*; **Bill Bramwell**, *gtr*; **Dick Smith**, *bass*; and **Danny Craig**, *drs*.

The loner

see **Le solitaire**

1137

The lonesome road

USA 1941 – 3 mins

Soundie featuring **Sister Tharpe**.

1138

The long goodbye

USA 1973 – 111 mins
dir Robert Altman

Outrageous screen adaptation of Raymond Chandler's novel transposed to a 1970's setting. The soundtrack features a title song – by John T. Williams and Johnny Mercer – performed by six different artists, one of whom is trumpeter **Jack Sheldon**.

The long ride home

see **A time for killing.**

1139

The long stripe

USA 196?

Porno movie for which The **Elvin Jones** Trio recorded about 50 minutes of soundtrack music – possibly not used in the final cut.

1140

Look back in anger

UK 1959 – 101 mins
dir Tony Richardson

Tony Richardson's first feature film – a relatively straightforward adaptation of John Osborne's famous play. Music by **Chris Barber** and His Band with **Pat Halcox**, *tpt*, and **Monty Sunshine**, *clar*.

1141

Lord love a duck

USA 1965 – 105 mins
dir George Axelrod

One of the most underrated movies of all time – an extremely witty satire of American morals and mores. Tuesday Weld's central performance is a revelation. Lively music score and title song by **Neal Hefti**.

1142

Lord Shango

USA 1975 – 91 mins
dir Raymond Marsh

Above average low-budget drama focusing upon the conflicts in black heritage: tribal roots vs Southern Christian tradition. Music score composed and conducted by **Howard Roberts** blending gospel and tribal rhythms.

1143

Lost in a harem

USA 1944 – 89 mins
dir Charles Reisner

Abbott and Costello farce, in an Eastern setting. **Jimmy Dorsey** and His Orchestra, including **Si Zentner**, *trb*, and **Bobby Schutz**, *drs*, are featured in two musical sequences; the first, very brief, has the band marching in Arab costume; the second, a good hard-swinging up-tempo number, while at least a self-contained sequence, utilises trick photographic effects which exploit the musicians, still in Arab costume, for all they're worth.

The lost lady

see **Safe in hell.**

1144

The lost man

USA 1969 – 122 mins
dir Robert Alan Aurthur

Disastrous adaptation of *Odd man out* updated to 1969. Music and songs by **Quincy Jones**.

1145

Louis Armstrong

USA 1963/4 – c30 mins
dir Richard Moore

Originally produced for US TV by Ralph J. Gleason in his Jazz Casual series on KQED, a programme devoted to the life and work of **Louis Armstrong** in which he discusses and demonstrates his music with R.J.G.

1146

Louis Armstrong

USA 1971 – 9 mins

A brief, efficient, biography of the entertainer using part of an interview with Satchmo himself, stills, newsreel material, TV recordings and a film clip of him singing 'I can't give you anything but love'. Includes footage of His All Stars in action.

1147

Louis Armstrong and The All Stars

USA 1961 – 25 mins
prod Mike Bryan

A programme by the title group, made in colour for the Goodyear Tyre Company. Musicians: **Louis Armstrong**, *tpt, voc;* **Trummy Young**, *trb;* **Joe Darensbourg**, *clar;* **Billy Kyle**, *pno;* **Billy Cronk**, *bass;* **Danny Barcelona**, *drs,* Jewell Brown, *voc.* Numbers: 'Sleepy time down South', 'C'est si bon', 'Some day', 'Jerry', 'Nobody knows the trouble I've seen' and 'The saints'.

1148

Louis Jordan Medley No.1 & No.2

USA c1944 – 9 mins each

Two compilations of Soundies, each consisting of three popular numbers played by **Louis Jordan** and His Band.

1149

Les loups dans la bergerie

France 1959 – 85 mins
dir Hervé Bromberger

Unprepossessing melodrama conceived upon familiar second-feature lines. Some good swinging jazz arrangements on soundtrack by Alain Goraguer.

1150

Love and hisses

USA 1937 – 84 mins
dir Sidney Lanfield

Second round in the screen feud, started in *Wake up and live*, between Walter Winchell and Ben Bernie, with Simone Simon supplying the romance. **Charlie Barnet** has a small acting part.

Love and other crimes

see **Alex and the gypsy.**

The love cage

see **Les félins.**

Love 65

see **Kärlek 65.**

1151

Love that brute

USA 1950 – 85 mins
dir Alexander Hall

Gangster comedy set in the Chicago of prohibition and gang war, though it conveys no sense of place or of 1920's atmosphere. Features **Zutty Singleton**.

1152

Love turns winter to spring

USA 1941 – 3 mins

Soundie in which an ice-skating number is sung by Martha Tilton backed by **Bobby Sherwood** and His Orchestra plus comedian Vince Barnett.

1153

Lover

USA c1952 – 3 mins

Telescription featuring **Jack Teagarden** playing the title number.

Lovers must learn

see **Rome adventure.**

1154

Love's got me in a lazy mood

USA c1952 – 3 mins

Telescription of The **Bobcats** playing the title number.

1155

Low down dog

USA 1944 – 3 mins

Soundie featuring **Meade Lux Lewis** playing the title number.

1156

Lucebert, dicter-schilder

Netherlands 1962 – 15 mins
dir Johan van der Keuken

Impressions of the Dutch poet and painter Lucebert; his work, his studio, his views on the world. Recorded music by Paul Hindemith and **John Coltrane** is used on the soundtrack.

L

1157
Lucky lady
USA 1975 – 118 mins
dir Stanley Donen

Conspicuously overproduced action picture set in Tijuana, 1930, providing only a few minutes of good old-fashioned entertainment. The music score by **Ralph Burns** uses, among other songs, 'Empty bed blues' by and sung by **Bessie Smith** and 'Ain't misbehavin'' by **Fats Waller** and Andy Razaf, sung by Burt Reynolds.

1158
Lucky Luciano
Italy/France 1973 – 115 mins
dir Francesco Rosi

An enquiry into the mechanics of power politics played around the story of an ex-Mafia activist. The song 'Moonlight serenade' by **Glenn Miller** and Mitchell Parish is strongly featured.

1159
Lucky Luke
France/Belgium 1971 – 76 mins
dir René Goscinny

A full-length colour cartoon based on the widely syndicated European comic-strip, combining many of the stock Western situations and characters into a vehicle for its chain-smoking hero – the laconic Lucky Luke. Music score by **Claude Bolling**.

1160
Luv
USA 1967 – 96 mins
dir Clive Donner

Embarrassingly inept adaptation of Murray Schisgal's play about the language of love in a Freud-ridden society. Music by and played by **Gerry Mulligan** with orchestrations by **Bill Holman**.

1161

Machine mon amie

France 1961 – 17 mins
dir Louis Daquin

Industrial short on the relationship between machine and man. Jazz score by **'Lucky' Thompson** accompanied by **Kenny Clarke, Martial Solal** and **Guy Pedersen**.

1162

Mackenna's gold

USA 1968 – 136 mins
dir J. Lee Thompson

Long, rambling and thoroughly cliché Western, not quite bad enough to be funny. Thumping music score and song 'Old turkey buzzard' by **Quincy Jones**.

1163

Mad at the world

USA 1955 – 63 mins
dir Harry Essex

Formula 'B' movie about juvenile delinquents with some arty photography and official police moralising thrown in for good measure. A band sequence features **Howard Rumsey**'s Lighthouse All Stars playing **Bob Cooper**'s 'Witch Doctor'.

The mad hatter
see **Breakfast in Hollywood.**

Madam Kitty
see **Salon Kitty.**

1164

Madame Bovary

USA 1949 – 114 mins
dir Vincente Minnelli

A grotesque distortion of Gustave Flaubert's novel with all his richly drawn characters reduced to the worst Hollywood cliché figures. The pianist heard frequently on Miklós Rósza's music track is **Mel Powell**.

1165

Madame Sin

UK 1972 – 90 mins
dir David Greene

A half-hearted attempt at a thriller, with a dull script, a wooden hero and an abysmal ending. Music score by **Michael Gibbs**.

1166

Made in Paris

USA 1966 – 103 mins
dir Boris Sagal

Light romantic comedy with music and dancing set in a Metrocolored Paris. Features **Count Basie** and His Octet, **Mongo Santamaria** and His Band and one song by **Quincy Jones**.

1167

The magic of music

UK 1955 – 13 mins
dir Horace Shepherd

A rather cheaply made musical kaleidoscope interesting only for a featured performance of **George Shearing**'s 'Lullaby of Birdland'.

1168
Le magnifique/How to destroy the reputation of the greatest secret agent
France/Italy 1973 – 93 mins
dir Philippe de Broca

Uneven, quirky, adventure spoof featuring a breezy, ineptly acrobatic Jean-Paul Belmondo. Music score by **Claude Bolling**.

1169
Magnum force
USA 1973 – 122 mins
dir Ted Post

Routine followup to *Dirty Harry* in which the non-conformist San Francisco detective tracks down a band of vigilante cops. **Lalo Schifrin** again provides a moody score.

1170
The Magus
UK 1968 – 116 mins
dir Guy Green

Disappointing screen adaptation by John Fowles of his own superb novel. Music score by **John Dankworth**.

1171
Mahalia Jackson
USA 1961

A composite reel of numbers selected from a series of shows originally produced for US TV: 'Down by the riverside', 'He's got the whole world in his hand', 'His eye is on the sparrow', 'It's no secret', 'I know it was the blood', 'Nobody knows the trouble I've seen', 'Precious Lord', 'Somebody bigger than you or I', 'To me it's so wonderful' and 'Tell it, sing it, shout it'.

Mahalia Jackson (1974)
see **Got to tell it: A tribute to Mahalia Jackson**.

1172
Mahalia Jackson No. 62
USA 1961 – 29 mins
prod Irving Townsend

Originally made for TV, a programme of religious songs subtitled 'Have thine own way Lord', featuring Louise Weaver, *pno;* **Barney Kessel**, *gtr;* **Red Mitchell**, *bass;* **Shelly Manne**, *drs;* and Edward C. Robinson, *org*.

1173
Mahalia Jackson No. 76
USA 1961 – 32 mins
prod Irving Townsend

A programme of religious songs, originally made for TV, subtitled **Bless this House**.

1174
Maidstone
USA 1970 – 110 mins
dir Norman Mailer

Mailer has described this very personal statement as 'a military operation . . . an attack on reality in which you discover what the reality of your attack is by attacking . . .' Music used on soundtrack by **Wes Montgomery** and The **Modern Jazz Quartet**.

1175
Les mains d'Orlac/The hands or Orlac
France/UK 1960 – 105 mins
dir Edmond T. Gréville

Limping up-dated version of Maurice Renard's lurid horror novel, previously filmed by Robert Wiene in 1924 with Conrad Veidt and remade some ten years later by Karl Freund with Peter Lorre. Has an excellent jazz soundtrack composed by **Claude Bolling** and played by His Orchestra.

1176
Make believe ballroom
USA 1949 – 78 mins
dir Joseph Santley

Routine musical but rich in jazz appearances. Features **Jimmy Dorsey** and His Orchestra, **Pee Wee Hunt** and His Band, **Charlie Barnet** and His Band, **Gene Krupa** and His Band and The **'King' Cole** Trio.

1177
Make mine music/Swing street
USA 1945 = 75 mins
dir J. Kinney, C. Geronimi, H. Luske, B. Cormack, J. Meador

Disney Technicolor revue in ten scenes with several memorable sequences involving music by **Benny Goodman**; The Quartet with 'After you've gone' and The Orchestra with 'All the cats join in'. Participating musicians include **Cozy Cole, Sid Weiss** and **Teddy Wilson**.

Making it
see **Les valseuses**.

1178
The making of a President, 1960
USA 1964 – 81 mins
dir Mel Stuart

Originally produced for US TV, a compilation project on the Kennedy/Nixon campaign and camera accounts of later political events. Music score by **Lalo Schifrin**.

1179

Mal Waldron

West Germany c1971 – 17 mins
dir Hans-Gert Hillgruber

Mal Waldron, *elec pno;* **Jimmy Jackson**, *org;* plus *elec bass* and *drs* work out in a studio. The pianist talks about his life and work.

1180

Malcolm X

USA 1972 – 91 mins
prod Marvin Worth, Arnold Perl

A film biography of Malcolm Little using stock footage, speeches, interviews and film clips together with early biographical details narrated by James Earl Jones and his funeral with Ossie Davis eulogizing. Excellent soundtrack includes **Billie Holiday**'s singing of 'Strange fruit' and 'God bless the child', **Duke Ellington**'s Orchestra playing 'The mooche', **Slim and Slam**'s 'Flat foot floogie' and a more contemporary song 'Nigggers are scared of revolution' sung by The Last Poets.

1181

Mama's dirty girls

USA 1974 – 80 mins
dir John Hayes

Witless comic-strip welter of murders and seductions, with a music score by **Don Bagley** and Steve Michaels.

1182

Mame

USA 1974 – 131 mins
dir Gene Saks

Screen adaptation of the 1966 musical play, based on the 1956 play, based on the 1954 novel, previously filmed in 1958, set in 1928. Orchestrations by **Ralph Burns** and **Billy Byers**. One party sequence features a Negro band consisting on camera of: Harland C. Evans, *pno;* William A. Allen, *clar;* **Andrew Blakeney**, *tpt;* Benjamin A. Booker, *tuba;* Bobby Price, *drs,* who are ghosted on soundtrack by **Sol Gubin**, *drs;* **Roland Bundock**, *bass;* Donald G. Aldrop, *tuba;* **Abe Most**, *clar;* **John Best**, *tpt;* Herbert Harper, *trb;* **Artie Kane**, *pno.*

Mammals
see **Ssaki.**

1183

Mammy

USA 1930 – 85 mins
dir Michael Curtiz

Music drama tailored for the talents of its star Al Jolson, from an earlier Irving Berlin musical comedy. Features pianist **Paul Lingle** and the songs 'To my mammy', 'Across the breakfast table looking at you', 'Let me sing and I'm happy' and 'Knights of the road'.

Mam'zelle Pigalle
see **Cette sacrée gamine.**

1184

Man and boy

USA 1971 – 98 mins
dir E. W. Swackhamer

Old-fashioned, sentimental, black Western with star Bill Cosby showing that there were some tough black folks in the Old West. Music score composed by **J. J. Johnson** and supervised by **Quincy Jones**.

1185

A man called Adam

USA 1966 – 103 mins
dir Leo Penn

Corny backstage melodrama about non-violence and the colour problem. The music is by **Benny Carter; Louis Armstrong** plays an ageing trumpeter and Sammy Davis Jnr mimes some good jazz – ghosted by **Nat Adderley**. Other musicians appearing include **Billy Kyle**, *pno;* **Buster Bailey**, *clar;* **Tyree Glenn**, *trb;* **Kai Winding**, *trb;* **'Pops' Foster**, *bass;* **Jo Jones**, *drs;* **Frank Wess** and Mel Tormé singing 'All that jazz'. Also the numbers 'Whisper to one', 'Back o'town blues', 'Someday sweetheart', 'Muskrat ramble', 'I want to be wanted' and 'Playboy theme'.

1186

The man called Flintstone

USA 1966 – 87 mins
dir Joseph Barbera, William Hanna

Crudely animated full length colour cartoon about the simple antics of Fred Flintstone and his friends. Music partly by **Marty Paich** and the song 'Pensate amore' sung by **Louis Prima**.

1187

Man on a swing

USA 1974 – 108 mins
dir Frank Perry

▲

*A party sequence in **Mame** in which Andrew Blakeney, tpt, and William A. Allen, clar, are miming to pre-recorded tracks by John Best, tpt, and Abe Most, clar.*

Talky, low-key, murder melodrama as much a puzzle to its characters as to its audience. Unimpressive music score by **Lalo Schifrin**.

1188

Man that's groovy

USA 1943 – 3 mins

Soundie featuring **Jimmy Dorsey** and His Band, with vocalist Helen O'Connell.

1189

The man who fell to earth.

UK 1976 – 138 mins
dir Nicolas Roeg

Screen adaptation of the novel by Walter Tevis and accurately described by one critic as 'an extremely photogenic mess'. Among the many recordings used on soundtrack are 'Blueberry hill', performed by **Louis Armstrong** and 'Stardust' by **Hoagy Carmichael** and Mitchell Parish, performed by **Artie Shaw** and His Orchestra.

1190

The man who had power over women

UK 1960 – 90 mins
dir John Krish

Superficial drama about the spiritual guilt and cowardice bred by commercial compromise. Music score by **Johnny Mandel**.

1191

Man with a funny horn

USA

Details unknown – a film impression of trombonist 'Snub' Mosley.

1192

The man with the golden arm

USA 1955 – 118 mins
dir Otto Preminger

Probably Sinatra's finest screen performance as Frankie Machine, aspiring jazz drummer, who tries to rid himself of his habit – the '40 pound monkey on his back'. Memorable music by Elmer Bernstein with jazz sequences arranged and played by **Shorty Rogers**, with **Shelly Manne, Pete Candoli, Milt Bernhart, Bud Shank, Frank Rosolino, Bob Cooper** and **Ralph Pena**, all of whom also appear in a rehearsal sequence which even gives **Rogers** a few lines of dialogue. **Shelly Manne**'s further functions on the movie are as 'personal assistant' to Mr Preminger and 'tutor' to Mr Sinatra.

1193

The man with the weird beard

USA 1946 – 3 mins
dir Dave Gould

Soundie in which vocalist Debby Claire sings the title number backed by **Ray Bauduc** and His Band.

1194

The Manchurian candidate

USA 1962 – 126 mins
dir John Frankenheimer

George Axelrod's brilliant and very faithful adaptation of Richard Condon's novel about brain-washing and political assassination. Music score by **David Amram**.

1195

La mandarine

France 1971 – 90 mins
dir Edouard Molinaro

Screen adaptation of the book by Christine de Rivoyre, about an inbred family running a posh hotel in Paris. Music by **Claude Bolling**.

1196

Mandingo

USA 1975 – 126 mins
dir Richard Fleischer

Screen adaptation of the novel by Kyle Onstott and the play by Jack Kirkland – a tale of Deep

South atrocities. The song 'Born in this time' is sung on soundtrack by **'Muddy' Waters**.

1197

Manhattan merry-go-round/Manhattan music box

USA 1937 – 78 mins
dir Charles F. Reisner

Musical comedy about a gangster who inherits a music company and tries to threaten his way to success. Features **Jack Jenney** and His Orchestra, **Cab Calloway** and His Cotton Club Orchestra, **Ted Lewis** and His Orchestra and **Louis Prima** and His Band.

Manhattan music box

see **Manhattan merry-go-round**.

1198

Mann with a flute

USA 1960 – 14 mins
dir Tom Craven

A portrait of jazz flautist **Herbie Mann**, made originally for US TV.

Människor möts och ljuv musik uppstär i hjärtet

see **Mennesker modes og sod musik opstår i hjertet**.

1199

Many happy returns

USA 1934 – 66 mins
dir Norman McLeod

Musical comedy based on the novel *Mr Dayton, darling* by Lady Mary Cameron (pseud.) featuring Burns and Allen with Guy Lombardo and His Royal Canadians. **Duke Ellington** actually plays piano on soundtrack though Guy Lombardo receives the credit.

1200

Maracaibo

USA 1958 – 88 mins
dir Cornel Wilde

Simple adventure story set in Venezuela that crams in water-skiing, flamenco dancing and spectacular fire fighting. Music by **Laurindo Almeida**.

1201

March of time 1st year no. 2

USA 1935 – 22 mins

Contains a sequence entitled *Leadbelly* charting **Huddie Leadbetter**'s prison sentence and his eventual pardon.

1202

March of time   3rd year no. 7
USA 1937 – 20 mins

One chapter is a 6 minute *reportage* entitled *The Birth of Swing* in which the main feature is the rediscovery of The **Original Dixieland Jazz Band** who are shown recording and playing their own 'Tiger rag'. Reference is made to **Red Norvo, Benny Goodman** and **Chick Webb**.

1203

March of time   9th year no. 8
USA 1943 – 16 mins

Subtitled *Upbeat in Music* this edition of the series deals with the status of music during the war, with reference to Captain **Glenn Miller** and His Army Band and maestros **Paul Whiteman** and **Tommy Dorsey**.

1204

March of time   10th year no. ?
USA 1944 – 16 mins

A chapter of the series subtitled *Music in America* dealing with the concert hall, recital room, opera, popular music and jazz. **Benny Goodman** lectures at Juillard and appears with His Band playing 'Henderson stomp' (**Gene Krupa**, *drs*); he recreated **Original Dixieland Jazz Band** works in a recording studio and **Art Tatum** appears at The Three Deuces plus The **Eddie Condon** All Stars and George Gershwin at the piano playing 'I got rhythm'.

1205

March of time   14th year no. 10
USA 1948 – 20 mins

Called *It's in the groove* this episode concentrates on a brief history of the recording industry, from Edison to the first LP. There are brief appearances by The **Original Dixieland Jazz Band, Eddie Condon**'s All Stars and **Paul Whiteman** and His Orchestra plus soundtrack use of 'Wow' by The **Lennie Tristano** Sextette.

1206

March of time   15th year no. 4
USA 1950 – 17 mins

A chapter examining the state of the world in 1950, subtitled *Mid century: halfway to where?* which briefly features The **Wild Bill Davison** Orchestra.

1207

Margie
USA 1946 – 94 mins
dir Henry King

Light, Technicolored, romantic comedy about middle class life in small-town America in the late 1920s. Features the song 'Wonderful one' by Dorothy Terriss, **Paul Whiteman** and Ferde Grofe.

1208

Marion Brown
West Germany c1971 – 23 mins

Colour study of **Marion Brown**, *reeds;* **Leo Smith**, *perc, tpt;* and 'assistants' working out in a studio and talking about their 'free' music.

1209

The Marseille contract
UK/France 1974 – 90 mins
dir Robert Parrish

Perfunctorily scripted and directed *policier* embroidered with glowing photography. Soundtrack use is made of ' 'Round midnight' by **Thelonius Monk, Cootie Williams** and Bernie Hanighen, performed by The Fellings Quartet.

1210

Mary Lou
USA 1948 – 65 mins
dir Arthur Dreifuss

Cheerful enough second-feature about an air hostess who becomes a nightclub vocalist. **Jack Costanzo** appears as a dancer.

1211

M-A-S-H
USA 1969 – 116 mins
dir Robert Altman

Wild, irreverent, blasphemous army comedy based on the novel by Richard Hooker: highly intelligent and extremely funny. Music and song 'Suicide is painless' by **Johnny Mandel** and a brief appearance by **Bobby Troup** in the role of Sgt. Gorman.

1212

Masks and memories
USA 1934 – 25 mins
dir Roy Mack

Vitaphone short set in New Orleans and starring Lillian Roth, which includes among its musical numbers **Duke Ellington**'s 'Sophisticated lady'.

1213

The master gunfighter
USA 1975 – 121 mins
dir Frank Laughlin (Tom Laughlin)

Western re-working of the 1969 Japanese samurai movie *Goyokin* – a violent revenge story. Music score by **Lalo Schifrin**.

Me, a groupie
see **Ich – ein Groupie.**

1214

Me and the boys
UK 1929 – 6 mins
dir Victor Saville

A British-produced music short, made in RKO's New York City studios by Victor Saville while he was adding dialogue to his silent picture, *Kitty*, and starring Estelle Brody whom he had brought with him from London. A band consisting of **Jimmy McPartland**, *tpt;* **Jack Teagarden**, *trb;* **Benny Goodman**, *clar;* Dick Morgan, *gtr;* Vic Breidis, *pno*; and **Ray Bauduc**, *drs*, accompanies Miss Brody while she sings 'Mean to me' and 'My suppressed desire': **McPartland, Teagarden** and Morgan are featured as a vocal trio in the second number.

1215

Medicine ball caravan/We have come for your daughters
USA/France 1971 – 88 mins
dir François Reichenbach

Yet another journey across contemporary America, this time 150 hippies in a caravan of buses, trucks, cars etc plus visits to music concerts of varying quality. Appearances by many pop artistes and **B. B. King**.

1216

Meet Danny Wilson
USA 1951 – 88 mins
dir Joseph Pevney

A cliché, jumbled story of an American crooner with an inferiority complex played, of course, by Frank Sinatra. Includes **Sy Oliver**'s song 'Lonesome man blues'.

1217

Meet me after the show
USA 1951 – 87 mins
dir Richard Sale

Formula Fox musical tailored for Betty Grable – extravagant, highly coloured and totally absurd. Bernie Billings's combo is featured visually only: Billings, *clar;* Jack Coon, *tpt;* **Brad Gowans**, *trb;* Don Owens, *pno;* Tommy Rundell, *drs*. They worked to playback of soundtrack recorded by Fox staff musicians. **Abe Most** soundtracked clarinet for Billings.

Meet Miss Bobby Socks
see **Meet Miss Bobby Sox.**

1218

Meet Miss Bobby Sox/Meet Miss Bobby Socks
USA 1944 – 68 mins
dir Glenn Tryon

Weak satirical comedy about a crooner and his 15-year-old pen-friend. The leading role is played by **Bob Crosby**.

1219

Meet the maestros
USA 1938 – 9 mins

A Paramount music short with **Cab Calloway** playing 'Zah-zuh-zaz' and **Isham Jones** and His Orchestra.

1220

The melancholy dame
USA 1929 – 20 mins
dir Arvid E. Gillstrom

Paramount short based on a story by Octavus Roy Cohen and featuring **Spencer Williams**.

1221

Melodies by Martin
USA 1955 – 16 mins

A Universal music featurette presenting Freddie Martin and His Orchestra who spotlight their drummer, **Buddy Rich**. Musical items include 'Jitterbug routine', 'Do do do', 'A man' and 'Somebody stole my gal'.

1222

Melody garden
USA 1943 – 15 mins
dir Vernon Keays

A Universal *Name band musical* featuring **Teddy Powell** and His Orchestra.

1223

Melody maestro
USA 1947 – 14 mins
dir Will Cowan

Universal music short featuring **Skinnay Ennis** and His Orchestra playing 'I don't know why I love you like I do', 'Echoes of Harlem', 'I'll never be the same' and 'All that glitters is not gold'.

1224

Melody parade
USA 1944 – 15 mins
dir Lewis D. Collins

M

Universal music featurette spotlighting **Charlie Barnet** and His Orchestra, in a stage setting, entertaining with support from The Pied Pipers, June Hutton, Dorothy Allen, Grey and Diane and Kay Starr. Numbers include 'How am I to know?', 'Redskin rhumba', 'Skyliner' and 'Washington whirligig'.

225

Melody time
USA 1946 – 18 mins
dir Jack Scholl

RKO music featurette with music from **Tex Beneke** and The **Glenn Miller** Orchestra. Numbers include 'Moonlight serenade', 'In the mood', 'Don't be that way' and 'The woodchuck song'.

226

Member of the wedding
USA 1953 – 89 mins
dir Fred Zinnemann

Rather dull and flat screen adaptation of the book and play by Carson McCullers with Julie Harris repeating her enthusiastically acclaimed stage performance. **Ethel Waters**'s presence inevitably enriched the proceedings.

227

Memphis Slim
Belgium 1960 – 35 mins
dir Yannick Bruynoghe

Film impression of the blues singer in action.

228

Men with wings
USA 1938 – 107 mins
dir William A. Wellman

The story of aviation from 1903, though told in fictional terms. Includes some really outstanding aerial battles enhanced by a genuinely creative use of colour. Frank Loesser and **Hoagy Carmichael** wrote the title song.

229

Mennesker modes og sod musik opstår i jertet/Människor möts och ljuv musik uppstar i hjärtat/People meet
Denmark/Sweden 1967 – 105 mins
dir Henning Carlsen

A frothy sex comedy adapted from a novel by Jens August Schade, with little to recommend it save an attractive performance by Harriet Andersson. The lush music score is by **Krzysztof Komeda**.

1230

The mercenaries
UK 1967 – 100 mins
dir Jack Cardiff

Conventional, thoroughly cliché adventure movie, with a music score by **Jacques Loussier**.

1231

Le metamorphose des cloportes
France 1965 – 102 mins
dir Pierre Granier-Deferre

Well-made but otherwise dull thriller about a gangster who, after serving a jail sentence, avenges himself on his former accomplices. Music score by **Jimmy Smith**.

1232

The Mexican suite
USA 1972
dir Gary Keys

Impressions of **Duke Ellington** and His Orchestra at concerts in Mexico, featuring a specially composed 22 minute suite.

1233

Michael Bryan
USA 1961 – 25 mins
dir Lee Rothberg

A studio bandstand programme produced for the Goodyear Tyre Company featuring **Georgie Auld**, *ten sax;* **'Doc' Severinsen**, *tpt;* **Michael Bryan**, *gtr;* **Derek Smith**, *pno;* **Harry Sheppard**, *vibs;* **Jack Lesberg**, *bass;* **'Mousie' Alexander**, *drs.* Numbers: 'Bennie's bugle', 'Blues in G', 'Seven come eleven', 'Ain't got time', 'Sweet Lorraine', 'Airmail special'. Introductory music: 'The good years of jazz' played by The **Duke Ellington** Orchestra.

1234

Mickey One
USA 1965 – 93 mins
dir Arthur Penn

A confused though stylish thriller about a club entertainer trying to escape from his guilty conscience. Plenty of soundtrack jazz composed by **Eddie Sauter** with magnificent improvisations by **Stan Getz**.

1235

Midnight cowboy
USA 1969 – 113 mins
dir John Schlesinger

Grotesque screen adaptation of the novel by James Leo Herlihy – a comment on the hideous society in which the two central characters are involved. **Jean 'Toots' Thielemans** is responsible for the splendid harmonica work on soundtrack.

A Milanese story

see   **Una storia Milanese.**

1236

Millenium jump

USA 1946 – 3 mins
dir William Forest Crouch

Soundie featuring **Joe Marsala** and His Orchestra backing dancer Judy Bakay.

1237

Million dollar notes

USA 1935 – 9 mins
dir Fred Waller

Paramount short with a brief appearance by **Red Nichols**.

1238

Mills Blue Rhythm Band

USA 1933 – 9 mins
dir Roy Mack

Vitaphone short featuring the title band playing 'The peanut vendor', 'Tony's wife', 'Love is the thing', 'Blue rhythm', 'Underneath the Harlem moon'. 'I would do anything for you' and 'There goes my headache'. Personnel: Shelton Hemphill, Wardell Jones, Edward Anderson, *tpts;* **George Washington,** Henry Hicks, *trbs;* Crawford Wethington, Gene Mikell, **Joe Garland**, *saxes;* **Edgar Hayes**, *pno;* Benny James, *gtr;* **Hayes Alvis**, *bass, tuba,* **O'Neill Spencer**, *drs;* Sally Gooding, *voc.*

1239

The Mills Brothers on parade

USA 1956 – 16 mins

Universal music featurette with The **Mills Brothers**, Gogi Grant, Jana Mason and Chuck Nelson. Numbers: 'Say si si', 'A diamond, a pearl and an ermine wrap', 'Slap leather', 'Who are we?', 'Paper doll' and 'Opus one'.

1240

Mingus

USA 1968 – 56 mins
dir Thomas Reichman

An honest and accurate interview with **Charlie Mingus** made at the time of his eviction from his downtown New York flat, intercut with footage of various **Mingus** groups performing in clubs with numbers including 'All the things you are', 'Secret love' and **Billy Strayhorn**'s 'Take the "A" train'. Otherwise music and poetry by **Charlie Mingus,** *bass, pno;* **Lonnie Hillyer, Walter Bishop, John Gilmore, Dannie Richmond** and **Charles McPherson.**

1241

Mini-midi/Hier, audjourd'hui, demain/World of fashion

France 1968 – 23 mins
dir Robert Freeman

A model strides gracefully through 60 years of fashion in a series of period sketches. Music backing is provided by use of **Paul Whiteman**'s recording of 'The black bottom'.

1242

Minnie and Moskowitz

USA 1971 – 115 mins
dir John Cassavetes

Quite brilliant comedy-drama about two lonely misfits exploring each other's hang-ups and emerging through a saga of rows and quarrels to a wedding bell finale. Superb performances, particularly from the beautiful Gena Rowlands, and some jazz on soundtrack contribute towards a memorable movie. Recordings used include **Lil Armstrong**'s 'Skit-dat-de-dat' and **Louis Armstrong**'s 'Yes, I'm in the barrel'.

1243

Minnie the moocher

USA 1932 – 6 mins
dir Dave Fleischer

A Paramount 'Song Cartoon' featuring Betty Boop and Bimbo. The music was recorded by **Cab Calloway** and His Orchestra who also appear in the opening sequence. Numbers: 'Minnie the moocher' and 'Tiger rag'.

1244

Minnie the moocher

USA 1942 – 3 mins

Soundie featuring **Cab Calloway** and His Orchestra with his classic interpretation of the title number.

1245

Minnie the moocher

USA 1950 – 3 mins

Snader Telescription in which the title number is performed by **Cab Calloway** and His Cabaliers, including **Jonah Jones**, *tpt;* Milt Hinton, *bass;* **'Panama' Francis**, *drs.*

1246

A miracle can happen/On our merry way

USA 1948 – 107 mins
dir King Vidor, Leslie Fenton

Multi-cast, episodic entertainment which includes an appearance by **Harry James**.

1247

Mirage

USA 1965 – 109 mins
dir Edward Dmytryk

Confused but intriguing and atmospheric thriller which is entertaining if nothing else. Music score by **Quincy Jones**.

1248

Mirrors

USA 1934 – 9 mins

Vitaphone music short featuring The Freddie Rich Orchestra with **Bunny Berigan**.

1249

Mirth and melody

UK 1951 – 36 mins
dir Horace Shepherd

Revue featuring popular entertainers of the day including **Stephane Grappelly** and His Quintet.

1250

Mission impossible vs the mob

USA 1969 – 89 mins
dir Paul Stanley

Cops and robbers movie based on the format and characters of the TV series, with theme music by **Lalo Schifrin**.

1251

Mississippi Delta Blues

USA 1974 – 18 mins
dir Bill & Josette Ferris

Produced by the Center for Southern Folklore: a selection of music best representing the richness of Mississippi Delta Blues.

1252

Mister Big/School for jive

USA 1943 – 74 mins
dir Charles Lamont

One of the splendid series of Universal musical comedies tailored for the talents of Donald O'Connor. Features Ray Eberle with **Eddie Miller**'s Bob Cats.

1253

Mister Brown

USA/France 1972 – 85 mins
dir Roger Andrieux

Written, produced, photographed and edited by the director, the story of a man who strives to start his own business only to see his dream fade and his relationship with his family dissipate until he ends up driving someone else's truck. Two original numbers composed and played by **John Lee Hooker** add depth to the mood.

1254

Mr Bug goes to town/Hoppity goes to town

USA 1941 – 78 mins
dir Dave Fleischer

Justly famous full-length animated cartoon in Technicolor containing a good deal of music and song with one number 'We're the couple in the castle' by Frank Loesser and **Hoagy Carmichael**.

Mr Co-ed

see **Bathing beauty.**

1255

Mr Jackson from Jacksonville

USA 1945 – 3 mins

Soundie featuring vocalist **June Richmond** singing the title number in a nightclub setting.

1256

Mr Music

USA 1950 – 114 mins
dir Richard Haydn

Routine backstage musical with Bing Crosby ambling agreeably through the songs and various guest stars including Peggy Lee making brief appearances. Features **Dave Barbour** in an acting role.

1257

Mr Ricco

USA 1974 – 98 mins
dir Paul Bogart

Tedious and corny hodge-podge about an attorney whose client is suspected of murder. Music score by **Chico Hamilton**.

1258

Mister Rock and Roll

USA 1957 – 74 mins
dir Charles Dubin

Usual scrappy plot and a series of musical numbers by current idols. **Lionel Hampton** is credited as musical director and also appears with his band.

1259

Mr X blues

USA 1945 – 3 mins

Soundie featuring **Cecil Scott** and His Band with the title number.

1260

Mrs Pollifax – spy

USA 1970 – 110 mins
dir Leslie Martinson

Uninspired parody of the cinema's recent spy mania: mainly a vehicle for its star Rosalind Russell. Music by **Lalo Schifrin**.

Mixed doubles

see **Ex: flame.**

1261

Model shop

USA 1968 – 92 mins
dir Jacques Demy

Initially disappointing first American movie by Jacques Demy, though Anouk Aimée is as dazzling as ever. Music direction by **Marty Paich**.

1262

The Modern Jazz Quartet

USA 1964 – 28 mins
prods Ralph J. Gleason, Richard Christian

Originally produced for US TV in KQED's `Jazz Casual` series, **John Lewis**, pianist and musical director of **The Modern Jazz Quartet**, discusses the use of jazz in motion pictures and in the ballet with particular reference to his own music for the ballet *Original Sin*.

1263

Modern Polish jazz groups

Poland 1964 – 5 mins each
dir J. Majewski

Six separate short films recording the work of Polish jazz groups: 1. The All Stars 2. Bossa Nova Combo 3. Warsaw Stompers 4. Namyslowski's Quartet 5. Trzaskowski's Quintet 6. **Komeda** Quintet.

1264

Modern rhythm

UK 1963 – 11 mins
dir Robert Henryson

Music short featuring The Hermanos Deniz Cuban Rhythm Band, **Tony Kinsey** with 'It's the bluest kind of blues my baby sings', and **Ted Heath** and His Band playing 'Paradise'.

1265

Modesty Blaise

UK 1966 – 119 mins
dir Joseph Losey

A paean to the mid-60s: a mixture of Op-art and pop fiction, based on the comic strip of the same name. Music composed and conducted by **John Dankworth** with songs partly by Benny Green.

1266

Molly and 'Lawless' John

USA 1972 – 97 mins
dir Gary Nelson

A matriarchal Western weepie, based on the timeless cliché that a naive but determined woman can win the heart of the most hardened, sinful roustabout. Music score by **Johnny Mandel**.

Moment for music

see **Sweet and low-down.**

1267

Momma don't allow

UK 1955 – 22 mins
dir Karel Reisz, Tony Richardson

The classic first film by two distinguished directors is an impression of an evening among the young members of the Wood Green Jazz Club at the Fishmonger's Arms. Features **Chris Barber**'s Band including **Monty Sunshine**, *clar;* **Pat Halcox**, *tpt;* Lonnie Donegan, *banjo;* **Jim Bray**, *bass;* **Ron Bowden**, *drs;* **Ottilie Patterson**, *voc.*

1268

Mon ami Pierrot

France 1960 – 19 mins
dir L. Grospierre

The story of Colombine, Pierrot and Harlequin transposed to the 20th century, with music by **Henri Crolla**.

1269

Mon chien

France 1955 – 25 mins
dir Georges Franju

The story of a pet dog, abandoned by his owners whilst on their holiday trip to the Côte d'Azur, and how he resourcefully finds his way back to his Parisian home. Music by **Henri Crolla**.

1270

Le monde sans soleil/World without sun

France/Italy 1964 – 93 mins
dir Jacques-Yves Cousteau

New discoveries in underwater exploration – a follow-up to the same director's earlier success *The silent world*. 'Additional' soundtrack music by **Henri Crolla** and **André Hodeir**.

1271

Il mondo di notte numero due/World by night no. 2

Italy 1961 – 118 mins
dir Gianni Proia, Mario Russo

Documentary successor to *World by night No. 1* devoted to cabaret and variety acts around the world. Includes a New Orleans sequence featuring **Al Hirt** and His Orchestra and **Paul Barbarin** and His Orchestra.

1272

Monique

UK 1969 – 87 mins
dir John Bown

Unconvincing sexual fairy tale, with a music score by **Jacques Loussier**.

1273

Monterey jazz

USA 1968 – 120 mins
prods Ralph J. Gleason, Richard Moore

Originally produced for US TV by KQED, an edited version of four one-hour specials covering the 10th annual Monterey Jazz Festival in 1967. Performers include The Cla.a Ward Singers with 'Dry bones'; bluesmen **'T-Bone' Walker** and **B.B. King**; **Carmen McRae**, *voc*, and **Ray Brown**, *bass*, with 'Satin doll'; **Woody Herman** and His Orchestra; **'Illinois' Jacquet**, *ten sax*, and **Louis Bellson**, *drs*, with 'Flyin' home'; **Jean-Luc Ponty**, *vln*, **Ray Nance**, *vln*, **Svend Asmussen**, *vln*, with 'C jam blues'; The **Don Ellis** Band and **Dizzy Gillespie**.

1274

Monterey jazz

USA 1973 – 81 mins
dir Norman Abbott

Film record of the 13th Annual Monterey Jazz Festival in 1970. An introduction includes **Duke Ellington** relaxing on the beach, **John Lewis** addressing the staff and rehearsing with The **Modern Jazz Quartet** 'Monterey mist'. Then, on stage, the Johnny Otis show – including Delmar 'Mighty Mouth' Evans, 'Sugarcane' Harris, **Gene 'The Mighty Flea' Connors** and Shuggie Otis – **'Big' Joe Turner** with 'Hide and go seek' and

'Roll 'em Pete'; Margie Evans with 'I may be wrong'; **Eddie 'Cleanhead' Vinson** with 'Cleanhead's blues'; Esther Phillips with 'I'm in the mood for love' and 'Release me'; **Jimmy Rushing** with 'Everyday I have the blues' and 'Sent for you yesterday'; The **M.J.Q.** (**John Lewis**, *pno;* **Milt Jackson**, *vibs;* **Percy Heath**, *bass;* **Connie Kay**, *drs*) with 'Walkin' stomp'; **Tim Weisberg**, *flute*, plus group with 'A day at the fair'; **Duke Ellington** and His Orchestra with 'Afro-Eurasian eclipse' (soloists **Harry Carney**, **Harold Ashby**), 'I got it bad and that ain't good' (soloist **Woody Herman**, *alt sax*) and 'Don't get around much anymore' (soloist **Joe Williams**, *voc*). Background instrumental use is made of 'Satin doll'. (A shortened version of this film, edited down to 50 mins has been transmitted several times by BBC TV).

1275

The mooche

USA 1952 – 3 mins

Snader Telescription in which the title number is played by **Duke Ellington** and His Orchestra, featuring **Jimmy Hamilton, Russell Procope, Willie Smith, Paul Gonsalves, Harry Carney**, *reeds,* **Ray Nance, Willie Cook, Cat Anderson**, *tpt;* **Juan Tizol, Quentin Jackson, Britt Woodman**, *trb,* **Wendell Marshall**, *bass;* **Louis Bellson**, *drs.*

1276

Mood indigo

USA 1952 – 3 mins

Snader Telescription of **Duke Ellington** and His Orchestra playing the title number, with solos from **Russell Procope**, *clar;* **Willie Cook**, *tpt;* **Ellington**, *pno;* also featuring **Willie Smith, Jimmy Hamilton, Harry Carney, Paul Gonsalves**, *reeds;* **Ray Nance. Cat Anderson**, *tpt;* **Juan Tizol, Quentin Jackson, Britt Woodman**, *trb;* **Wendell Marshall**, *bass;* **Louis Bellson**, *drs.*

1277

Moon zero two

UK 1969 – 100 mins
dir Roy Ward Baker

The first 'space Western' appealing only to undemanding juvenile audiences. A totally inappropriate music score by **Don Ellis** mixes heavy electric rock/jazz with big band stratospherics and a female vocalist with heavenly chorus.

1278

Moonlight masquerade

USA 1942 – 3 mins

Soundie featuring **Stan Kenton** and His Orchestra plus radio star James Newell.

1279
The moonshine war

USA 1970 – 100 mins
dir Richard Quine

Adaptation by Elmore Leonard of his own novel about moonshiners in hillbilly country. Features **Joe Williams** in an acting role.

1280
Mop

USA 1946 – 3 mins
dir William Forest Crouch

Soundie featuring **Red Allen** and **J. C. Higginbotham** with their version of the title number.

1281
Morgan, a suitable case for treatment

UK 1966 – 97 mins
dir Karel Reisz

Not entirely successful screen adaptation by David Mercer of his own satirical play, but quite enjoyable. Music by **John Dankworth**.

1282
Mother Goose goes to Hollywood

USA 1938 – 8 mins

Walt Disney cartoon caricaturing famous personalities of the day including **Cab Calloway, Fats Waller** and The Andrews Sisters.

1283
Mother, Jugs & Speed

USA 1976 – 98 mins
dir Peter Yates

Opportunistic comedy set in the world of competing Los Angeles ambulance companies, too near the M.A.S.H. format for comfort. Among the recordings used on soundtrack is 'My soul is a witness' by **Billy Preston** and Joe Greene.

1284
Move

USA 1951 – 3 mins

Snader Telescription in which the title number is played by **George Shearing**, *pno;* **Joe Roland**, *vibs;* **Chuck Wayne**, *gtr;* **Al McKibbon**, *bass;* **Denzil Best**, *drs.*

The moving target
see **Harper.**

1285
Le mur de l'Atlantique

France/Italy 1969 – 100 mins
dir Marcel Camus

Comedy set in Normandy during the war tracing the adventures of an R.A.F. pilot among the local villagers. Music score by **Claude Bolling**.

1286
Murder at the Vanities

USA 1934 – 87 mins
dir Mitchell Leisen

Stylish, thoroughly enjoyable comedy-thriller set behind the scenes of a spectacular musical show. One splendid production number features **Duke Ellington** and His Orchestra with 'Ebony rhapsody'. Personnel: **Otto Hardwicke, Harry Carney, Johnny Hodges, Barney Bigard**, *reeds;* **Freddie Jenkins, Cootie Williams, Arthur Whetsol**, *tpts;* **Sam Nanton, Juan Tizol, Lawrence Brown**, *trbs;* **Fred Guy**, *gtr;* **Wellman Braud**, *bass;* **Sonny Greer**, *perc;* Ellington, *pno.*

1287
Murder in swingtime

USA 1937 – 10 mins

An RKO Radio band short with an all Negro cast featuring **Les Hite** and His Orchestra plus **June Richmond**, *voc.*

1288
The murder men

USA 1962 – 75 mins
dir John Peyser

Routine underworld thriller involving a nightclub singer and her jazz trumpeter husband. Appearances and music by **Shelly Manne, Red Mitchell, Conte Candoli** and **Al Hendrickson**.

1289
Murder on Lenox Avenue

USA 1941
dir Arthur Dreifuss

Low-budget, B-plot picture produced for black audiences featuring vocalist **Mamie Smith**.

1290
Murder with music

USA c1941

All black production featuring **Bob Howard, Noble Sissle** and His Orchestra and the song 'I'm a cute little banji from Ubangi'.

▲

*A posed publicity shot of Duke Ellington at Paramount
Studios in 1934.*

1291

Murderer's Row

USA 1966 – 108 mins
dir Henry Levin

The further adventures of Matt Helm with Dean
Martin as wittily relaxed as ever. Music and song
'I'm not the marrying kind' by **Lalo Schifrin**.

1292

Music

UK 1968 – 43 mins
dir Michael Tuchner

A somewhat disorganised *mélange* of music past
and present thrown together for the National
Music Council of Great Britain. Contains brief
appearances by **John Dankworth** and **Lol
Coxhill**.

The music box

see **Sing as you swing.**

1293

Music for millions

USA 1945 – 117 mins
dir Henry Koster

Formula vehicle for Margaret O'Brien with José
Iturbi's orchestra supplying numerous musical
'classics'. Orchestrations partly by **Calvin
Jackson**.

1294

Music: from popular to concert stage

USA c1970 – 15 mins
dir Sidney Galanty

An instructional movie for school children
produced by Communications Group West which
tries to explain the development of various
musical styles, including jazz, but except for the
narrator reeling off the names of the great jazz
innovators it never gets off the ground.

1295

The music goes 'round

USA 1936 – 88 mins
dir Victor Schertzinger

Musical comedy about a showboat troupe in New York. Features The **Les Hite** Orchestra plus Eddie 'Rochester' Anderson and Jimmy Taylor with an eccentric dance and acrobatic taps from Nyas Berry.

1296

Music in Manhattan

USA 1944 – 81 mins
dir John H. Auer

Comedy with music and a particularly tiresome plot. Features **Charlie Barnet** and His Orchestra.

1297

Music man

USA 1948 – 66 mins
dir Will Jason

Musical romance about a successful songwriting team who feud over a girl. Features **Jimmy Dorsey** and His Orchestra.

1298

Music power

USA 1970

One of two documentaries about the Amougies Festival held in October 1969 featuring **Joachim Kühn, Anthony Braxton** and **John Surman**.

1299

Musical miracle

USA 1948 – 11 mins

One in a series of 'Pacemaker' shorts. This features **Paul Whiteman** presenting a musical biography of singer Patti Clayton.

1300

Music-hall parade

France 1958 – 20 mins
dir Michel Gast

Variety show presenting popular artistes including **Maxim Saury**.

1301

Muskrat ramble

USA c1952 – 3 mins

Telescription of The **Bobcats** playing the title number.

My bed is not for sleeping
see **Negresco – eine todliche Affaire.**

1302

My blue heaven

USA 1950 – 96 mins
dir Henry Koster

Betty Grable and Dan Dailey as a stage couple involved in a series of attempts to acquire a family and ending up as TV stars. The **Benny Carter** Band did the soundtrack but are not seen. Musicians involved include **Benny Carter**, *alt sax, arr;* **Ernie Royal**, *tpt;* **Britt Woodman**, *trb;* **'Bumps' Myers**, *ten sax;* **Gerry Wiggins**, *pno;* **Ulysses Livingston**, *gtr;* **Lee Young**, *drs.*

1303

My bottle is dry

USA 1946 – 3 mins
dir William Forest Crouch

Soundie in which **June Richmond** presents her interpretation of the title number.

1304

My gal loves music

USA 1944 – 63 mins
dir Edward Lilley

Comedy with music and not much else, with the leading role played by **Bob Crosby**.

My heart goes crazy
see **London town.**

1305

My lost horizon

USA 1941 – 3 mins

Soundie in which an original composition is played by The **Les Brown** Orchestra with singer Doris Day.

1306

My, my, ain't that somethin'

USA 1944 – 3 mins

Soundie in which **Gene Rodgers** dances and plays the title number on piano.

1307

My new gown

USA 1944 – 3 mins

Soundie with Lena Horne singing the title number backed by **Albert Ammons** and Pete Johnson on piano plus **Teddy Wilson** and His Orchestra.

1308

Die Nacht vor der Premiere/The night before the premiere

West Germany 1959 – 98 mins
dir George Jacoby

Colour musical tailored for the talents of its star, Marika Rökk. Features **Louis Armstrong, Trummy Young, 'Peanuts' Hucko, Mort Herbert**, Billy Kyle and **Danny Barcelona**. Numbers: 'Kisses in der Nacht', 'Ain't misbehavin'' and 'Honeysuckle rose'.

Naked hearts
see **Les coeurs verts.**

1309

Naked sea

USA 1955 – 69 mins
dir Allen H. Miner

Brilliantly photographed Pathécolor documentary: an account of a 16-week tuna-fishing trip in the waters off Panama, the Galapagos Islands and the coast of Peru. Soundtrack music by **Laurindo Almeida**, *gtr*, and George Fields, *hca*.

1310

The naked world of Harrison Marks

UK 1965 – 84 mins
dir George Harrison Marks

Long, repetitive and exceedingly boring movie about the director, photographer of nudes. Music score by **Johnny Hawksworth**.

1311

Nancy Wilson

USA 1962 – 20 mins
dir Steve Binder

Introduced by Oscar Brown, Jnr, and originally produced for Jazz Scene USA by US TV, a bandstand programme by vocalist **Nancy Wilson**, accompanied by **Lou Levy**, *pno;* **Al McKibbon**, *bass;* **Kenny Dennis**, *drs*. Numbers: 'Happy talk', 'Little girl blue', 'Put on a happy face', 'Never will I marry', 'Guess who I saw today' and 'I believe in you'.

1312

Naples au baiser de feu/Naples kissed by fire

France 1937 – 81 mins
dir A. Gargour

Romantic tale, with songs, of a philandering Neapolitan café singer and his loves, tailored for its star Tino Rossi. **Django Reinhardt** participates.

Naples kissed by fire
see **Naples au baiser de feu.**

Nat Gonella and His Georgians
see **Pity the poor rich.**

1313

Nat 'King' Cole and Joe Adams's Orchestra

USA 1951 – 15 mins
dir Will Cowan

Universal-International music short in which, accompanied by the all coloured Joe Adams Orchestra, **Nat 'King'Cole** sings three numbers: 'Destination Moon', 'Too young' and 'That's my girl'.

1314

Nat 'King' Cole and Russ Morgan's orchestra
USA 1953 – 18 mins
dir Will Cowan

A conventional music short from Universal Studios in which **Nat 'King' Cole** plays and sings a programme of songs. Filmed in 3-D a trombonist's slide is frequently pushed out into the audience's face.

1315

Nat 'King' Cole and The 'King' Cole Trio
USA 1951 – 18 mins
Snader Telescriptions featuring the title group.

1316

The Nat 'King' Cole musical story
USA 1955 – 18 mins
dir Will Cowan

A colour and 'Scope featurette purporting to re-tell the story of **Nat 'King' Cole**'s discovery as a jazz pianist and the events leading to fame. Songs include 'Sweet Lorraine', 'Route 66', 'Pretend' and 'Straighten up and fly right'. Actor Jeff Chandler delivers the commentary.

1317

National Aquarium Presentation
USA 1967 – 10 mins
dir Charles and Ray Eames

A film report to the Secretary of the Interior on the new National Aquarium; its architecture, its programme, its general philosophy. Music score by **Buddy Collette**.

1318

Naturally, it's rubber
UK 1964 – 24 mins
dir Peter Hopkinson

An account of the rubber producing industry in Malaysia showing how scientific development has improved productivity. Music score by **Kenneth Graham**.

1319

The naughty 'nineties
USA 1945 – 75 mins
dir Jean Yarbrough

Routine vehicle for Abbott and Costello, set on a Mississippi showboat and featuring The **Ted Lewis** Orchestra.

1320

Negresco – eine todliche Affaire/My bed is not for sleeping
West Germany 1967 – 93 mins
dir Klaus Lemke

Routine thriller, aptly summed up in its English title. Brief guest appearance by **Erroll Garner**.

1321

Neiges
France 1955 – 20 mins
dir Jean-Jacques Languepin

An impression of winter sports, with music by **Henri Crolla**.

1322

The Neptune factor – An undersea odyssey
Canada 1973 – 98 mins
dir Daniel Petrie

Contrived, formula undersea rescue drama with a dull script, dreary direction and a cast of familiar faces for whom one can feel only embarrassment. An original music score by William McCauley was scrapped during post-production and **Lalo Schifrin** was called in to fabricate an atrocious travesty on *that* famous Richard Strauss composition, which is repeated with all the subtlety of a fire alarm.

1323

Le neutron et la fission
France 1965 – 19 mins
dir Manuel Otero, Jacques Leroux

Documentary about nuclear reactions, with music by **Martial Solal**.

1324

Nevada Smith
USA 1966 – 131 mins
dir Henry Hathaway

Disjointed, episodic Western drama telling the early adventures of the silent movie cowboy who was to become a character in *The Carpetbaggers*. The excellent music score by Alfred Newman includes contributions from **Ted Nash**, *bas-flute;* **Vince de Rosa**, *Fr horn;* **Dick Nash**, *trb;* Carl Fortina, *acc;* **Red Mitchell**, *fender bass;* **Laurindo Almeida** and **Al Hendrickson**, *gtrs.*

1325

Never bug an ant
USA 1969 – 6 mins
dir Gerry Chiniquy

Poor colour cartoon in the *Ant and the Aardvark* series. Doug Goodwin's bouncy music is played by **Pete Candoli, Billy Byers, Ray Brown, Jimmy Rowles, Tommy Tedesco** and **Shelly Manne**.

Never give an inch
see **Sometimes a great notion.**

1326

Never love a stranger

USA 1957 – 91 mins
dir Robert Stevens

Confused and episodic melodrama adapted from a novel by Harold Robbins, mixing crime documentary, anti-semitism, religion, sentimentality, beatings up, sex, psychology and delinquency. Music by **Raymond Scott** who also provides the title song and the song 'Oh, baby'.

1327

Never too old to swing

USA 1945 – 3 mins

Soundie featuring **Tiny Grimes** and His Band supported by a dancing team.

1328

The new Centurians/Precinct 45 – Los Angeles Police

USA 1972 – 103 mins
dir Richard Fleischer

Slick, rugged, unsatisfying screen adaptation of Joseph Wambaugh's novel by Stirling Silliphant who, years ago, trod much the same ground with *Naked City* – routine police work – though with far greater assurance and success. The music score by **Quincy Jones** is equally disappointing, though this may be explained by its having been composed in three days, following the last minute rejection of a score written by **Don Ellis**.

New clothes
see **Ubranie prawie nowe.**

New face in hell
see **P.J.**

1329

New faces of 1937

USA 1937 – 100 mins
dir Leigh Jason

Pleasant musical comedy from the story *Shoestring* by George Bradshaw. Features the song 'Peckin'' by **Ben Pollack** and **Harry James**.

1330

A new kind of love

USA 1963 – 109 mins
dir Melville Shavelson

Very weak romantic comedy set in Hollywood's idea of wicked, irresistible Paris. Part of the music score is written by **Erroll Garner**.

1331

New Orleans

USA 1947 – 90 mins
dir Arthur Lubin

Conventional musical in every way except for its cast which contains many top jazz personnel of the time including **Woody Herman** and His Orchestra (with **Sonny Berman, Bill Harris** and **'Flip' Phillips**); **Louis Armstrong, Barney Bigard, Kid Ory, Russell Moore, Charlie Beal, Mutt Carey, Red Callender, Meade Lux Lewis, Bud Scott, Zutty Singleton** and **Billie Holiday** in her only feature film role singing 'Do you know what it means to miss New Orleans'. Other songs: 'Endie', 'The Blues are brewin'', 'West End blues', 'Buddy Bolden's blues', 'Honky tonk train blues', 'Dippermouth blues', 'New Orleans stomp', 'Where the Blues were born in New Orleans', 'Basin Street blues', 'Farewell to Storyville', 'Mahogany Hall stomp', 'Maryland, my Maryland'. (**George Lewis** with **Kid Howard**'s Brass Band took part in the filming but was edited out of the final release prints).

1332

New Orleans blues

USA 1943 – 15 mins
dir Josef Berne

A Universal Name Band Musical featuring **Louis Prima** and His Orchestra.

1333

New Orleans funeral

USA 1962 – 6 mins

A film record of a traditional Negro funeral, made by the New Orleans Jazz Club, with music by **Bunk Johnson**'s Brass Band.

1334

The New Orleans Jazz Museum

USA 1967 – 14 mins
prod Donald R. Perry

Documentary film record of the New Orleans Jazz Museum opened in 1961 containing some 10,000 jazz souvenirs. Contains footage of many local musicians, dancers and parades including **Pete Fountain** and His Half Fast Walking Club and The **Eureka Brass Band** with snatches of various musical numbers.

Louis Armstrong and Kid Ory among the musicians in New Orleans.

1335
New York eye and ear control
USA 1964 – 34 mins
dir Michael Snow

Subtitled *The Walking Woman Work*, an independently produced experimental movie by the filmmaker who was later to make such a name for himself with his prizewinning *Wavelength*. Music track by **Don Cherry, Albert Ayler, Roswell Rudd** and **John Tchicai**.

1336
New York, New York
USA 1977
dir Martin Scorsese

Currently in production, a drama with music set in the Big Band era and featuring Robert DeNiro and Liza Minnelli. Music composed and conducted by **Ralph Burns**, with **Georgie Auld** as musical adviser to Robert DeNiro.

1337
Niewinni czarodzieje/Innocent sorcerers
Poland 1960 – 86 mins
dir Andrzej Wajda

A model piece of intimate film-making – an account of adolescent lethargy and rebellion in a threatening world, with impeccable performances by all concerned. **Krzysztof T. Komeda** supplies the jazzy soundtrack score and also appears briefly.

Night affair
see **Le désordre et la nuit.**

The night before the premiere
see **Die Nacht vor der Premiere.**

Robert DeNiro leads the big band in **New York, New York.**
▼

1338

Night club girl

USA 1945 – 61 mins
dir Eddie Cline

A couple of kids from Missouri try to crash Hollywood with a song and dance act. Features The **Delta Rhythm Boys** with 'Vingo jingo' and 'One o'clock jump' and other numbers 'Pagan love song' and 'Wo-ho'.

Night club girl (1948)

see **Glamour girl.**

1339

Night in Harlem

USA 1947 – 10 mins

An all black production featuring **Dizzy Gillespie** and His Bebop Orchestra (**Milt Jackson**, *vibs*) presenting 'He beeped when he should 'a' bopped' and 'A night in Tunisia', with Ray Sneed, Audrey Armstrong and Phil Harris.

1340

The night of the following day

USA 1968 – 93 mins
dir Hubert Cornfield

Straightforward kidnapping thriller set in France adapted from the novel *The Snatchers* by Lionel White. Stanley Myers and **Jon Hendricks** supply the song 'One early morning' sung on soundtrack by **Annie Ross**.

1341

Night of the quarter moon/Flesh and flame

USA 1959 – 96 mins
dir Hugo Haas

Vulgar, sensational and humanly false melodrama bearing absolutely no relation to reality. Features **Nat 'King' Cole** and **Ray Anthony**, the former also contributing music for a song: 'To whom it may concern'.

1342

Night song

USA 1947 – 102 mins
dir John Cromwell

Intelligent, entertaining melodrama with Dana Andrews as a blind pianist/ composer who graduates from a dance band to the Philharmonic. Features **Hoagy Carmichael**, as the band leader, switching from clarinet to piano/vocal for his own song 'Who killed 'er'. Leith Stevens provides the rest of the music, including his Piano Concerto played by Rubinstein.

1343

The night they raided Minsky's

USA 1968 – 99 mins
dir William Friedkin

Uneven, but quite enjoyable screen adaptation of the book by Rowland Barber, set in New York in 1925 and evoking the burlesque shows of the period. Among the musicians playing for the film are **Eddie Barefield, Cliff Jackson, Sonny Greer, Al Hall** and **Lammar Wright**.

1344

Night tide

USA 1961 – 95 mins
dir Curtis Harrington

Impressive first feature by a highly talented director, telling of a love affair with super-natural overtones. David Raksin provides the music score, with a jazz sequence featuring **Joe Gordon** and **Paul Horn.**

Night train

see **Pociag.**

1345

Night train to Memphis

USA 1946 – 67 mins
dir Lesley Selander

An outdoor adventure produced by Republic – an excuse for hillbilly songs and music. **Nina Mae McKinney** has a minor role.

1346

Night train to Paris

UK 1964 – 64 mins
dir Robert Douglas

Flat-footed espionage melodrama with weak invention, mundane playing and nondescript direction. Music score by **Kenny Graham.**

1347

Night without sleep

USA 1952 – 77 mins
dir Roy Baker

20th Century Fox psychological melodrama, with the participation of **Benny Carter.**

1348

Nightmare

USA 1956 – 88 mins
dir Maxwell Shane

Preposterous, old-fashioned melodrama set in New Orleans, with the leading character a session clarinetist for **Billy May** who is featured with His Orchestra as well as being responsible for vocal and instrumental arrangements – though his own trumpet solos are actually dubbed by **Dick Cathcart**. Actor Kevin McCarthy is ghosted by **Skeets Hurfurt**, while **Meade Lux Lewis** appears briefly in a club sequence, has one line of dialogue and then tinkles away off camera.

1349
Nine o'clock folks
USA c1934 – 9 mins

Vitaphone short featuring The Mound City Blue Blowers playing, among other numbers, **W. C. Handy**'s 'St Louis blues'.

1350
No leave, no love
USA 1946 – 118 mins
dir Charles Martin

Formula musical comedy with the bands of Lombardo and Cugat plus a very early appearance by **'Sugar Chile' Robinson**. Partly orchestrated by **Calvin Jackson**.

No sun in Venice
see **Sait-on jamais?**

1351
No way out
USA 1950 – 102 mins
dir Joseph L. Mankiewicz

One of the many 'colour problem' pictures of the period in which the plot's development is curiously clumsy, the desired central conflict being arrived at by an almost tortuous series of coincidences. In one sequence Linda Darnell, trapped in a flat, turns up the radio as loud as possible in order to attract attention – the tenor player thus featured is **Eddie Miller**, announced by the unseen disc jockey Gene Norman.

1352
Noble Sissle and Eubie Blake
USA 1927 – 9 mins

Vitaphone music short in which the title artistes interpret 'I wonder where my sweetie can be' and other numbers.

1353
Noble Sissle and Eubie Blake
USA 1927 – 9 mins

Vitaphone music short in which 'The big parade' and other numbers are interpreted by the title artistes.

1354
Nobody knows the trouble
USA c1952 – 3 mins

Snader Telescription featuring **Jack Teagarden** playing the title number.

1355
Noi insistiamo/We insist
Italy 1965 – 15 mins
dir Gianni Amico

A visual interpretation of extracts from the 'We insist – freedom now' suite by **Max Roach** and Oscar Brown Jnr using still shots. Solos from **Coleman Hawkins**, *ten sax;* **Booker Little**, *tpt;* **Walter Benton**, *ten sax;* **Julian Priester**, *trb;* Abbey Lincoln, *voc;* **Max Roach**, *drs;* Michael Olatunji, *perc.*

1356
Norman . . . is that you?
USA 1976 – 91 mins
dir George Schlatter

Uneven, sporadically amusing comedy adaptation of the play by Ron Clark and Sam Bobrick, with Redd Fox and **Pearl Bailey** as the perplexed and estranged parents of a 'gay' son and his white lover.

Notes for a film on jazz
see **Appunti per un film sul jazz.**

Notes for an African Oresteia
see **Appunti per un Orestiade Africana.**

1357
Nothing sacred
USA 1937 – 75 mins
dir William A. Wellman

Witty and outrageous satire, written by Ben Hecht, about mercenary journalism ready to use death for a tear-jerking stunt. As near a perfect movie comedy as one could wish for. Novelty music by The **Raymond Scott** Quintet.

1358
Nowhere to go
UK 1958 – 87 mins
dir Seth Holt

Above average thriller, faithfully adapted from Donald Mackenzie's novel by the director and Kenneth Tynan. Jazz score by **Dizzy Reece**, played by His Quartet - **'Tubby' Hayes**, *ten sax, bar sax;* Lloyd Thompson, *bass;* **Phil Seamen**, *drs;* **Dizzy Reece**, *tpt, tom-tom.*

Robert DeNiro mimes tenor sax with Liza Minnelli in **New York, New York**.

1359

Noz w wodzie/Knife in the water

Poland 1962 – 94 mins
dir Roman Polanski

Cool, economical, symmetrical drama involving three people out for a weekend on a yacht – Polanski's remarkable first feature film. **Krzysztof Komeda** supplies the excellent jazz score featuring **Bernt Rosengren**, *ten sax*; Roman Dylag, *bass*; L. Dudziak, *drs*; and **Komeda** himself on piano.

1360

Une nuit à Saint-Germain-des-Prés

France 1949 – 16 mins
dir Jean Laviron, Fred Savdié

Short story set in a Paris Left Bank cellar featuring a group of musicians that includes **James Moody** and **Don Byas**.

1361

La nuit est une sorcière

France 1960 – 17 mins
dir Marcel Martin

Film record of the ballet originally staged at the Théâtre des Champs-Elysées in 1955. Music composed and played by **Sidney Bechet**.

1362

La nuit la plus longue

France 1964 – 90 mins
dir José Bénazéraf

Two kidnappers threaten to kill an industrialist's daughter unless a ransom is paid by dawn . . . Music score by **Chet Baker**, *tpt*, who also solos on soundtrack.

1363

Number one/Pro

USA 1969 – 104 mins
dir Tom Gries

Well-intentioned vehicle for Charlton Heston as a fading star quarterback of the New Orleans Saints football team. In a nightclub sequence **Al Hirt** and His Group play 'Down by the riverside' and there's an acting appearance by **Bobby Troup**.

1364

The nutty professor

USA 1963 – 107 mins
dir Jerry Lewis

Probably the best, and surely the funniest, of all the Jerry Lewis comedies – a vague parody of *Dr Jekyll and Mr Hyde*. Features **Les Brown** and His Band of Renown and the evergreen 'Stella by starlight'.

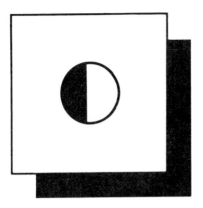

1365

Ô saisons, Ô châteaux/Castles through the ages

France 1958 – 22 mins
dir Agnès Varda

Colourful impression of some of France's most beautiful castles, imaginatively photographed. Music score by **André Hodeir**.

1366

Objectifs temps

France 1965 – 12 mins
dir Dr Michel Meignant

Documentary recording the experience of spending time underground, with music by **André Hodeir**.

1367

The odd couple

USA 1967 – 105 mins
dir Gene Saks

Brilliantly successful adaptation by Neil Simon of his own play, with definitive performances by Walter Matthau and Jack Lemmon. Bright, lightly swinging music score composed, arranged and conducted by **Neal Hefti**.

1368

Odds against tomorrow

USA 1959 – 96 mins
dir Robert Wise

An efficient but unnecessarily portentous thriller with socially significant overtones. **John Lewis** wrote the excellent music score performed by a large orchestra which includes **Milt Jackson**, *vibs;* **Percy Heath**, *bass;* **Connie Kay**, *drs;* **Bill Evans**, *pno,* and **Jim Hall**, *gtr.*

1369

Of men and demons

USA 1970 – 10 mins
dir John Hubley

An animated cartoon recounting the human battle to overcome the problems of environment, produced for Expo '70 in Osaka. Music by **Quincy Jones**.

Off the beaten track

see **Behind the eight ball.**

1370

Off the main road

UK 1970 – 27 mins
dir James O. Pines

An examination of the dilemma of choosing between personal idealism and political prerogatives within the context of black militancy. Soundtrack music played by The **Chris McGregor** Group.

Oh! Alfie

see **Alfie darling.**

1371

Oh dad, poor dad, moma's hung you in the closet and I'm feelin' so sad

USA 1966 – 86 mins
dir Richard Quine

Clumsy and vulgar screen version of the play by Arthur L. Kopit, with music score by **Neal Hefti**.

Oh! For a man!

see **Will success spoil Rock Hunter?**

1372

Oh! Frenchy

USA 1946 – 3 mins
dir Dave Gould

Soundie featuring the title number sung by Paula Kelly with **Glenn Miller**'s Modernaires.

1373

Oh! look

USA 1943 – 3 mins

Soundie featuring **Jimmy Dorsey** and His Band with vocalists Helen O'Connell and Bob Eberly.

1374

Oklahoma crude

USA 1973 – 111 mins
dir Stanley Kramer

Formula fable about human greed set in the Oklahoma oilfields in 1913. Henry Mancini's music track features **Dick Nash**, *trb, bar horn*.

1375

Old grey mare

USA 1945 – 3 mins
dir William Forest Crouch

Soundie featuring vocalist Joan Cavanaugh backed by The Swing Stars – pianist/leader **Johnny Guarnieri**.

1376

Old man Mose

USA 1942 – 3 mins

Soundie in which the title number is performed by **Louis Jordan** and His Band.

1377

The old man of the mountain

USA 1933 – 6 mins
dir Dave Fleischer

A Paramount 'Song Cartoon' featuring the ever-popular Betty Boop. The music was recorded by **Cab Calloway** and His Orchestra.

1378

On a clear day you can see forever

USA 1970 – 143 mins
dir Vincente Minnelli

Long – and subsequently shortened – screen adaptation of Alan Jay Lerner's musical play, with music by Burton Lane arranged and conducted by Nelson Riddle. Drummer on soundtrack: **John Guerin**.

On Friday at eleven

see **An einem Freitag um halb zwölf.**

1379

On Her Majesty's Secret Service

UK 1969 – 140 mins
dir Peter Hunt

The least successful of the James Bond movies, that is, the first one without Sean Connery. **Louis Armstrong** sings the John Barry/Hal David song 'All the time in the world'.

1380

On n'enterre pas le dimanche

France 1959 – 95 mins
dir Michel Drach

The story of a Negro writer, isolated in Paris, who falls in love with a Swedish girl. Music by **Eric Dixon** and **Kenny Clarke**.

On our merry way

see **A miracle can happen.**

1381

On the mellow side

USA 1944 – 15 mins
dir Lewis D. Collins

Universal music short presenting, in a stage setting, Emil Coleman and His Orchestra playing 'Amour', 'Goodnight sweetheart', 'Bingo, jingle' and 'Git aboard the 'A' train'; The Dewey Sisters, acrobatic dancers, and The **Delta Rhythm Boys**.

1382

On the road special: the 1955 show

UK 1975 – 21 mins
dir Simon Albury

Originally produced for Granada TV. **George Melly** and Derek Taylor of Warner Bros records return to the North West where they lived and worked in 1955. They revisit a lot of their old haunts in an effort to recapture their past.

1383

On the road with Duke Ellington

USA 1974 – 58 mins
prod Drew Associates

Excellent colour documentary on **Duke Ellington** at 68, originally produced in 1967 and updated after his death. **Ellington** talks about his childhood and family, is shown on the road, composing, relaxing, recording with his Orchestra, receiving his Doctorate at Yale University and at Morgan State and performing at the piano a variety of items, including 'Satin doll', 'Sophisticated lady', 'Mood indigo', 'Take the 'A' train', 'Solitude', 'Salute to Morgan State', 'Traffic jam', 'Soda fountain rag', 'I let a song go out of my heart' and part of a sacred work. Among the many musicians appearing are **Louis Armstrong, Jimmy Hamilton, Harry Carney, Billy Strayhorn, Mercer Ellington, Paul Gonsalves, Johnny Hodges** and **Russell Procope**. A clip is included from the film *Reveille with Beverly* in which the band plays 'Take the 'A' train'.

1384

On velvet

UK 1938 – 70 mins
dir Widgey Newman

Musical evolving around the setting up of an amateur TV station, featuring **Nina Mae McKinney**.

1385

On with the show

USA 1929 – 108 mins
dir Alan Crosland

Large scale revue in the early Technicolor process described at the time as the 'first dialogue motion picture in natural colours'. It featured many top artistes of the time including **Speed Webb** and His Orchestra and **Ethel Waters** singing 'Am I blue?'.

1386

Once a thief/Les tueurs de San Francisco

USA/France 1965 – 106 mins
dir Ralph Nelson

A cliché-ridden script doesn't help this melodramatic and hysterical thriller to get up off the studio floor. The relentless jazz score by **Lalo Schifrin** includes a frantic opening sequence of jazz drumming by Russell Lee.

1387

Once over lightly

USA 1941 – 3 mins

Soundie in which a musical programme is presented by **Les Brown** and His Orchestra with vocals by Doris Day and Jimmy Palmer.

Once there was a war

see **Der var engang en Krig**.

1388

One flew over the cuckoo's nest

USA 1975 – 134 mins
dir Milos Forman

Excellent screen adaptation of the novel by Ken Kesey, set in a State Mental Hospital. Original music composed by Jack Nitzsche; additional music arranged and conducted by Ed Bogas with sax solo on 'Call of the west' by **Stanley Turrentine**.

1389

One for my baby

USA 1950 – 3 mins

Cab Calloway and His Cabaliers interpret the title song in a nightclub setting. A Snader Telescription.

1390

The one I love belongs to somebody else

USA 1941 – 3 mins

Soundie with singer Mary Healy backed by **Ben Pollack**'s Orchestra.

1391

One o'clock jump

USA c1950 – 3 mins

Snader Telescription in which The **Count Basie** Sextet interpret the title number: **Basie**, *pno;* **Clark Terry**, *tpt;* **Buddy DeFranco**, *clar;* **Wardell Gray**, *ten sax;* **Freddie Green**, *gtr;* **Jimmy Lewis**, *bass;* **Gus Johnson**, *drs.*

1392

One rainy afternoon

USA 1936 – 78 mins
dir Rowland V. Lee

Inconsequential romantic comedy set in Paris and featuring Ida Lupino. Contains an appearance by **Seger Ellis**.

1393

The only game in town

USA 1969 – 113 mins
dir George Stevens

Sluggish screen adaptation by Frank D. Gilroy of his own unsuccessful play about two Las Vegas drifters who find love with each other. There's a rather noisy music score composed and conducted by Maurice Jarre with beautiful flugel horn solos by **Bobby Bryant**.

1394

Oop boop sh'bam

USA 1947 – 10 mins

An all black production featuring **Dizzy Gillespie** and His Bebop Orchestra (**Milt Jackson**, *vibs*) playing the title number, plus two others. backing Taylor and Burley with The Hubba Hubba Girls and Ray Sneed.

1395

Op med humøret

Denmark 1943
dir Ole Berggreen

A filmed revue featuring many popular entertainers of the time. **Svend Asmussen**'s Quintet
and **Leo Mathison** supply music for the soundtrack.

1396

The open window

USA 1972 – 12 mins
dir Richard Patterson

A careful screen version of the story by Saki
produced for the American Film Institute. John
Green's 'straight' music score is played by a
group that includes **Larry Bunker** and **Ronny
Lang**.

Opening tomorrow

see **Jutro premiera.**

1397

Operation heartbeat

USA 1973 – 79 mins
dir Boris Sagal

Conventional hospital drama packed with tear-
jerker clichés, with a music score by **Lalo
Schifrin**.

1398

Opération MJC

France 1965 – 20 mins
dir Henri Pialat

A look at the activities of French Youth and
Cultural Hostels, with music by **André Hodeir**.

Operation time bomb

see **Le vent se lève.**

1399

Operation 13/Spy 13

USA 1934 – 90 mins
dir Richard Boleslavsky

MGM historical romance told against a panorama
of the American Civil War, featuring The **Mills
Brothers**.

1400

The opposite sex

USA 1956 – 116 mins
dir David Miller

Extremely unattractive musical remake of Cukor's
The women, from the play by Clare Boothe.
Harry James guests with His Orchestra in a
flashback to wartime sequence playing 'The
young man with a horn'.

1401

Opus jazz

Poland 1963 – 12 mins
dir Janusz Majewski

Award-winning impression of a Polish studio
during the recording of a jazz session.

1402

Opus 1

Denmark 1948 – 4 mins
dir Jörgen Roos

Drawn shapes and images synchronised to a jazz
score, similar in style to Norman McLaren's early
experiments. Traditional jazz supplied by pianist
Bent Fabricius-Bjerre, substituting for a **Jelly Roll
Morton** recording discarded for copyright
reasons.

1403

Orchestra wives

USA 1942 – 98 mins
dir Archie Mayo

A slight story about an inexperienced orchestra
wife serves as a background to some good
numbers played by **Glenn Miller** and His
Orchestra, with **Tex Beneke** and The
Modernaires. Included are 'At last', 'Serenade in
blue', 'Kalamazoo', 'Chattanooga choo choo',
'People like you and me', 'American patrol' and
'Bugle call rag'. **Bobby Hackett** and **Ernie
Caceres** are in the Orchestra and **'Doc'
Goldberg** ghosted bass for Jackie Gleason.

1404

L'Ordinateur des pompes funèbres

France/Italy 1976 – 95 mins
dir Gérard Pirès

A feeble black comedy of murder based on the
book by Walter Kempley. Music score by **Claude
Bolling**.

1405

L'Ordre des choses ou mort un matin

France 1962 – 14 mins
dir Henry Lange

Fictional short about a man on the run, with music
by **Kenny Clarke** and **Lou Bennett**.

1406

The organisation

USA 1971 – 107 mins
dir Don Medford

The second movie in the series spawned by the success of *In the heat of the night*, marginally better than its immediate predecessor but still a long way after its original inspiration. Music score by **Gil Mellé**.

1407

Orphéon

France 1966 – 7 mins
dir Jean-Charles Meunier

The rehearsal of a choral group told with animated geometric forms, with music by **Martial Solal**.

The other side of the tracks

see **De l'autre côté du chemin de fer.**

1408

Ouest

France 1963 – 18 mins
dir Louis Grospierre

Documentary on the French regions of Poitou and Charentes, with music score by **Jacques Loussier**.

1409

Our latin thing

USA 1972 – 144 mins
dir Leon Gast

Performance documentary on salsa, shot during a show at Cheetah, the New York disco, and featuring Ray Barretto, Willie Colon, Larry Harlow, Johnny Pacheco, Roberta Roena, Bonny Valentin, Celia Cruz, José Feliciano, **Mongo Santamaria** and others.

1410

Our man Flint

USA 1965 – 107 mins
dir Daniel Mann

Inventive and genuinely funny example of super-Bondery that carries its audience along by the sheer mad technical ingenuity of it all. Music composed and conducted by Jerry Goldsmith using the talents of **Shelly Manne**, *drs;* **Ronnie Lang**, *alt sax;* **Bob Bain** and **Al Hendrickson**, *gtrs.*

1411

Our time no.1

UK 1965/7 – 26 mins
dir Caterina Arvat, Anthony West

A study of life in Britain's new office blocks and housing projects showing how people adjust to automated and mechanised surroundings. Music score by **Kenny Graham** played by The **Ronnie Scott** Quartet.

Out of the blacks, into the blues

see **En remontant le Mississippi.**

1412

The outfit

USA 1973 – 102 mins
dir John Flynn

Violent crime movie adapted from a novel by Richard Stark which includes a brief appearance by **Anita O'Day**, as a nightclub *chanteuse.*

1413

The outline of jitterbug history

USA 1942 – 3 mins

Soundie featuring Whitey's Lindy Hoppers and **Stan Kenton**.

1414

The out-of-towners

USA 1969 – 97 mins
dir Arthur Hiller

Not completely successful Neil Simon comedy but it does have its good moments. Music by **Quincy Jones**.

1415

The outskirts of town

USA 1942 – 3 mins

Soundie featuring the hit title number played by **Louis Jordan** plus some comedy from Theresa Harris and Dudley Dickerson.

Övergreppet

see **Le viol.**

1416

Oversexed

USA c1974 – 75 mins
dir Joe Sarno

Softcore sexploitation marginally based on *Dr Jekyll and Mr Hyde*. Music score partly played by The **Ruby Braff-George Benson** Quartet.

1417

P.J./New face in hell

USA 1967 – 109 mins
dir John Guillermin

Thoroughly entertaining spy thriller, not meant to be taken too seriously. Music score by **Neal Hefti**.

1418

La P . . . . respectueuse/The respectable prostitute

France 1952 – 86 mins
dir Marcello Pagliero, Charles Brabant

Dreary screen adaptation of the play by Jean-Paul Sartre, containing an appearance by trumpeter **Bill Coleman**.

1419

Le pain du ciel

France 1962 – 20 mins
dir Philippe Agostini

Documentary on the problems of world hunger and the part that engineers and chemists are playing to help provide food for the exhausted soil. Music by **Hubert Rostaing**.

1420

The pajama game

USA 1957 – 99 mins
dir Stanley Donen

Light-hearted and friendly musical spoof of the management versus labour battle, adapted from its successful stage counterpart. Some orchestral arrangements are by **Buddy Bregman**, undoubtedly the swinging big band backing to the show-stopper 'Steam heat' and the big band source music in 'Hernando's hideaway'.

1421

Pal Joey

USA 1957 – 112 mins
dir George Sidney

Disappointingly revised and watered-down screen adaptation of John O'Hara's musical play lacking some of Rodgers and Hart's original songs and generally substituting bounce for bite, but there's still much to be enjoyed, particularly a ruthless, demanding Sinatra. His vocals are backed by The **Bobby Sherwood** Orchestra (though this doesn't apply to the so-called 'original soundtrack' album which used studio musicians instead).

1422

Le palais idéal

France 1959 – 17 mins
dir Ado Kyrou

Short story set in an old castle, with music by **André Hodeir**.

1423

La paloma

West Germany 1959 – 100 mins
dir Paul Martin

A filmed revue featuring mainly German entertainers such as The Kessler Twins, but also **Louis Armstrong**.

1424

Panama

USA c1952 – 3 mins

Snader Telescription of The **Bobcats** playing the title number.

1425

Panama hattie

USA 1942 – 79 mins
dir Norman Z. McLeod

Comedy musical based on the stage play by Herbert Fields and B. G. DeSylva, with music and lyrics by Cole Porter and musical numbers staged by Vincente Minnelli. Cast includes Lena Horne singing 'Just one of those things' and **Leo Watson**.

1426

Panic in the streets

USA 1950 – 95 mins
dir Elia Kazan

One of the best of the then current series of location thrillers, shot mainly in New Orleans using local people for minor roles, and concerning the search for a suspected carrier of bubonic plague. Featured prominently on soundtrack are **Benny Carter**, *alt sax, arr;* **Ziggy Elman, Teddy Buckner**, *tpts;* **Britt Woodman**, *trb;* **'Bumps' Myers, Eddie Miller**, *ten sax;* Russ Cheever, *clar;* Bill Elliott, *bas-sax;* **Hal Schaefer**, *pno;* **Ulysses Livingston**, *gtr;* Charlie Drayton, *bass;* **Lee Young**, *drs.* Frank Beach, *tpt,* is heard on the main title theme and in one sequence **Helen Humes**, accompanied by Freddie Slack, is the featured voice off screen.

1427

The paper doll

USA 1942 – 3 mins

Soundie featuring The **Mills Brothers** with dancer Dorothy Dandridge.

1428

Paper moon

USA 1973 – 103 mins
dir Peter Bogdanovich

Highly successful screen adaptation of Joe David Brown's novel *Addie Pray*, in which the visuals are accompanied on soundtrack by a non-stop stream of musical evergreens that include extracts from 'A picture of me without you' and 'Mississippi mud' performed by **Paul Whiteman** and His Orchestra; 'About a quarter to nine' by Ozzie Nelson and His Orchestra; 'Georgia on my mind' by **Hoagy Carmichael** and Stuart Gorrell, performed by **Hoagy Carmichael** and His Orchestra; 'After you've gone' performed by **Tommy Dorsey** and His Orchestra and 'The music goes round and round' performed by **Nat Gonella** and His Georgians.

1429

Parade of the bands

UK 1955 – 29 mins
dir Michael Carreras

Musical entertainment in colour and 'Scope featuring six popular bands of the time: Malcolm Mitchell, Frank Weir, Eric Jupp, Francisco Cavez, **Freddy Randall** and **Johnny Dankworth** with **Cleo Laine**.

1430

Paradise in Harlem

USA 1939 – 70 mins
dir Joseph Seiden

Black produced gangster-cum-musical movie set against a back-drop of jazz spots, featuring **Lucky Millinder** and His Orchestra with **Mamie Smith**, *voc.*

1431

Parallèles

France 1962 – 17 mins
dir Louis Daquin

Impressions of everyday experiences – lights, crowds, trains and the parallel lines of the rails. Music partly by **Pierre Michelot**.

1432

Paramount pictorial magazine

USA 1937 – c15 mins

Contains a five minute sequence entitled 'Record making with Duke' featuring **Duke Ellington** and His Orchestra.

1433

Paramount pictorial magazine no 837/The world at large

USA 1933 – c15 mins

Sandwiched in between Barron Lee and His Blue Rhythm Band are short segments of **Cab Calloway** and His Orchestra playing 'Echoes of the jungle' and **Duke Ellington** and His Orchestra with excerpts from 'Creole rhapsody', all introduced by Irving Mills.

1434

Pardon my rhythm

USA 1944 – 62 mins
dir Felix Feist

Rather stupid story of American adolescence, mainly a vehicle for displaying the questionable talents of Gloria Jean. Features **Bob Crosby** and his Orchestra (Mel Tormé, *drs*).

▲

Director Sidney Lumet, Paul Newman and Duke Ellington on location for **Paris blues**.

1435

Paris blues

USA 1961 – 98 mins
dir Martin Ritt

Paul Newman, as an unlikely jazz trombonist, moons around tourist Paris whilst Sidney Poitier mouths interminable platitudes about the 'colour problem'. Music score by **Duke Ellington**, supervised by **Billy Byers**, and jazz sequences feature **Louis Armstrong**. Controversy rages as to exactly which musicians are responsible for individual sequences but **Paul Gonsalves** and **Murray McEachern** ghosted the two principals; otherwise the collective personnel includes **Clark Terry, Willie Cook, Cat Anderson, Ray Nance, Ed Mullens, Lawrence Brown, Britt Woodman,** Louis Blackburn, **Juan Tizol, Jimmy Hamilton, Russell Procope,** Johnny Hodges, Oliver Nelson, 'Babe' Clark, **Harry Carney,** Bob Smiles, **Billy Strayhorn, Les Spann, Aaron Bell, Jimmy Johnson, Sam Woodyard, Max Roach,** Dave Jackson,'**Philly**'**Joe Jones, Guy Lafitte, Christian Garros, Jimmy Gourley,** Eugene Vees, **Joseph Reinhardt,** Jack Butler and **Guy Pedersen.**

1436

Le Paris des mannequins

France 1963 – 11 mins
dir François Reichenbach

Documentary about Paris fashion photographers, with music score by **Jacques Loussier.**

1437

Le Paris des Scandinaves

France 1964 – 15 mins
dir Jean-Jacques Fauré

Report on the lives of Scandinavian girls in Paris, with music by **Jacques Loussier**.

1438

Une Parisienne

France/Italy 1957 – 87 mins
dir Michel Boisrond

Lively Technicolor comedy with Brigitte Bardot giving one of her most animated performances, pouting, undressing and even fighting, all to good effect. A good jazz soundtrack by **Henri Crolla, Hubert Rostaing** and **André Hodeir**, with scat vocals by Christiane Legrand.

1439

Part 2, Sounder

USA 1976 – 98 mins
dir William Graham

Respectable sequel to *Sounder* using William H. Armstrong's novel as source once again. **Taj Mahal** not only provides the music score but also has a leading role as a folk singer.

1440

The party's over

UK 1963 – 94 mins
dir Guy Hamilton (uncredited)

Unconvincing and equally unrewarding tale of Chelsea layabouts. Title song sung by **Annie Ross**.

1441

Pas de caviar pour tante Olga

France 1965 – 100 mins
dir Jean Becker

Unoriginal and flatly routine comedy-thriller revolving around a lost roll of microfilm. Music by **Jacques Loussier**.

1442

Passing the buck

USA 1932 – 15 mins
dir Roy Mack

Vitaphone short featuring **Nina Mae McKinney** and 'Tiger rag'.

Passionate demons

see **Line.**

1443

Pat Garrett and Billy the Kid

USA 1973 – 106 mins
dir Sam Peckinpah

Fred Katz, *cello*, is credited as working on Bob Dylan's score for Peckinpah's return to his familiar territory of Western myth-making and – breaking.

1444

Patate/Friend of the family

France/Italy 1964 – 90 mins
dir Robert Thomas

Routine movie adaptation of the play by Marcel Achard, with music arrangements by **Hubert Rostaing**.

1445

Patience and fortitude

USA 1946 – 3 mins
dir Dave Gould

Soundie in which the much-recorded title number is interpreted by **Valaida Snow** backed by The Ali Baba Trio.

1446

Patterns in jazz

USA 1963 – 10 mins

Educational depiction of the life and work of a young jazz trumpet player engaged in performing, studying and teaching with the emphasis on jazz as a discipline worthy of serious study.

1447

The pawnbroker

USA 1964 – 115 mins
dir Sidney Lumet

Relentlessly dramatic exposition of the enormous moral question-mark over the problem of human responsibility, with a memorable performance by Rod Steiger. Excellent music score composed, arranged and conducted by **Quincy Jones** – his first for an American picture. Some arrangements and orchestrations by Dick Hazard and **Billy Byers**; solos by **Freddie Hubbard**, *tpt.*

The pay-off

see **T-bird gang.**

1448

Peacemeal

USA 1967 – 7 mins
dir Albert Allotta

Visual impression of an anti-war demonstration held in New York City, with music by **Chico Hamilton**.

1449

Il peccato di Anna/The sin of Anna

Italy 1952 – 85 mins
dir Camillo Mastrocinque

A minor, commercial melodrama with tentative and unconvincing racial overtones, featuring The **Roman New Orleans Jazz Band**.

1450

Péché de jeunesse/Sins of youth

France 1958 – 77 mins
dir Louis Duchesne

Totally unsubtle problem picture about a possessive mother and her son's relationship with a shop-girl. Music score by **Henri Crolla** and **André Hodeir**.

1451

Peggy Lee and The Dave Barbour Quartet

USA 1950 – 19 mins

Snader Telescriptions featuring the title artistes.

The penguin
see **Pingwin.**

1452

Pennies from heaven

USA 1936 – 80 mins
dir Norman Z. McLeod

Comedy-romance with music starring Bing Crosby. A nightclub sequence features **Louis Armstrong** and His Orchestra, with the participation of **Teddy Buckner** and an appearance by **Lionel Hampton** – the number is 'Skeleton in the closet'.

1453

The penthouse

UK 1967 – 96 mins
dir Peter Collinson

Screen adaptation of the play *The meter man* by C. Scott Forbes on the theme of the outsider who insinuates himself into a household in a subordinate position and proceeds gradually to assume control. Music track by **John Hawksworth** and the song 'World full of lonely men' by **Hawksworth** and Harold Shaper.

1454

People are funny

USA 1946 – 83 mins
dir Sam White

Second-feature comedy about a Hollywood radio show, featuring Ozzie Nelson and His Orchestra with the number 'Every hour on the hour' by Don George and **Duke Ellington**.

People meet
see **Mennesker modes og sod musik opstär i hjertet.**

1455

People people people

USA 1975 – 4 mins
dir John Hubley

A condensed recap of the population process on the North American continent from 1776 BC to 1976, told in the form of an animated cartoon. Music composed and conducted by **Benny Carter**.

1456

Perdido

USA c1952 – 3 mins

Sarah Vaughan, backed off-screen by a big band, sings the title number – a Snader Telescription.

1457

Perfect Friday

UK 1970 – 95 mins
dir Peter Hall

Unattractive, routine bank robbery movie played for laughs – or rather, for brave smiles. Music composed, arranged and conducted by **John Dankworth**, though much credit must go to orchestrator Ken Gibson.

1458

Permission to kill

USA/Austria 1975 – 97 mins
dir Cyril Frankel

Screen adaptation by Robin Estridge of his own novel; a suspense thriller involving secret agents from Western Intelligence. Richard Rodney Bennett's music score is played by the Vienna Volksoper Orchestra, featuring **Art Farmer**, *fl horn*.

Personal column
see **Pièges.**

1459

Pete Fountain Sextet

USA 1962 – 23 mins
dir Steve Binder

Originally produced for Jazz Scene USA by US TV and hosted by Oscar Brown, Jnr, a bandstand performance of five numbers by **Pete Fountain**, *clar;* John Propst, *pno;* Bobby Gibbons, *gtr;* **Morty Corb**, *bass;* **Jack Sperling**, *drs;* Godfrey Hirsch, *vibs.* 'Avalon', 'Do you know what it means to miss New Orleans?', 'St Louis blues', 'Lazy river' and 'Creole gumball'.

1460
Pete Kelly's blues
USA 1955 – 95 mins
dir Jack Webb

The story of a jazz-age trumpeter who clashes with a gang of racketeers. A great opening sequence of a Negro cornetist's funeral, Peggy Lee, and two fine numbers from **Ella Fitzgerald** backed by **Don Abney**, *pno;* **Joe Mondragon**, *bass;* and **Larry Bunker**, *drs.* Jazz arrangements are by **Matty Matlock** with participating musicians: **Teddy Buckner**, *cor;* **George Van Eps, Moe Schneider**, *trbs;* **Matty Matlock**, *clar;* **Eddie Miller**, *ten sax;* Ray Sherman, *pno;* Jud de Naut, *bass;* **Nick Fatool**, *drs;* **Joe Venuti, Thomas Jefferson**; Harper Goff, Perry Bodkin and **Dick Cathcart** dubbing trumpet for Jack Webb. Musical numbers: 'Pete Kelly's blues',

'Sing me a rainbow', 'He needs me', 'Oh, didn't he ramble', 'I never knew', 'Hard hearted Hannah', 'Sugar', 'Bye bye blackbird' and 'Somebody loves me'.

Pete, Pearl and the pole
see **Piazza pulita.**

1461
Pete's place
USA 1966 – 17 mins

A music short presenting an impression of **Pete Fountain** in action during the Mardi Gras festival in New Orleans.

1462
Photo souvenir
France 1960 – 18 mins
dir Henri Fabiani

Dick Cathcart ghosted cornet for Jack Webb in **Pete Kelly's blues.**

▼

While developing his customer's photographs, a photographer imagines what these same photos could have looked like had they been taken with a modicum of taste and imagination. Music by **Henri Crolla**.

1463
Piaf/The sparrow of Pigalle
France 1974 – 105 mins
dir Guy Casaril

Thoroughly old-fashioned film biography of Edith Piaf's early career, curiously lacking in sensitivity. Musical direction by **Ralph Burns** who also supplies one song *Sur tes lèvres*, sung by Betty Mars.

1464
Pianorama
UK 1973 – 22 mins
dir Richard Taylor

Scrappy comedy subtitled *Six scenes in the life of a very upright piano*, with music score by **John Dankworth**.

1465
Piazza pulita/Pete, Pearl and the pole
USA 1973 – 96 mins
dir Vance Lewis (Luigi Vanzi)

Belated attempt to jump on the thirties gangster bandwagon, featuring soundtrack use of **Louis Armstrong**'s recording of 'The Sheik of Araby'.

1466
Pick up
France 1968 – 16 mins
dir Bernard Eisenschitz

Fictional short story about a young girl living in Paris who steals a dress and becomes involved with a boy. Music by **Gato Barbieri**.

1467
Picnic
USA 1955 – 113 mins
dir Joshua Logan

Over-blown transcription by Daniel Taradash of William Inge's famous play; entertaining by virtue of the splendid playing by its strong cast. Pianist **Stan Wrightsman** is prominently featured on George Duning's memorable music track.

1468
Pie, pie, blackbird
USA 1932 – 9 mins
dir Roy Mack

Vitaphone short featuring **Eubie Blake** and His Band with **Nina Mae McKinney**, *voc*, and the tap-dancing Nicholas Brothers. Numbers: 'Black Maria', 'Blackbird pie', 'Memories of you', 'Everything I've got belongs to you', 'You rascal you' and 'China boy'.

1469
The pied piper of Basin Street
USA 1944 – 7 mins
dir James Culhane

Universal Lantz Technicolor cartoon about a trombone player who rids a town of rats, with soundtrack music by **Jack Teagarden**.

1470
Piedalu deputé
France 1953 – 95 mins
dir Jean Loubignac

The third in the series of Piedalu domestic comedies, enlivened by appearances from **André Réwéliotty** and His Orchestra, **Sidney Bechet**, **Claude Luter** and Le Quadrille de Be-Bop de Saint Germain-des-Prés.

1471
Pièges/Snares/Personal column
France 1939 – 115 mins
dir Robert Siodmak

A Parisian playboy is almost convicted of murder. Nightclub sequences feature **Freddie Johnson** and **Valaida Snow**.

The pig's war
see **La guerra del cerdo**.

1472
Pillow to post
USA 1945 – 94 mins
dir Vincent Sherman

Screen adaptation of the stage play by Rose Simon Kohn, in which Ida Lupino made her debut as comedienne. Contains an appearance by **Herb Flemming**, *trb*.

1473
Pin up girl
USA 1943 – 83 mins
dir Bruce Humberstone

Routine Fox romantic comedy in Technicolor, with musical interludes – a vehicle for Betty Grable. Charlie Spivak and His Orchestra, (**Alvin Stoller**, *drs*), are featured in several numbers which include 'You're my little pin up girl', 'Once too often', 'The story of the very merry widow', 'Don't carry tales out of school' and 'Time will tell'.

474

Pingwin/The penguin

Poland 1965 – 85 mins
dir Jerzy Stefan Stawinski

Limpid tale of a timid, lonely young man who eventually faces up to the corruption around him. Music score by **Krzystof Komeda**.

475

The pink panther

USA 1963 – 114 mins
dir Blake Edwards

Amusing, though erratic, comedy which chronicles the misadventures of an incompetent but zealous official of the Sûreté on the trail of a celebrated international jewel thief. Henry Mancini's bouncy music score includes plenty of soundtrack tenor sax from **Plas Johnson**.

476

The pink panther strikes again

UK 1976 – 103 mins
dir Blake Edwards

Number 4 in Edwards's Pink Panther series, full of prat falls and equally tired and uninspired jokes, redeemed only by Richard Williams's witty and inventive animated credit sequence and by Henry Mancini's bouncy music track on which is featured soloists **Tony Coe**, *ten sax*, and **Don Lusher**, *trb*.

477

Pinky

USA 1949 – 102 mins
dir Elia Kazan

Intelligent, beautifully played, drama based on a novel by Cid Ricketts Sumner on the controversial theme of racial prejudice. Contains a memorable performance by **Ethel Waters** and an appearance by **Nina Mae McKinney** plus the song 'Blue (with you or without you)'.

478

The pirate

USA 1948 – 102 mins
dir Vincente Minnelli

Classic MGM Technicolor musical with Judy Garland and Gene Kelly plus a great Cole Porter score. Features **Wilbur De Paris**, *trb*.

1479

Pity the poor rich/Nat Gonella and His Georgians

UK 1935 – 22 mins
dir Ian Walker

In a nightclub setting, **Nat Gonella** and His Georgians play four numbers with solos and vocals by the leader, *tpt*: 'Georgia on my mind', 'I'm gonna wash my hands of you', 'Troublesome trumpet' and a thinly disguised 'Tiger rag'. Musicians include: Monia Liter, *pno*; Eric Ritty, *alt sax*; Don Barrigo, *ten sax*; and 'Tiny' Winters, *bass*.

1480

Play it again, Sam

USA 1972 – 86 mins
dir Herbert Ross

Very funny, thoroughly entertaining screen version of Woody Allen's play with the author repeating his Broadway performance as an erratic, self-deprecating film buff vicariously living through Humphrey Bogart's movie roles. The soundtrack features 'Blues for Allan Felix' written and performed by **Oscar Peterson**.

1481

Play misty for me

USA 1971 – 96 mins
dir Clint Eastwood

Competent but fairly conventional thriller, more entertaining than its predictable script would suggest. **Erroll Garner**'s interpretation of his own number 'Misty' is used extensively on the sound-track and part of **Ellington**'s classic 'Squeeze me' is heard. The **Cannonball Adderley** Quintet is seen and heard briefly while at the Monterey Jazz Festival. Also on soundtrack is **Roberta Flack** singing 'The first time I ever saw your face'.

1482

Playback – André Previn

USA 1963 – 4 mins
dir Tim Kiley

A brief promotional telerecording made by CBS records in which Previn talks about his career and, accompanied by **Red Mitchell**, *bass*, and **Frankie Capp**, *drs*, plays 'Perdido'. 'Like love' and 'Hindemith sonata'.

1483

Playback – Dave Brubeck and His Quartet

USA 1963 – 5 mins
dir Tim Kiley

Promotional telerecording made by CBS records in which The Quartet play 'Thank you', 'Dziekujo' and 'Blue rondo à la Turk'.

1484

Playback – Duke Ellington

USA 1963 – 4 mins
dir Tim Kiley

Promotional telerecording made by CBS records
in which **Ellington** leads his Band in a swinging
version of a section from the *Nutcracker suite*.
Soloing are **Paul Gonsalves**, *ten sax;* **Lawrence
Brown**, *trb;* **Shorty Baker**, *tpt;* **Sam Woodyard**,
drs.

1485

Playback – Mahalia Jackson

USA 1963 – 4 mins
dir Tim Kiley

Promotional telerecording made by CBS records
in which **Mahalia Jackson** talks about her music
and her plans for an interdenominational temple.
With immense power and sincerity she sings
'Holding my Saviour's hand'.

1486

Playback – Teddy Wilson

USA 1963 – 4 mins
dir Tim Kiley

Promotional telerecording made by CBS records
in which the pianist discusses his style and plays
a lively version of 'Tea for two'.

1487

Playing the environment game

UK 1973 – 30 mins
dir Mick Csàky

Arts Council account of the efforts of three
pressure groups to alter development plans in
Central London. Music used on soundtrack: 'Birds
of fire' played by The Mahavishnu Orchestra; 'As
time goes by' sung by **Billie Holiday**.

1488

Playing the thing

UK 1972 – 30 mins
dir Christopher Morphet

Exuberant, joyful celebration of the multiple
sounds, moods and pleasures which can be
obtained from that somewhat despised
instrument, the harmonica. Features, among
many artistes, **Sonny Terry** playing an
improvised blues and also two of his own
compositions: 'Fox chase' and 'Uncle Bud'.

1489

The pleasure seekers

USA 1964 – 107 mins
dir Jean Negulesco

A re-hash of 'Three coins in the fountain' – but set
in Spain for a change. Orchestrations by **Billy
May**.

1490

Plein air

France 1956 – 20 mins
dir Jean Vénard

Impressions of camping sports, with music by
Henri Crolla.

1491

Plod

UK 1972 – 20 mins
dir Michael Cort

An agreeable piece of Liverpudlian whimsy, based
on the 'P. C. Plod' poems by Roger McGough.
Musical direction by **John Hawksworth**.

1492

Les plus belles escroqueries du monde

France/Italy/Japan 1962 – 90 mins
dirs J-L Godard, C. Chabrol, U. Gregoretti, R.
Polanski, H. Horikawa

A five-part anthology film dramatising examples of
cheating throughout the world. Polanski's episode
set in Amsterdam, was scored by **Krzystof
Komeda**.

1493

Pociag/Night train

Poland 1959 – 100 mins
dir Jerzy Kawalerowicz

Excellent drama set primarily on a train; half
thriller, half psychological study of the
separateness of human beings. Andrzej
Trzaskowski's music score is based on 'Moon
rays' by **Artie Shaw**.

1494

Pocomania

USA 1939 – 65 mins
dir Arthur Leonard

All Negro production filmed on location in
Jamaica, with **Nina Mae McKinney**.

1495

Poem posters

USA 1967 – 24 mins
dir Charles Henri Ford

An experiment in multi-media: artwork, living
portraits, jazz, poetry, reportage. Music: **John
Handy**.

496

Point blank

USA 1967 – 92 mins
dir John Boorman

Enjoyable adaptation of Richard Stark's excellent
novel *The hunter*, with suitable atmospheric music
by **Johnny Mandel**.

497

Pojken i trädet/Boy in the tree

Sweden 1961 – 86 mins
dir Arne Sucksdorff

A stilted tale of a misunderstood teenager who
becomes friendly with two delinquent game
poachers – the first feature with live actors by this
famous maker of nature films. **Quincy Jones**
music score was his first motion picture
assignment.

498

The polyolefins

UK 1964 – 25 mins
dir Alan Pendry

Experiments made with plastics reveal their
suitability to replace more expensive or less
efficient traditional materials. Music by **Johnny
Hawksworth**.

499

Population explosion

Canada 1967 – 14 mins
dir Pierre Hébert

Instructional animated cartoon depicting the
demographic problems of the world and
suggesting how wealthier nations might help. It's
hard work to watch and extraordinary to hear with
original soundtrack music by **Ornette Coleman**
played by **Coleman**, *alt sax;* **David Izenzon**,
bass; and **Charles Moffett**, *drs*.

500

Porgy and Bess

USA 1959 – 138 mins
dir Otto Preminger

Extravagantly produced adaptation of Gershwin's
stage operetta featuring **Pearl Bailey**, with André
Previn as music director and **Russ Freeman**
assisting with underscoring.

501

Les portes claquent

France 1960 – 90 mins
dir Jacques Poitrenaud, Michel Fermaud

A light comedy about an eccentric family, with
music by Michel Legrand and featuring **Maxim
Saury**.

1502

Portrait of a bushman

Denmark c1968 – 8 mins
dir Niels Holt

A short study of pianist **Dollar Brand** in
Copenhagen and at the Jazzhus Montmartre,
accompanied by unidentified *bass* and **M.
Ntshoko**, *drs*.

1503

Portrait robot, ou échec à l'assassin

France 1961 – 85 mins
dir Paul Paviot

Adaptation of a novel by Michel Lebrun about a
journalist who finds himself suspected of murder,
with music score by **Bill Byers**.

1504

Le poulet/The chicken

France 1963 – 16 mins
dir Claude Berri

Simple, uncomplicated story of a little boy's
attachment to a chicken and how he saves it from
the dinner table. Music by **René Urtreger**.

1505

Pourquoi l'Amérique?/Why America?

France 1969 – 100 mins
dir Frédéric Rossif

A documentary on the USA between the two
world wars charting the rise of the country
towards world power status. Old footage used
includes material on **Louis Armstrong**.

1506

The Powers girl/Hello! beautiful

USA 1942 – 94 mins
dir Norman Z. Mcleod

Extravagant musical about a girl's rise to fame as
a Powers model. Features **Benny Goodman** and
His Orchestra which includes **Lou McGarity,
Dave Barbour** and **Louis Bellson**. Numbers:
'The lady who didn't believe in love' (Peggy Lee,
voc), 'One o'clock jump', 'Roll 'em', 'I know that
you know', 'Three dreams', 'Out of this world',
'Partners' and 'We're looking for the big bad wolf'.

Precinct 45 – Los Angeles police
see **The new Centurions.**

1507

La première fois

France 1976 – 85 mins
dir Claude Berri

Semi-autobiographical sequel to the same director's *The two of us*, with the Jewish boy now 17 experiencing his first frustrations. Music by **René Urtreger**.

1508

The present

UK 1971 – 36 mins
dir Don Higgins

A sponsored film stating the case for the use of labelling machines in the factory, with music by **Johnny Hawksworth**.

1509

Presenting Lily Mars

USA 1943 – 104 mins
dir Norman Taurog

MGM musical romance based on a novel by Booth Tarkington and tailored for its star, Judy Garland. **Bob Crosby** and His Orchestra appear in a nightclub sequence backing two vocals by Garland plus an instrumental 'Paradise'. **Tommy Dorsey** and His Orchestra appear in the film's final dance sequence 'Broadway rhythm'. One of Garland's younger sisters is played by Annabelle Logan (**Annie Ross**).

1510

The President's analyst

USA 1967 – 103 mins
dir Theodore J. Flicker

A sharp and witty satire of contemporary America, helped considerably by a splendid performance from James Coburn. Music by **Lalo Schifrin**.

1511

Pretty maids all in a row

USA 1971 – 95 mins
dir Roger Vadim

Pointless black comedy which tends to spring into life only when Angie Dickinson is on the screen. Music and song 'Chilly winds' by **Lalo Schifrin**.

1512

Pretty poison

USA 1968 – 89 mins
dir Noel Black

Fascinating black comedy from the book *She let him continue* by Stephen Geller, with a memorably fine performance by Tuesday Weld. Music by **Johnny Mandel**.

1513

Prima della rivoluzione/Before the revolution

Italy 1964 – 112 mins
dir Bernardo Bertolucci

A complex and richly romantic drama conceived with all the passion and narcissism of a precocious intellectual, establishing the director as one of the most important film-makers to emerge in the sixties. Several sequences receive added power from **Leandro 'Gato' Barbieri**'s cool tenor sax work on the soundtrack playing his own 'Walking with GA', 'Invention for Fabrizio' and 'Gina'.

1514

Prime cut

USA 1972 – 86 mins
dir Michael Ritchie

In spite of severe production difficulties, a splendidly formal gangster movie set in unconventional locations – the cattle-pens and wheat fields of Kansas. Great fun until the lame final reel. Suitably forceful music score by **Lalo Schifrin**.

1515

Prime of my life

USA c1960 – 3 mins

Scopitone, in colour, of **Billy Eckstine** singing the title number.

1516

Les primitifs du XIIIe

France 1960 – 26 mins
dir Pierre Guilbaud

Prize-winning documentary about children at a Paris nursery school and how, through drawing, they learn to see, to remember, to read and write and prepare themselves for life in the larger world outside. Music by **Henri Crolla** and **André Hodeir**.

1517

Printemps à Paris

France 1956 – 85 mins
dir Jean-Claude Roy

A provincial girl visiting Paris acts as an excuse for a series of variety acts representing *Paris la nuit*. Participants include **Bill Coleman** and **Maxim Saury**.

1518

The prisoner of Second Avenue

USA 1975 – 98 mins
dir Melvin Frank

Screen adaptation by Neil Simon of his own play. **Pete Candoli** takes the trumpet solos on Marvin Hamlisch's music track.

1519

Private buckaroo

USA 1942 – 69 mins
dir Edward F. Cline

Conventional, low-budget comedy with music,
featuring **Harry James** and His Music Makers
and The Andrew Sisters.

1520

Private hell 36

USA 1954 – 80 mins
dir Don Siegel

Routine, though efficiently made, melodrama about
a cop who succumbs to dishonesty because of a
desirable woman. Excellent soundtrack music by
Leith Stevens incorporates jazz by leading West
Coast musicians: **Sal Franzella, Lennie Niehaus,
Bob Cooper, Jimmy Giuffre, Bob Gordon, Bud
Shank,** *saxes;* **Pete Candoli,** Charlie Grifford,
Shorty Rogers, Carlton MacBeth, *tpts;* **Milt
Bernhart, Harry Betts, Bob Enevoldsen,
George Roberts,** *trbs;* **John Graas,** *Fr horn;*
Paul Sarmento, *tuba;* **Claude Williamson,** *pno;*
Joe Mondragon, *bass;* **Shelly Manne,** *drs.*

Pro

see **Number one.**

1521

Le procès/The trial

France/Italy/West Germany 1962 – 118 mins
dir Orson Welles

Fascinating screen adaptation of Kafka's
nightmarish novel *The trial* which Welles has
turned into his own particular style of baroque
exercise. Jazz arrangements are by Jean Ledrut
and feature The **Martial Solal** Trio.

1522

**A program of songs by 'Lightnin'' Sam
Hopkins**

USA 1971 – 8 mins

An informal performance of three songs by
'Lightnin'' **Hopkins,** country-blues guitarist,
produced by the University of Washington
Archives of Ethnic Music and Dance.

1523

The proper time

USA 1959 – 75 mins
dir Tom Loughlin

Uneven *tour de force* by a young actor-writer-
director, about student problems at U.C.L.A. that
almost comes off. Driving jazz score by **Shelly
Manne,** played by **Joe Gordon,** *tpt;* Richie
Kamuca, *ten sax;* **Victor Feldman,** *vibs;* **Russ
Freeman,** *pno;* **Monte Budwig,** *bass;* **Shelly
Manne,** *drs.*

1524

The prowler/Cost of loving

USA 1951 – 91 mins
dir Joseph Losey

A rivetingly cool, clean thriller about the trap
which inexorably closes on a woman unhappily
married to a rich husband, and the cop
summoned to deal with the prowler who lingers to
get rid of the husband and take both wife and
money for himself. Radio sequences on
soundtrack feature a band headed by **Randy
Brooks,** *tpt;* and including **Clyde Hurley,** *tpt;*
Benny Carter, *alt sax;* Don Ferris, *pno;* Vince
Terri, *gtr;* Larry Breen, *bass;* **Alvin Stoller,** *drs.*
Lynn Murray is composer, arranger and
conductor.

1525

Pudgy boy

USA 1942 – 3 mins

Soundie featuring **Les Hite** and His Orchestra
with their interpretation of the title number – vocal
by **Les Hite.**

1526

Pull my daisy

USA 1959 – 28 mins
dir Robert Frank, Alfred Leslie

Hilarious adaptation of an unproduced play by
Jack Kerouac *The beat generation* with an
ad-libbed narration that is little short of a major
masterpiece. Music, including a swinging jazz
intro and song 'The crazy daisy' sung by Anita
Ellis, is by **David Amram** who also has a leading
role in the movie.

1527

Punishment park

USA 1971 – 89 mins
dir Peter Watkins

Another of this director's 'reconstructions of the
future' – documentary fiction in allegorical form.
Music track by **Paul Motian.**

1528

Pussycat, pussycat, I love you

USA 1970 – 100 mins
dir Rod Amateau

Creaking comedy that bears more than a surface
likeness to *What's new, pussycat?* . . . Music and
a song, 'Groove into it', by **Lalo Schifrin.**

1529

Put-put-put (your arms around me)

USA 1942 – 3 mins

Soundie in which the title song is sung by Rufe
David, backed by **Sonny Dunham.**

1530

Quand c'est parti, c'est parti/J'ai mon voyage

Canada/France 1973 – 89 mins
dir Denis Héroux

Mild comedy about the latter-day discovery of Canada by an adventurer who has his wife and two boys as company in the car. Music by **Claude Bolling**.

1531

Quand les fleuves changent de chemin

France 1960 – 21 mins
dir Daniel Lecomte

The life of specialist workmen on site, with music by **André Hodeir**.

1532

Que s'est-il passé en mai?

France 1969 – 18 mins
dir Jean-Paul Savignac

The events of May 1968 in Paris viewed in retrospect, with music by **Christian Garros** and **Guy Pedersen.**

A question of rape
see **Le viol.**

1533

Qui/Il cadavere dagli artigli d'acciaio

France/Italy 1970 – 77 mins
dir Léonard Keigel

Poor thriller adding nothing new to the genre. Music score by **Claude Bolling**.

1534

Quicksand

USA 1951 – 79 mins
dir Irving Pichel

Shop-soiled melodrama with Mickey Rooney as a garage mechanic involved in robbery, murder and other degenerate activities. With an appearance by **Red Nichols** and His Band.

Quiet days in Clichy
see **Stille dage in Clichy.**

1535

Race for the golden flag

UK 1969 – 11 mins
prod Roy Simpson

Impressions of the 1967 500 mile sports car race at Brands Hatch, Kent. Music by **Johnny Hawksworth**.

1536

Racing world

USA 1968 – 30 mins
dir Sam Shaw

Documentary showing paintings and sketches of racecourses by Dégas, Forain, Dufy and others. Music score written and performed by **Duke Ellington** – with complete musical freedom. Soundtrack musicians include: **Harold Ashby**, *ten sax;* **Harry Carney**, *clar, bar sax;* **Willie Cook** and **Chuck Connors**.

1537

Radio melodies

USA 1943 – 15 mins
dir Reginald LeBorg

A Universal 'Name Band' music short featuring **Stan Kenton** and His Orchestra playing 'Production on theme', 'Reed rapture' and Charlie Shirley arrangements of 'Ride on' and 'Hip, hip hooray' (Dolly Mitchell, voc). Personnel: Ray Borden, John Carroll, **Buddy Childers**, Dick Morse, Frank Payne, *tpts;* **Harry Forbes**, George Faye, *trbs;* **Bart Varsalona**, *bas-trb;* Eddie Meyers, Arnold Stanley, *alt sax;* 'Red' Dorris, Ted Vargas, *ten sax;* **Bob Gioga**, *bar sax;* **Stan Kenton**, *pno;* **Bob Ahern**, *gtr;* Clyde Singleton, *bass;* Joe Vernon, *drs.*

Radio revels of 1942
see **Swing it soldier.**

1538

Radio stars on parade

USA 1945 – 69 mins
dir Leslie Goodwins

Minor RKO musical but does contain two nice songs: 'I couldn't sleep a wink last night' and 'That old black magic' and features **Skinnay Ennis** and His Band.

1539

Rafferty and The Gold Dust Twins

USA 1974 – 91 mins
dir Dick Richards

Sterile comedy-drama about the 'ordinary people' of America. **Louis Prima** and His Band appear briefly in a casino sequence.

1540

Rage

USA 1972 – 99 mins
dir George C. Scott

A sluggish, tired and tiring melodrama, with George C. Scott in his screen directorial debut as a father wreaking vengeance for the death of his son after a chemical warfare experimental accident. Music score by **Lalo Schifrin**.

1541

The ragman's daughter

UK 1972 – 94 mins
dir Harold Becker

Charming, bitter-sweet, love story set in Nottingham, adapted by Alan Sillitoe from his own short story – firmly rooted in the regional social realism which, in film terms, gained prominence at the beginning of the sixties. Kenny Clayton's excellent score is interpreted by some top jazz talent including **Danny Moss**, *ten sax;* Chris Taylor, *flute, picc;* Tony Campo, *bass;* **Kenny Clare**, *drs.*

1542

Raintree County

USA 1957 – 166 mins
dir Edward Dmytryk

A long, rambling narrative adapted from a novel of the Civil War by Russ Lockridge Jnr. Only the battle scenes reflect any visual skill or vigour but John Green's superior music score has become one of the all-time classics. It includes a vocal 'The song of Raintree County' with lyrics by Paul Francis Webster sung on soundtrack by Nat **'King' Cole**. The superb harmonica solos on soundtrack are by George Fields.

1543

Rak

France 1972 – 90 mins
dir Charles Belmont

Drama about a woman suffering from cancer and her desire to fight for recovery. Music score by **André Hodeir**.

1544

Ramblin'

USA 1970 – 15 mins
dir D. A. Pennebaker

A film of performers Jack Elliott, Michael Pollard, **Odetta**, Kris Kristofferson and Bobby Neuwirth.

1545

Rambling 'round Radio Row No 1

USA 1932 – 9 mins

Popular entertainers, including The **Boswell Sisters**, present a musical programme: 'Louisiana waddle', 'Whistle and blow your blues away', 'Put that sun back in the sky', 'My mother's eyes' and 'Too many tears'.

1546

Rambling 'round Radio Row no 7

USA 1934 – 9 mins

Paul Whiteman's Rhythm Boys are among the popular radio personalities who entertain with a programme including 'Just you and I' and 'How'm I doin'?'.

1547

Rambling 'round Radio Row no 8

USA 1934 – 9 mins

Radio personalities behind the scenes perform several numbers including **W. C. Handy**'s 'St Louis blues'.

1548

The rat race

USA 1960 – 105 mins
dir Robert Mulligan

Uneven, wisecracking tale of a young jazz musician in New York, scripted by Garson Kanin from his own play. Features **Gerry Mulligan, Joe Bushkin, Paul Horn** and Bryan Clark.

1549

Ration blues

USA 1944 – 3 mins

Soundie featuring **Louis Jordan** and His Band.

1550

Ray Anthony and His Orchestra

USA 1947 – 11 mins
dir Harry Foster

One in the 'Thrills of Music' series in which a disc jockey chatters in between selections from the Orchestra. Numbers include: 'I'll close my eyes', 'Let's go back and kiss the boys again' and 'Finiculi, finicula'.

1551

Ray Anthony and His Orchestra

USA 1950 – 14 mins
dir Will Cowan

In a nightclub setting, **Ray Anthony** and His Orchestra provide a programme of music supported by a vocal group, The Starlighters, and a tap dancing xylophonist Jimmy Vey. Numbers include 'Toot toot tootsie goodbye' and 'Come to the fair'.

1552

Ray McKinley and His Orchestra

USA 1946 – 10 mins
dir Harry Foster

A Columbia 'Thrills of Music' short in which the title orchestra shows its paces with a musical programme that includes 'Hoodle addle', 'Tabu' and 'Comin' out'.

1553

Ray McKinley and His Orchestra

USA 1948 – 8 mins
dir Jay Bonafield

One of the RKO 'Jamboree' series – a routine programme of music by the title orchestra with the accent on the leader's drumming. Numbers include 'St Louis blues', 'Big boy', 'Yank, yankee doodle' and 'Jive bomber'.

1554
Le réacteur nucléaire

France 1966 – 14 mins
dir Manuel Otéro, Jacques Leroux

The working of a nuclear reactor, with music by **Martial Solal**.

1555
Readin', 'ritin' and rhythm

USA 1939 – 10 mins
dir Milton Schwarzwald

An RKO Radio short featuring **Don Byas, Lucky Millinder** and **Frankie Newton** with orchestrations by Jack Schaindlin. Includes an interpretation of the number 'Ride red ride'.

Rebel with a cause
see **Loneliness of the long distance runner.**

1556
Reckless

USA 1935 – 97 mins
dir Victor Fleming

Somewhat turgid melodrama with music featuring Jean Harlow, with an appearance by **Nina Mae McKinney.**

1557
Record hop

USA 1957 – 15 mins

Universal music featurette with **Ella Mae Morse**, The Lancers, Tex Williams, Alan Copeland plus **Charlie Barnet** and His Orchestra.

1558
Record party

USA 1947 – 15 mins
dir Will Cowan

Universal featurette with singer Connie Haines, The Pied Pipers, The Page Cavanaugh Trio and mimic Jackie Green.

1559
Red Nichols and His Five Pennies

USA 1950 – 15 mins
dir Will Cowan

A Universal-International programme filler featuring the title group with June Hutton, *voc;* The Skylarks, *voc harmony*; Bob Hopkins, *comedy;*and Burns Twins & Evelyn, *taps.* Numbers include: 'Three blind mice', 'Do it again', 'Vaudeville is back', 'The entry of the gladiators' and 'I got tookin''.

1560
Red Nichols and His Five Pennies

USA 1950 – 19 mins

Snader Telescriptions featuring the title group.

1561
Red Nichols and His World Famous Pennies

USA 1936 – 9 mins
dir Joseph Henabery

A programme of music from the title group supported by The Wallace Sisters and Bob Carter. 'Wail of the winds', 'Get happy', 'Cryin' for the Carolines', 'Sleepytime down South', 'Troublesome trumpet', 'Can't you hear me calling' and 'Carolina in the morning'.

1562
The red shoes

UK 1948 – 136 mins
dir Michael Powell, Emeric Pressburger

One of the few truly great British movies with Moira Shearer as dancer Vicky Page caught between two loves and eventually dancing to her death. Brian Easdale's music score incorporates trumpet work by **Kenny Baker.**

1563
Red sky at morning

USA 1970 – 112 mins
dir James Goldstone

Bearable melodrama, set in 1944, that emphasises the good-humoured but tough down-to-earth ways of country folk. Music arrangements by **Benny Carter.**

The red wagon
see **They live by night.**

Redneck
see **Senza Ragione.**

1564
Redskin rhumba

USA 1948 – 15 mins
dir Will Cowan

Universal-International featurette spotlighting **Charlie Barnet** and His Orchestra, in a garden setting, supported by Clark Dennis and Virginia Maxey, vocalists. Numbers: 'Redskin rhumba', 'Skyliner', 'Jeepers creepers', 'Peg o' my heart' and 'Jealousy'.

1565
Reed rapture

USA 1942 – 3 mins

Soundie featuring **Stan Kenton**'s hit number.

1566
Reet, petite and gone

USA 1947
dir Bud Pollard

An all Negro production featuring **Louis Jordan**.

1567
Refuges

France 1963 – 14 mins
dir J. J. Languepin, R. Vernadet

The construction of mountain refuges for climbers, with music by **Jacques Loussier**.

Rendez-vous à Antibes-Juan-les-Pins
see **Antipolis.**

1568
Rendez-vous à Melbourne

France 1956 – 95 mins
dir René Jucot

Documentary on the 1956 Olympic Games in Melbourne, with music score by **Christian Chevallier** played by His Big Band.

1569
Rendez-vous de Juillet

France 1949 – 68 mins
dir Jacques Becker

Sketchy study of young people in post-war Paris: their ambitions, their loves, their family conflicts etc. Features **Claude Luter** and His Musicians playing music by **Mezz Mezzrow**, with **Rex Stewart** much in evidence.

1570
Repulsion

UK 1965 – 104 mins
dir Roman Polanski

Polanski's first British movie – a casebook study of madness. Music by **Chico Hamilton** whose jazz contributions to the film being neither motivated by dramatic necessity nor by decorative need, seem quite superfluous.

1571
Requiem

USA c1970 – 5 mins
dir Jeff Dell

Images of young people, violence, persecution and death, produced to the memory of Martin Luther King. A recording of **Billie Holiday** singing 'Strange fruit' is used as backing on soundtrack.

The respectable prostitute
see **La P . . . réspectueuse.**

1572
Return from the ashes

UK 1965 – 104 mins
dir J. Lee Thompson

Depressingly weary psychological melodrama based on the novel by Jubert Monteilhet. Music by **John Dankworth**.

1573
The return of the pink panther

UK 1975 – 115 mins
dir Blake Edwards

The third in Blake Edwards's series of Pink Panther comedies and probably the most successful in terms of distinction. Henry Mancini again provides a bouncy big band score, with tenor sax solos by **Tony Coe**.

1574
Return to Macon County/Highway girl

USA 1975 – 89 mins
dir Richard Compton

A sequel in name and setting only to *Macon County line* – little more than a potboiling *American Graffiti* with a period soundtrack utilising recordings by sundry artistes including **Jimmy Dorsey**, with **Fats Domino** opening and closing the movie with 'I'm gonna be a wheel someday'.

1575
Reveille with Beverly

USA 1943 – 77 mins
dir Charles Barton

Low-budget musical with lots of fine music, about a local radio station and a disc jockey's ambition. Features **Duke Ellington** and His Orchestra (**Sonny Greer**, *drs*) playing 'Take the 'A' train', written by **Billy Strayhorn** especially for the movie; Bob Crosby's Dixieland Band with **Ray Bauduc** and **Bob Haggart** doing their 'Big noise from Winnetka'; **Count Basie** and His Band (**Vernon Alley**, *bass*) playing 'One o'clock jump'; **Ray McKinley's** Orchestra; Frank Sinatra singing 'Night and day'; Freddie Slack's orchestra; **Ella Mae Morse** with 'Cow cow boogie'; The **Mills Brothers** and The Radio Rogues.

1576
Reverend Gary Davis
USA 1967 – 26 mins

A film portrait of the great blues-turned-gospel singer and guitarist **Gary Davis**. Numbers include 'Candy man', 'Twelve gates to the city' and 'Stove pipe rag'.

1577
Rhapsody in black and blue
USA 1932 – 9 mins
dir Aubrey Scotto

Tasteless music short featuring **Louis Armstrong** and His Orchestra in which Satchmo, dressed in a leopard skin and standing in soap bubbles, performs 'I'll be glad when you're dead you rascal you' and 'Shine'.

1578
Rhapsody in blue
USA 1945 – 139 mins
dir Irving Rapper

Pedestrian film biography of George Gershwin for which Warner Bros '. . . faithfully reconstructed the scenes of his life (58 interiors, 23 exteriors) . . Appearances by **Paul Whiteman** and His Orchestra and pianist **Hazel Scott**.

1579
Rhapsody in wood
USA 1947 – 9 mins
dir George Pal

Cartoon featuring a mixture of puppet animation and a live-action **Woody Herman** explaining the origin of his clarinet. **Herman** plays solo clarinet throughout.

1580
Rhino!
USA 1963 – 91 mins
dir Ivan Tors

Routine wild-life picture with a particularly silly story and music by **Lalo Schifrin**.

1581
Rhythm and blues revue
USA 1956 – 70 mins

Musical extravaganza featuring Negro entertainers, among which are **Nat 'King' Cole, Count Basie, Sarah Vaughan** and **Lionel Hampton**. A compilation of previously issued shorts made for US TV?

Paul Whiteman and His Orchestra feature in **Rhapsody in blue**.

1582

Rhythm in the ranks

USA 1941 – 10 mins
dir George Pal

A Paramount short, in the Madcap Model series, in which wooden soldiers come to life and march off in smart military fashion to a swing version of **Raymond Scott**'s 'The toy trumpet'.

1583

Rhythm inn

USA 1951 – 70 mins
dir Paul Landres

Formula musical from Monogram involving a Dixieland jazz band with a would-be song writer and a budding girl vocalist. Featured both visually and musically are **Pete Daily**, *cor;* '**Wingy' Manone**, *tpt;* **Joe Yukl**, *trb;* **Matty Matlock**, *clar;* **Walter Gross**, *pno;* Budd Hatch, *bass;* **Barrett Deems**, *drs.* Ramez Idriss soundtracked the single-string electric guitar solos for Ralph Peters. Also featured is The Anson Weeks Band in scenes originally shot for, but not used in, another film and pulled off the shelf for this one. Songs: 'Swing low, sweet chariot', 'Window wiper's song' sung by Jane Frazee; 'With a twist of the wrist', 'It's a big wide wonderful world' and 'Love' sung by Lois Collier.

1584

Rhythm masters – A decade of band hits

USA 1948 – 15 mins
dir Will Cowan

A Universal-International compilation from previous music shorts featuring **Jack Teagarden** and **Joe Sullivan** with 'Basin Street blues'; the bands of **Sonny Dunham; Henry Busse** (**Chubby Jackson**, *bass*); **Louis Prima** (with 'That old black magic'); Frankie Masters (with 'Stompin' at the Savoy'); Harry Owens and **Stan Kenton** ('Artistry in rhythm').

1585

Rhythm on the range

USA 1936 – 85 mins
dir Norman Taurog

Paramount vehicle for Bing Crosby, containing a brief appearance by **Louis Prima**.

1586

Rhythm on the river

USA 1944 – 3 mins

Soundie in which the title number is played by '**Wingy' Manone** and His band – instrumentalists include **Santo Pecora**, *trb.*

1587

Rhythm parade

USA 1942 – 70 mins
dir Howard Bretherton

Monogram musical revue featuring Ted Fiorito and His Orchestra and The **Mills Brothers**.

Rhythm romance

see **Some like it hot (1939).**

1588

Riddles in rhythm

USA 1956 – 15 mins

Universal featurette with The Nelson Riddle Orchestra, The Lancers, Matt Dennis, Leigh Snowden, Kay Brown, Earl Barton, Augie & Margo and **Jack Costanzo**.

1589

Ride 'em, cowboy

USA 1941 – 85 mins
dir Arthur Lubin

Rodeo extravaganza with music, tailored for the talents of its stars, Abbott and Costello. Features **Ella Fitzgerald** singing 'A tisket, a tasket'.

1590

Ride on, ride on

USA 1944 – 3 mins

Soundie featuring vocalist **June Richmond** accompanied by Roy Milton and His Orchestra.

1591

Rig move

UK 1964 – 25 mins
dir Don Higgins

A description of the removal of a giant drilling rig and all the maintenance and housing units required by the crew of 100 men to a new site in the Libyan desert. Music by **Johnny Hawksworth**.

1592

Rigoletto blues

USA 1941 – 3 mins

Soundie in which The **Delta Rhythm Boys** do a comedy operatic number.

1593

Riley the cop

USA 1928 – 76 mins
dir John Ford

Louis Prima, seated with trumpet, waits for his cue in
Rhythm on the range.

Beautifully conceived and executed comedy about
a loveable Irish policeman from New York who is
assigned to the job of extraditing a suspect from
Europe . . . with hilarious consequences. A Paris
nightclub sequence briefly features **Speed Webb**
and His Orchestra.

1594

The Rimacs Rhumba Orchestra

USA 1935 – 9 mins
dir Joseph Henabery

Vitaphone exhibition of rhumba dancing by the
title band which includes a performance of the
O.D.J.B.'s 'Tiger rag'.

1595

Rio bravo

USA 1959 – 141 mins
dir Howard Hawks

One of the really great movies of all time – a long,
conventionally outlined Western set within the
confines of a small Texas bordertown. On the
soundtrack, **Mannie Klein**'s trumpet work broods
sadly and ominously over much of the action with
the unforgettable 'De guello'.

1596

Riot

USA 1968 – 96 mins
dir Buzz Kulik

Violent drama adapted from ex-convict Frank
Elli's novel about an actual incident in a
Minnesota prison. Music score and song '100
years' by **Christopher Komeda**.

1597

Riot in rhythm

USA 1957 – 15 mins
dir Will Cowan

Universal-International music featurette with **Harry James** and His Music Makers supporting Johnny O'Neill and The DeCastro Sisters, *voc*, with Ralph and Lorraine, dancers. Numbers include 'Teach me tonight', 'Heartbreak hotel' and 'Jericho'.

1598
The rise and fall of the Third Reich
USA 1967 – 58 mins
dir Jack Kaufman

Originally produced for US TV by David Wolper, a reconstructed documentary, with music score by **Lalo Schifrin**.

Rites of passage
see **Bernice bobs her hair.**

1599
La rivière du hibou/Incident at Owl Creek
France 1961 – 27 mins
dir Robert Enrico

Prize-winning screen adaptation of Ambrose Bierce's story *An occurence at Owl Creek bridge* set during the American Civil War. A light jazz score includes contributions from **Kenny Clarke** and **Jimmy Gourley**.

1600
Road show
USA 1941 – 87 mins
dir Hal Roach

Crazy comedy with a circus background starring Adolphe Menjou and Carole Landis. Presents four songs by **Hoagy Carmichael**: 'Calliope Jane', 'I should have known you years ago', 'Slav Annie' and 'Yum! yum!'.

1601
Road to Bali
USA 1952 – 92 mins
dir Hal Walker

The sixth film in the 'Road' series, and the first in Technicolor – a mixture of burlesque, slapstick, surrealism and exotic South Sea islands. Contains a brief appearance by **Bob Crosby** and soundtrack use of **Stan Kenton**'s Capitol recording of 'Artistry in rhythm'. Participating on the recording of the soundtrack was **Chico Hamilton**.

1602
Road to Zanzibar
USA 1945 – 92 mins
dir Victor Schertzinger

Routine comedy vehicle for Hope, Crosby and Lamour set in Paramount's idea of the African interior. **Charles Mingus** worked in one sequence as an extra but was eventually edited out in the final cut.

Rock around the world
see **The Tommy Steele story.**

1603
Rock 'n' roll revue/Harlem rock 'n' roll
USA 1955 – 65 mins
dir Joseph Kohn

A misleading title, as this is mainly an assembly of jazz items by such performers as **Lionel Hampton, Duke Ellington, Nat 'King' Cole, Joe Turner**, The **Delta Rhythm Boys** and **Dinah Washington** (the last named was cut from the British release version).

1604
Rock, pretty baby
USA 1956 – 87 mins
dir Richard Bartlett

One of the routine melodramas in vogue at the time about misunderstandings between teenagers and their parents, here laced with rock 'n' roll. Henry Mancini's score includes two songs written by **Bobby Troup**: 'Rockabye lullaby blues' and 'Picnic by the sea'.

1605
Rock, rock, rock
USA 1956 – 85 mins
dir Will Price

A slim plot provides a rather ineffective link for a collection of rock 'n' roll numbers – interesting as an early production by Milton Subotsky and for an early appearance by Tuesday Weld. Drummer Walter Conyers is featured backing Lavern Baker.

1606
Rock you sinners
UK 1957 – 59 mins
dir Denis Cavanagh

Cheapo teenage musical with a negligible plot and much rock 'n' roll footage featuring such illustrious exponents of their art as Art Baxter and His Rockin' Sinners, **Tony Crombie** and His Rockets and Don Sollash and His Rockin' Horses, with music by Jeffrey S. Kruger.

1607
Rockabilly baby
USA 1957 – 82 mins
dir William F. Claxton

A slight story of local snobbery, with the novel combination of water polo and rock 'n' roll. Features **Les Brown** and His Band.

1608
Rockin' chair
USA 1942 – 3 mins
Soundie featuring **Hoagy Carmichael**'s classic title number, interpreted by The **Mills Brothers**.

1609
Rockin' chair
USA c1952 – 3 mins
Snader Telescription featuring **Jack Teagarden** with the title number.

1610
Roll 'em
USA 1944 – 3 mins
Soundie featuring **Meade Lux Lewis** in a boogie number, augmented by Dudley Dickerson and dancers.

1611
The Roman Spring of Mrs Stone
UK 1961 – 103 mins
dir José Quintero
Unemotional adaptation of Tennessee Williams's 1937 novel, richly designed and photographed. Features **Cleo Laine**.

1612
Romance without finance
USA 1945 – 3 mins
dir William Forest Crouch
Soundie featuring **Tiny Grimes** and His Orchestra backing a vocalist in the title number.

1613
Romantic rhythm
USA c1946 – c9 mins
An Official Films compilation of previously issued Soundies including **Stan Kenton** and His Orchestra with 'This love of mine'.

1614
Rome adventure/Lovers must learn
USA 1962 – 118 mins
dir Delmer Daves
Glossy, tasteless, romantic fantasy based on the novel by Irving Fineman, with an appearance by **Al Hirt**.

1615
Rooftops of New York
USA 1960 – 10 mins
dir Robert McCarty
Impressions of life at penthouse level above New York City. Joseph Liebman's music is interpreted on vibes by **Lionel Hampton**.

1616
Rookies on parade
USA 1941 – 70 mins
dir Joseph Santley
Forgettable Army comedy with music, featuring **Bob Crosby**.

1617
Roosevelt Sykes
USA 1972 – 30 mins
dir P. Buba, D. Nelson
An impression of the life and work of **Roosevelt Sykes**, shown in concert, at home in New Orleans and relaxing by the sea. Among the piano/vocal numbers are 'Night time is the right time', 'Hoochie coochie yes ma'am', 'Drivin' wheel' and 'Blue moon'.

1618
Roosevelt Sykes 'the honeydripper'
Belgium 1961 – 27 mins
A film record of the pianist/singer, shot in a Brussels studio by Jazz Films SPRL.

1619
Roots of American music part 3
USA 1971 – 20 mins
dir Robert Garfias
Performances by bluesman **'Mississippi' Fred McDowell** of 'Louisa', 'Keep your lamp trimmed and burning' and other numbers.

1620
Rose of Washington Square
USA 1939 – 86 mins
dir Gregory Ratoff
Elaborate but routine Fox musical of the period giving its stars, Alice Faye, Tyrone Power and Al Jolson, a further opportunity to give the public what it wanted. Features **Louis Prima** and His Band. Songs include: 'Rockabye your baby to a Dixie melody', 'Mammy', 'Pretty baby', 'The vamp', 'My man' and 'I never knew heaven could speak'.

1621

Rosemary's baby

USA 1968 – 137 mins
dir Roman Polanski

Basing his screenplay on the novel by Ira Levin, Polanski brings an impressive subtlety and maturity to this study of a lonely, frightened woman's struggle to retain her sanity. Music score by **Krzysztof Komeda**.

1622

La Rosita

USA 1943 – 3 mins

Soundie featuring **Jimmy Dorsey** and His Band with vocalist Helen O'Connell.

1623

La route de Suède

France 1952 – 25 mins
dir Pierre Demarne

Impressions of the journey between Paris and Stockholm, with music by **Claude Luter**.

1624

La route du bonheur

France/Italy 1952 – 92 mins
dir Maurice Labro, Giorgio Simonelli

Musical comedy consisting of little more than a series of musical items with participating artistes that include **Louis Armstrong** and His Orchestra, **Sidney Bechet, Claude Luter, Django Reinhardt** and **Hubert Rostaing**.

1625

Route 66

USA c1952 – 3 mins

Nat 'King' Cole, plus Trio, interprets the title number – a Snader Telescription.

Royal flush

see **Two guys from Milwaukee.**

1626

Rufus Jones for President

USA 1933 – 16 mins
dir Roy Mack

Vitaphone all black burlesque on politics featuring **Ethel Waters** – and a very young Sammy Davis.

1627

Rural rhapsody

USA 1946 – 9 mins
dir Thomas Mead

A general interest featurette which includes an item on **Paul Whiteman** in his capacity as owner/manager of a 700 acre farm in Rosemont, New Jersey.

1628

The Russians are coming, the Russians are coming

USA 1965 – 125 mins
dir Norman Jewison

Coy comedy about a Russian submarine captain who accidentally grounds his ship near an island off the US coast. Music composed and conducted by **Johnny Mandel** and lyric for vocal 'The shining sea' by Peggy Lee.

The sad young men
see **Los jovenes viejos.**

1629
Sadie Hawkins's day
USA 1942 – 3 mins
Soundie featuring comedienne Mabel Todd with the title number, backed by **Sonny Dunham**.

1630
Safe in hell/The lost lady
USA 1931 – 69 mins
dir William A. Wellman
Perfectly adequate screen adaptation of a popular stage play, with an acting performance and one song from **Nina Mae McKinney**.

1631
Saharan venture
UK 1965 – 28 mins
dir Harry Woof
An account of the project for obtaining natural gas from the Sahara, transporting it by tanker and distributing it to the consumer in Britain. Music by **Kenneth Graham**.

1632
The sailor who fell from grace with the sea
UK 1976 – 105 mins
dir Lewis John Carlino
Dismally misconceived and cheaply executed screen adaptation of Mishima Yukio's 1963 novel *Gogo no Eiko*, with little to recommend it save a delicate music score by **Johnny Mandel**.

1633
Saint-Germain-des-Prés
France 1953 – 19 mins
dir Marcel Pagliero
The cafés and cabarets of Paris's Left Bank including a sequence in The Vieux-Colombier with **Claude Luter** and His Orchestra.

1634
St Ives
USA 1976 – 94 mins
dir J. Lee Thompson
Dull, plodding Charles Bronson vehicle in which our hero becomes involved with a wealthy crime dilettante and his female partner, based on the novel *The Procane Chronicle* by Oliver Bleeck. **Lalo Schifrin** provides a gently swinging and easy-to-listen-to music track.

1635
St James Infirmary
USA 1942 – 3 mins
Soundie featuring **Stan Kenton**, with the title number.

1636
St James Infirmary
USA 1950 – 3 mins
Snader Telescription in which the title number is played by **Cab Calloway** and His Cabaliers, including **Jonah Jones**, *tpt;* **Milt Hinton**, *bass;* **Panama Francis**, *drs.*

1637
St Louis blues
USA 1929 – 16 mins
dir Dudley Murphy

S

A dramatised interpretation of the classic Blues, with an all Negro cast and **Bessie Smith**, in her only film appearance, as the wronged wife. **W. C. Handy** was music director as well as co-author of the script, and the music is played by **James P. Johnson**'s Orchestra consisting almost entirely of members of The **Fletcher Henderson** Band with The **W. C. Handy** Choir. **James P. Johnson** appears on screen as the pianist. The movie was made in Astoria, Long Island, during late June 1929.

1638

St Louis blues/Best of the Blues

USA 1939 – 90 mins
dir Raoul Walsh

Musical romance set aboard a Mississippi showboat and nothing to do with **W. C. Handy**'s composition. Features **Maxine Sullivan**, Matty Malneck and His Orchestra and The Hall Johnson Choir. Numbers include 'Loch Lomond' and 'St Louis blues' (vocal arrangement by Hall Johnson); 'Let's dream in the moonlight' by Matty Malneck and Raoul Walsh, 'Junior'; 'I go for that' by Matty Malneck and Frank Loesser; 'Blue nightfall'; 'Kinda lonesome' by **Hoagy Carmichael**, Leo Robin and Sam Coslow.

1639

St Louis blues

USA 1941 – 3 mins

Soundie in which Alvino Rey and His Orchestra, plus The King Sisters, interpret **W. C. Handy**'s classic.

1640

St Louis blues

USA 1958 – 93 mins
dir Allen Reisner

Patronising screen biography of **W. C. Handy**, played by **Nat 'King' Cole** – but some of the footage shows a feeling for jazz. Also features **Pearl Bailey, Cab Calloway, Mahalia Jackson, Ella Fitzgerald, Barney Bigard, Teddy Buckner, Red Callender, Curtis Counce, Lee Young** and **Billy Preston** as the boy **W. C. Handy**. The music, arranged and conducted by Nelson Riddle, is based on themes and songs by **Handy**.

1641

Saint-Paul-de-Vence

France 1949 – 20 mins
dir Robert Mariaud

Nat 'King' Cole on cornet as W. C. Handy in **St Louis Blues** *(1958).*

▼

The story of the old fortified town, with music by **Henri Crolla**.

1642

Saint-Tropez blues

France/Italy 1960 – 95 mins
dir Marcel Moussy

Colourful and unpretentious diversion about spongers, gigolos, surrealist painters, film directors (Chabrol makes a brief appearance), youth-seeking elders and a riding-school, with an irrepressible performance from Marie Laforêt. Music score by **Henri Crolla**.

1643

Saint-Tropez, devoir de vacances

France 1952 – 25 mins
dir Paul Paviot

A short story centred on the famous resort, with music by **André Hodeir** played by **Hubert Rostaing**, *clar, alt sax;* **Bernard Peiffer**, *pno;* Christian Bellest, *tpt;* **Pierre Michelot**, *bass;* **Géo Daly**, *vibs;* **Bobby Jaspar**, *ten sax;* Pierre Lemarchand, *drs;* William Boucaya, *bar sax;* Nat Peck, *trb.*

1644

Les saintes nitouches/Wild living

France/Italy 1962 – 95 mins
dir Pierre Montazel

Vague, inconsequential and zany melodrama centred around a kleptomaniac jewel thief and her surreal adventures. Music by **Hubert Rostaing** and **André Hodeir**.

1645

The saints come marching in

USA 1943 – 3 mins

Soundie featuring **Wingy Manone** and His Mardi Gras Band, with vocal from the leader.

1646

Sait-on jamais?/When the devil drives/No sun in Venice

France/Italy 1957 – 90 mins
dir Roger Vadim

Probably Vadim's best movie, set in an affectionately photographed Venice, and containing one of the most appropriate and satisfactory scores ever written. **John Lewis** takes the credit and performs with the other members of the quartet – **Milt Jackson, Percy Heath** and **Connie Kay**.

1647

Sal-à-malle-ek

France 1965 – 18 mins
dir P. Daniel, G. Nadeau

Fictional story of two gangsters who attempt to kidnap a young girl at Orly. Music by **Mal Waldron**.

1648

Sally, Irene and Mary

USA 1938 – 85 mins
dir William A. Seiter

Thin musical with only average songs and dances, adapted from a Broadway success and featuring **Charlie Barnet** in an acting role.

1649

Salon Kitty/Madam Kitty

Italy/West Germany/France 1975 – 110 mins
dir Giovanni Tinto Brass

Elegantly produced, often amusing through sometimes repulsive, softcore melodrama about sordid goings-on in a World War II Nazi brothel. The music score consists mainly of Viennese waltzes and period tunes orchestrated by Fiorenzo Carpi but also song lyrics by Derry Hall sung on screen by actress Ingrid Thulin but dubbed by **Annie Ross**.

1650

Salsa

USA 1976 – 80 mins
dir Jerry Masucci, Leon Gast

Latin American pop music documentary covering an electric concert in Yankee Stadium in 1973 and another in the same year in San Juan, plus movie clips depicting Hollywood stereotypes of Latin performers such as Desi Arnaz, Carmen Miranda, Al Jolson. Performers in concert include drummer **Billy Cobham**, percussionist **Mongo Santamaria** and Cameroonian saxophonist Manu Dibango.

1651

Salt and pepper

UK 1968 – 101 mins
dir Richard Donner

Excruciatingly unfunny comedy, best forgotten. Music score by **John Dankworth**.

1652

Salute to Duke Ellington

USA 1950 – 15 mins
dir Will Cowan

S

Salute to Duke Ellington

Fine Universal-International music short featuring band performances by **Duke Ellington** and His Orchestra, spotlighting **Johnny Hodges, Ray Nance, Harry Carney, Tyree Glenn** and **Lawrence Brown**. Numbers include 'Things ain't what they used to be', 'A history of jazz in three minutes', 'She wouldn't be moved' (soloists **Wendell Marshall**, *bass;* **Sonny Greer**, *drs*), 'Violet blue' (soloists Kay Davis, *voc;* **Johnny Hodges**, *alt sax*), 'Take the "A" train' and vocalist Chubby Kemp. Intros are by the leader and other personnel include **Al Killian**, *tpt;* **Quentin Jackson**, *trb;* **Charlie Rouse** and **Jimmy Forrest**, *ten sax.*

1653

Salute to song

USA 1957 – 15 mins

Universal featurette with The **Cal Tjader** Quintet, Johnny Cochran, Ralph Anthony and The Martin Men, with Freddy Martin and His Orchestra.

1654

Sanctuary

USA 1960 – 90 mins
dir Tony Richardson

Uneven adaptation of William Faulkner's *Sanctuary* and *Requiem for a Nun*, retaining little of the vitality and horror of the originals. Features **Odetta** in the role of Nancy.

1655

Sanders of the river

UK 1935 – 96 mins
dir Zoltan Korda

Adaptation of Edgar Wallace's story of the work of Commissioner Sanders, the King's Representative, among some of the tribes of British West Africa. Features **Nina Mae McKinney**.

1656

The sandpiper

USA 1965 – 117 mins
dir Vincente Minnelli

Silly and pretentious melodrama, surprisingly co-scripted by Dalton Trumbo. Music and song 'The shadow of your smile' by **Johnny Mandel**, and memorable trumpet passages from **Jack Sheldon**.

1657
Sands of the Kalahari

UK 1965 – 119 mins
dir Cy Endfield

South African desert epic that hardly attains to the level of a poor comic-strip. Music by **Johnny Dankworth**.

1658
Sapphire

UK 1959 – 92 mins
dir Basil Dearden

Flatly written and directed whodunit, used as a peg on which to hang a colour bar problem story. **John Dankworth** takes the alto sax solos on Philip Green's music track.

1659
Sarah Vaughan and Herb Jeffries/Kid Ory and His Creole Jazz Band

USA 1950 – 15 mins
dir Will Cowan

Universal-International featurette with **Sarah Vaughan** singing 'Don't blame me' and 'I cried for you' backed on camera by **Herb Jeffries** and His Band (**Britt Woodman**, *trb*) though it is patently a different band on soundtrack; **Kid Ory** and His Creole Jazz Band with 'Muskrat ramble' (**Kid Ory**, *trb*; **Teddy Buckner**, *cor*; **Joe Darensbourg**, *clar*; **Lloyd Glenn**, *pno*; **Ed Garland**, *bass*; **Minor Hall**, *drs*); The Treniers with 'You're a sweetheart' and **Herb Jeffries** with 'A woman is a worrisome thing'.

1660
Sarge goes to college

USA 1947 – 66 mins
dir Will Jason

A routine comedy of college life, except that there is an abundance of swing. Appearances by Russ Morgan's Orchestra and Jack McVea's Orchestra with musicians Les Paul, **Jess Stacy**, Jerry Wald, Abe Lyman, **Wingy Manone, Conte Candido** and **Joe Venuti.** Jack McVea's song 'Open the door Richard' was introduced in this movie.

1661
Satan in high heels

USA 1962 – 89 mins
dir Jerald Intrator

Low-budget exploitation feature banned in Great Britain as being 'immoral and vicious'. Music by **Mundell Lowe**.

1662
Satchmo the Great

USA 1956 – 64 mins
prod Edward R. Murrow, Fred W. Friendly

A compilation of footage shot for an Ed Murrow TV programme, which follows **Louis Armstrong** and His All Stars on their tour of Europe and Africa. Features **W. C. Handy, Edmond Hall**, *clar;* **Trummy Young**, *trb;* **Barrett Deems**, *drs;* **Billy Kyle**, *pno;* **Arvell Shaw**, *bass;* **Velma Middleton**, *voc;* **Claude Luter**, *clar;* **Jack Lesberg**, *bass.* Numbers include 'The saints', 'When it's sleepytime down south', 'That's my desire', 'Blueberry hill', 'Kokomo', 'Mop mop', 'C'est si bon', 'Struttin' with some barbecue', 'Mack the knife', 'Royal garden blues', 'Black and blue', 'St Louis blues' and 'Ole miss'.

1663
Saturday night and Sunday morning

UK 1960 – 89 mins
dir Karel Reisz

Fictional view of life in an English industrial town, based on Alan Sillitoe's autobiographical novel. Music score and song, 'Let's slip away', by **John Dankworth**, played by His Orchestra.

1664
The Saturday night swing club

USA 1938 – 9 mins
dir Lloyd French

Vitaphone music short with Paul Douglas introducing Leith Stevens and His Orchestra, **Bobby Hackett** and His Boys (**Eddie Condon**, *gtr*), and drummer **Chauncey Morehouse**. Numbers include 'Bob White', 'Dipsy doodle' and 'At the jazzband ball'.

1665
Le saumon atlantique

France 1956 – 20 mins
dir Georges Franju

The life of the salmon, with music by **Henri Crolla**.

1666
The Sauter-Finegan Orchestra

USA 1955 – 18 mins

A Universal music featurette presenting a programme of arrangements by the title group, supported by vocalists. Numbers: 'Doodletown pipers', 'Doodletown races', 'Hold back tomorrow',

'Midnight sleighride', 'John Henry' and 'Thunderbreak'.

1667
The savage is loose
USA 1974 – 115 mins
dir George C. Scott

Survival drama set on some tropical island in the early years of this century, following a shipwreck. Effective and haunting music score by **Gil Mellé**.

1668
Save the children
USA 1973 – 123 mins
dir Stan Lathan

Film record of the 1972 Black Exposition in Chicago. Among the many performers presented are The **'Cannonball' Adderley** Quintet with 'Country preacher'; **Roberta Flack** and **Quincy Jones** with 'On a clear day' and 'Killer Joe' and **Ramsey Lewis**.

1669
Save the tiger
USA 1972 – 100 mins
dir John G. Avildsen

A day in the decline of a middle-aged business-man who suddenly finds the ethics of a lifetime lying in ruins. A witty script suffocated by a heavy-handed message. The soundtrack uses 'Airmail special' by **Benny Goodman**, Jimmy Mundy and **Charlie Christian**; 'Stompin' at the Savoy' by **Benny Goodman, Chick Webb** and Edgar Sampson and 'I can't get started'.

1670
Savoy blues
USA c1952 – 3 mins

Snader Telescription of The **Bobcats** playing the title number.

1671
Say it in French
USA 1938 – 69 mins
dir Andrew L. Stone

A comedy of deception and its consequences which features Helen Meinardi and **Hoagy Carmichael**'s song 'April in my heart'.

1672
Scandal
c1934

Black-produced movie; details unknown except that it featured **Lucky Millinder** and His Orchestra.

1673
The scarlet hour
USA 1955 – 94 mins
dir Michael Curtiz

Conventional melodrama with a particularly complicated and ingenious plot which is rather let down by the inexperience of its leading players. **Nat 'King' Cole** makes a guest appearance singing 'Never let me go'.

1674
Scene nun, take one
UK 1964 – 26 mins
dir Maurice Hatton

Amusing, irreverent entertainment with Susannah York playing a nun with a film unit in the East End storming off location in a temper and realising that she is assumed to be the genuine article. Music score by **Kenny Graham**.

1675
Schlagerparade
West Germany 1953 – 95 mins
dir Eric Ode

A slight plot and 16 musical numbers featuring prominent local singers combine to produce a German *Broadway Melody*. There is a two minute appearance by The **Stan Kenton** Orchestra.

1676
Die Schleuse
West Germany 1962 – 10 mins
dir Harry Kramer

An impression of Harry Kramer's mobile sculptures as seen against the skyline in Cologne. An excellent soundtrack by **Art Blakey**.

School for jive
see **Mister Big.**

1677
The score
USA c1971 – 59 mins

A film documentary exploring the process of writing music for the movies and for TV, produced by BMI. Contributors include Hugo Friedhofer, Earle Hagen, **Lalo Schifrin** (engaged in the collection of sounds for *The Hellstrom chronicle* and visiting **Emil Richards**'s studio), **Quincy Jones** (at work on his score for *In cold blood*), Jerry Goldsmith (conducting and dubbing his music for *The Mephisto waltz*).

1678

Scorpio rising

USA 1963 – 31 mins
dir Kenneth Anger

A study of the myth of the American motor-cyclist: the costume and accessories, the tribal rites, the element of self-destruction. The soundtrack uses one **Ray Charles** number.

1679

Scratch a tiger

USA 1969 – 6 mins
dir Hawley Pratt

Feeble colour cartoon in the *Ant and the aardvark* series. Doug Goodwin's bouncy music is played by **Pete Candoli, Billy Byers, Jimmy Rowles, Tommy Tedesco, Ray Brown** and **Shelly Manne**.

1680

Scrub me mama with a boogie beat

USA 1941 – 7 mins
dir Walter Lantz

A Universal Lantz Cartune in Technicolor, drawn to synchronise with the tempo of the popular swing number of the title.

1681

Screaming Mimi

USA 1957 – 71 mins
dir Gerd Oswald

Lurid and confused thriller, over-melodramatic in every way. Features **Red Norvo**.

1682

Screen snapshots no 6

USA 1935 – 10 mins

Columbia short devoted to snippets from a Hollywood benefit show featuring among the many personalities The **Boswell Sisters**.

1683

Search and research

UK 1967 – 23 mins
dir Eric Marquis

An impression of the creative effort involved over the broad field of research and product testing in the oil industry, with music by **Johnny Hawksworth**.

1684

Sebastian

UK 1967 – 100 mins
dir David Greene

Conventional spy thriller with an unconvincing script and little to recommend it save some spirited performances from its leading players. Composer Jerry Goldsmith provides one song, 'Comes the night', which is arranged by **Marty Paich** and is interesting for its early use of varitone trumpet.

1685

Second chance

USA c1970 – 10 mins
dir John Hubley

An essay on the sea, its history and man's abuse of it, told in the form of an animated cartoon, with music by **Bill Russo**.

1686

Second chorus

USA 1940 – 85 mins
dir H. C. Potter

Routine comedy-romance with musical interludes featuring Fred Astaire and Burgess Meredith as a couple of trumpeters trying to get work in **Artie Shaw**'s Band and win Paulette Goddard at the same time. **Artie Shaw** has a featured role, provides the music and appears with his band in several numbers including 'Dig it', 'Sweet Sue', 'Poor Mr Chisholm', 'Swing concerto' and 'The love of my love'. **Nick Fatool** is prominent on drums and there is soundtrack participation by **Johnny Guarnieri, Bobby Hackett** (ghosting Fred Astaire) and **Billy Butterfield** (ghosting Burgess Meredith).

1687

La seconde verité

France/Italy 1966 – 90 mins
dir Christian-Jaque

Unmemorable melodrama which takes the notorious Jaccoud affair as its inspiration but the result is nowhere as imaginative as the original. Music by **Jacques Loussier**.

Secret French prostitution report
see **Dossier prostitution.**

1688

The secret fury/Blind spot

USA 1950 – 86 mins
dir Mel Ferrer

Silly story about a woman who is forced by a complicated and wholly incredible conspiracy to doubt her own sanity. **Dave Barbour** appears briefly in an acting role as the killer's victim and also as guitarist in a short jazz sequence together with **Ernie Royal**, *tpt*; **Vido Musso**, *ten sax*; **Hal Schaefer**, *pno*; Walt Yoder, and **Alvin Stoller**, *drs*.

S

Secret interlude

see **A view from Pompey's head.**

1689

The secret life of an American wife

USA 1968 – 92 mins
dir George Axelrod

Beautifully controlled comedy of character, witty and compassionate, fantastic and totally convincing, helped by superb performances from Walter Matthau and Anne Jackson and a music track by **Billy May**.

1690

The secret of the purple reef

USA 1960 – 81 mins
dir William N. Witney

Repetitious action thriller set in the West Indies, adapted from a Saturday Evening Post story by Dorothy Cottrell. **Buddy Bregman**'s score includes a battery of South American percussion.

1691

Secrets

UK 1971 – 107 mins
dir Philip Saville

Totally unbelievable and thoroughly synthetic romantic drama memorable only as a technical experiment – it was the first British commercial feature to be shot in Super-16, which gives film-making the advantages of TV film production. Uninteresting music score by **Mike Gibbs**.

1692

See here, Private Hargrove

USA 1944 – 101 mins
dir Wesley Ruggles

The experiences of a reporter following his call-up in the army, featuring **Bob Crosby**.

1693

See my lawyer

USA 1945 – 69 mins
dir Eddie Cline

Rather tired farce tailored for the weary talents of Olsen and Johnson. Features The **King Cole** Trio and the song 'Man on the little white keys' by Joe Greene and **Nat 'King' Cole**.

See you in hell, darling

see **An American dream.**

See you tomorrow

see **Do widzenia do jutra.**

1694

Segar Ellis and His Embassy Club Orchestra

USA 1929 – 10 mins

A Vitaphone music short featuring the song 'How can I love again' and other numbers played by the title band. Personnel: 'Fuzzy' Farrer , *tpt;* **Arthur Schutt**, *pno;* **Eddie Lang**, *gtr;* Al Duffy, *vln;* Stan King, *drs;* **Jimmy Dorsey**, *alt sax;* **Tommy Dorsey**, *trb.*

1695

Senior prom

USA 1958 – 82 mins
dir David Lowell Rich

Low-budget, fragile musical featuring a large number of well-known American TV and record stars, with guest appearances by **Bob Crosby, Louis Prima** and **Connee Boswell.**

Sensations

see **Sensations of 1945.**

1696

Sensations of 1945/Sensations

USA 1944 – 85 mins
dir Andrew Stone

Enjoyable musical spectacular with Eleanor Powell, featuring **Woody Herman** and His Orchestra (**Cliff Leeman**, *drs*), **Cab Calloway** and His Orchestra and appearances by **Eugene Rodgers** and **Dorothy Donegan**.

1697

Sentimental journey

USA 1946 – 95 mins
dir Walter Lang

Lachrymose weepie with John Payne and Maureen O'Hara, featuring the song 'Sentimental journey' by **Les Brown**, Ben Homer and Bud Green.

1698

The sentinel

USA 1976 – 92 mins
dir Michael Winner

Opportunistic screen adaptation of the novel by Jeffrey Konvitz – a grubby, grotesque excursion into religious psychodrama. Music score composed by **Gil Mellé**.

1699

Senza ragione/Redneck

Italy/Great Britain 1972 – 87 mins
dir Silvio Narizzano

Formula chase movie that tries hard, but fails, to conjure surrealist atmosphere from the landscape. Includes a song by John Cacavas sung by **Marian Montgomery**.

1700

Sepia Cinderella

USA 1947 – 75 mins
dir Arthur Leonard

All Negro musical comedy entertainment featuring, among others, **John Kirby**'s Band with music score prepared by **Charlie Shavers**.

1701

7 morts sur ordonnance

France/Spain/West Germany 1975 – 106 mins
dir Jacques Rouffio

A dramatic tale of the medical profession and small town repression, with music score by Philippe Sarde directed by **Hubert Rostaing**.

1702

Serail

France 1975 – 90 mins
dir Eduardo de Gregorio

Impressive directorial debut by an Argentine screenwriter, a sort of Gothic romp – part erotic fairy tale, part supernatural thriller; with a music score by **Michel Portal**.

1703

The sergeant

USA 1968 – 108 mins
dir John Flynn

Straightforward man loves boy tale: static, clumsy and uninspiring. Brief appearance by **Memphis Slim** as a nightclub singer.

1704

Sergeants 3

USA 1961 – 112 mins
dir John Sturges

Comic Western vehicle for Frank Sinatra and his clan – actually a re-working of Gunga Din. Music score composed by **Billy May**.

1705

Série noire

France 1955 – 88 mins
dir Pierre Foucard

Derivative and imitative gangster movie with only Erich von Stroheim's presence to hold the attention. Features **Sidney Bechet** and **André Réwéliotty**.

1706

The servant

UK 1963 – 115 mins
dir Joseph Losey

Satanic comedy brilliantly scripted, by Harold Pinter, about class and sex, power, corruption and personality change. **John Dankworth** provides the fine music track and also makes a brief appearance playing a blues number, supported by **Alan Branscombe**, *pno;* **Kenny Napper**, *bass;* **Johnny Butts**, *drs.* His song, 'All gone', is sung on soundtrack by **Cleo Laine**.

1707

Seven days leave

USA 1942 – 87 mins
dir Tim Whelan

An engaging musical comedy featuring Victor Mature and Lucille Ball which takes more than a casual swipe at radio producers. Features **Les Brown** and His Orchestra and the numbers: 'Can't get out of this wood', 'I get the neck of the chicken', 'A touch of Texas', 'Soft hearted', 'Please won't you leave my girl alone' and 'You speak my language'.

1708

The seven minutes

USA 1971 – 115 mins
dir Russ Meyer

Crude and vulgar screen adaptation of Irving Wallace's novel – of no interest at all. The song, 'Seven minutes', is sung on soundtrack by **B. B. King**.

1709

1776

USA 1972 – 141 mins
dir Peter H. Hunt

Americana for all ages. A handsomely produced screen version of Peter Stone's play; a dramatisation of the background to the Declaration of Independence. Sherman Edward's music, supervised and conducted by Ray Heindorf, was arranged by **Eddie Sauter**.

1710

The Seven-ups

USA 1973 – 103 mins
dir Philip D'Antoni

Skillful thriller about some underground cops who get caught in a series of gangland kidnappings. Has an extremely good forties-style score by **Don Ellis**.

1711
Several Africas
Italy c1975 – 60 mins each part
dir Andrea Andermann

Originally produced for TV, a five part film about darkest Africa made according to an itinerary that follows more or less that of André Gide in 1925. The music commentary includes sounds by **Gato Barbieri** and **Baden Powell**. Title music by **Gato Barbieri**.

1712
Sex and the single girl
USA 1964 – 110 mins
dir Richard Quine

Highly amusing romantic comedy based on the book by Helen Gurley Brown. Music composed and conducted by **Neal Hefti** and appearances by **Count Basie** and His Orchestra backing 'The anniversary song' during a nightclub sequence and rehearsing 'What is this thing called love'.

1713
Shadows
USA 1958/9 – 81 mins
dir John Cassavetes

Cassavetes's remarkable first feature film, conceived without a script, and shot on 16mm on New York locations. Music track by **Charles Mingus** with horn solos by **Shafi Hadi** (pseud) and the soundtrack participation of **Phineas Newborn Jnr**.

1714
Shaft
USA 1971 – 100 mins
dir Gordon Parks

A fast, slick private-eye thriller, based on the novel by Ernest Tidyman, which transposes a traditionally white genre into an all Negro context. Isaac Hayes receives screen credit for the music but the movie's musical director, Tom McIntosh, claims credit for the score adding that **J. J. Johnson** was also involved as orchestrator.

1715
Shaft's big score
USA 1972 – 105 mins
dir Gordon Parks

A repeat of the previously successful *Shaft* with, if anything, even more destructible hardware than before but otherwise barely distinguishable from the original. Gordon Parks's thunderous music track includes three songs: 'Blowin' your mind', 'Don't misunderstand' and 'Move on in' belted out by **O. C. Smith**. There is also some splendid work on the soundtrack from **Freddie Hubbard**, *tpt;* **Marshall Royal**, *alt sax;* and **Joe Pass**, *gtr.*

1716
Shake, rattle and rock!
USA 1956 – 75 mins
dir Edward L. Cahn

Cheaply produced story of a disc jockey's defence of a youth club against stuffy reformers, featuring **Joe Turner** and **Fats Domino**.

1717
Shakey: an experiment in robot planning and learning
USA 197? – 25 mins
prods Peter Hart, Nils Nilsson

Produced at the Stanford Research Institute, California, an educational film showing the progress of an experiment with a laboratory robot. The soundtrack uses **Dave Brubeck**'s 'Take five' recording.

1718
Shall we dance?
USA 1937 – 108 mins
dir Mark Sandrich

RKO Radio vehicle for Fred Astaire and Ginger Rogers with words and music by George and Ira Gershwin. The **Jimmy Dorsey** Band, augmented to 50 pieces, worked on the soundtrack. Numbers: 'Slap that bass', 'Walking the dog', 'Beginner's luck', 'They all laughed', 'Let's call the whole thing off', 'They can't take that away from me' and 'Shall we dance?'.

1719
Shelly Manne and His Men
USA 1962 – 20 mins

Originally produced for US TV as one of their Jazz scene U.S.A. shows, and hosted by Oscar Brown, Jnr, a programme of music by **Shelly Manne**, *drs,* with **Conte Candoli**, *tpt,* **Russ Freeman**, *pno,* and **Richie Kamuca**, *ten sax.*

1720
Sherlock Jones
Netherlands 1975 – 94 mins
dir Nicolaï van der Heijde

Routine comedy about an amateur sleuth who gets mixed up with professional thieves. Music by **'Toots' Thielemans**.

1721
She's too hot to handle
USA 1944 – 3 mins

Soundie in which the title number is sung by **Bob Howard**.

1722

Shine

USA 1942 – 3 mins

Soundie featuring **Louis Armstrong** with his interpretation of the title number.

1723

Shine

USA 1944 – 3 mins

Soundie in which **Bob Howard** sings and plays the title number.

1724

Shine on your shoes

USA 1946 – 3 mins
dir Dave Gould

Soundie featuring **Ray Bauduc** and His Orchestra with vocalist Debby Claire.

1725

The shining future

USA 1944 – 15 mins
dir Leroy Prinz

Warner Bros short made to promote Canada's Sixth Victory Loan featuring personalities of the time including Frank Sinatra, Cary Grant and **Benny Goodman** (a film clip dating from 1937).

1726

The shining hour

USA 1938 – 80 mins
dir Frank Borzage

Silly romantic melodrama redeemed only by the presence of Margaret Sullavan and one sequence in which Joan Crawford breaks into an impromptu dance to **Duke Ellington**'s 'Solitude'.

1727

Ship ahoy!

USA 1942 – 95 mins
dir Edward Buzzell

Bright, lively and typically well-polished MGM musical featuring **Tommy Dorsey** and His Band, with orchestrations partly by **Sy Oliver**. One number, 'I'll take Tallulah', teams **Buddy Rich** with Eleanor Powell.

1728

The shooting of Dan McGrew

USA 1966 – 7 mins
dir Ed Graham

Animated version of the famous ballad set to music by The **George Shearing** Trio.

1729

Shorty Rogers and His Giants

USA 1962 – 20 mins
dir Steve Binder

Meadowlane Production for *Jazz scene USA* hosted by Oscar Brown, Jnr and featuring **Shorty Rogers**, *fl horn;* **Gary Lefever**, *flute, ten sax;* **Lou Levy**, *pno;* **Gary Peacock**, *bass;* **Larry Bunker**, *drs;* playing 'Greensleeves', 'Time was', 'Martians go home' and 'The outsider'.

1730

Shout sister, shout

USA 1941 – 3 mins

Soundie presenting **Sister Tharpe** backed by **Lucky Millinder** and His Orchestra.

1731

Show of shows

USA 1929 – 130 mins
dir John G. Adolfi

Lavish musical revue in Technicolor featuring virtually every Warner Bros star of the period. **Ted Lewis** and His Band appear on a picturesque pirate ship with an array of leading ladies. Numbers: 'Singing in the bathtub', 'Lady luck', 'Motion picture pirates', 'If I could learn to love', 'Pingo-pongo', 'If your best friends won't tell you', 'The only song I know', 'My sister', 'Your mother and mine', 'You were meant for me', 'Just an hour of love', 'Li-po-li', 'Military march', 'Rock-a-bye your baby with a Dixie melody', 'Jumping jack' and 'Your love is all I crave'.

1732

Shuffle rhythm

USA 1942 – 15 mins
dir Reginald LeBorg

A Universal music short presenting **Henry Busse** and His Orchestra, supported by various vocal groups including Six Hits and a Miss and The Jivin' Jacks and Jills, playing 'Shrine of St Cecilia', 'Hot lips', 'Ramona', 'Zoot suit', 'I'll see you in my dreams', 'Swanee river', 'Ciribiribin' and 'Rose room'.

1733

Si j'avais quatre dromadaires

France/West Germany 1966 – 73 mins
dir Chris Marker

Photo-documentary from some 800 stills reflecting the director's personal outlook in his search to find hope and love. Music by The **Barney Wilen** Trio.

1734

Si le vent te fait peur

Belgium 1960 – 105 mins
dir Emile Degelin

Revealing drama giving an account of an incestuous relationship between brother and sister without any sensationalism, with dignity and sympathy. Music score composed by **Martial Solal**.

1735

Signalet

Denmark 1966 – 26 mins
dir Ole Gammeltoft

A study in loneliness typified by a man alone in his flat waiting for the doorbell to ring. Soundtrack music by **Bill Evans**.

1736

Silent movie

USA 1976 – 87 mins
dir Mel Brooks

Limp comedy about which the less said the better. The bouncy music score is by John Morris, orchestrated by the composer and **Bill Byers**.

The silent stranger

see **Step down to terror.**

The sin of Anna

see **Il peccato di Anna.**

1737

Sing as you swing/Swing tease/The music box

UK 1937 – 82 mins
dir Redd Davis

Musical about competing radio stations featuring popular entertainers of the day including The **Mills Brothers** and **Nat Gonella** and His Georgians.

1738

Sing, sing, sing

USA 1944 – 3 mins

Soundie in which the title number is played by **Wingy Manone** and His Band.

1739

Sing Sing Thanksgiving

USA 1973 – 90 mins
dir David Hoffman, Harry Wiland

An array of performers give a concert for the inmates of Sing Sing the day before Thanksgiving, including **B.B. King.**

1740

Sing sinner sing

USA 1933 – 74 mins
dir Howard Christy

The eternal triangle theme once again: a singer accused of her husband's murder is cleared at the eleventh hour when her boyfriend comes forward as a witness. Features The **Les Hite** Orchestra: Geo Orendorff, James Porter, *tpt;* Marvin Johnson, Charles Jones, *saxes;* Joe Bailey, *bass;* Sonny Craven, *trb;* Bill Perkins, *banjo;* **Lionel Hampton**, *drs;* **Marshall Royal**, *alt sax;* Harold Brown, *pno.*

1741

Sing, you sinners

USA 1938 – 91 mins
dir Wesley Ruggles

Musical comedy with Bing Crosby and Donald O'Connor which features the song 'Small fry' by Frank Loesser and **Hoagy Carmichael**.

1742

Singin' the Blues

USA 1948 – 8 mins
dir Benjamin R. Parker

A film in the *Sing and Be Happy* series which tells the story of the Blues from the days of the great **W. C. Handy**. Numbers include 'Blues in the night', 'Am I blue?', 'Moanin' low' and 'Wabash blues'.

1743

The singing kid

USA 1936 – 85 mins
dir William Keighley

Typical vehicle for Al Jolson who tends to burst into song at every conceivable opportunity. It does however include an appearance by **Cab Calloway** and His Orchestra with The Four Yacht Club Boys and a performance of Irving Mills's and **Cab Calloway**'s number 'Keep that hi-de-ho in your soul'.

1744

The singing sheriff

USA 1944 – 63 mins
dir Leslie Goodwins

Comedy-Western with a few songs from its star, **Bob Crosby**. Also featured is Spade Cooley and His Orchestra.

1745

Sins of the fathers

USA 1928 – 88 mins
dir Ludwig Berger

Drama about a German-American restaurateur who becomes a bootlegger only to reform when his son goes blind drinking his hootch! Briefly features **Speed Webb** and His Orchestra.

Sins of youth
see **Péché de jeunesse.**

1746
Sis Hopkins
USA 1941 – 98 mins
dir Joseph Santley

Republic musical comedy featuring **Bob Crosby** and His Band, including **Muggsy Spanier**. Numbers: 'Crackerbarrel County', 'If you're in love', 'It ain't hay, it's the USA', 'Well, well' and 'Look at you, look at me'.

1747
Six faces of Terylene
UK 1964 – 20 mins
dir David Evans

Documentary that highlights the properties of Terylene and points an amusing contrast between the fashions of the 1900's and the practical, easy-to-care-for clothes of today. Music by **Johnny Hawksworth**.

1748
6.5 special/Calling all cats
UK 1958 – 85 mins
dir Alfred Shaughnessy

An almost continuous flow of musical numbers by current favourites – for a change, a shrewd producer has virtually dispensed with a story. Among the featured performers are **Johnny Dankworth** and His Orchestra and **Cleo Laine**.

1749
Sizzle with Sissie
USA 1946 – 3 mins
dir William Forest Crouch

Soundie with **Noble Sissle** and His Orchestra and the title number, plus Mabel Lee.

Young Johnny Dankworth jams in **6.5 special**.

The ski raiders
see **Snow job.**

1750
Ski total

France 1962 – 16 mins
dir Jacques Ertaud

Documentary on the preparation, training and
participation in competition skiing, with music by
André Hodeir.

1751
Ski troop attack

USA 1960 – 62 mins
dir Roger Corman

Very low-budget war movie which just about gets
by when it sticks to action. Music score by **Fred
Katz**.

1752
Skinnay Ennis and His Orchestra

USA 1940 – 10 mins
dir Jean Negulesco

Skinnay Ennis leads His Band and provides the
vocals in a programme consisting of 'La plight',
'Three little words', 'Let's do it' and 'Birth of the
Blues'.

1753
Skinnay Ennis and His Orchestra

USA 1949 – 15 mins
dir Will Cowan

Universal-International music featurette presenting
the title band supported by The Bachelors, vocal
trio; Marion Colby, vocal; Hightower and Ross,
acrobatic dancers; Landre and Verna, dance duo.
Numbers include 'Remember me', 'It's a good
day' and 'St Louis blues'.

1754
Skirts ahoy!

USA 1952 – 109 mins
dir Sidney Lanfield

Glossy MGM portrait of life in the WAVES with
Esther Williams's aquatics and Harry Warren's
'Hold me close to you', 'What good is a gal',
'What makes a WAVE' and 'The navy waltz'.
Music partly orchestrated by **Peter Rugolo** with
Lee Young responsible for a drum speciality.

1755
Skullduggery

USA 1969 – 105 mins
dir Gordon Douglas

A traditional jungle adventure, set mainly in New
Guinea, with a dash of science fiction thrown in
for good measure. Music score by **Oliver Nelson**.

1756
The skunk song

USA 1942 – 3 mins

Cab Calloway and His Band (**Tyree Glenn**, *trb;*
Cozy Cole, *drs*, prominent) – plus vocal quartet,
with their interpretation of the title song. A
Soundie.

1757
Sky high

USA 1931 – 9 mins

Vitaphone music short presenting popular
entertainers, including Larry Adler, with **W. C.
Handy**'s 'St Louis blues' among its musical items.

1758
Sky riders

USA 1976 – 91 mins
dir Douglas Hickox

Absurd, though surprisingly lively, opportunistic
venture combining lyrical hang-gliding interludes
with no-nonsense plot development. Effective and
lively music score by **Lalo Schifrin**.

1759
Skylark

USA 1942 – 3 mins

Soundie featuring **Sonny Dunham** and His
Orchestra plus vocalist Harriett Clark.

1760
Skyliner

USA 1951 – 3 mins

Snader Telescription in which the title number is
played by **Charlie Barnet** and His Orchestra,
including **Claude Williamson**, *pno;* **Bill Holman**,
ten sax; **Dave Wells**, *trb;* **Bob Dawes**, *bar sax*.

1761
Skyscraper

USA 1959 – 20 mins
dir Shirley Clarke. Willard Van Dyke, Irving
Jacoby

Inspired documentary approach to the changing
face of New York in general and the building of a
new skyscraper in particular. Music by **Teo
Macero**.

1762

Slambert

Denmark 1966 – 7 mins
dir Flemming Quist Møller, Jannik Hastrup

An animated fantasy about a trouble-maker whose thoughts work havoc among innocent people. Music by The **Contemporary Jazz Quartet**.

1763

Slaughter

USA 1972 – 90 mins
dir Jack Starrett

Formula thriller involving a black Vietnam veteran with an underworld syndicate. The theme song 'Slaughter' composed and sung by **Billy Preston**.

1764

Sleeper

USA 1973 – 88 mins
dir Woody Allen

Nutty futuristic comedy in which Woody Allen is brought back to life 200 years hence to find himself a wanted man in a totally regulated society. Music score by Woody Allen playing clarinet with The **New Orleans Funeral and Ragtime Orchestra** and The **Preservation Hall Jazz Band**.

1765

Sleepy lagoon

USA 1942 – 3 mins

Soundie featuring **Sonny Dunham** and His Orchestra with vocalist Ray Kellogg and dancer Anita Camargo.

1766

Sleepytime down south

USA 1942 – 3 mins

Soundie featuring **Louis Armstrong** and His Orchestra with their interpretation of the title number.

1767

Sleepytime gal

USA 1941 – 82 mins
dir Albert S. Rogell

Cheaply produced Republic musical comedy featuring **Skinnay Ennis** and His Orchestra with numbers: 'Sleepytime gal', 'Barrelhouse Bessie', 'When the cat's away' and 'I don't want anybody at all'.

1768

The slender thread

USA 1965 – 98 mins
dir Sydney Pollack

Suspenseful thriller showing in documentary fashion the attempts to trace a suicide's telephone call. Music by **Quincy Jones**.

1769

Slim Gaillard Trio

USA c1952 – 3 mins each

Two numbers, recorded in a nightclub, by **Slim Gaillard**, *pno;* **Zutty Singleton**, *drs;* and unidentified *bass* – 'Hoboken bounce' and 'Spanish melody swing'. Snader Telescriptions.

1770

Sliphorn king of Polaroo

USA 1945 – 7 mins
dir Dick Lundy

Universal Lantz Technicolor cartoon about a trombone player shipwrecked on an Arctic iceberg, with soundtrack music by **Jack Teagarden**.

1771

Slippery when wet

USA 1959
dir Bruce Brown

Surfing movie little seen outside the USA, with soundtrack music composed and played by **Bud Shank**, *alt sax, flute;* with **Billy Bean**, *gtr;* **Gary Peacock**, *bass;* **Chuck Flores**, *drs.*

1772

Slither

USA 1973 – 96 mins
dir Howard Zieff

Amiable romp, part spoof and part straight thriller, taking in a wide variety of established movie targets. A number of big band recordings are used on soundtrack including **Count Basie**'s 'One o'clock jump' and 'Stompin' at the Savoy'.

1773

The small back room

UK 1948 – 106 mins
dir Michael Powell, Emeric Pressburger

Sensitive and restrained wartime drama, from Nigel Balchin's novel, about a back-room boy in a research station, his personal and professional problems. In nightclub sequences music is provided by The **Ted Heath/Kenny Baker** Swing Group, with **Johnny Gray**, *ten sax.*

S

1774

Small band jazz

UK 1961 – 9 mins
dir Robert Henryson

In a bandstand setting, The **Tony Kinsey** Quartet play three numbers: **John Lewis**'s 'The golden striker', 'Little chick' and 'Didn't we'.

1775

The small propeller

UK 1967 – 23 mins
dir John Spencer

The various uses of small boats all over the world, for transport in Venice, speed and surfing in Australia, pleasure in Stockholm and carrying medical supplies in Singapore. Music by **Johnny Hawksworth**.

1776

Small town girl

USA 1953 – 93 mins
dir Leslie Kardos

A pleasant but uninspired musical cut to the usual pattern, though the musical numbers are well staged by Busby Berkeley. Features **Nat 'King' Cole** singing the background song, with **Jack Costanzo**.

1777

The small world of Sammy Lee

UK 1962 – 107 mins
dir Ken Hughes

Implausible but quite enjoyable drama set mainly in the streets and clubs of Soho, adapted by the director from his TV play *Sammy*. Music score by **Kenny Graham**.

Smart politics

see **Campus sleuth.**

1778

Smash your baggage

USA 1933 – 9 mins
dir Roy Mack

A tritely plotted Vitaphone short featuring The **Elmer Snowden** Band (as Small's Paradise Entertainers) cast as baggage porters, plus hordes of energetic tap dancers. Identified musicians include: Leonard Davis, **Roy Eldridge**, *tpts;* **Dicky Wells, George Washington,** *trbs;* **Otto Hardwick, Al Sears, Wayman Carver,** *reeds;* **Elmer Snowden,** *banjo;* Dick Fulbright, string and brass *bass;* **Don Kirkpatrick,** *pno;* **Sid Catlett,** *drs.* Numbers include: 'Bugle call rag', two versions of 'Tiger rag' and 'My man's gone' sung by an unidentified torch singer.

1779

Smashing time

UK 1967 – 96 mins
dir Desmond Davis

A clumsy, vulgar attempt to create a female comedy team and to cash in on the myth of the non-existent Swinging London scene. The script is by **George Melly**, who also wrote the songs together with John Addison.

1780

Smile

USA 1974 – 113 mins
dir Michael Ritchie

Hugely enjoyable but ultimately shallow putdown of American teenage beauty contests. **Nat 'King' Cole**'s recording of Charles Chaplin's 'Smile' is used on soundtrack during the credit titles.

Snares

see **Pièges.**

1781

Snoqualomie Jo Jo

USA 1945 – 3 mins

Soundie in which The **Delta Rhythm Boys**, backed by a girls chorus, interpret the title number.

1782

Snow

UK 1964 – 8 mins
dir Geoffrey Jones

Railwaymen, trains and travellers in the snow. Individual scenes are composed in a kind of choreography so as to form a unity with an electronically edited and arranged jazz composition by **Johnny Hawksworth** and Daphne Oram.

1783

Snow job/The ski raiders

USA 1971 – 90 mins
dir George Englund

Weak crime melodrama about a bank robbery at a ski resort, redeemed only by some excellent location photography. Music score by **Jacques Loussier**.

1784

The snows of Kilimanjaro

USA 1952 – 114 mins
dir Henry King

Ernest Hemingway's classic short story expanded into a long, lush saga, a kind of intellectual

S

'Rake's Progress'. One nice jazz sequence features **Benny Carter**, with rhythm section, playing an Alfred Newman item, 'Love is Cynthia' (later recorded with full orchestra as 'Blue mountain').

1785
Snow-White
USA 1933 – 6 mins
dir Dave Fleischer

A Paramount Song Cartoon featuring Betty Boop, based on the fairy tale of the same name. One sequence uses, on soundtrack, **Cab Calloway** singing 'St James Infirmary blues'.

1786
Sol Madrid/The heroin gang
USA 1967 – 89 mins
dir Brian G. Hutton

Forgetable, though efficiently made, thriller about the Mafia, with music score by **Lalo Schifrin**.

1787
Soldaterkammerater
Sweden/Denmark 1958 – 84 mins

Army farce, with an appearance by **'Papa' Bue** and His Viking Jazz Band.

1788
Soleil de pierre
France 1967 – 15 mins
dir Jean-Pierre Baux

On the Nile delta archaeologists discover a town and local farmers attempt to bring life back to it. Music by **Michel Portal**.

1789
Solid jive
USA 1946 – 3 mins
dir Dave Gould

Soundie featuring the drumming of **Ray Bauduc** with His Orchestra, plus dancer Charles Whitty Jnr.

1790
Le solitaire/The loner
France 1973 – 95 mins
dir Alain Brunet

Tired thriller about a lone safecracker who pines for his daughter during his jail term. Music score by **Claude Bolling**.

1791
Solitude
USA 1952 – 3 mins

Snader Telescription in which **Duke Ellington** and His Orchestra play the title number, featuring Jimmy Grissom, *voc;* **Harry Carney, Jimmy Hamilton, Willie Smith, Russell Procope, Paul Gonsalves,** *reeds;* **Willie Cook, Ray Nance, Cat Anderson,** *tpt;* **Quentin Jackson, Britt Woodman, Juan Tizol,** *trb;* **Wendell Marshall,** *bass;* **Louie Bellson,** *drs.*

1792
Solo
1965
dir Jørn Winther

Louis Armstrong and His All Stars play 'Sleepytime down south', 'Struttin' with some barbecue', 'I've got a lot of livin' to do', 'Avalon', 'My man', 'Mack the Knife' and 'Ole miss'. **Armstrong,** *tpt;* **Tyree Glenn,** *trb, vibs;* **Buster Bailey,** *clar;* **Billy Kyle,** *pno;* **Buddy Catlett,** *bass;* **Danny Barcelona,** *drs;* Jewell Brown, *voc.*

1793
Some call it loving
USA 1973 – 103 mins
dir James B. Harris

Obtuse, quirky adaptation of the short story by John Collier, 'The Sleeping Beauty', about the erotic fantasies of a young white jazz musician. An excellent music track by Richard Hazard has **Ronnie Lang** ghosting the baritone sax solos for the leading actor accompanied on soundtrack by **Conte Candoli,** *tpt;* **Bob Brookmeyer,** *trb;* Dave Grusin, *elec pno;* **Ray Brown,** *bass;* **Stan Levey,** *drs.* Bassist **Leroy Vinegar** appears in a rehearsal sequence and source music is provided by **Bud Shank** plus strings. Soundtrack use is made of **Nat 'King' Cole**'s recording of 'The very thought of you'.

1794
Some came running
USA 1959 – 136 mins
dir Vincente Minnelli

Luckless adaptation of James Jones's novel about the writer's place in American society. **Ted Nash** participated on Elmer Bernstein's music track.

1795
Some kind of nut
USA 1969 – 89 mins
dir Garson Kanin

Very weak comedy with little but Angie Dickinson's presence to recommend it. Music score by **Johnny Mandel**.

S

1796

Some like it hot/Rhythm romance

USA 1939 – 65 mins
dir George Archainbaud

Comedy with music, starring Bob Hope, and in no way related to the 1959 classic of the same name. Features **Gene Krupa** and His Band and the songs: 'Some like it hot' by Frank Loesser, **Gene Krupa** and Remo Biondi, and 'The lady's in love with you'.

1797

Some like it hot

USA 1959 – 121 mins
dir Billy Wilder

Fast, extravagant comedy, brilliantly scripted by Billy Wilder and I.A.L. Diamond, set in 1929, with memorable performances from Tony Curtis and Jack Lemmon as involuntary witnesses to the St Valentine's Day massacre enlisting in an all girl band in Florida. Matty Malneck's soundtrack orchestra includes **Art Pepper, Barney Kessel, Leroy Vinegar** and **Shelly Manne**.

1798

Some of these days

USA 1942 – 3 mins

Soundie in which the title song is interpreted by **Maxine Sullivan**.

1799

Somebody nobody loves

USA 1942 – 3 mins

Soundie featuring pianist **Claude Thornhill**, assisted by girls with toy pianos, putting over the title number.

1800

Something nice to eat

UK 1967 – 21 mins
dir Sarah Erulka

Luxurious cooking by the expert in a way that will make the ordinary person realise that the art of cooking is by no means beyond him. Music by **Johnny Hawksworth**.

1801

Something to shout about

USA 1943 – 90 mins
dir Gregory Ratoff

Columbia backstage musical featuring a variety of popular performers including boogie woogie pianist **Hazel Scott; Teddy Wilson** and His Band and six Cole Porter songs: 'You'd be so nice to come home to', 'Something to shout about', 'Hasta luego', 'Lotus bloom', 'I always knew' and 'Through thick and thin'.

1802

Sometimes a great notion/Never give an inch

USA 1971 – 114 mins
dir Paul Newman

Coherent screen adaptation of the novel by Ken Kesey. Henry Mancini's music track features instrumentalists **Plas Johnson**, *ten sax*; and **Carol Kaye**, *Fender bass*.

1803

Son House

USA 1969 – 25 mins

Rare performances on film by the great Mississippi Delta bluesman **Son House** produced by The Seattle Folklore Society. Numbers: 'Death letter blues', 'John the revelator', 'I'm gonna get me religion' and 'I want to live so God can use me'.

1804

Song hits on parade

USA 1936 – 10 mins
dir Fred Waller

A Paramount music short featuring the band of Freddie Rich, including both **Bunny Berigan** and **Adrian Rollini** with the former soloing on 'Until today'.

1805

A song is born

USA 1939 – 9 mins
dir Leslie Roush

Five numbers from Larry Clinton and His Orchestra, with vocalists, introducing, among other numbers, 'Heart and soul' by **Hoagy Carmichael** and Frank Loesser.

1806

A song is born

USA 1948 – 112 mins
dir Howard Hawks

Hawks's colour remake of his own 1941 movie *Ball of fire,* itself an adaptation of *Snow White and the seven dwarfs.* **Benny Goodman** plays a leading role, supported by **Louis Armstrong, Tommy Dorsey, Lionel Hampton, Charlie Barnet, Mel Powell, Harry Babasin, Benny Carter, Al Hendrickson, Louie Bellson,** Buck Washington and **Kenny Dorham**. Numbers include: 'Flying home', 'Stealin' apples' and 'A song is born'.

1807

Songs of the range

USA 1944 – 9 mins

The famous music lesson sequence in **A song is born** *(1948).*

A programme of Western songs by a variety of performers, including **Henry Busse** and His Orchestra with 'Along the Santa Fe trail'.

808

'Sonny Boy' Williamson

Denmark c1970 – 12 mins

Sonny Boy' Williamson, *hca*, sings and plays three blues numbers accompanied by guitar and bass. A studio performance.

809

Sonny Dunham and His Orchestra

USA 1944 – 10 mins
dir Jack Scholl

A Warner Bros music short in the Melody Masters series, charting the rise to fame of **Sonny Dunham** and His Orchestra, with vocals from Angela Greene and The Pied Pipers. Numbers: 'Sweet Georgia Brown', 'Annie Laurie', 'Memories of you', 'Bob White', 'Liza' and 'Someday I'll meet you again'.

1810

'Sonny Ford'

USA 1969 – 42 mins
dir Bill and Josette Ferris

A film about **James 'Sonny Ford' Thomas**, with **J.W. 'Sonny Boy' Watson** and **Shelby 'Poppa Jazz' Brown**.

1811

Sonny Rollins live at Laren

Netherlands 1973 – 37 mins
dir Frans Boelen

Excellent colour *reportage* made for Dutch TV of The **Sonny Rollins** Quintet performing four numbers at The International Jazzfestival at Laren in August 1973. Personnel: **Sonny Rollins**, *ten sax;* **Matsuo**, *gtr;* **Walter Davis Jnr**, *pno;* **Bob Cranshaw**, *Fender bass;* **David Lee**, *drs*. Numbers: 'There is no greater love' by Isham Jones, Marty Symes, 'Alfie', 'St Thomas' by **Sonny Rollins** and 'Don't stop the carnival'.

1812
Sonny Rollins, musician
UK 1968 – 30 mins
dir Dick Fontaine

Good documentary attempting to express the relationship that exists between **Rollins** and his music; the thoughts and feelings of this extra-ordinarily gifted and sensitive musician. Also features **Paul Jeffrey**.

1813
Sons and daughters
USA 1967 – 98 mins
dir Jerry Stoll

Counterposes images of death and life in order to stimulate discussion of the war in Vietnam. Music: Virgil Gonsalves and **Jon Hendricks**.

1814
Sophisticated lady
USA 1952 – 3 mins

Snader Telescription of **Duke Ellington** and His Orchestra playing the title number with solos by **Harry Carney**, *bas-clar;* **Willie Smith**, *alt sax* and Ellington, *pno;* also featuring **Jimmy Hamilton, Russell Procope, Paul Gonsalves**, *reeds;* **Willie Cook, Cat Anderson, Ray Nance**, *tpt;* **Britt Woodman, Juan Tizol, Quentin Jackson**, *trb;* **Wendell Marshall**, *bass;* **Louie Bellson**, *drs.*

1815
So's your uncle
USA 1943 – 64 mins
dir Jean Yarbrough

Light comedy dependent largely on the skilled playing of its star, Billie Burke. Features **Jack Teagarden** and His Orchestra.

1816
Le souffle au coeur/Dearest love
France/Italy/West Germany 1971 – 118 mins
dir Louis Malle

Beautifully observed story of a boy's adolescence, his mother's adultery, and their own highly sensitive relationship with each other, set in 1954. Recordings by **Charlie Parker, Sidney Bechet** and **Henri Renaud** figure prominently on the soundtrack.

1817
Soul to soul
USA 1971 – 96 mins
dir Denis Sanders

Film record of a rock/jazz concert held in Ghana to celebrate the country's 14th Anniversary. Among the many performers appearing are **Roberta Flack, Les McCann** and **Eddie Harris**.

1818
The sound and the fury
USA 1959 – 115 mins
dir Martin Ritt

Meandering, platitudinous screen adaptation of William Faulkner's novel about bitchiness in the Deep South, with a formula performance from **Ethel Waters**.

1819
The sound of jazz
USA 1957 – 60 mins
dir Jack Smight

Originally produced for US TV, by Nat Hentoff and Whitney Balliett, a great musical package: **Henry 'Red' Allen** and The All Stars, **Billie Holiday** with The **Mal Waldron** All Stars, **Count Basie**'s All Stars with **Jimmy Rushing**, The **Jimmy Giuffre** Trio and **Thelonius Monk**. Musicians include **Lester Young, Coleman Hawkins, Ben Webster, Earle Warren, Gerry Mulligan, Vic Dickenson, Roy Eldridge, 'Doc' Cheatham, Rex Stewart** and **Dickie Wells**. Numbers: 'Wild man blues', 'Rosetta', 'Fine and mellow', 'I left my baby', 'The train and the river' and 'Dickie's dream'.

1820
Sounder
USA 1972 – 105 mins
dir Martin Ritt

Conventional screen adaptation of the novel by William H. Armstrong, about a family of Negro sharecroppers living out the Depression somewhere in the South. Music and an appearance by **Taj Mahal** and a song, 'Needed time', sung on soundtrack by **'Lightnin'' Hopkins**.

1821
Sounder II
USA 1975
dir William Graham

Originally produced for US TV but subsequently thought good enough for cinema release, a followup to the previously successful *Sounder.* **Taj Mahal** again has a featured part. Title changed on release to *Part II Sounder,*

1822
Sounds of the seventies
UK 1971 – 42 mins
prod Richard W. Jackman

Monotonous, brash record of a concert at The Royal Albert Hall, London, given by four American pop groups and originally recorded on videotape. Features bluesman **Taj Mahal** with two of his own songs: 'Riverside' and 'Oh, Susannah'.

S

1823

Soup run

UK 1975 – 11 mins
dir Guy Magar

The story of The St Mungo Community Trust, used by some 15,000 homeless people in London as an opportunity for eating and talking. Music performed by Tony Desborough and **Bruce Turner**.

1824

Sous-sol

France 1953 – 14 mins
dir J. C. Roy, S. Malaussena

The cafés and cabarets of St Germain-des-Prés, including a sequence in Les Trois Maillots with **'Peanuts' Holland** and **Lil Armstrong**, supported by **Michel Attenoux** and His Band.

1825

Southern comfort

USA 1946 – 3 mins
dir William Forest Crouch

Soundie in which **Joe Marsala** and His Orchestra backs vocalist Earl Oxford with Betty Underwood.

1826

Southern scandal

USA 1946 – 3 mins
dir William Forest Crouch

Soundie featuring **Stan Kenton** and His Orchestra playing the title number.

The sparrow of Pigalle

see   **Piaf.**

1827

Sparrows can't sing

UK 1962 – 94 mins
dir Joan Littlewood

Fresh and vigorous screen adaptation of Stephen Lewis's play *Sparrers can't sing* as irrepressibly spirited as the Cockneys depicted. Musicians featured include **Ken Wray**, *trb;* **Les Condon**, *tpt;* **Brian Dee**, *pno;* **Malcolm Cecil**, *bass;* **Tony Carr**, *drs.*

1828

Special delivery

USA 1976 – 99 mins
dir Paul Wendkos

Routine drama featuring Bo Svenson as a Vietnam veteran who engineers a bank robbery. Music score by **Lalo Schifrin**.

1829

The specialist

USA 1975 – 93 mins
dir Hikmet Avedis

Turgid and unconvincing screen adaptation of the novel *Come now the lawyers* by Ralph B. Potts, with music score by **Shorty Rogers** and a title song by Sammy Fain, Paul Francis Webster.

1830

Spirit of Boogie woogie

USA 1942 – 3 mins

Soundie in which pianist **Meade Lux Lewis** backs Katherine Dunham and Her Dancers in the title number.

1831

Splendor in the grass/Splendour in the grass

USA 1961 – 124 mins
dir Elia Kazan

Case-history study in repression by William Inge, with all the lavish elements of Victorian melodrama. A superb music score composed and conducted by **David Amram**, and a brief appearance by **Buster Bailey**.

Splendour in the grass

see   **Splendor in the grass.**

1832

The split

USA 1968 – 89 mins
dir Gordon Flemyng

Amoral thriller, adapted from the novel by Richard Stark, *The seventh*. Music score by **Quincy Jones** who also supplies three songs: 'A good woman's love', 'The split' and 'It's just a game, love', the latter two with vocals from **Billy Preston**.

1833

The spook who sat by the door

USA 1973 – 102 mins
dir Ivan Dixon

As yet unreleased in the UK, an adaptation of Sam Greenlee's novel charting the exploits of a black, ex-CIA super-hero. Evocative music score by **Herbie Hancock**.

1834

The Sportsmen and Ziggy Elman's Orchestra

USA 1951 – 15 mins
dir Will Cowan

Universal-International production in which **Ziggy Elman** and His Orchestra provide most of the backing for a series of popular entertainers: The Mel Henke Trio with 'In a little Spanish town'; The Knight Sisters, dance duo; The Sportsmen, vocal quartet. The Band provides 'And the angels sing'.

1835
Springtime in the Rockies

USA 1942 – 91 mins
dir Irving Cummings

One of the series of formula Technicolor musicals that Fox produced in the 1940's – this one with Betty Grable, featuring **Harry James** and His Orchestra.

Spy 13
see **Operator 13.**

1836
Squeeze a flower

Australia 1969 – 102 mins
dir Marc Daniels

A particularly lifeless comedy from down under, about an Italian adrift in Australia. The title song is by Tommy Leonetti and **Bobby Troup**.

1837
Ssaki/Mammals

Poland 1962 – 10 mins
dir Roman Polanski

An engaging anecdote about two men with a sledge in a snowy waste. Music by **K.T. Komeda**.

1838
Stage door canteen

USA 1943 – 133 mins
dir Frank Borzage

All-star vaudeville comedy which contains brief appearances by some 60 well-known entertainers, including **Ethel Waters** singing 'Quicksand' with **Count Basie** and His Orchestra and The **Benny Goodman** Band with 'Bugle call rag' and 'Why don't you do right?' (vocal Peggy Lee). Also the bands of Kay Kyser, Guy Lombardo, Xavier Cugat and Freddie Martin. Among participating musicians are **Jack Jenny**, *trb*, and **Lee Castle**, *tpt*.

1839
Stage entrance

USA 1951 – 7 mins
dir Bill Seasman

A sequence from a Dumont Production for US TV in which Leonard Feather presents Downbeat Awards for 1951 to **Charlie Parker**, *alt sax*, and

Dizzy Gillespie, *tpt*, who then play 'Hot house' supported by **Dick Hyman**, *pno*, plus bass and drums.

1840
Stagecoach

USA 1966 – 114 mins
dir Gordon Douglas

Pallid and graceless adaptation of Dudley Nichols's screenplay for John Ford's 1939 classic Western of the same name. The vocal 'Stagecoach to Cheyenne' was orchestrated by **Shorty Rogers**.

1841
Stakeout on Dope Street

USA 1957 – 82 mins
dir Irvin Kershner

Excellent, low-budget, independently-made thriller about three young men who find a suitcase containing heroin, and a gang of dope pedlars. Music score by Richard Markowitz, featuring The **Hollywood Chamber Jazz Group**.

1842
Stallion Road

USA 1947 – 97 mins
dir James V. Kern

Veterinary surgeon Ronald Reagan nearly loses future wife Alexis Smith over life of racehorse. Features The **Ray Bauduc** Quintet playing 'Flusie'.

1843
Stan Kenton

USA c1942 – 3 mins

Soundie number 7906, details unknown.

1844
Stan Kenton

USA c1942 – 3 mins

Soundie number 5601, details unknown.

1845
Stan Kenton and His Orchestra – artistry in rhythm

USA 1945
dir Jack Scholl

A Warner Bros Melody Master Bands short featuring **Stan Kenton** and His Orchestra playing 'If I could be with you' (**Pete Rugolo**, *arr*); 'Somebody loves me' and 'Original blues' (**Gene Roland**, *arr*; **June Christy**, *voc*); 'I been down in Texas' (**Gene Roland**, *arr*; **June Christy, Gene Howard, Ray Wetzel, Stan Kenton**, *voc*); 'Don't blame me' (**Gene Howard**. *arr, voc*); and 'Artistry in rhythm' (Gerri Gale, dancer). Personnel: **Buddy Childers, Ray Wetzel, John Anderson,** Russ Burgher, Bob Lymperis, *tpt;* Ray Klein, **Freddie Zito,** Milt Kabak, *trb;* **Bert Varsalona,** *bas-trb;* Al Anthony, **'Boots' Mussulli,** *alt sax;* **Vido Musso, Bob Cooper,** *ten sax;* **Bob Gioga,** *bar sax;* **Stan Kenton,** *pno;* **Bob Ahern,** *gtr;* **Eddie Safranski,** *bass;* Ralph Collier, *drs.*

1846

Stan Kenton and His Orchestra

USA 1962 – 24 mins
dir Steve Binder

A *Jazz scene USA* programme originally produced for US TV and introduced by Oscar Brown, Jnr. Bandstand performances of five numbers by **Stan Kenton**'s Mellophonium Orchestra: 'Limehouse blues', *arr* **Bill Holman**; 'All the things you are', *arr* **Stan Kenton**; 'The waltz of the prophets', composed by **Dee Barton**; 'Maria', *arr* **Johnny Richards**; 'Malaguena', *arr* **Bill Holman**. Prominent in the band are **Don Menza,** *ten sax;* **Dee Barton,** *drs.*

1847

Les stances à Sophie

France 1971 – 97 mins
dir Moshe Mizrahi

Smoothly-made and played comedy-drama about a girl who marries a stuffy management type only to rebel and eventually gain her independence. Music by The **Art Ensemble of Chicago**.

1848

Stand up and be counted

USA 1972 – 99 mins
dir Jackie Cooper

A rather thin-valued production fumbling its way amusingly if awkwardly through the subject of women's liberation and the effect of that contemporary movement on several male-female relationships. **Ernie Wilkins**'s music track, including a song, 'I am woman', is disappointingly rock-type bombast laid on with a trowel.

Stand up and sing

see **Earl Carroll sketchbook**.

1849

Star dust

USA 1940 – 85 mins
dir Walter Lang

Romantic comedy with music about talented young hopefuls trying to crash Hollywood. Songs include 'Star dust' by **Hoagy Carmichael** and Mitchell Parish.

1850

A star is born

USA 1954 – 154 mins
dir George Cukor

Expensive CinemaScope musical remake of William Wellman's brilliant 1937 Hollywood melodrama. Includes an appearance by pianist **Buddy Cole**.

1851

The star reporter in Hollywood

USA 1936 – 10 mins

Paramount music short about talent discovery, with music from **Louis Prima**.

1852

Star spangled rhythm

USA 1942 – 100 mins
dir George Marshall

Star-studded Paramount vehicle promoting the studio, its most glamorous stars and the war effort. **Slim Gaillard,** *pno,* appears for about two seconds in a Harlem production number. Musical items include 'A sweater, a sarong and a peek-a-boo bang', 'Hit the road to dreamland', 'Old glory' and 'That old black magic'.

1853

Starlift

USA 1951 – 102 mins
dir Roy Del Ruth

Nearly every star at Warners who could sing, dance or be reasonably attractive was roped in to entertain the 'boys' at an air base, where there was a constant stream of aircraft to and from Korea. Doris Day and Gordon MacRae singing 'You're gonna lose your gal' are backed by a trio headed by **Buddy Cole,** *pno;* Jane Wyman does 'I may be wrong' with The **Ernie Felice** Quintet.

1854

Stars and violins

. USA 1944 – 15 mins
dir Vernon Keays

The trombone of **Jack Teagarden** leads his orchestra in a programme of popular favourites including 'Stars and violins', 'Let's love again' and 'A dream ago'.

1855

Stars fell on Alabama

USA c1952 – 3 mins

Snader Telescription of **Jack Teagarden** playing the title number.

1856
Stars on parade
USA 1944 – 62 mins
dir Lew Landers

Musical comedy. A slight plot links a series of musical and variety tunes, including The **'King' Cole** Trio, The Ben Carter Choir and the song 'Jumpin' at the jubilee' by Ben Carter and Mayes Marshall.

1857
Start cheering
USA 1937 – 79 mins
dir Albert S. Rogell

Formula comedy from Columbia tailored for its star, Jimmy Durante and featuring **Louis Prima**.

1858
Step down to terror/The silent stranger
USA 1957 – 75 mins
dir Harry Keller

Desperately contrived and low-budget remake of Hitchcock's classic *Shadow of a doubt*, with music score by **Buddy Bregman**.

1859
Stephane Grappelly and His Quintet
UK 1946 – 14 mins
dir Horace Shepherd

A flat but nonetheless valuable film record of The Quintet playing 'The Stephane blues', 'Piccadilly stomp', 'Wendy', 'Sweet Georgia Brown' and 'Evelyn'. Personnel: **Stephane Grappelly**, *vln;* **George Shearing**, *pno;* **Dave Goldberg**, *gtr;* **Coleridge Goode**, *bass;* Ray Ellington, *drs.* (An additional number, 'Red-o-ray', exists from the same session but was presumably edited out of the final print at some stage of the production).

1860
Steppenwolf
USA 1974 – 105 mins
dir Fred Haines

Erratic but visually rich screen adaptation of the novel by Hermann Hesse, with a music track by **George Gruntz**: participating musicians include **Charlie Mariano, Tony Oxley, Mark Murphy, Paul Rutherford** and Piano Conclave.

Actor Pierre Clementi on tenor sax in **Steppenwolf**.
▼

S

1861

Stille dage i Clichy/Quiet days in Clichy

Denmark 1969 – 90 mins
dir Jens Joergen Thorsen

Screen adaptation of Henry Miller's erotic-idyllic reminiscences in Paris between the wars. A nightclub sequence features **Ben Webster** and the soundtrack **'Papa' Bue**'s Viking Jazz Band. Numbers include **Ben Webster**'s 'Blue miller'.

1862

The sting

USA 1973 – 129 mins
dir George Roy Hill

Thoroughly old-fashioned, highly professional entertainment about a pair of confidence tricksters in the Chicago of the 1930's. An excellent music score employs rags by **Scott Joplin** and John Philip Sousa – although perhaps a decade too early for the emphasized thirties period. Joplin pieces heard in part include 'The entertainer', 'Easy winners', 'Pineapple rag', 'The ragtime dance' and 'Gladiolus rag' – the pianist is Marvin Hamlisch, musical supervisor on the picture and adaptor of some four minutes of the music. Some seven minutes-worth of music was adapted, uncredited, by **Gunther Schuller**.

1863

The stolen feast

Denmark 1967/8 – c30 mins
dir Peter Refn

Featurette, details unknown, but the soundtrack music was recorded by **Kenny Drew**, *pno;* **Niels Ørsted Henning Pederson**, *bass;* and a Danish backing group.

1864

Stolen hours

USA/UK 1963 – 97 mins
dir Daniel M. Petrie

Tired and tiresome remake of *Dark Victory* which was Hollywood professionalism at its tasteful best. Contains an appearance by **Chet Baker**, *tpt,* who provides some of the music.

1865

Stompin' for Mili

USA 1955 – 9 mins
dir Gjon Mili

A session with The **Dave Brubeck** Quartet.

1866

Stopforbud

Denmark 1963 – 12 mins

An experimental film portrait of pianist **Bud Powell** shown both at leisure and at work in Copenhagen, backed by **Niels-Henning Orsted Pedersen**, *bass,* and unidentified *drs.* Commentary spoken by **Dexter Gordon**.

1867

Una storia Milanese/A Milanese story

Italy 1962 – 93 mins
dir Eriprando Visconti

Routine story of a teenager love affair, set in Milan. Original music score by **John Lewis** (composed before shooting began) and played by **Lewis**, *pno;* **Bobby Jaspar**, *flute, ten sax;* **René Thomas**, *gtr;* Giovanni Tommaso, Jozsef Paradi, *bass;* 'Buster' Smith, *drs;* and The Quartetto di Milano.

1868

The stork club

USA 1945 – 99 mins
dir Hal Walker

Comedy tailored for the brassy talents of Miss Betty Hutton, featuring two songs by Paul Francis Webster and **Hoagy Carmichael**: 'Doctor, lawyer, Indian chief' and 'Baltimore oriole'.

1869

Stormy weather

USA 1943 – 78 mins
dir Andrew Stone

Imaginatively photographed – and released in sepia tone – though otherwise conventional all-Negro musical featuring a host of top musical performers including Lena Horne, Bill Robinson, **Fats Waller, Cab Calloway** and His Band, **Zutty Singleton, 'Slam' Stewart, Benny Carter** (on trumpet), Alton Moore, **Irving Ashby, Ada Brown, Eugene Porter** and **Ethel Waters**. Numbers include 'Greechy Joe' by Jack Palmer, Andy Gibson and **Cab Calloway**; 'There's no two ways about love' by Ted Koehler and **James P. Johnson**; 'That ain't right' by **Nat 'King' Cole** and Irving Mills; 'Ain't misbehavin'' by Harry Brooks, Andy Razaf and **Fats Waller**; 'Dica dica doo'; 'Can't give you anything but love'; 'Linda Brown', **Cab Calloway**'s 'Rhythm cocktail'; 'My, my, ain't that somethin'' and 'Stormy weather'.

1870

Straight on till morning

UK 1972 – 96 mins
dir Peter Collinson

Pretentious and derivative Hammer thriller with such an absurd plot that nothing can really be taken seriously. A character called Liza is played by **Annie Ross**, who also provides and sings the title song.

1871

Street girls

USA 1974
dir Michael Miller

As yet unreleased New World exploitation movie about delinquent girls and with 'additional music' by **'Muddy' Waters**.

1872

Strictly dynamite

USA 1934 – 74 mins
dir Elliott Nugent

Tedious comedy vehicle for Jimmy Durante, about a young poet who achieves quick fame by writing for a couple of radio comics. Features a short solo spot for The four **Mills Brothers**.

1873

Strike up the band

USA 1940 – 119 mins
dir Busby Berkeley

Routine MGM musical vehicle for its two young stars, Mickey Rooney and Judy Garland. A birthday party sequence features **Paul Whiteman** and His Orchestra, with the leader having some dialogue scenes with Mickey Rooney. **Lee Young** ghosted drums for Mickey Rooney.

1874

The strip

USA 1951 – 86 mins
dir Leslie Kardos

Murder mystery with a background of Sunset Strip and Mickey Rooney as a jazz drummer. Features the orchestras of **Louis Armstrong** and **Jack Teagarden**, with **Earl Hines** and **Barney Bigard**. **Cozy Cole**, *drs;* **Buddy Cole**, *nova;* and **Red Norvo**, *vibs*, are heard on soundtrack, as is **Eddie Beal** who played double piano with **Earl Hines**. Musical items include: 'Basin Street blues', 'A kiss to build a dream on' and 'Don't blame me'. **Pete Rugolo** worked as arranger and assistant to musical director George Stoll.

1875

The student body

USA 1975 – 90 mins
dir Gus Trikonis

New World exploitation picture plotting the adventures of a group of delinquent teenage girls at college. Music score partly by **Don Bagley**.

1876

The subterraneans

USA 1960 – 89 mins
dir Ranald MacDougall

A silly, novelettish adaptation of Jack Kerouac's book about the 'new Bohemians'. Contains some jazz, of a kind, written by André Previn and he appears together with **Carmen McRae, Gerry Mulligan, Bob Enevoldsen, Art Pepper, Art Farmer, Russ Freeman, Red Mitchell, Dave Bailey, Shelly Manne, Bill Perkins** and **Chico Hamilton**. **Gerry Mulligan** also has a few lines of dialogue in his role as a friendly neighbourhood clergyman (sic). **Buddy Clark**, *bass*, participated on soundtrack.

1877

Suddenly it's jazz

UK 1963 – 14 mins
dir Jeremy Summers

A dramatised featurette with **Dick Charlesworth** and The City Gents, during which they ecord 'Brown skin girl'.

1878

Sud-express

France 1963 – 23 mins
dir Jean Leherissey

Documentary on French Railways' Southern Express, with music by **Jacques Loussier**.

1879

'Sugar Chile' Robinson – Billie Holiday – Count Basie and His Sextet

USA 1950 – 15 mins
dir Will Cowan

Superior Universal-International music short, introduced by **Count Basie**, in which **Billie Holiday** sings 'God bless the child' and 'Now baby, or never'; **'Sugar Chile' Robinson**, *pno, voc*, provides 'Numbers boogie' and 'After school boogie' and The **Basie** Sextet plays 'One o'clock jump'. Personnel: **Basie**, *pno;* **Clark Terry**, *tpt;* **Marshall Royal**, *clar;* **Wardell Gray**, *ten sax;* **Freddie Green**, *gtr;* **Jimmy Lewis**, *bass;* **Gus Johnson**, *drs*.

1880

Sugar is a business

UK 1971 – 17 mins
dir Arthur G. Wooster

The changes in the sugar business since the families of Tate and Lyle joined forces in the 1920's to form the foundation of their world wide trading interests. Music by **Johnny Hawksworth**.

1881

The sugarland express

USA 1974 – 109 mins
dir Steven Spielberg

▲
Gerry Mulligan plays the role of a horn-playing preacher in **The subterraneans***.*

'Sugar Chile' Robinson – Billie Holiday – Count Basie and His Sextet.

▼

Splendidly entertaining chase movie – a sort of live action, feature length *Roadrunner* cartoon, marred only by a silly, artless ending. John Williams's music track features harmonica solos by **'Toots' Thielemans**.

1882
Suivez l'oeuf
France 1963 – 16 mins
dir Pierre Robin

A satirical report on poultry raising on an industrial scale, with music by **Jacques Loussier**.

1883
Sullivan's empire
USA 1967 – 85 mins
dir Harvey Hart, Thomas Carr

Conventional jungle adventure yarn, extended from a TV pilot. Music by **Lalo Schifrin**.

1884
Sult/Hunger
Denmark/Norway/Sweden 1966 – 110 mins
dir Henning Carlsen

A remarkably successful attempt to capture the flavour of Knut Hamsun's brilliant, virtually unfilmable, first novel – a study of a mind on the brink of dissolution. Music score by **Krzysztof Komeda**.

1885
Summer wishes, winter dreams
USA 1973 – 87 mins
dir Gilbert Cates

Dismal attempt to communicate the feeling of middle-aged American emptiness; the more tedium captured, the more the film drags. Music score by **Johnny Mandel**.

1886
Sun Valley serenade
USA 1941 – 86 mins
dir H. Bruce Humberstone

Musical romance built around the personality of skating star Sonja Henie, featuring almost continuously **Glenn Miller** and His Orchestra with **Tex Beneke** and The Modernaires. The band includes: Paul Tanner, Jimmy Priddy, Frank D'Anolfo, *trb;* **'Chummy' MacGregor**, *pno;* **Ernie Caceres, Hal McIntyre**, Willie Schwarz, **Tex Beneke, Al Klink**, *saxes;* Ralph Brewster, **Ray Anthony**, Mickey McMickle, **Johnny Best, Billy May**, *tpt;* Jack Lathrop, *gtr;* **Maurice Purtill**, *drs;* **'Trigger' Alpert**, *bass;* Paula Kelly and Ray Eberle, *voc.* Arrangements by **Bill Finegan** and a dance sequence from The Nicholas Brothers with Dorothy Dandridge. Musical items include: 'In the mood', 'Chattanooga choo choo', 'I know why', 'Moonlight serenade' and 'It happened in Sun Valley'.

1887
Sunday sinners
USA 1941
dir Arthur Dreifuss

Low-budget, B-plot movie produced for black audiences, featuring vocalist **Mamie Smith**.

1888
The sun's gonna shine
USA 1967 – 10 mins
dir Les Blank

Words, music and images are combined to form an impression of **'Lightnin'' Hopkins**'s life, using material originally intended for the same director's longer study *Blues accordin' to 'Lightnin'' Hopkins*. Two of the subject's songs, 'The sun's gonna shine' and 'Freight train' are used on soundtrack.

1889
The super cops
USA 1973 – 94 mins
dir Gordon Parks

Routine thriller adaptation of the book by L.H. Whittemore, about novice cops posted to the dreaded 21st Precinct. **'Snooky' Young** is featured on Jerry Fielding's music track.

1890
Supershow
UK 1969/70 – 93 mins
dir John Crome

Crude film record of a series of group appearances in London, mainly pop, but also features 'Under the jasmin tree' and 'Visitor from Venus' by The **Modern Jazz Quartet**; 'Mary had a little lamb', 'Hoochie coochie man' and 'My time after a while' by **Buddy Guy**; 'Primitive Ohio' and 'I say a little prayer' by The **Roland Kirk** Quartet; 'Stormy Monday' and 'Kansas City' by **Buddy Guy** and **Roland Kirk**; 'Slate 27' by Eric Clapton and **Roland Kirk**; 'Eric and Buddy's blues' by Eric Clapton and **Buddy Guy**.

1891
Support your local gunfighter
USA 1971 – 92 mins
dir Burt Kennedy

Light comedy follow-up to the highly successful *Support your local sheriff*, with music score by Jack Elliott and **Allyn Ferguson**.

Multi-instrumentalist Roland Kirk appears in **Supershow**.

S

1892

Survival in the sea

USA 1968 – 29 mins
dir Richard Wormser

Documentary dealing with the struggle for survival in the sea, derived from the Life Nature Library book *The fishes*. The soundtrack uses 'Three king fishers' and 'Love is blue' performed by guitarist **Gabor Szabo**.

1893

Sven Klangs Kvintett

Sweden 1976 – 109 mins
dir Stellan Olsson

Screen adaptation of the play by Henric Holmberg and Ninne Olsson about an amateur jazz group gigging in small towns in southern Sweden in the late 1950's. The music is by Christer Boustedt and Jan Lindell and consists mainly of jazz standards including **Neal Hefti**'s 'Splanky', **Horace Silver**'s 'The preacher', **Kid Ory**'s 'Muskrat ramble', **Thelonius Monk**'s 'Well you needn't', **Benny Golson**'s 'Whisper not', **Charlie Parker**'s 'Confirmation' and 'Now's the time', **Dizzy Gillespie**'s 'Bebop' and **Monk**'s 'Blue Monk'. Other music includes 'Whispering', 'Ramona', Isle of Capri', 'American patrol', 'Fascination', 'Over the rainbow', 'As time goes by', 'True love', 'Jailhouse rock', 'Twilight time' and 'Some other Spring'.

1894

Svenska flickor i Paris

Sweden 1960 – 78 mins
dir Barbro Boman

Pointless and unsympathetic sexploitation production with some coldly effective images of Parisian low life and a jazz score by **Martial Solal**.

1895

Swamp women

USA 1956 – 70 mins
dir Roger Corman

Meagre melodrama set in the bayou area of Louisiana, with music score by **Willis 'Bill' Holman**.

1896

Swedish pastry

USA 1951 – 3 mins

Snader Telescription in which the title number is played by **George Shearing**, *pno;* **Joe Roland**, *vibs;* **Chuck Wayne**, *gtr;* **Al McKibbon**, *bass;* **Denzil Best**, *drs*.

1897

Sweet and low-down/Moment for music

USA 1944 – 76 mins
dir Archie Mayo

Silly story of a slum-bred musician who falls for socialite, but the film's saving grace is the almost non-stop appearance of **Benny Goodman** and His Orchestra, featuring the quartet of **Goodman, Jess Stacy, Sid Weiss** and **Morey Feld**. Also participating is trombonist **Bill Harris**. Numbers include: 'Rachel's dream' and 'Ten days with baby' (Lorraine Elliott, *voc*).

1898

Sweet charity

USA 1968 – 149 mins
dir Bob Fosse

Screen adaptation of the hit Broadway musical that was itself adapted from the screenplay for Fellini's *Notti di Cabiria* – a bitter-sweet fairy tale of a golden-hearted prostitute trapped in a profession not of her choosing. Orchestrations by **Ralph Burns**.

1899

Sweet jam

USA 1943 – 15 mins
dir Vernon Keays

Universal music short presenting the orchestra of Jan Garber;The **Delta Rhythm Boys**; vocalist Liz Tilton and dancer Louis DaPron.

1900

Sweet love, bitter/It won't rub off, baby

USA 1966 – 92 mins
dir Herbert Danska

Adaptation of the novel *Night song* by John Williams, seemingly inspired, at least in part, by the death of **Charlie Parker**. The leading role of the jazz musician is played by Dick Gregory and ghosted on soundtrack by **Charles McPherson**: the latter is seen briefly in a nightclub scene together with Dave Burns, *tpt;* **Chick Corea**, *pno;* **Al Dreares**, *drs;* and Steve Swallow, *bass*. The movie's music score is by **Mal Waldron**.

1901

Sweet movie

France/Canada/West Germany 1973/4 – 90 mins
dir Dusan Makavejev

The fifth feature from Europe's most controversial filmmaker – a continuous string of visual oaths aimed at anyone who cares to watch. **George Melly** appears briefly in the Paris sequence, as a movie director.

▲

Jess Stacy, Benny Goodman, Sid Weiss and Morey Field in **Sweet and low-down**.

1902
Sweet November

USA 1968 – 113 mins
dir Robert Ellis Miller

Quite nauseating romance with an embarrassingly simple-minded message about poetry and the little things, with Sandy Dennis piling on the kooky charm. **Shelly Manne** and **Ray Brown** participated on Michel Legrand's music track.

1903
The sweet ride

USA 1967 – 110 mins
dir Harvey Hart

Unconvincing attempt to reveal all about the Malibu beach set; particularly disappointing coming from such a talented director. Also disappointing is the music score by **Pete Rugolo**.

1904
Sweet serenade

USA 1950 – 15 mins
dir Will Cowan

Universal-International music short presenting **Tex Beneke** and His Orchestra supported by The Moonlight Serenaders, *voc;* and Maurice &

Maryea, dancers. The leader solos extensively and takes the vocal on 'You turned the tables on me'. Other numbers: 'Swing low, sweet chariot', 'Pin-striped pants', 'Tuxedo junction', 'St Louis blues march' and, as introduction, 'Moonlight serenade'.

1905
The sweet smell of success

USA 1957 – 93 mins
dir Alexander Mackendrick

Elmer Bernstein's music score, with generous contributions from **Chico Hamilton**'s Quintet, provides a suitable background to the esoteric world of New York columnists and publicity men and their constant atmosphere of menace and corruption. Features **Frank Rosolino, Carson Smith, Curtis Counce, Paul Horn, Buddy Clark, Conte Candoli** and superb ghosting by **Jim Hall**. Songs by **Chico Hamilton** and **Fred Katz**.

1906
Sweet swing

USA 1944 – 15 mins
dir Josef Berne

Universal Name Band music short featuring **Eddie Miller** and His Orchestra.

1907

Sweetheart of Sigma Chi

USA 1941 – 3 mins

Soundie featuring Marlyn Stewart with The Sigma Chi Quartette, which includes **Slim Gaillard**.

1908

Sweetheart of the campus/Broadway ahead

USA 1941 – 65 mins
dir Edward Dmytryk

Cheapo comedy of college life with seven musical numbers by Ozzie Nelson and His Band, featuring The Spirits of Rhythm.

Swing and sway

see **Swing in the saddle.**

1909

Swing cat's jamboree

USA 1938 – 10 mins
dir Roy Mack

Vitaphone short with **Louis Prima** and His Band, supported by vocalist Shirley Lloyd plus dancers. Numbers: 'I can't give you anything but love', 'Loch Lomond' and 'You're an education'.

1910

Swing fever

USA 1944 – 81 mins
dir Tim Whelan

Musical comedy about a songwriter who uses hypnotism to help a boxer win his fight. Contains brief appearances by **Tommy Dorsey** and **Harry James** acting as sidemen in Kay Kyser's Band. Lena Horne is also featured with 'You're indifferent'. Other items: 'I planted a rose' and 'Mississippi dreamboat'.

1911

Swing high, swing sweet

USA 1945 – 15 mins
dir Lewis D. Collins

A Universal Name Band musical presenting Jam Savitt and His Orchestra plus **Ella Mae Morse** with 'Cow cow boogie'; The **Delta Rhythm Boys** with 'What a difference a day makes' and Jan Savitt's violin solo, 'Caprice'.

1912

Swing hostess

USA 1944 – 76 mins
dir Sam Neufeld

Hackneyed story about a jobless singer and her search for success with a big band. The leading role is taken by singer Martha Tilton.

1913

Swing in the saddle/Swing and sway

USA 1944 – 69 mins
dir Lew Landers

Conventional low-budget musical Western presenting a number of popular radio favourites, including The **'King' Cole** Trio.

1914

Swing it

USA 1936 – 17 mins
dir Leslie Goodwins

An RKO music short featuring **Louis Prima**, *tpt*, *voc;* **'Pee Wee' Russell**, *clar;* plus rhythm trio (*pno, bass, gtr*) clowning their way through five numbers, including: 'Way down yonder in New Orleans', 'Basin Street blues', 'Up a lazy river' and 'Dinah'.

1915

Swing it soldier/Radio revels of 1942

USA 1941 – 66 mins
dir Harold Young

Standard low-budget musical introducing current radio favourites, including **Skinnay Ennis** and His Orchestra.

1916

Swing, monkey, swing

USA 1937 – 8 mins
prod Charles Mintz

Columbia colour cartoon set in monkeyland in which the prolific animals play all the instrumentals in a rendering of **W. C. Handy**'s 'St Louis blues'.

1917

Swing parade of 1946

USA 1946 – 74 mins
dir Phil Karlson

Cheaply produced Monogram musical comedy, with The Three Stooges and other entertainers, charting the rise to fame of a girl singer. Features **Louis Jordan** and His Tympany Five with 'Don't worry about the mule'; **Connee Boswell** with 'Just a little fond affection' and 'Stormy weather'; Will Osborne and His Orchestra with 'A tender word will mend it all'. Also 'Oh! brother' and 'On the sunny side of the street'.

Swing street

see **Make mine music.**

S

1918

Swing styles

USA 1939 – 10 mins
dir Lloyd French

Vitaphone featurette presenting three musical groups: **Adrian Rollini**'s, Milt Herth's, and Tito's plus The Frazee Sisters, *voc*, and Charles Troy and Joe Lynn, dancers. Numbers include 'It had to be you'.

Swing, teacher, swing

see **College swing.**

Swing tease

see **Sing as you swing.**

1919

The swinger

USA 1966 – 81 mins
dir George Sidney

Ugly, unwholesome vehicle for Ann-Margret's strained sex-kitten personality, without a spark of life. Music by **Marty Paich.**

1920

Swingin' along

USA 1960/2 – 74 mins
dir Charles Barton

Salvaged, re-issued version of a movie originally entitled *Double trouble* to which a few musical items have been added. Features **Ray Charles** and his song 'What'd I say?'.

1921

Swingin' and singin'

USA 1957 – 15 mins

Universal music featurette with Peggy Ryan and Ray McDonald, dancers, plus The Sabres, Russ Arno and The DeCastro Sisters, *voc*, backed by **Maynard Ferguson** and His Orchestra.

1922

Swingin' in the groove

USA 1945 – 3 mins

Soundie in which a team of girls go into their dance, backed by **Tiny Grimes** and His Band.

1923

Swingin' on nothin'

USA 1942 – 3 mins

Soundie presenting **Louis Armstrong** and His Orchestra with **Velma Middleton** and George Washington, interpreting the title number.

The swinging set

*see***Get yourself a college girl.**

1924

Swing's the swing

USA 1942 – 15 mins
dir Reginald LeBorg

Universal music short presenting Del Courtney and His Orchestra with vocalist Carol Bruce singing **W. C. Handy**'s 'St Louis blues'.

1925

Swingtime holiday

USA 1944 – 15 mins
dir Larry Ceballos

Universal Name band musical with Gus Arnheim and His Orchestra, spotlighting The **Delta Rhythm Boys**. Numbers: 'Pagan love song', 'You're my dish', 'Shake well before using', 'Do nothin' till you hear from me', 'Jersey bounce' and 'Rhythm rhapsody'.

1926

Sylvia

USA 1964 – 115 mins
dir Gordon Douglas

Flashback story of a prostitute who loathes promiscuity and men, from the novel by E. V. Cunningham. Musicians heard on Walter Scharf's music track include **Dick Nash, Larry Bunker** and **Shelly Manne.**

1927

Symphonie sous le ciel

France 1952 – 21 mins
dir L. Fehr-Lutz

Film record of **Sidney Bechet**'s wedding, on the Côte d'Azur, attended by his friends from Paris, including **Claude Luter** and His Orchestra.

1928

Symphony in black

USA 1934 – 9 mins
dir Fred Waller

Elegant Paramount music short featuring **Duke Ellington** and His Orchestra, with **Billie Holiday**, playing 'The laborers', 'A triangle (Dance -- Jealousy-Big city blues)', 'A hymn of sorrow' and 'Harlem rhythm'. Personnel: **Arthur Whetsol, Freddy Jenkins, Cootie Williams**, *tpt;* **Joe Nanton, Lawrence Brown, Juan Tizol**, *trb;* **Barney Bigard, Johnny Hodges, Otto Hardwicke, Harry Carney**, *reeds;* **Fred Guy**, *gtr;* **Wellman Braud**, *bass;* **Sonny Greer**, *perc;* **Ellington**, *pno.*

1929
Symphony in swing

USA 1949 – 15 mins
dir Will Cowan

Universal-International short subject featuring **Duke Ellington** and His Orchestra, supported by The **Delta Rhythm Boys**, *voc*; Kay Davis, *voc;* The Edwards Sisters, dancers. **Ellington** introduces the programme, in a bandstand setting, and numbers include 'Take the "A" train', 'Turquoise cloud', 'Knock me a kiss', 'Frankie and Johnny' and 'Suddenly it jumped'. Personnel: **Ellington**, *pno;* **Al Killian, Shorty Baker, Francis Williams, Shelton Hemphill, Ray Nance**, *tpt;* **Lawrence Brown, Tyree Glenn, Quentin Jackson**, *trb;* **Johnny Hodges, Russell Procope, Jimmy Hamilton, Ben Webster, Harry Carney**, *reeds;* **Wendell Marshall**, *bass;* **Sonny Greer**, *drs.*

1930
Synanon/Get off my back

USA 1965 – 106 mins
dir Richard Quine

Romanticised biography of Synanon House, an organisation founded to help drug addicts to get off the hook and back to normal life. Music by **Neal Hefti**.

1931
Syncopation

USA 1942 – 88 mins
dir William Dieterle

Musical romance tracing in fictional form the development of jazz from 1906. Many musicians are featured including **Benny Goodman, Charlie Barnet, Joe Venuti, Gene Krupa, Harry James, Rex Stewart**, Alvino Rey, **Jack Jenny, Connee Boswell** and The Hall Johnson Choir. Some soundtrack ghosting was done by **Bunny Berigan** (for Jackie Cooper) and by **Stan Wrightsman** (for Bonita Granville). Leith Stevens provided several songs.

1932
Sytten minutter Grønland

Denmark 1967 – 17 mins
dir Jørgen Roos

Standard documentary which tries to answer questions about Greenland today – its people, its industries etc. Music by **Erik Moseholm**.

1933
Szklana Gòra/The glass mountain

Poland 1960 – 90 mins
dir Pawel Komorowski

Routine psychological melodrama about a young woman doctor and her affair with an engineer from a local stone quarry. Music by **Krzystof Komeda-Trzciński**.

1934

T. G. boogie woogie

USA 1945 – 3 mins
dir William Forest Crouch

Soundie featuring **Tiny Grimes** and His Orchestra with a supporting team of dancers.

1935

THX 1138

USA 1970 – 95 mins
dir George Lucas

Orwellian science fiction movie, which, though stunning visually, tends to leave a great many questions unanswered. Music score by **Lalo Schifrin**.

1936

T. R. Baskin/A date with a lonely girl

USA 1971 – 89 mins
dir Herbert Ross

Dull and erratic tragi-comedy with Candice Bergen learning the hard way how impersonal contemporary life is. Music score by Jack Elliott and **Allyn Ferguson**.

1937

TV special

USA 1951 – 3 mins

Snader Telescription in which the title number is played by **Lionel Hampton** and His Orchestra.

1938

Taffy and the jungle hunter

USA 1964 – 87 mins
dir Terry O. Morse

Adventure story set in East Africa – strictly for the children. Music score and theme song by **Shorty Rogers**.

1939

Tailgate man from New Orleans

France 1956 – 12 mins
dir Thomas L. Rowe

A film, made in English, featuring '**Kid**' **Ory**, in which he plays, and talks about his early life and the beginnings of jazz, with support from **Alvin Alcorn, Minor Hall** and **Wellman Braud**.

1940

Take a girl like you

UK 1970 – 101 mins
dir Jonathan Miller

Flaccid screen adaptation of the novel by Kingsley Amis, scripted by **George Melly**.

1941

Take me back, baby

USA 1941 – 3 mins

Soundie in which the title number is played by **Count Basie** and His Orchestra, with **Jimmy Rushing**.

1942

Take one baby

UK 1968 – 17 mins
dir Sarah Erulkar

Documentary intended for housewives showing the value of sugar in a balanced diet, with music by **Johnny Hawksworth**.

T

1943

Take the 'A' train

USA 1941 – 3 mins

Soundie in which the title number is sung by The **Delta Rhythm Boys**.

1944

The taking of Pelham One Two Three

USA 1974 – 104 mins
dir Joseph Sargent

Highly enjoyable suspense drama enlivened with crisp, laconic dialogue and splendid performances from all concerned. David Shire provides an exciting music track played by a 35 piece band that includes: **Don Menza**, Don Griestleib, **Ronnie Lang**, *saxes;* Chuck Findley, **John Audino, Tony Terran**, *tpt;* **Dick Nash, Lloyd Ulyate**, Tom Shepherd, *trb;* **Vince DeRosa**, *Fr. horn;* Dave Cohen, *gtr;* **Chuck Demanica**, *Fender bass;* **Artie Kane**, *key;* **Shelly Manne, Larry Bunker**, *drs;* **Emil Richards, Milt Holland**, *perc.*

1945

Tales of Manhattan

USA 1942 – 118 mins
dir Julien Duvivier

Portmanteau picture, the linking device being the adventures of an evening tail-coat bringing good luck to some and tragedy to others. Features **Ethel Waters**, Paul Robeson and The Hall Johnson Choir.

1946

Talk about a lady/Duchess of Broadway

USA 1946 – 72 mins
dir George Sherman

Simple romantic comedy about a small-town girl with a taste for singing who unwittingly inherits both a fortune and Forrest Tucker. One sequence features The **Stan Kenton** Orchestra playing 'Avocado' (**'Boots' Mussulli**, *arr;* **June Christy;** **Gene Howard**, *voc*); 'The mist is over the moon' and 'I never had a dream come true' (**Gene Roland**, *arr*) and 'You gotta do watcha gotta do' (**Gene Howard**, *arr, voc*). Personnel: **Buddy Childers, Ray Wetzel, John Anderson**, Russ Burgher, Bob Lymperis, *tpt;* Ray Klein, **Freddie Zito**, Jimmy Simms, Milt Kabak, *trb;* **Bart Varsalona**, *bas-trb;* Al Anthony, **'Boots' Mussulli**, *alt sax;* **Vido Musso, Bob Cooper**, *ten sax;* **Bob Gioga**, *bar sax;* **Stan Kenton**, *pno;* **Bob Ahern**, *gtr;* **Eddie Safranski**, *bass;* Ralph Collier, *drs.*

1947

Tall story

USA 1960 – 91 mins
dir Joshua Logan

Despite the presence of Jane Fonda this is a very flat, laboured adaptation of Howard Nemerov's book *The homecoming game*. Title song composed by **Shelly Manne** and André Previn.

1948

Tampico

USA 1945 – 3 mins

Soundie featuring the title number (**Gene Roland**, *arr*), played by **Stan Kenton** and His Orchestra with **June Christy**, *voc.*

1949

Tan and terrific

USA 1947

Dizzy Gillespie and His Bebop Orchestra backing three numbers: 'My man blues' sung by **Helen Humes** and two dance creations by Sahji.

1950

Tant d'amour perdu

France/Italy 1958 – 90 mins
dir Léo Joannon

Domestic melodrama about a rich industrialist and his concern for his two daughters' happiness, especially the one involved with a jazz musician. Soundtrack jazz recorded by **Jimmy Giuffre, Bob Brookmeyer** and **Jim Hall**.

1951

Tant qu'il y aura de l'angoisse

France 1966 – 14 mins
dir Manuel Otéro, Jacques Leroux

An animated cartoon on the theme 'as long as there is life, there will be sorrow'. Music by **Martial Solal**.

1952

Tant qu'il y aura des capricornes

France 1961 – 12 mins
dir Jean Barral

A light-hearted account of the way Capricorn subjects are expected to behave in life. Music by **Martial Solal**.

1953

Tarzan the ape man

USA 1959 – 80 mins
dir Joseph Newman

Incredibly cheap-looking remake of the first Tarzan sound film with a former basket-ball star as the twelfth screen ape man. Music by **Shorty Rogers**.

1954

Tatu bola/Isabel is death

Italy 1972 – 90 mins
dir Glauber Rocha Group

Originally produced for RAI TV, an extraordinary story about Brazilian magic rites. Contains a brief appearance by **Gato Barbieri**.

1955

Taxi driver

USA 1975 – 114 mins
dir Martin Scorsese

Frighteningly plausible case history of a quiet ex-marine with an oppressive sense of alienation from the corruption and filth of New York who exorcises himself in a series of brutal killings. Bernard Herrmann's glorious music score – on which he finished work the night before he died – contains a haunting urban blues refrain beautifully played on alto sax by **Ronny Lang** (*not* Tom Scott as is suggested on the tasteless, so-called 'original soundtrack' album, which is in effect a re-recording of the original music).

1956

T-bird gang/The pay-off

USA 1958 – 75 mins
dir Richard Harbinger

Pathetic teenage quickie whose plot seems to have been lifted from the superior *Street with no name*. Jazz score by **Shelly Manne**.

1957

Tea for two

USA 1950 – 97 mins
dir David Butler

Pleasant enough screen adaptation of the play *No, no, Nanette*, with a dozen or so songs sung by Doris Day and Gordon MacRae. Several of the songs are backed by The **Ernie Felice** Quartet: **Felice**, *acc;* Dick Anderson, *clar;* Dick Fisher, *gtr;* **Rolly Bundock**, *bass.* Bongo drummers seen and heard in 'Crazy rhythm' are Emanuel Vanderhans and Onest Conley, formerly with Katherine Dunham. **Buddy Cole**, *pno,* is featured extensively on soundtrack.

Teacher Nansen

see   **Timelaerer Nansen**.

1958

Technik – 3 Studien in Jazz

West Germany 1961 – 10 mins
dir Hans H. Hermann

Rather pretentious study of a Krupp steel works, clumsily cut to big band jazz by **Pete Rugolo** and His Orchestra.

1959

Ted Heath and his music

UK 1961 – 9 mins
dir Robert Henryson

Music short featuring **Ted Heath** and His Orchestra in a bandstand setting playing 'Cherokee', **Fats Waller**'s 'Bond Street' and 'Rockin' in Morocco'. The personnel includes Duncan Campbell, Eddie Blair, Ronnie Simmonds, Bert Ezard, *tpts;* **Don Lusher**, *trb;* Ronnie Chamberlain, **Bob Efford**, *reeds;* Derek Warne, *pno;* **Johnny Hawksworth**, *bass;* **Ronnie Verrell**, *drs.* (An additional number, 'Ill wind', exists from this same session but was presumably edited out of the final print at some stage of production).

1960

Teddy Powell and His Band

USA 194?

Three numbers from **Teddy Powell** and His Band with vocalists Allan Courtney, Peggy Mann and Tommy Taylor.

1961

Un témoin dans la ville/Witness in the city

France/Italy 1959 – 90 mins
dir Edouard Molinaro

Complicated thriller about a man who kills his wife's murderer. Beautifully melodic jazz score composed by **Barney Wilen** and played by an ensemble consisting of **Barney Wilen**, *saxes;* **Kenny Clarke**, *drs;* **Kenny Dorham**, *tpt;* **Duke Jordan**, *pno;* Paul Rovere, *bass.*

1962

Les temps d'une nuit

France 1963 – 28 mins
dir Francis Bouchet

One night in the life of a performing rights inspector, as he works his way around French jazz circles. Music by **Maxim Saury, Martial Solal** and **Guy Lafitte**.

1963

Le temps redonné

France 1967 – 46 mins
dir H. Fabiani, J. L. Lévi-Alvares

T

Documentary about a pilot sanatorium at Beauroune specialising in psychological illness. Music partly by **Henri Crolla**.

1964
Ten bob in winter
UK 1964 – 12 mins
dir Lloyd Reckord

Ten shillings goes from hand to hand amongst three young, poor, coloured compatriots relieving some of their difficulties and creating others. Music by **Joe Harriott**.

1965
10 Rillington Place
UK 1970 – 111 mins
dir Richard Fleischer

Very dull screen adaptation of the book by Ludovic Kennedy – a case history of pathological murder. Music score composed and conducted by **John Dankworth**.

The tenant
see Le locataire.

1966
The tender game
USA 1958 – 7 mins
dir John Hubley

Beautifully designed, now-classic colour cartoon of 'boy meeting girl', with excellent soundtrack by The **Oscar Peterson** Trio accompanying **Ella Fitzgerald** with 'Tenderly'.

1967
Teorema/Theorem
Italy 1968 – 98 mins
dir Pier Paolo Pasolini

A complex intellectual parable, adapted by the director from his own novel, in which Marx and Christ become interchangeable symbols of self-destruction. The music track by Ennio Morricone features trumpet work by **Ted Curson**.

1968
Teresa Brewer and The Firehouse Five Plus Two/The Firehouse Blues Five Plus Two
USA 1951 – 16 mins
dir Will Cowan

Universal-International music short featuring the title performers supported by **Joe Venuti**. *vln*; The Mercer Brothers, dance duo; and Leo Diamond, *hca*. Teresa Brewer was inexplicably deleted from the British release version which was shortened to 9 minutes. Numbers: 'Music, music, music', 'Old man Mose', 'Everybody loves my baby',

'Johnson rag', 'Hot canary', 'Fantasy in blue' and 'When you bump into someone you know'.

1969
Terre fleurie
France 1956 – 10 mins
dir Robert Mariaud

Impressions of Cannes and its environs, with music by **Henri Crolla** and **André Hodeir**.

1970
Terres et flammes/Vallauris
France 1951 – 18 mins
dir Robert Mariaud

Ceramic and pottery studios, including Picasso's, in Vallauris. Music by **Henri Crolla** and **André Hodeir**.

1971
Le testament d'Orphée
France 1959 – 83 mins
dir Jean Cocteau

Cocteau's 'farewell to the screen', a fashionable, but magical fairy tale. Features a short piano interlude by **Martial Solal**.

1972
Testing oils for two-stroke engines
UK 1963 – 13 mins
dir Derek Stewart, Julian Cooper

Documentary about the testing of specially designed lubricating oils to prove their qualities. Music by **Stan Tracy** and **Harold McNair**.

1973
Tex Beneke
USA c1948 – 18 mins

The **Tex Beneke** Band plays 'Moonlight serenade', 'In the mood', 'Don't be that way', 'Five minutes more', 'Serenade in blue', 'American patrol' and 'Some other time'.

1974
Tex Beneke and His Orchestra
USA 1948 – 15 mins
dir Will Cowan

A Universal-International featurette in which the title band entertain, supported by Garry Stevens and The Moonlight Serenaders. Numbers include: 'Moonlight serenade', 'Over the rainbow', 'Too late' and 'Kalamazoo'.

1975

Tex Beneke and Orchestra

USA 1948 – 10 mins
dir Jack Scholl

Martin Block tells the story behind The **Tex Beneke** Band who are presented playing several numbers, including 'Makin' love mountain style'. Starts with a brief sequence of **Glenn Miller** and His Orchestra playing 'Moonlight serenade'.

1976

Tex Beneke and The Glenn Miller Orchestra

USA 1946 – 17 mins
dir Will Cowan

One of the best of the Universal music shorts, extensively featuring **Tex Beneke**, *ten sax, voc,* with The **Glenn Miller** Orchestra plus strings, supported by Artie Malvin, Bobby Nichols and Lillian Lane – The Crew Chiefs. Numbers: 'Chattanooga choo choo', 'Meadowlands', 'Cynthia's in love', 'Little brown jug' and 'Hey! ba-ba-re-bop'.

1977

Texas carnival

USA 1951 – 75 mins
dir Charles Walters

Lively, good humoured MGM Technicolor musical with Esther Williams in her swimming pool, Ann Miller and Howard Keel. One sequence features The **Red Norvo** Trio.

1978

Thanks a million

USA 1935 – 85 mins
dir Roy Del Ruth

Routine musical tailored for Dick Powell's engaging personality and featuring **Paul Whiteman** and His Orchestra, with **Jack Teagarden**.

1979

Thanks for the boogie ride

USA 1942 – 3 mins

Soundie featuring **Gene Krupa** and His Orchestra with vocal by **Anita O'Day** assisted by **Roy Eldridge**.

1980

Thanks for the memory

USA 1938 – 78 mins
dir George Archainbaud

Domestic comedy about a newly married couple (Bob Hope and Shirley Ross); their quarrels and subsequent reconciliations. Includes the song 'Two sleepy people' by Frank Loesser and **Hoagy Carmichael**.

1981

That certain feeling

USA 1956 – 103 mins
dir Norman Panama, Melvin Frank

Effective screen adaptation of the Broadway play *King of hearts* by Jean Kerr and Eleanor Brooke, with a particularly well judged performance from Bob Hope. Features a very relaxed **Pearl Bailey**.

1982

That cold day in the park

Canada 1969 – 115 mins
dir Robert Altman

Interesting, though not wholly successful, adaptation of Richard Miles's novel with an excellent performance by Sandy Dennis. Music by **Johnny Mandel**.

1983

That girl from Paris

USA 1936 – 105 mins
dir Leigh Jason

Comedy-musical with opera star Lily Pons following a band from Paris to the USA, featuring **Jimmy Dorsey**.

1984

That ol' ghost train

USA 1942 – 3 mins

Soundie presenting **Les Hite** and His Orchestra.

1985

That's a plenty

USA c1952 – 3 mins

Snader Telescription of **Jack Teagarden** playing the title number.

1986

That's entertainment!

USA 1974 – 137 mins
dir Jack Haley Jr

Lavish compilation of MGM musicals which includes footage of virtually every star the company ever employed, including Lena Horne singing 'Honeysuckle rose' by Andy Razaf and **Fats Waller**, from *Thousands cheer*. **Ethel Waters** is credited but does not appear – presumably a sequence from *Cabin in the sky* has been edited out.

1987

That's entertainment! part 2

USA 1976 – 133 mins
dir (new sequences) Gene Kelly

Dull and unimaginative sequel to *That's entertainment!* using left-overs from the MGM vaults. Includes 'Taking a chance on love' sung by **Ethel Waters** and Eddie Anderson, from *Cabin in the sky*; 'The lady is a tramp' sung by Lena Horne from *Words and music*; 'Now you has jazz' sung by Bing Crosby and **Louis Armstrong** from *High society*.

1988
That's jazz
UK 1973 – 28 mins
dir Leslie Timmins

Bandstand performances by The **Freddy Randall-Dave Shepherd** All Stars, originally recorded on colour V/T and apparently sponsored by a church. The septet play 'Uncertain blues' (**Freddy Randall**, *voc*), 'Lonesome road', 'Beale Street blues', 'Sugar' (Jeanie Lambe, *voc*), 'Wolverine', 'Nobody knows you when you're down and out'(Jeanie Lambe, *voc*) and 'Mood indigo', plus the backing for a religious story. Besides **Freddy Randall**, *tpt*, and **Dave Shepherd**, *clar*, the soloists include **Danny Moss**,*ten sax;* **Brian Lemon**, *pno;* and **Ken Baldock**, *bass*.

1989
That's my baby
USA 1945 – 67 mins
dir William Burke

Feeble comedy about a comic-magazine magnate who suffers from a constant state of depression. Features pianist **Eugene Rodgers**.

1990
That's my desire
France 1950 – 10 mins

Origin and French title unknown – a film record of **Louis Armstrong**'s All Stars, featuring **Jack Teagarden** and **Cozy Cole**.

1991
That's the spirit
USA 1933 – 9 mins
dir Roy Mack

A fictional short produced by Vitaphone featuring The **Noble Sissle** Band with **Wendell Culley** and Clarence Brereton, *tpt;* **Wilbur De Paris**, *trb;* **Buster Bailey**, *clar;* Edward 'Jelly' Coles, *tuba;* The Washboard Serenaders and tap-dancer Cora La Redd. Musical items include: 'St Louis blues', 'Tiger rag' and 'A shanty in old shanty town'.

1992
That's what makes the world
USA c1952 – 3 mins

Snader Telescription featuring **Jack Teagarden** playing the title number.

1993
Theater for a story
USA 1959 – 30 mins
prod Robert Herridge

Originally made for US TV, a half-hour show featuring The **Miles Davis** Quintet – **John Coltrane**, *ten sax;* **Wynton Kelly**, *pno;* **Paul Chambers**, *bass;* **Jimmy Cobb**, *drs;* with 'So what?' and **Miles Davis** with **Gil Evans** and His Orchestra in three numbers: **Brubeck**'s 'The Duke', **Evans**'s own 'Blues for Pablo' and **Ahmad Jamal**'s 'New rhumba'.

1994
Theatre Royal
UK 1943 – 101 mins
dir John Baxter

Comedy vehicle for Flanagan and Allen, charting their efforts to get a show staged. Appearances by **George Shearing** and **Victor Feldman**.

Theorem
see **Teorema.**

1995
These things I offer you
USA c1952 – 3 mins

Snader Telescription in which the title number is sung by **Sarah Vaughan**.

1996
They call me Mister Tibbs
USA 1970 – 108 mins
dir Gordon Douglas

Routine, but efficient, urban thriller featuring Virgil Tibbs, the phlegmatic Negro cop from *In the heat of the night*. Music by **Quincy Jones**.

1997
They live by night/The red wagon
USA 1948 – 96 mins
dir Nicholas Ray

Beautifully played and intelligently directed story of a young man's attempt to go straight against overwhelming odds. Contains an appearance by vocalist **Mary Bryant**.

1998
They raided the joint
USA 1946 – 3 mins
dir William Forest Crouch

Soundie in which the title song is sung by **Vanita Smythe** backed off-screen by boogie piano.

They shoot horses, don't they?
USA 1969 – 120 mins
dir Sydney Pollack

Tricksy, pretentious screen adaptation of Horace McCoy's novel centred around a dance marathon in 1932. Music director John Green incorporates many popular numbers of the time: 'Easy come, easy go', 'Sweet Sue', 'Paradise', 'Coquette', 'I'm yours', 'The Japanese sandman', 'By the beautiful sea', 'Between the devil and the deep blue sea', 'The best things in life are free', 'Body and soul', 'I cover the waterfront', 'Brother, can you spare a dime?', 'I found a million dollar baby', 'Out of nowhere' and 'California, here I come'. Soundtrack musicians include: **Gus Bivona, Ronnie Lang, Ted Nash, Gene Cipriano, Teddy Edwards**, *reeds;* **Mannie Klein, Johnny Audino**, *tpt;* **Lloyd Ulyate**, Thurman Green, Gil Falco, *trb;* **Shelly Manne**, *drs;* **Larry Bunker**, *vibs;* **Ray Brown, Joe Mondragon**, *bass;* **Ronnell Bright**, Paul Smith, John Green, *pno;* Steve Paietta, *acc;* Carl Lamagna, *vln.*

2000

The thief of Bagdad
USA 1924 – 140 mins
dir Raoul Walsh

Magnificent adventure fantasy tailored for Douglas Fairbanks, with memorable art direction by William Cameron Menzies. Somewhere in the crowd scenes **Jesse Fuller** made his first screen appearance as an extra.

2001

The thief of Bagdad
UK 1940 – 110 mins
dir Ludwig Berger, Michael Powell, Tim Whelan

Remarkable Arabian Nights fantasy, full of colour spectacle and inspired invention. Miklós Rózsa's magnificent score features three songs 'Sailor's song', 'Sabu's song' and 'The princess's song' one of which is sung by **Adelaide Hall. Cleo Laine** is an extra, somewhere in the crowd.

2002

The third alibi
UK 1961 – 68 mins
dir Montgomery Tully

Economical thriller, cleverly worked out and with a powerful twist ending. Includes a guest appearance by **Cleo Laine** singing 'Now and then' by Don Banks and David Dearlove.

2003

The third voice
USA 1959 – 79 mins
dir Hubert Cornfield

Quite watchable thriller with a well-tried but still serviceable theme: the planning and execution of an apparently perfect murder. Music by **Johnny Mandel**.

2004

This could be the night
USA 1957 – 104 mins
dir Robert Wise

Charming fairy-tale of a fresh young *ingénue* who finds her way into and reforms a sophisticated nightclub world. Features **Ray Anthony** and His Orchestra.

2005

This love of mine
USA 1942 – 3 mins

Soundie in which The **Stan Kenton** Band play the title number (Joe Rizzi, *arr;* Dolly Mitchell, *voc*) Personnel: Ray Borden, John Carroll, **Chico Alvarez**, Frank Payne, *tpt;* **Joe Howard, Harry Forbes**, George Faye, *trb;* Eddie Meyers, Bill Lahey, *alt sax;* Ted Romersa, 'Red' Dorris, *ten sax;* **Bob Gioga**, *bar sax;* **Stan Kenton**, *pno;* Al Costi, *gtr;* Bill Walther, *bass;* Joe Vernon, *drs.* The dancers are Charisse and Gary Leon.

2006

This time for keeps
USA 1947 – 104 mins
dir Richard Thorpe

Formula vehicle for swimmer Esther Williams, with comedy supplied by Jimmy Durante. Orchestrations partly by **Calvin Jackson**.

2007

Those blues
USA 1932 – 9 mins

Vincent Lopez and His Orchestra entertain with a programme of popular musical items that includes **W. C. Handy**'s 'St Louis blues'.

2008

A thousand clowns
USA 1965 – 115 mins
dir Fred Coe

Charming and very funny comedy by Herb Gardner, based on his own play. Title song composed by Judy Holliday and **Gerry Mulligan**.

2009

Thousands cheer

USA 1943 – 126 mins
dir George Sidney

All star MGM Technicolor musical extravaganza, produced as a wartime morale booster. Among the many popular entertainers appearing are Virginia O'Brien, June Allyson and Gloria DeHaven singing 'In a little Spanish town' with **Bob Crosby** and His Orchestra; 'I dug a ditch' by Kay Kyser and His Orchestra and Andy Razaf and **Fats Waller**'s 'Honeysuckle rose' sung by Lena Horne backed by **Benny Carter** and His Band, with **Eugene Porter**, *ten sax*.

2010

Three blind mice

USA c1952 – 3 mins

Snader Telescription of **Red Nichols** playing the title number.

2011

Three for the show

USA 1955 – 92 mins
dir H. C. Potter

Musical screen adaptation of W. Somerset Maugham's play, *Home and beauty*, realised as a vehicle for its star, Betty Grable. Among the many standard numbers used is **Hoagy Carmichael** and Harold Adamson's 'Down boy'.

2012

Three little bops

USA 1956 – 8 mins
dir Friz Freleng

Amusing Warner Bros colour cartoon in which The Three Little Pigs are rock 'n' roll musicians and The Wolf blows a hot trumpet. The music is composed and played by **Shorty Rogers**.

2013

Thrill of a romance

USA 1945 – 104 mins
dir Richard Thorpe

Lavish colour musical from MGM in which Esther Williams does her swimming and diving bit, featuring **Tommy Dorsey** and His Orchestra. There are also some orchestrations by **Calvin Jackson**.

2014

The thrill of Brazil

USA 1946 – 81 mins
dir S. Sylvan Simon

Pleasant enough musical comedy of errors with Evelyn Keyes, featuring **Jack Costanzo**. The third screen version of *The front page*.

2015

The tiger makes out

USA 1967 – 95 mins
dir Arthur Hiller

Unsuccessful adaptation of Murray Schisgal's one act play, originally for two characters. Music and title song composed and conducted by **Milton 'Shorty' Rogers**.

2016

Tiger rag

Netherlands c1960 – 4 mins

Sponsored music short featuring The **Dutch Swing College Band**.

2017

'Til the butcher cuts him down

USA 1971 – 53 mins
dir Philip Spalding

Particularly fine colour documentary about the late trumpeter **Ernest Punch Miller**, made during his appearance at the 1971 New Orleans Heritage Jazz Festival. Features a blues by **'Kid' Thomas** and His Algiers Stompers: **'Kid' Thomas Valentine**, *tpt;* **Louis Nelson**, *trb;* Sam Dutrey, *clar;* Emanuel Paul, *ten sax;* Charlie Hamilton, *pno;* Joe Butler, *bass;* Alonso Stewart, *drs;* 'Algiers strut' and 'Over the waves' performed by The Algiers Stompers (Albert Burbank replaces Sam Dutrey on *clar*); 'Oh, didn't he ramble' and 'The old rugged cross' by **Dejan's Olympia Brass Band**, including Milton Batiste, **George 'Kid Sheik' Cola**, Edmund Foucher, *tpt;* Paul Crawford, Gerald Joseph, *trb;* Harold Dejan, *alt sax;* Emanuel Paul, *ten sax;* Andrew Jefferson, Nowell 'Papa' Glass, *snare drs;* Henry 'Booker T Glass, *bass drs;* 'When it's sleepytime down south' by **Dizzy Gillespie** with rhythm section; 'Exactly like you', 'I wanna be a rug-cutter', 'Eight, nine and ten', 'You can depend on me' and 'That's my home' by **'Punch' Miller**, *tpt, voc;* **Bobby Hackett**, *cor;* **Raymond Burke**, *clar;* **Don Ewell**, *pno;* **Emmanuel Sayles**, *banjo, voc;* Freddie Kohlman, *drs;* and unidentified bass. There's also an appearance by an ailing **'Kid' Ory** and the informative commentary is by William Russell of Tulane University's Jazz Archive.

2018

Till then

USA 1944 – 3 mins

Soundie featuring The **Mills Brothers** with the title number.

Kid Ory and Punch Miller appear together briefly in **'Til the butcher cuts him down.**

2019

Tillie

USA 1945 – 3 mins

Soundie in which **Louis Jordan** interprets the title number.

2020

Timber move

UK 1965 – 5 mins
dir Norman Prouting

Documentary on timber handling, in which a ship is turned round in record time at Hull docks. Good swinging music score by **Kenny Graham**.

2021

Timber – Øk i Canada

Denmark 1967 – 23 mins
dir Ole Roos

Documentary about the work of a timber company in Canada, with music score by **Martial Solal**.

2022

Timberjack

USA 1954 – 92 mins
dir Joe Kane

A standard Western plot transposed to a timber county story – conventional and undistinguished. **Hoagy Carmichael**, somewhat subdued, plays the saloon piano-player, Jingles, contributing five songs.

2023

Time flies

UK 1944 – 88 mins
dir Walter Forde

Comedy about a return to Mediaeval days in a professor's time machine, featuring **Stephane Grappelly** as a troubadour.

2024

A time for killing/The long ride home

USA 1967 – 83 mins
dir Phil Karlson

American Civil War drama, originally started by director Roger Corman who left the production shortly after filming began. Music score by **Mundell Lowe**.

2025
Time takes care of everything
USA 1946 – 3 mins
dir William Forest Crouch

Soundie in which the title song is sung by **June Richmond**.

2026
Timelaerer Nansen/Teacher Nansen
Denmark 1968 – 11 mins
dir Kirsten Stenbaek

Short story charting the romantic experiences of a master at a girls school, with music by **Erik Moseholm**.

2027
Timothy Leary's wedding/You're nobody 'til somebody loves you
USA 1964 – 12 mins
dir D. A. Pennebaker

Improvised impression of Dr Timothy Leary's marriage, in which **Charlie Mingus** appears briefly playing piano.

2028
Tired of waiting for you
USA 1943 – 3 mins

Soundie featuring **Jimmy Dorsey** and His Orchestra, with vocalists Helen O'Connell and Bob Eberly.

2029
To be free
USA 1972 – 82 mins
dir Ned Bosnick

Superbly photographed, independently produced feature on the theme of sexual frigidity. Music score by **Lalo Schifrin**, performed by The Los Angeles String Quartet.

2030
To have and have not
USA 1944 – 100 mins
dir Howard Hawks

One of the really great movies – a screen adaptation of the novel by Ernest Hemingway, which shot Lauren Bacall to stardom and clinched her partnership with Bogart, both on and off screen. **Hoagy Carmichael** co-stars in one of his most memorable roles and provides, with Johnny Mercer, the song 'How little we know' sung on screen by Bacall but thought to have been ghosted by Andy Williams. Also the numbers 'Hong Kong blues' and 'Am I blue'.

To love
see **Att alska.**

2031
Tommy
UK 1975 – 108 mins
dir Ken Russell

Screen adaptation of the rock opera by Pete Townshend and The Who. Among the many

Tommy Dorsey and His Orchestra

▼

soundtrack musicians are **Bob Efford** and **Ronnie Ross**.

2032
Tommy Dorsey and His Orchestra
USA 1951 – 15 mins
dir Will Cowan

Universal-International production in which **Tommy Dorsey** and His Orchestra (**Ray Wetzel**, *tpt*), in a bandstand setting, play a programme consisting of 'You left your brown eyed baby', 'Opus no.1', 'Diane', 'The hucklebuck' (soloist **Charlie Shavers**, *voc, tpt*) and 'Boogie woogie', supported by vocalists Frances Irvin and Bob London.

2033
The Tommy Steele story/Rock around the world
UK 1957 – 82 mins
dir Gerard Bryant

Reconstructed documentary telling the story of the entertainer's discovery and rise to fame as a teenage rock 'n' roll idol. Features **Humphrey Lyttleton** and His Band, Chas McDevitt Skiffle Group and Nancy Whiskey. Numbers include 'Bermondsey bounce' by **Humphrey Lyttelton**; 'Freight train' by Paul James, Fred Williams; 'It's fun finding out about London' by Roger Paul; 'Narrative calypso' by Russell Henderson.

2034
The Tony Kinsey Quartet
UK 1961 – 9 mins
dir Robert Henryson

Music short featuring the title group, in a bandstand setting, playing three numbers: 'The clock on the wall', 'Dinner for one, please, James' and 'Autobahn'.

2035
Tony Rome
USA 1967 – 110 mins
dir Gordon Douglas

Highly watchable attempt to revive the successful 1940's formula of the private-eye thriller, adapted from the book *Miami mayhem* by Marvin H. Albert. Music score by **Billy May**, who also supplies two songs: 'Something here inside me' and 'Hard times'.

2036
Too late blues
USA 1961 – 103 mins
dir John Cassavetes

A sadly underrated movie that effectively captures the edgy *camaraderie* between its central group of characters – a jazz combo. Superb music score

The final club sequence in **Too late blues**.

▼

by David Raksin, with the participation of **Benny Carter, Uan Rasey, Jimmy Rowles, Milt Bernhart, Red Mitchell** and **Shelly Manne**. On screen, in an early party sequence, **Slim Gaillard** is prominent.

2037
Top flight
UK 1964 – 26 mins
dir Julian Spiro

Documentary, made for BOAC, about the part played by ground controllers and staff of distant airfields in ensuring the safety and comfort of air passengers. Music score by **Johnny Dankworth**.

2038
Top man
USA 1943 – 83 mins
dir Charles Lamont

One of the excellent series of comedy musicals that Donald O'Connor made with Universal in the 1940's. Features **Count Basie** and His Orchestra and the numbers: 'Basie boogie', 'Wrap your troubles in dreams' and 'Dark eyes'.

2039
Top of the heap
USA 1972 – 88 mins
dir Christopher St. John

As producer, writer, director and star Christopher St. John must take full responsibility for this contrived drama of a Washington, DC, cop, mistrusted and despised by his own black people. Effective music score by **J. J. Johnson**.

2040
Topper
USA 1927 – 96 mins
dir Norman Z. McLeod

The first in the series of Hal Roach 'Topper' movies, based on a story by Thorne Smith, with Constance Bennett and Cary Grant involved in ghostly escapades. **Hoagy Carmichael** makes a brief appearance and provides the music and lyrics for the song 'Old man moon'.

Tops is the limit
see **Anything goes.**

2041
Tormented
USA 1960 – 75 mins
dir Bert I. Gordon

Undistinguished, low-budget ghost story about a jazz pianist haunted by the death of his mistress, with a jazz score by **Calvin Jackson**.

2042
Toronto jazz
Canada 1964 – 27 mins
dir Donald Owen

A very poor impression of the Toronto jazz scene with interviews, rehearsals and club performances by a cross-section of the groups in the city, including: The Lenny Breau Trio, The Don Thompson Quintet and The Alf Jones Quartet. Music includes 'Mike's music' by Mike Snow.

2043
Touch of evil
USA 1957 – 107 mins
dir Orson Welles

Justly renowned baroque narcotics thriller, set in a Mexican border town, with Welles indulging himself to the full, both in his playing of the corrupt obsessed cop and in his virtuoso direction. **Barney Kessel** and **Dave Pell** participated in Henry Mancini's atmospheric music track.

2044
A touch of larceny
UK 1959 – 92 mins
dir Guy Hamilton

Amiable comedy about a naval commander who arranges his disappearance hoping that the press will brand him as a traitor enabling him to bring a profitable libel action. **Hoagy Carmichael**'s 'The nearness of you' is used on soundtrack.

2045
Tracks
USA 1975 – 100 mins
dir Henry Jaglom

Drama set almost entirely aboard a train during a journey from Los Angeles to San Diego in the spring of 1973 immediately following Nixon's 'peace with honour' announcement. Recorded music on soundtrack includes 'Praise the lord and pass the ammunition' by Kay Kyser and His Orchestra; 'Say it over and over again' sung by Dinah Shore; 'These foolish things' sung by Bing Crosby; 'This love of mine' by **Tommy Dorsey** and His Orchestra with Frank Sinatra; 'He wears a pair of silver wings' by Kay Kyser and His Orchestra; 'My sister and I' by **Jimmy Dorsey** and His Orchestra and 'The way you look tonight' sung by Fred Astaire.

2046
Trader Horn
USA 1973 – 105 mins
dir Reza S. Badiyi

A laughably inane remake of the 1931 classic with Rod Taylor caught in the African phase of World War I and faced with a series of cardboard perils and much stock footage. **Shelly Manne** supplies the jazz-flavoured music score.

2047
Le train
France/Italy 1973 – 100 mins
dir Pierre Granier-Deferre

Love story, set in 1940, involving refugees earmarked for Germany, with orchestrations by **Hubert Rostaing**.

2048
Transatlantic merry-go-round
USA 1934 – 92 mins
dir Benjamin Stoloff

Comedy set on an ocean liner, from a story by Leon Gordon, and featuring The **Boswell Sisters**.

2049
Transit supervan
UK 1969 – 22 mins
dir Bob Shearer

A light-hearted story of what happens when a party of Ford salesmen descend on a village to sell the local tradesmen a range of Transit vans. Music score by **Johnny Hawksworth**.

2050
Trauma
USA 1962 – 92 mins
dir Robert Malcolm Young

Routine low-budget chiller that just isn't good enough to be either interesting or exciting. Music score by **Buddy Collette**.

The trial
see **Le procès**.

2051
Trial by combat/A choice of weapons
UK 1976 – 90 mins
dir Kevin Connor

Abysmal comedy with an eminent cast struggling manfully with woefully written material. Music score by Frank Cordell employing a hand-picked symphony orchestra that included Alan Civil, Jack Brymer, **Kenny Baker, Stan Roderick, Don Lusher** and **Ray Premru**.

2052
The trial of the Catonsville Nine
USA 1972 – 85 mins
dir Gordon Davidson

Independently produced (by Gregory Peck) screen adaptation of Father Philip Berrigan's play about a group of men on trial for burning draft records. Music score by **Shelly Manne**.

2053
Les tricheurs/Youthful sinners
France 1958 – 125 mins
dir Marcel Carné

Old-timer Marcel Carné's exploitation of the juvenile delinquent theme, or beatnik amorality as it was known in 1958. There is plenty of recorded jazz on the soundtrack from **Stan Getz, Roy Eldridge, Dizzy Gillespie, Coleman Hawkins, Ray Brown, Herb Ellis, Oscar Peterson, Sonny Stitt, Gus Johnson** and **Maxim Saury**.

Trip to kill
see **Clay pigeon**.

2054
Les tripes au soleil
France/Italy 1958 – 105 mins
dir Claude-Bernard Aubert

Controversial and much-banned melodrama on a racial theme, set in a doomed mythical city. Jazz score by **André Hodeir**.

2055
Trois chambres à Manhattan
France 1964 – 110 mins
dir Marcel Carné

Disappointing screen adaptation of the novel by Georges Simenon – a story of romantic intrigue set in New York. Music by **Mal Waldron**.

Tropicana
see **The heat's on**.

2056
True to life
USA 1943 – 94 mins
dir George Marshall

Comedy about two radio writers looking for realistic material. Contains four songs by Johnny Mercer and **Hoagy Carmichael**: 'There she was', 'Old music master', 'Mister Pollyanna' and 'Sudsy suds theme song'.

True to the army
see **Trumpet serenade**.

2057
Trumpet player's tribute
USA 1970
dir George Wein, Sidney J. Stiber

One of three documentaries produced around **Louis Armstrong**'s final performances at Newport.

2058
Trumpet serenade/True to the army
USA 1942 – 15 mins
dir Reginald LeBorg

A Universal featurette spotlighting **Harry James**, his trumpet and His Music Makers, in a club setting, supported by Helen Forrest, *voc;* Grace McDonald, dancer, and The Jivin' Jacks and Jills. Numbers include: 'You made me love you'.

2059
Tryptyk jazzowy/Jazz triptych
Poland c1960 – 20 mins
dir G. Lasota

Embarrassingly arty-crafty impression of a Polish jazz club, with numbers from The Hagow Instrumental Group, The Kurylewicz Quintet and The Novi Vocal Group with Wanda Warska.

2060
Tu seras terriblement gentille
France 1967 – 94 mins
dir Dirk Sanders

Colour supplement whimsy about which the less said the better. Music score by **Jacques Loussier**.

2061
Tubby Hayes
UK c1964 – 25 mins
dir Robin Scott

Originally produced for BBC TV, a performance from The Marquee Club, London, featuring The **Tubby Hayes** Quintet with guest vocalist **Betty Bennett**, introduced by Steve Race. The group includes **Bert Courtley**, *tpt, mello;* and **Alan Ganley**, *drs;* with **Tubby Hayes**, *ten sax, vibs, flute.* Numbers include: 'The syndicate', 'With the wind and the rain in your hair' and 'Down in the village'.

2062
Tubby the tuba
USA 1975

Currently in production, a feature-length animated cartoon, using the voice of **Pearl Bailey**.

2063
Tue. afternoon with The New York Improvisation Ensemble
USA 1967 – 32 mins

Depicts the lives of modern jazz musicians as reflected in the personal experiences of members of The New York Improvisation Ensemble.

Les tueurs de San Francisco
see **Once a thief.**

2064
Tumbleweed tempos
USA 1946 – 15 mins
dir Will Cowan

Universal featurette with Spade Cooley's Orchestra backing songs from **Ella Mae Morse** and comic turns by 'Smokey' Rogers. Numbers: 'The Campbells are coming', 'The life of the party', 'Turn my picture upside down', 'Crazy 'cause I love you' and 'Don't move'.

2065
Tweed me
USA 1942 – 3 mins

Soundie featuring The Chocolateers with one of their crazy dance routines. Among the backing musicians is **John Kirby**.

2066
Twenty million sweethearts
USA 1934 – 89 mins
dir Ray Enright

Routine Warner Bros musical, with Dick Powell and Ginger Rogers, set in and around a radio station and featuring The **Mills Brothers**.

2067
Twilight of honor/The charge is murder
USA 1963 – 104 mins
dir Boris Sagal

Predictable courtroom drama adapted from the novel by Al Dewlen. John Green's music track features alto solos by **Ronny Lang**.

2068
Twilight on the prairie
USA 1944 – 62 mins
dir Jean Yarbrough

Cheaply made comedy about a cowboy band stranded in Texas, featuring **Jack Teagarden** in a leading role as well as appearing with his big band in three numbers including his own song 'The blues'.

2069
Twist all night/The young and the cool
USA 1961 – 85 mins
dir William J. Hole

T

A sketchy story serves as a peg on which to hang a succession of 'Twist' numbers by various popular artistes, one of whom is **Louis Prima**.

Two are guilty
see **Le glaive et la balance.**

2070
Two girls and a sailor
USA 1944 – 124 mins
dir Richard Thorpe

Musical romance in the best escapist manner, providing an excuse to introduce a series of star turns, including **Harry James** and His Orchestra, with Lena Horne and Virginia O'Brien, and Xavier Cugat's Orchestra. Numbers include 'A-tisket, a-tasket' by Al Feldman and **Ella Fitzgerald**.

2071
Two guitars in jive
USA 1942 – 3 mins

Soundie featuring the title number played by **Stan Kenton**, backing dancer Amarillo.

2072
Two guys from Milwaukee/Royal flush
USA 1946 – 91 mins
dir David Butler

Formula comedy about a Balkan prince living it up in New York. Features the song: 'And her tears flowed like wine' by Charles Lawrence, Joe Greene and **Stanley Kenton.**

2073
Two guys from Texas/Two Texas knights
USA 1948 – 84 mins
dir David Butler

Mild musical about two nightclub entertainers stranded on a Texas ranch, featuring **Joe Venuti** and the songs: 'Every day I love you a little bit more', 'Hankerin'', 'I don't care if it rains all night', 'At the rodeo', 'I never met a Texan' and 'I wanna be a cowboy in the movies'.

2074
Two Latins from Manhattan
USA 1941 – 65 mins
dir Charles Barton

Second-feature musical comedy with a South American slant, featuring the song 'Daddy' by **Bobby Troup**.

2075
Two left feet
UK 1963 – 93 mins
dir Roy Baker

Modest but well observed romantic drama, based on the novel *In my solitude* by David Stuart Leslie, featuring **Bob Wallis** and His Storyville Jazzmen and music played by **Sandy Brown** and **Kenny Baker**.

Two men and a wardrobe
see **Dwaj ludzie z szafa.**

2076
Two people
USA 1973 – 100 mins
dir Robert Wise

As yet unreleased in the UK, a story of two people – their coming together and their separation, while travelling from Africa to France and on to the USA. Composer David Shire used some top jazz musicians for his music track, including **Ronnie Lang, Larry Bunker, Shelly Manne** and **Emil Richards**.

2077
Two shadows
USA 1938 – 20 mins
dir Lloyd French

Vitaphone music short presenting popular entertainers that include **Sharkey Bonano**'s Swing Band.

Two Texas knights
see **Two guys from Texas.**

2078
Two tickets to Broadway
USA 1951 – 106 mins
dir James V. Kern

Bouncy Technicolor musical on familiar lines – the college girl who finds romance, adventure and success on Broadway. Features **Bob Crosby** and His Bobcats and the song 'Let's make comparisons' by Sammy Cahn and **Bob Crosby**. The **Red Norvo** Trio cut a non-visual sequence backing a vocal by Ann Miller.

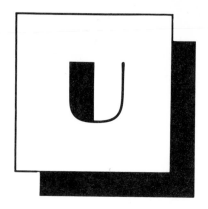

2079

Ubranie prawie nowe/A hand-me-down suit/New clothes

Poland 1963 – 95 mins
dir Wlodzimierz Haupe

Thoroughly unlikeable and unpleasant production about an elderly, ugly housemaid saving money for years to provide herself with a dowry for a successful marriage. Music score by **Krzystof T. Komeda**.

2080

L'Ultima donna/La dernière femme/The last woman

Italy/France 1976 – 109 mins
dir Marco Ferreri

Rather grim but honest and deeply felt expression of psychic imprisonment played out by a childish and oafish earthy hero. Spare music score by Philippe Sarde, directed by **Hubert Rostaing**.

2081

The ultimate warrior

USA 1975 – 94 mins
dir Robert Clouse

Violent, futuristic fantasy proposing that the ecological disasters being perpetrated will lead in the next century to devastation akin to an atomic war. Music score by **Gil Mellé**.

2082

Ultimo tango a Parigi/Last tango in Paris

Italy/France 1972 – 130 mins
dir Bernardo Bertolucci

Bold, controversial, impeccable study of sexual passion with a truly remarkable performance by Marlon Brando as an ageing and failed widower who involves himself in a purely carnal relationship with a young girl. Brilliant music score by **Gato Barbieri**, played by His Orchestra with the leader soloing on tenor sax throughout. Arranger and conductor, **Oliver Nelson**.

2083

Unchained

USA 1955 – 74 mins
dir Hall Bartlett

Adaptation of the book *Prisoners are people* by Kenyon Scudder, set in the famous Chino prison-without-bars in California. **Dexter Gordon**, an inmate at the time, appears playing tenor sax but the soundtrack was ghosted by a studio musician. He also has a few lines of dialogue which were ultimately to be the start of his acting career.

2084

Underneath the Broadway moon

USA 1934 – 10 mins
dir Fred Waller

Paramount music short featuring **Isham Jones** and His Orchestra, supported by Vera Vann and The Four Eton Boys.

2085

Uneasy terms

UK 1948 – 91 mins
dir Vernon Sewell

Stale, unexciting adaptation of a Peter Cheyney thriller with Michael Rennie as Slim Callaghan. The **Ted Heath** Band, with **Jack Parnell**, *drs*, prominent, is featured in the nightclub sequences.

086

Unlucky woman

USA 1944 – 3 mins

Soundie in which Lena Horne sings the title
number, supported by **Teddy Wilson**'s Band.
This is actually one sequence from the longer
Boogie woogie dream.

087

The unsinkable Molly Brown

USA 1964 – 127 mins
Dir Charles Walters

Likeable screen adaptation of the musical play,
with Debbie Reynolds giving a deliciously
attractive performance and an occasional touch of
the old MGM brilliance. Orchestrations partly by
Calvin Jackson.

088

The unsuspected

USA 1947 – 90 mins
Dir Michael Curtiz

Highly polished and thoroughly enjoyable thriller in
the best Warner Bros tradition, with a chilling
performance by Claude Rains. A nightclub
sequence features 'I got rhythm' played by a jazz
group lead by **Jo Jones**, *drs*.

089

Upkeep

USA 1973 – 10 mins
Dir John Hubley

A short history of the world as lived by the
repairman from that invention of the wheel to the
cities of tomorrow, told in the form of an animated
cartoon, with music by **Benny Carter**.

090

Urbanissimo

USA 1967 – 6 mins
Dir John Hubley

Animated cartoon – a comic allegory depicting a
runaway city devouring its environs, produced for
Expo '67 in Montreal. Music by **Benny Carter**.

091

Use your imagination

USA 1933 – 15 mins
Dir Roy Mack

Vitaphone short presenting popular entertainers of
the day, including among its musical numbers the
O.D.J.B.'s 'Tiger rag'.

2092

V.I.P.'s boogie

USA 1952 – 4 mins

Snader Telescription in which **Duke Ellington** and His Orchestra present the title number, featuring **Harry Carney**, *bar sax;* **Jimmy Hamilton**, *clar;* **Willie Cook**, *tpt;* **Paul Gonsalves**, *ten sax;* **Ray Nance**, *tpt;* **Britt Woodman**, *trb;* **Russell Procope**, *alt sax;* **Cat Anderson**, *tpt;* **Quentin Jackson**, *trb;* **Juan Tizol**, *trb;* **Willie Smith**, *alt sax;* **Louie Bellson**, *drs;* **Wendell Marshall**, *bass.*

2093

La valise

France 1973 – 100 mins
dir Georges Lautner

Undistinguished spy thriller, with music orchestrated by **Hubert Rostaing**.

Vallauris

see **Terres et flammes.**

2094

Valley of the redwoods

USA 1960 – 70 mins
dir William N. Witney

Second-feature robbery movie with a ragged and unlikely plot and superficial characterisation. Jazz score composed and conducted by **Buddy Bregman**.

2095

Les valseuses/Making it

France 1974 – 118 mins
dir Bertrand Blier

Entertaining, anarchic tale of two drifters who live off their wits, women, extortion and theft. Splendid hard-swinging soundtrack jazz score composed and played by **Stephane Grappelli**, *vln;* backed by Maurice Vander, *pno, org, harpsichord;* Philippe Catherine, *gtr;* Marc Hemmeler, *pno;* **Guy Pedersen**, *bass;* **Daniel Humair**, *drs.*

2096

Vampire

France 1945 – 9 mins
dir Jean Painlevé

A remarkable science film about parasites, with a macabre sequence of a bat sucking blood from a living rabbit. **Duke Ellington**'s 'Black and tan fantasy' is used on the soundtrack as an experiment with its rhythmic possibilities.

2097

Variety girl

USA 1947 – 93 mins
dir George Marshall

Star-filled musical comedy about young hopefuls in Hollywood, featuring **Pearl Bailey** singing 'Tired'.

2098

Vauxhall, Bedford, England

UK 1965 – 22 mins
dir Arthur G. Wooster

Sponsored documentary describing Vauxhall's motor works, showing the scope of their resources and activities. Music by **Johnny Hawksworth**.

V

2099

Vedettes en pantoufles

France 1953 – 20 mins
dir Jacques Guillon

Diverse personalities from the entertainment world
presented in informal surroundings, including
Claude Luter and His Orchestra, **Cab Calloway**
and **Mezz Mezzrow**.

2100

Le vent se lève/Operation time bomb

France/Italy 1958 – 91 mins
dir Yves Ciampi

Mediocre seafaring melodrama set in Hamburg
and around the Kiel canal. Music score by **Henri
Crolla** and **André Hodeir**.

2101

The Venetian affair

USA 1966 – 92 mins
dir Jerry Thorpe

Rather unexciting spy thriller set in Venice
locations, beautifully photographed as they always
seem to be. Music score and song by **Lalo
Schifrin**.

2102

Verdensberømetheder i København

Denmark 1939

A short programme filler compiled from newsreel
material and featuring many celebrities of the day,
including **Duke Ellington**.

2103

Véridiquement vôtre

France 1968 – 12 mins
dir Jean Leduc

The story of consumer protection since the co-
operative societies of the nineteenth century.
Music by **Martial Solal**.

2104

Vibes boogie

USA 1951 – 3 mins

Snader Telescription in which the title number is
played by **Lionel Hampton** and His Orchestra.

2105

La vie à deux/Life together

France 1958 – 103 mins
dir Clément Duhour

A diverting entertainment fashioned out of the last
writing of the great Sacha Guitry, with a generous
all star cast of top French players. Music score by
Hubert Rostaing.

2106

La vie à l'envers/Life upside down

France 1964 – 92 mins
dir Alain Jessua

Quiet, infinitely peaceful and often funny movie
about an office worker who attains a kind of
Nirvana. A pleasing music track by **Jacques
Loussier** includes several choruses of jazz piano.

2107

La vie continue

France 1952 – 14 mins
dir C. Vilardebo

Short story about a young couple who meet in an
old provincial castle, with music by **Claude Luter**.

2108

La vie des criquets

France 1965 – 14 mins
dir Pierre Roger Lousteau

The story of the desert locust – the 'seventh
plague of Egypt'. Music by **Jacques Loussier**.

2109

La vie des oiseaux en Mauritanie

France 1963 – 16 mins
dir Jean Dragesco

The work of French ornithologists, with music by
Jacques Loussier.

2110

A view from Pompey's head/Secret interlude

USA 1955 – 97 mins
dir Philip Dunne

A New Yorker returns to the scenes of his
childhood – a rather theatrical adaptation of the
novel by Hamilton Basso. With the participation of
Benny Carter.

2111

Le village de la colère

France 1946 – 90 mins
dir Raoul André

Rural drama about a young man settling in a
small village ruled by superstition and ignorance.
Music arranged by **André Hodeir** and **Django
Reinhardt**.

2112

Vine Street blues

USA 1943 – 3 mins

Soundie in which the title number is sung by Anna
Lee, accompanied by **Wingy Manone** and His
Band.

2113
Le viol/Övergreppet/A question of rape
Sweden/France 1967 – 84 mins
dir Jacques Doniol-Valcroze

A positive and precise exploration of the no man's land between illusion and reality; a strikingly beautiful movie, superbly directed and acted. An excellent music track by **Michel Portal**.

2114
Violet er blå/Violets are blue
Denmark 1975 – 120 mins
dir Peter Refn

A moving portrait of a group of professional people unable to accept their roles in modern society. Music director Bent Fabricius Bjerre uses as source music two **Duke Ellington** small group recordings featuring **Johnny Hodges** plus **Ben Webster** playing 'How long has this been going on?'.

Violets are blue
see **Violet er blå.**

2115
Virginia, Georgia and Caroline
USA 1942 – 3 mins

Soundie featuring **Cab Calloway** and His Orchestra with their famous interpretation of the title number.

2116
Visage des P.T.T.
France 1964 – 16 mins
dir Sylvain Dhomme

Documentary on the French Post Office, with music by **Memphis Slim**.

2117
Visit to a small planet
USA 1959 – 85 mins
dir Norman Taurog

Inoffensive vehicle for the grimaces and zany chatter of Jerry Lewis, adapted from the satirical play by Gore Vidal. Contains appearances by **Frank Socolow, Don Bagley** and **Jack Costanzo**.

2118
Vitaphone Varieté
USA 1936 – 10 mins
dir Roy Mack

Entertaiment from variety performers including **Louis Prima** and His Orchestra. Numbers: 'Full steam ahead', 'Lonely gondolier', 'Sleepytime down south', 'Are you from Dixie', 'Smile' and 'Chinatown, my Chinatown'.

2119
Vitrine sous la mer
France 1960 – 15 mins
dir Georges Alépée

The capturing of fish for a museum in Monaco, with music by **Henri Crolla** and **André Hodeir**.

2120
Viva Max
USA 1969 – 92 mins
dir Jerry Paris

Damp comedy saga about a platoon of Mexican soldiers who recapture the Alamo in 1969. The music score by Hugo Montenegro, Ralph Dino and John Sembello – blaring, brassy and martial – is performed by **Al Hirt**.

2121
Vivre la nuit
France/Italy 1967 – 90 mins
dir Marcel Camus

Potboiler about young lovers caught up in nightlife cynicism, corruption and mendacity. Music by **Claude Bolling**.

2122
Voice in the mirror
USA 1958 – 102 mins
dir Harry Keller

Rather unsatisfactory presentation of the problems of alcoholism – drama based on fact – but with an intelligent performance from Julie London, who also provides the title song in collaboration with **Bobby Troup**.

2123
The voice of Britain
UK 1935 – 56 mins
dir Stuart Legg

A GPO Film Unit production, highlighting some of the facts and figures behind BBC radio, with the emphasis on its cultural and entertainment qualities. Among the performers, **Nina Mae McKinney** sings 'Dinah' during a 'Music hall' broadcast and, for the record, Henry Hall and The BBC Dance Orchestra play 'Piccadilly ride'.

V

2124

The voice that thrilled the world

USA 1943 – 17 mins
dir Jean Negulesco

Warner Bros short tracing the rise of talking
pictures, illustrated by clips from studio output,
including **Ethel Walters** singing 'Am I blue' from
the 1929 *On with the show.*

2125

Voici le ski

France 1961 – 34 mins
dir Jacques Ertaud

Documentary on skiing techniques as practised in
France, including a survey of former conventions.
Music by **André Hodeir.**

2126

**Voulez-vous danser avec moi?/Come dance
with me**

France/Italy 1959 – 91 mins
dir Michel Boisrond

Conventional, but colourful *policier*, adapted from
the novel *The blonde died dancing* by Kelley
Roos, boasting a few neat twists and surprises.
Music by **Henri Crolla** and **André Hodeir.**

2127

Le voyage à Khonostrov

France 1962 – 11 mins
dir Claude Ligure

Fictional short about six characters who are
brought together in a railway compartment. Music
by **Jacques Loussier.**

2128

Le voyage de noces

France 1975 – 88 mins
dir Nadine Trintignant

Rambling and verbose melodrama about a
married couple whose mutual infidelities are
revealed during a second honeymoon trip to North
Africa. Music by Michel Legrand and **Christian
Chevallier.**

2129

Voyage of the damned

UK 1976 – 155 mins
dir Stuart Rosenberg

Long, sluggish all-star melodrama with formula
characters involved in a story of a ship carrying
Jews away from Nazi Germany. Music score by
Lalo Schifrin.

2130

Voyage to next

USA 1974 – 10 mins
dir John Hubley

Animated cartoon fable in which Mother Earth and
Father Time (soundtracked by Maureen Stapleton
and **Dizzy Gillespie**) observe the state of life on
planet Earth. Music composed and conducted by
Dizzy Gillespie.

2131

Voyage vers la lumière

France 1969 – 18 mins
dir Pierre Unia

Science fiction featurette about a man's
experiments with hallucinogens – and the
consequences. Music by **Martial Solal.**

2132

W

USA 1973 – 95 mins
dir Richard Quine

Trite mystery-thriller with Twiggy being terrorized by an invisible maniac given to daubing his initial on his destructive handiwork. Music score by **Johnny Mandel**.

2133

WUSA

USA 1970 – 117 mins
dir Stuart Rosenberg

Miscalculated attempt at incisive satire of America's right-wing backlash and media manipulation, bearable only because of some sufficiently vivid performances. Music score by **Lalo Schifrin** and an appearance by The **Preservation Hall Jazz Band** of New Orleans.

2134

W.W. and The Dixie Dancekings

USA 1975 – 94 mins
dir John G. Avildsen

Likeable comedy set in the Deep South during the mid-1950's, utilising on soundtrack many popular recordings of the time, including 'I'm walkin'' by **'Fats' Domino** and Dave Bartholomew. **'Furry' Lewis** appears and contributes the traditional song 'Dirty car blues'.

2135

Wabash Avenue

USA 1950 – 93 mins
dir Henry Koster

Robust musical set in the saloons of Chicago during the World's Fair of 1893, with cross-play and double cross for Betty Grable between Phil Harris and Victor Mature. There is a featured spot for **Red Nichols** and The Five Pennies backing Betty Grable on 'I wish I could shimmy like my sister Kate', and they are heard elsewhere on soundtrack.

2136

The wackey world of numberrs

USA 1970 – 7 mins
dir Steven Clark

Colour cartoon adatation of the book of the same name, in which numbers are used in comedy form to demonstrate a variety of situations. Music composed and directed by **Shorty Rogers**.

Wake up and dream

see **What's cookin'?.**

2137

Walk, don't run

USA 1966 – 114 mins
dir Charles Walters

Lightweight comedy remake of George Stevens's classic *The more the merrier*. Music score by **Quincy Jones**, with vocals by The **Don Elliott** Voices.

2138

The walking hills

USA 1949 – 78 mins
dir John Sturges

Routine Western set in Death Valley and tailored for its star, Randolph Scott. Features **Josh White** singing and providing his own guitar accompaniment.

2139

Walking with my honey

USA 1945 – 3 mins

Soundie in which **Cab Calloway** interprets the title number.

2140

War dance for wooden Indians

USA 1941 – 3 mins

Soundie in which **Raymond Scott**'s title number is illustrated by Nucomi and Neeahtha, accompanied by **Ben Pollack**'s Orchestra.

2141

War hunt

USA 1961 – 83 mins
dir Denis Sanders

Extremely honest and strikingly effective war movie, shot on a very low budget in only 15 days. Music score by **'Bud' Shank**.

2142

Warnung vor einer heiligen Nutte

West Germany 1970 – 103 mins
dir Rainer Werner Fassbinder

Subtitled 'Pride comes before a fall', a drama involving a group of people making a movie – their confusion, their self-revelation. Among the recordings used on soundtrack is one by **Ray Charles**.

2143

The wasp woman

USA 1959 – 73 mins
dir Roger Corman

Modest shocker, made on an incredibly low budget, about the owner of a cosmetics firm who, undergoing specialised beauty treatment, starts turning into a wasp-faced fiend. Music score by **Fred Katz**.

2144

Watch the birdie

USA 1942 – 3 mins

Soundie featuring the title song interpreted by Virginia Cornell, backed by **'Sonny' Dunham**.

2145

Watched

USA 1974 – 93 mins
dir John Parsons

Erratic attempt to make a worthwhile statement about surveillance, falling far short of *The conversation*. Music by **Weather Report**.

2146

Way down yonder in New Orleans

USA c1952 – 3 mins

Snader Telescription featuring **Jack Teagarden** playing the title number.

2147

The way of all freshmen

USA 1933 – 15 mins
dir Joseph Henabery

Vitaphone music short presenting several numbers, including **W. C. Handy**'s 'St Louis blues'.

Way of the wicked
see **Ce corps tant désiré.**

2148

Way . . . way out

USA 1966 – 105 mins
dir Gordon Douglas

Science fiction comedy with Jerry Lewis that is so unfunny it's embarrassing. Music score and title song by **Lalo Schifrin**.

2149

Wayward

USA 1932 – 76 mins
dir Edward Sloman

Family drama about a jealous mother-in-law, from the novel *Wild beauty* by Mateel Howe Farnham, featuring The **Claude Hopkins** Orchestra.

2150

We are the Lambeth boys

UK 1959 – 52 mins
dir Karel Reisz

Outstanding social documentary about a youth club in Kennington; a toughly optimistic personal impression by the film's director. Music by **Johnny Dankworth**.

2151

We are young

Canada 1967 – 22 mins
prods Francis Thompson, Alexander Hammid

Experimental production made for the Canadian National Pacific-Cominco Pavilion at Expo '67 and shown on a cluster of six curved screens. Music by **David Amram**.

We have come for your daughters
see **Medicine Ball caravan.**

We insist
see **Noi insistiamo.**

2152

We the cats shall hep ya

USA 1945 – 3 mins

Soundie in which **Cab Calloway** sings the title number.

2153

Weekend

Denmark 1962 – 84 mins
dir Palle Kjaerulff-Schmidt

The movie that heralded the Danish *nouvelle vague*, a story based on inter-marital musical chairs, heavily influenced by Antonioni. Jazz score by bassist **Erik Moseholm.**

2154

A well spent life

USA 1971 – 44 mins
dir Les Blank, Skip Gerson

A portrait of the 75-year-old Texas blues singer and guitarist **Mance Lipscomb** in which he talks about his attitudes to life and to his music and performs both for the camera and for a club audience. Numbers included 'Asked my captain', 'Tom Moore's farm', 'Big boss man', 'Doorbell blues' and 'Baby take me back'.

2155

We're stepping out tonight

USA 1945 – 3 mins

Soundie featuring vocalist **June Richmond** with the title number, supported by dancers.

2156

De werkelijkheid van Karel Appel

Netherlands 1962 – 15 mins
dir Jan Vrijman

Portrait of the Dutch action painter at work and at play, with music track partly by **Dizzy Gillespie.**

2157

West 11

UK 1963 – 93 mins
dir Michael Winner

Ambitious attempt to make something out of a potentially interesting subject – an aimless London drifter – which somehow tails off into melodrama. Title theme partly composed and played by **Acker Bilk.**

2158

The West Point story/Fine and dandy

USA 1950 – 105 mins
dir Roy Del Ruth

Slickly produced musical romance with James Cagney conquering Virginia Mayo and army regulations in order to mount West Point's annual show. Also featured is Doris Day who, singing '10,000 sheep', is backed on soundtrack by **Buddy Cole**, *pno;* Vince Terri, *gtr;* and Artie Bernstein, *bass.*

2159

What the country needs

USA 1941 – 3 mins

Soundie featuring vocalist Martha Tilton, backed by **Bobby Sherwood** and His Orchestra, and actor Vince Barnett in a comedy sketch.

2160

What to do

USA 1942 – 3 mins

Soundie in which vocalist Savannah Churchill shares the spotlight with **Les Hite** and His Orchestra, plus dancers.

2161

Whatever happened to Uncle Fred?

UK 1967 – 5 mins
dir Bob Godfrey

An amusing child's view of adultery, in the form of an animated colour cartoon, with music by **John Hawksworth.**

2162

What's cookin'?/Wake up and dream

USA 1942 – 60 mins
dir Edward Cline

Routine comedy with some 14 musical numbers from popular entertainers of the day. Features **Woody Herman** and His Orchestra, and The Andrews Sisters, and includes 'Woodchopper's ball' by Joe Bishop and **Woody Herman.**

—

2163

Wheel of fortune

USA c1952 – 3 mins

Snader Telescription featuring **Jack Teagarden** playing the title number.

2164

When my sugar walks down the street

USA 1942 – 3 mins

Soundie featuring vocalist Linda Keene, accompanied by Henry Levine and His Dixieland Jazz Band.

2165
When Roobard made a spike
UK 1973 – 5 mins
dir Bob Godfrey
Crude colour cartoon about a dog and his attempt to fly with the birds. Soundtrack music by **Johnny Hawksworth**.

2166
When the boys meet the girls
USA 1965 – 97 mins
dir Alvin Ganzer
A new version of the 1943 *Girl crazy* but dull and feeble: the fine Gershwin numbers hardly survive. Features **Louis Armstrong** with **Tyree Glenn**, *trb;* **Buster Bailey**, *clar;* **Billy Kyle**, *pno;* **Buddy Catlett**, *bass;* **Danny Barcelona**, *drs;* and a song by **Armstrong** and **Billy Kyle**.

When the devil drives
see   **Sait-on jamais?**

2167
When there wasn't treasure
UK 1974 – 6 mins
dir Peter Green, Bob Godfrey
Further dull adventures of cheapo cartoon character Roobard the dog, with music by **Johnny Hawksworth**.

2168
When you're in love/For you alone
USA 1936 – 110 mins
dir Robert Riskin
Entertaining comedy with music in which opera star Grace Moore sings **Cab Calloway**'s 'Minnie the Moocher' in approved jazz fashion.

2169
When you're smiling
USA 1950 – 74 mins
dir Joseph Santley
A slight story is used as the peg on which to hang a number of songs, performed by a variety of bands and singers. Features **Bob Crosby** and The Modernaires with soundtrack backing from: **Zeke Zarchy, Mannie Klein**, *tpt;* **Lou McGarity**, *trb;* **Eddie Miller**, *ten sax;* **Matty Matlock**, *clar;* **Jess Stacy**, *pno;* **Nappy Lamare**, *gtr;* Manny Stein, *bass;* **Nick Fatool**, *drs*.

2170
Where angels go . . . trouble follows
USA 1967 – 94 mins
dir James Neilson
Moderately enjoyable sequel to *The trouble with angels*, all about those naughty nuns. Music and title song by **Lalo Schifrin**.

2171
Where has my little dog gone?
USA 1942 – 3 mins
Soundie in which the title number is played by **Claude Thornhill** and His Orchestra.

2172
Where has poor Mickey gone?
UK 1964 – 59 mins
dir Gerry Levy
Better than average low-budget second-feature with some nicely macabre script developments. The title song composed and sung by **Ottilie Patterson**.

2173
Where it's at
USA 1969 – 106 mins
dir Garson Kanin
Routine, sentimental comedy which tries to deal seriously with the problems of the generation gap in America. Music score by **Benny Golson**.

2174
Where the boys are
USA 1960 – 99 mins
dir Henry Levin
Wildy contemporary picture of undergraduates at play in an affluent, sex-obsessed society. Original 'dialetic' jazz by **Pete Rugolo**.

2175
Where's poppa?/Going ape
USA 1970 – 84 mins
dir Carl Reiner
Hilarious though brutally cold-blooded analysis of the tactics of familial war with a brilliantly witty script by Robert Klane, from his own novel. Music score by Jack Elliott with **Allyn Ferguson**, who include on soundtrack 'The goodbye song' sung by **Harry 'Sweets' Edison**.

2176
The white cliffs of Dover
USA 1942 – 3 mins
Soundie featuring **Stan Kenton**, with the title number.

2177
White line fever
USA 1975 – 89 mins
dir Jonathan Kaplan

Ineffectual tale of an individual up against the corporate moneymen, told in terms of a road movie with an unending series of fancy stunts. the music director on David Nichtern's score is **Billy Byers**.

2178
Who cares
USA 1951 – 3 mins

Snader Telescription in which the title number is played by **Lionel Hampton** and His Orchestra.

2179
Who dunit to who
USA 1946 – 3 mins
dir William Forest Crouch

Soundie in which the title song is sung by **June Richmond**.

Jimmy Dorsey and musicians pose for a studio publicity shot at Paramount.

▼

2180
Who is Harry Kellerman and why is he saying those terrible things about me?
USA 1971 – 108 mins
dir Ulu Grosbard

A sensitive and witty comedy on the theme of rat-race paranoia, with memorable performances from Dustin Hoffman, as a millionaire rock composer, and the ever delightful Barbara Harris. **Ray Charles**'s song 'Don't tell me your troubles' is used on soundtrack.

2181
Who killed Mary whats'ername?
USA 1971 – 90 mins
dir Ernie Pintoff

Thriller in which an amateur sleuth, who is also a diabetic, solves a Greenwich Village murder that is apparently being treated with indifference by everyone concerned – including the police. Atmospheric music score by **Gary McFarland**.

2182
A whole bunch of something
USA 1943 – 3 mins

Soundie featuring **Jimmy Dorsey** and His Orchestra, with vocalists Helen O'Connell and Bob Eberly.

2183

Whooping the Blues

USA 1969 – 14 mins
dir Jack Agins, Rick Paup

Sitting in an hotel room in Broadway Street, Oakland, California, the world's greatest blues harmonica player, **'Sonny' Terry**, sings a few songs and tells a few stories about his life. Numbers: 'My baby done chained the lock on the door', 'Sweet little girl' and 'Callin' my mama' – all composed by **'Sonny' Terry**.

2184

Who's been eating my porridge?

USA 1944 – 3 mins

Soundie featuring vocalist Ida James singing the title number, backed by The **'King' Cole** Trio.

2185

Who's crazy?

USA 1965 – 83 mins
dir Allan Zion, Thomas White

Improvisations by The Living Theatre Company of New York on a generally decided theme and series of happenings – filmed in Belgium. Improvised music on soundtrack from **Ornette Coleman**.

2186

Who's enchanted?

USA c1962

Documentary about blind children for which pianist **Joe Sullivan** composed and recorded about 30 minutes of appropriate soundtrack music.

2187

Who's minding the mint?

USA 1966 – 97 mins
dir Howard Morris

Pleasing comedy about a humble employee of the US Mint who accidentally destroys $50,000 in new bills and his scheme to reprint them. Lightly swinging jazz score by **Lalo Schifrin**.

2188

Who's sorry now?

USA c1952 – 3 mins

Snader Telescription of The **Bobcats** playing the title number.

Why America?
see **Pourquoi l'Amérique?**

2189

Wild and wonderful

USA 1963 – 87 mins
dir Michael Anderson

Embarrassingly unfunny comedy set in Hollywood's very own Gay Paree, featuring in a small part **Shelly Manne**.

Wild living
see **Les saintes nitouches.**

2190

The wild one/Hot blood

USA 1953 – 79 mins
dir Laslo Benedek

Rather overrated motorcycle movie but contains what is surely the definitive Marlon Brando performance. Probably the first movie ever to use source music dramatically throughout, the score is by Leith Stevens using **Shorty Rogers** and His Giants for the jukebox jazz sequences. Soundtrack musicians include Roger Short (**Shorty Rogers**), *tpt;* Bob Cooper, *ten sax;* **Milt Bernhart**, *trb;* **Bud Shank**, *alt sax, ten sax;* **Jimmy Giuffre**, *bar sax;* **Russ Freeman**, *pno;* **Carson Smith**, *bass;* Manny Shell (**Shelly Manne**), *drs.*

2191

The wild party

USA 1956 – 82 mins
dir Harry Horner

Cheap melodrama set partly in jazz clubs where the characters are all lost, derelict or unreal and where the action is lurid and largely incomprehensible. Features almost continuous jazz on soundtrack composed and conducted by **Buddy Bregman** incorporating solo piano work by **Pete Jolly**. Screen appearance by a rather embarrassed-looking **Buddy DeFranco** Quartet – **DeFranco**, *clar;* **Pete Jolly**, *pno;* **Frank DeVito**, *drs;* unknown bass. Also a brief appearance in a club group by **Teddy Buckner**. Also contains two memorable and highly quotable lines of lunatic dialogue: 'Girl, can you tell me where Flip Phillips is playing tonight?' and 'Have you heard Oscar Peterson at Sardi's?'

2192

The wildest

USA 1957 – 15 mins

Universal music featurette filmed at Lake Tahoe, with **Louis Prima**, Keely Smith, Sam Butera and The Witnesses.

2193

Will success spoil Rock Hunter?/Oh! for a man!
USA 1957 – 95 mins
dir Frank Tashlin

Quite routine screen adaptation of the play by George Axelrod, with a few good jokes and not much else. One song is credited to **Bobby Troup**.

2194

Willie Dynamite
USA 1973 – 102 mins
dir Gilbert Moses

Average black morality play about the decline and fall of an urban pimp. Music score by **J.J. Johnson**, songs by **J.J. Johnson** and Gilbert Moses 3rd, sung by Martha Reeves and The Sweet Things. Keyboard contributions from **Pete Jolly**.

Woody Herman and his Orchestra exploited to the full in **Wintertime.**
▼

2195

Windjammer
USA 1958 – 123 mins
dir Louis de Rochemont, Bill Colleran

Tame sea travelogue: the first film in the short-lived Cinemiracle wide screen process. Features **Wilbur De Paris**, *trb*.

2196

Wintertime
USA 1943 – 82 mins
dir John Brahm

Simple vehicle for skating star Sonja Henie, but plenty of music from **Woody Herman** and His Orchestra, including 'I like it here', 'Dancing in the dawn', 'Later tonight' and 'Wintertime'.

Witchcraft through the ages
see **Häxan.**

Within southern Louisiana
see **Dedans le sud de la Louisiane.**

2197

Without love
USA 1945 – 111 mins
dir Harold S. Bucquet
MGM domestic melodrama based on the play by
Philip Barry and featuring **Nina Mae McKinney.**

Witness in the city
see **Un témoin dans la ville.**

2198

Wolf
USA 1971 – 30 mins
dir Len Sauer
Rare performance on film by Delta bluesman
Howlin' Wolf including the songs 'Goin' dead
slow', 'I asked her for water', 'I am the wolf' and
'Evil'. Also appearing are **Hubert Sumlin, Fred
Below** and **Sunnyland Slim** and producer Ralph
Bass.

2199

Wolverine blues
USA c1952 – 3 mins
Snader Telescription featuring **Jack Teagarden**
playing the title number.

A woman needs loving
see **Eine Frau sucht Liebe.**

Women of the world
see **Wow.**

2200

Won Ton Ton, the dog who saved Hollywood
USA 1975 – 92 mins
dir Michael Winner
Clumsy, strained comedy remotely inspired by the
surprise success of Rin Tin Tin in silent pictures
some 50 years ago and featuring over 60 formerly
prominent film personalities in cameo roles. Music
scored by **Neal Hefti.**

2201

Woody Herman and His Orchestra
USA 1938 – 9 mins
dir Roy Mack
Vitaphone music short featuring the title band
playing 'Carolina in the morning', 'Holiday', 'You
must have been a beautiful baby', 'The shag' and
'Doctor jazz', supported by dancers and vocalist
Lee Wiley.

2202

Woody Herman and His Orchestra
USA 1948 – 15 mins
dir Will Cowan
Universal-International featurette spotlighting the
title band, supported by The Modernaires, Don
and Beverly – a dance duo – and The
Woodchoppers. Numbers: 'Blue flame', 'Sabre
dance', 'Caldonia' (solos from **Woody Herman**,
voc, clar; **Stan Getz**, *ten sax*), 'Jingle bell polka',
'Cane walk', and 'Northwest passage' (solos by
Woody Herman, *clar;* **Stan Getz**, *ten sax;*
Shorty Rogers, *tpt*). Prominent in the band are
'Zoot' Sims, *ten sax;* **Al Cohn**, *ten sax;* **Serge
Chaloff**, *bar sax;* **Chubby Jackson**, *bass;* **Don
Lamond**, *drs.*

2203

Woody Herman and The Swingin' Herd
USA 1963 – c30 mins
dir Richard Moore
Originally produced by US TV for Ralph J.
Gleason's *Jazz casual* series on KQED, a
programme of music by **Woody Herman** and His
Orchestra featuring soloists **Bill Chase**, *tpt* and
Sal Nistico, *reeds.* Music includes 'El torre
grande', 'Lonesome old town' and 'That's where it
is'.

2204

Woody Herman and The Swingin' Herd
USA 1963 – c30 mins
dir Richard Moore
A second programme of music by **Woody
Herman** and His Orchestra, produced originally
by US TV, in which the band play 'Deep purple',
'Early autumn', 'Blue flame', 'Satin doll', 'Mood
indigo' and 'A taste of honey'.

2205

Woody Herman's varieties
USA 1951 – 14 mins
dir Will Cowan
Universal-International music short, with a
fairground setting, in which **Woody Herman** and
His Orchestra play '99 guys' (soloists **Bill
Perkins, Dick Hafer**) and provide backing for The
Double Daters, *voc;* Nils and Nadynne, dancers;
The Langs, acrobats, and eventually launch into
their own 'Apple honey'.

The world at large
see **Paramount Pictorial Magazine no 837.**

2206

The world at three

UK 1965 – 23 mins
dir Frederic Goode

Colour documentary made for P & O Orient Lines,
with music by **Johnny Dankworth**.

World by night no. 2

see **Il mondo di notte numero due.**

2207

A world of beauty

USA 1955 – 18 mins
dir Will Cowan

Universal-International music short presenting the
Miss Universe Beauty Competition winners of
1955, supported by **Pete Rugolo**'s Orchestra and
vocalist **June Christy**.

World of fashion

see **Mini-midi.**

A world of strangers

see **Dilemma.**

World without sun

see **Le monde sans soleil.**

2208

Wow/Women of the world

USA 1975 – 10 mins
dir John Hubley

Animated cartoon presenting a global view of the
changing relationships between male and female
in world history, with music composed and
conducted by **Bill Russo**.

2209

The wrath of God

USA 1972 – 111 mins
dir Ralph Nelson

Solid, action-adventure movie adapted from
James Graham's novel, about a renegade priest
who frees a Latin American town of fear and
terror during a Twenties rebellion. Original music
score by **Lalo Schifrin**.

2210

Yamekraw

USA 1930 – 9 mins

Dramatic screen adaptation of the symphonic tone poem for orchestra, chorus, jazzband and solo piano by Harlem pianist **James P. Johnson**. No musicians appear on screen though there is some open trumpet soloing during the nightclub scenes.

2211

Yankee doodle swing shift

USA 1942 – 6 mins
dir Alex Lovy

Highly imaginative Walt Lantz *Swing symphony* colour cartoon, in which Swing is brought to one of Uncle Sam's armament factories by The 'Zoot Suit Swing Cats'.

2212

Yes sir, Mr Bones

USA 1951 – 54 mins
dir Ron Ormond

Low-budget production about minstrels on a showboat, featuring vocalist **Monette Moore**.

2213

You always hurt the one you love

USA 1944 – 3 mins

Soundie in which the title number is sung by The **Mills Brothers**.

2214

You can't have everything

USA 1937 – 99 mins
dir Norman Taurog

A Gregory Ratoff story about a small-town girl in New York, played by Alice Faye. Features **Louis Prima** and His Band with the songs: 'Rhythm on the radio' by **Louis Prima** and 'It's a southern holiday' by **Louis Prima**, Jack Loman and Dave Franklin.

2215

You must be joking!

UK 1965 – 100 mins
dir Michael Winner

Low-budget comedy involving army personnel, with music score by Laurie Johnson. There are also two songs by **Buddy Bregman**: 'I'm with you' and 'I'll be true to you, baby'.

2216

You were meant for me

USA 1947 – 92 mins
dir Lloyd Bacon

Formula 20th Century-Fox musical with Jeanne Crain and Dan Dailey, which includes the song 'Ain't misbehavin'' by Andy Razaf and **Fats Waller** and features **Eddie Miller** on soundtrack.

2217

You'll like my mother

USA 1972 – 93 mins
dir Lamont Johnson

Slightly above average screen adaptation of the novel by Naomi A. Hintze, with a good performance from Patty Duke as the helpless, persecuted heroine. Music score by **Gil Mellé**.

2218

Young Americans

USA 1967 – 103 mins
dir Alex Grasshoff

Inconsequentially padded semi-documentary about the work of a large vocal and instrumental teenage ensemble, with music by **Billy Byers**.

The young and the beat

see **A cool sound from hell.**

The young and the cool

see **Twist all night.**

2219

Young Billy Young

USA 1969 – 89 mins
dir Burt Kennedy

Very disappointing Western from such an obviously talented director, though there are some good performances. Straight music score by **Shelly Manne**.

2220

Young Dillinger

USA 1964 – 99 mins
dir Terry O. Morse

Uninspired gangster movie bringing together John Dillinger, 'Pretty Boy' Floyd and 'Baby Face' Nelson. Music composed and conducted by **Shorty Rogers**.

Young killers

see **High school confidential!**

Young man of music

see **Young man with a horn.**

2221

Young man with a horn/Young man of music

USA 1949 – 112 mins
dir Michael Curtiz

Typically wishy-washy Hollywood melodrama, obviously inspired by **Bix Beiderbecke**'s life only the names have been changed. **Harry James**, as well as being musical adviser, dubbed the trumpet solos for Kirk Douglas. **Hoagy Carmichael** plays his usual role of the melancholy but friendly pianist and there is an appearance by **Jack Jenney**. Songs include: 'Get happy', 'Moanin' low', 'The very thought of you' and 'Too marvellous for words'. Soundtrack musicians include: **Jimmy Zito, Willie Smith, 'Babe' Russin, Corky Corcoran**, Archie Rosate, **Hoyt Bohannon, Buddy Cole, Stan Wrightsman**, Artie Bernstein and **Nick Fatool**.

2222

The young savages

USA 1961 – 103 mins
dir John Frankenheimer

Overloaded tale of juvenile delinquency set in New York, based on Evan Hunter's novel *A matter of conviction*. Music score by **David Amram**.

2223

The young sinner

USA 1962 – 81 mins
dir Tom Laughlin

Pretentious, but effective, study of American youth when it strays off the straight and narrow. Music score by **Shelly Manne**.

2224

Your feet's too big

USA 1941 – 3 mins

Soundie in which **Fats Waller** plays and sings the title number. Recorded 7th November 1940.

2225

You're a sweetheart/Broadway jamboree

USA 1937 – 96 mins
dir David Butler

Universal musical comedy with Alice Faye, that also features jazz harpist **Casper Reardon**.

2226

You're never too young

USA 1955 – 103 mins
dir Norman Taurog

Routine vehicle for Dean Martin and Jerry Lewis. in VistaVision and Technicolor. **Johnny Mandel** worked on Arthur Schwartz's music score.

You're nobody 'til somebody loves you

see **Timothy Leary's wedding.**

2227

Youth and jazz

Norway 1962 – 13 mins
dir Ulf Balle Royem

Impressions of jazz clubs in Norway, featuring trumpeter **Rowland Greenberg**.

Youthful sinners

see **Les tricheurs.**

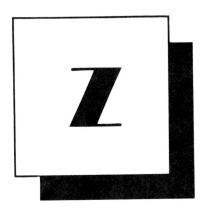

2228

Zachariah

USA 1970 – 93 mins
dir George Englund

The first so-called 'electric Western' – in which
most of the secondary characters are played by
musicians – is no less than a Biblical parable,
working out the contemporary tensions between
the two extremes of wasteful violence and
ecology. **Elvin Jones** plays a character called
Job Cain and takes a drum solo on John
Rubinstein's 'Camino waltz'.

2229

Zeta one

UK 1969 – 82 mins
dir Michael Cort

Positively appalling attempt at a sex comedy, with
science fiction overtones, adapted from a story in
the ill-fated *Zeta* magazine. Heavy, big band,
semi-rock score composed and conducted by
Johnny Hawksworth.

2230

Zigzag/False witness

USA 1970 – 104 mins
dir Richard A. Colla

A competently directed and ingeniously plotted
thriller which finally lets itself down by failing to
compel interest in its two-dimensional characters.
The music is composed, arranged and conducted
by **Oliver Nelson** and features **Artie Kane**, *pno;*
Buddy Collette, *saxes;* **Joe Mondragon**, *bass;*
John Guerin and Victor Feldman, *drs.* **Anita
O'Day** appears briefly.

Late Entries

2231

Brothers

USA 1977 – 105 mins
dir Arthur Barron

Fictionalised dramatization of the recent 'Soledad Brothers' case involving San Quentin prisoners and black activist Angela Davis. Music score composed and arranged by **Taj Mahal** who also plays keyboards. guitars and handles the lead vocals.

2232

Eraserhead

USA 1976 – 100 mins
dir David Lynch

An exercise in bad taste concerning a father and his horribly mutilated child. made over a period of 5 years under the auspices of the American Film Institute. The music track consists of recordings by **Fats Waller**.

2233

If you got the feelin'

USA 1973 – 52 mins
dir John Dominic

Intended for TV, a film portrait of veteran blues pianist **Jack Dupree**, produced in association with pop performer Elton John.

2234

Mon coeur est rouge

France 1976 – 105 mins
dir Michele Rosier

A day in the life of an humane and progressive heroine with various incidents and meetings that build a sort of tract for women's lib. Music score by **Keith Jarrett**.

2235

North Kensington laundry blues

UK 1974 – 11 mins
dir Robin Imray

Produced by the Polytechnic of Central London, a lament for the loss of a rare building and local amenity, using **Bessie Smith** vocals on soundtrack.

2236

Les passagers

France 1976 – 102 mins
dir Serge Leroy

Screen adaptation of the novel by K. R. Dwyer – a superficial, though slickly made, psychological/chase thriller with more than a nod towards Spielberg's *Duel*. Music score by **Claude Bolling**.

2237

Scott Joplin

USA 1976 – 96 mins
dir Jeremy Paul Kagan

A film biography of the composer. made on a low budget and shot in only 20 days. intended originally for TV. Billy Dee Williams has the leading role. Appearances by **Eubie Blake** and **Taj Mahal**. Music is mainly by **Scott Joplin**. arranged and performed by **Dick Hyman**: also 'Hang over blues' by Harold Johnson.

2238

The silver bears

UK 1977
dir Ivan Passer

Currently in production. the exploits of a Las Vegas crime syndicate accountant on the world silver markets. with a music score by **Claude Bolling**.

2239

Twilight's last gleaming

USA/West Germany 1976 – 146 mins
dir Robert Aldrich

Intriguing and intelligent adaptation of Walter Wager's novel *Viper three*. set in 1981, about a cashiered USAF officer who seizes a nuclear missile site for political ends. Music score by Jerry Goldsmith, whose uses **Billy Preston** singing 'America, my country 'tis of thee' over the main and end titles.

Index of Jazz Musicians

Gomez, Eddie 187, 970

Gonella, Nat 1428, 1479, 1737

Gonsalves, Paul 65, 95, 314, 339, 552, 553, 770, 1275, 1276, 1383, 1435, 1484, 1791, 1814, 2092

Goode, Coleridge 970, 1859

Goodman, Benny 59, 158, 176, 254, 277, 553, 622, 687, 825, 837, 838, 1177, 1202, 1204, 1214, 1506, 1669, 1725, 1806, 1838, 1897, 1931

Goodman, Harry 825

Goodman, Irving 158

Gordon, Bob 1520

Gordon, Dexter 497, 1866, 2083

Gordon, Joe 1344, 1523

Gordon, Justin 402, 619

Gourley, Jimmy 1435, 1599

Gowans, Brad 325, 1217

Gozzo, Conrad 158

Graass, John 1520

Guerin, John 1087, 1378, 2230

Graham, Kenny 309, 311, 319, 437, 629, 659, 679, 1028, 1318, 1346, 1411, 1631, 1674, 1777, 2020

Grappelly, Stéphane 518, 580, 643, 1056, 1121, 1132, 1249, 1859, 2023, 2095

Gray, Johnny 1773

Gray, Wardell 135, 756, 1391, 1879

Green, Benny 339

Green, Freddie 135, 136, 359, 756, 813, 1391, 1879

Green, Mel 91

Green, Urbie 158, 238, 553, 972

Greenberg, Roland 2227

Greer, Sonny 153, 196, 200, 288, 300, 351, 865, 948, 1286, 1343, 1575, 1652, 1928, 1929

Grey, Al 1117

Grey, Sonny 712

Griffin, Chris 158

Griffin, Johnny 83, 970

Grimes, Henry 972

Grimes, Tiny 108, 1327, 1612, 1922, 1934

Gross, Walter 1583

Grossman, Steve 941

Gruntz, George 1860

Gryce, Gigi 1089

Guarnieri, Johnny 27, 1375, 1686

Gubin, Sol 208, 1182

Guerin, John 1087, 1378

Guy, Buddy 225, 355, 586, 1890

Guy, Fred 153, 196, 288, 300, 351, 1286, 1928

H

Hackett, Bobby 238, 1403, 1664, 1686, 2017

Hadi, Shafi 1713

Hafer, Dick 2205

Hagemann, Henry 485

Haggart, Bob 236, 1106, 1575

Halcox, Pat 361, 362, 1136, 1140, 1267

Hall, Adelaide 45, 447, 513, 515, 2001

Hall, Al 1343

Hall, Edmond 129, 200, 294, 806, 1662

Hall, Jim 405, 490, 553, 972, 1368, 1905, 1950

Hall, Minor 1659, 1939

Hambro, Lennie 479

Hamilton, Chico 395, 405, 410, 972, 1257, 1448, 1570, 1601, 1876, 1905

Hamilton, Jimmy 65, 95, 250, 314, 552, 770, 1275, 1276, 1383, 1435, 1791, 1814, 1929, 2092

Hampton, Lionel 21, 138, 158, 622, 756, 825, 965, 1116, 1117, 1118, 1258, 1452, 1581, 1603, 1615, 1740, 1806, 1937, 2104, 2178

Hancock, Herbie 216, 476, 941, 1087, 1833

Hand, Dent 656

Handy, John 256, 1002, 1495, 2147

Handy, W.C. 111, 426, 480, 525, 577, 586, 729, 761, 801, 931, 1090, 1349, 1547, 1637, 1638, 1639, 1640, 1662, 1742, 1757, 1916, 1924, 2007

Hanna, Ken 1107

Hardwicke, Otto 153, 300, 1286, 1778, 1928

Harper, Herbert 1182

Harriott, Joe 1964

Harris, Bill 561, 792, 1331, 1897

Harris, Eddie 1817

Harvey, Eddie 721

Hastings, Lennie 39

Haven, Alan 1007, 1053

Hawkins, Coleman 27, 200, 387, 431, 906, 1355, 1819, 2053

Hawkins, Erskine 495, 844

Hawksworth, John (Johnny) 64, 76, 125, 372, 408, 439, 487, 641, 718, 762, 786, 1029, 1052, 1115, 1310, 1453, 1491, 1498, 1508, 1535, 1591, 1683, 1747, 1775, 1782, 1800, 1880, 1942, 1959, 2049, 2098, 2161, 2165, 2167, 2229

Hayes, Edgar 1238

Hayes, Tubby 40, 47, 523, 1358, 2061

Haynes, Roy 972

Heard, J.C. 250

Heath, Percy 1274, 1368, 1646

Heath, Ted 340, 443, 932, 963, 1123, 1264, 1773, 1959, 2085

Hefti, Neal 131, 239, 550, 561, 760, 850, 951, 1073, 1141, 1367, 1371, 1417, 1893, 1930, 2200

Heider, Werner 900

Hemphill, Shelton 1929

Henderson, Fletcher 158, 1637

Henderson, Rudi 970

Hendricks, Jon 554, 970, 1340, 1813

Hendrickson, Al 208, 619, 657, 874, 1288, 1324, 1410, 1806

Herbert, Mort 1308

Herfurt, Skeets 657, 1348

Herman, Woody 561, 622, 772, 792, 814, 961, 1273, 1274, 1331, 1579, 1696, 2162, 2196, 2202, 2203, 2204, 2205